ASTROLOGY FOR EVERYONE

KRISTI,
A small gift
for a
great person.

ASTROLOGY FOR EVERYONE

Edward Lyndoe

Introduction by

Joanne Clancy

Editor, *American Astrology Magazine*

New Revised Edition

NEW YORK

E. P. DUTTON & CO., INC.

1970

Revised edition first published in the U.S.A. 1970 by E. P. Dutton & Co., Inc.
Copyright © 1970, 1959 by Edward Lyndoe
Introduction copyright © 1960, by E. P. Dutton & Co., Inc.
All rights reserved. Printed in the U.S.A.

10   9   8   7

Published in England under the title *Everyman's Astrology*
Library of Congress Catalog Card Number: 60-12089

SBN 0-525-05919-9

INTRODUCTION

THIS, AS THE AUTHOR INSISTS, is a do-it-yourself book. It is aimed at gratifying your natural curiosity about astrology and what it may have to say about your present and future. As you will find, it provides the answer to many of the perplexing questions of day-to-day living which have troubled you.

Astrology helps to contribute to the development of the individual by giving him opportunities to take advantage of trends of the moment. In turn this permits him to bring out the best and strongest potentials he possesses, also teaching him how to control negative traits which may be present. He can then guide his actions so that he gains maturity, as well as a deeper understanding of life.

Lyndoe's book is just what its title implies: astrology placed within the reach of everyone. Using simplified terms and modern methods it enables a person who starts with no knowledge of astrology to set up his (or her) own birth-chart and to judge its prominent factors.

A prolific writer whose readers throughout the world cover circulations amounting to some 50 millions, Lyndoe during his many years of newspaper work has had an annual mail in excess of 100,000 letters. One may feel, therefore, that he has an intimate knowledge of the average person's problems. Obviously, he knows his subject well and in setting out to supply this do-it yourself manual on astrology he has made a major contribution by eliminating heavy mathematics and cutting a way through to the quick of the matter, as it were.

Usually to set up a birth-chart several expensive texts are

needed: an ephemeris, a table of houses, etc. With "Astrology for Everyone" in your possession you do not need any additional material. This one book alone is sufficient.

As the editor of *American Astrology Magazine,* now (1970) in its 38th year of publication, it has been my pleasure and privilege to present Lyndoe's writing to the American public each month as one of our regular contributors. His consistently accurate analysis of prominent figures in the news, as well as his interpretation of current affairs, has made him a respected personality in the field of astrology.

In my judgment there is no better way to start on the subject than with "Astrology for Everyone." By following its directions carefully the reader is bound to derive pleasure, comfort, and wisdom.

JOANNE S. CLANCY
Editor, *American Astrology Magazine*

PRELIMINARIES

" We wish to publish a work which gives the essentials of astrology for the person with little mathematics and less astronomy. The aim would be to produce the means for setting up a map such as is used in astrology, showing in as simple a form as possible how the reader can make his or her own birth chart and judge it, what it means for the immediate period, and what it indicates for the future.

" This implies a minimum of calculation and will probably involve the creation of very simple formulae which can be assimilated as the reader proceeds.

"Above everything, it is desired that you shall show the reader how you set up a chart yourself using the results of the latest research into astrology. We understand that you have courageously discarded antiquated methods and we would like to have the modern ones given prominence."—THE PUBLISHERS.

A GREAT DEAL OF MYSTERY has always attached to astrology. This is not because the subject is in any wise mysterious but because it has suited the pretensions of the professionals to make it seem so. Some such process is found in most of the sciences. Every operation has a dog-Latin appellation (or worse, a Greek-Latin monstrosity), and this lends a spurious air of importance to the subject. It does more than that: it makes perfectly simple matters difficult to understand, and thereby provides tutors with a livelihood, as well as limiting the possible competition which practitioners would otherwise suffer.

It would be excusable for scientific men to use their language of techniques if the English language were incapable of simpler terms. In most instances this is not so. Certainly there is no necessity for astrology to imitate what, after all, is only learned pomposity. We have Latin enough in our language without adding to it, especially where the object is only to appear cleverer than we are.

So far as the early stages of astrology go, there is nothing which cannot be understood by any person of reasonable intellect, provided the mystique is dropped and the task approached as an ordinary job of work. No other-worldly intimations are involved; no special capabilities are called for; no ivory-tower trance conditions are required. Shown how, an average schoolboy could set up a map. That is exactly the measure of mathematical and other abilities demanded.

Are there, then, no difficulties? That could not be affirmed. In the astronomical factors which lie behind some of the processes very considerable difficulties have to be faced; but the point is that *it is not necessary for the beginner to face them.* They are more for later study, as and when the individual feels a desire to know upon what basis his first steps were taken. One does not expect a baby to know the ball-and-socket principle of his joints before he is allowed to walk. He is aided and guided *so that he may walk.* He can go on for the rest of his life without knowing why his legs work as they do—and some people manage to be that ignorant without being in any way restricted in their walking.

This work, therefore, is designed solely to aid and guide. It does not expect the reader to get immersed in technical problems, though it contains a hope that he will become interested enough to do so at some rather distant date.

Again, it would be ridiculous not to say that the diagnosis which is used in reading off the indications in maps is not easy. It calls for a specialized synthesis of numerous factors and can only be performed well with long experience. On the other hand, the person only at the beginnings can be shown how to judge a map for its prominent factors, these being remarkably simple to master. In much the same manner, we do not demand that a boy at his geography lesson shall be able to take a highly detailed map and comprehend

all that it means to a cartographer. We give him a simplified
form of map and instruct him first of all in its bare outlines,
getting him to note the chief rivers and ports, and showing
him what conclusions he may draw from a relatively small
array of factors. He will not be able to discuss navigation,
nor will he be aware of the political implications which arise
from a country's location; but he will know in a very little
time where he himself is located on the globe and how this
position affects him during the seasons and in his daily food.
To the expert cartographer this is most elementary; but the
things that boy learns are valuable to him and will carry him
far. The finer points he can investigate later, building on the
knowledge acquired, when he needs them. So with this
subject.

Leave technicalities alone. They will only confuse you.

The requirements laid down by the Publishers have been
met by three principal methods:

(1) The few calculations needed for setting up a map have
been made over in terms of simple arithmetic. There is no
more of it than every twelve-year-old could manage. The
process has been carried to the extent of working in whole
degrees so far as possible. By and large the loss of accuracy is
fractional and would make little difference even were the
expert to follow the same methods.

(2) Modern systems (of what are known as house-division
and progression) were placed under discussion with experts.
It was felt that the simplest house-division system—that of
Morinus, which is not modern at all but is nevertheless
extremely trustworthy—should be used. In progressions it
was felt that the modern Tertiary System should have use.
This is mentioned here merely to explain in advance what is
done, but you need not be worried about the meanings of
terms used at this stage. Your interest should be only in the
fact that extreme simplification has been introduced.

(3) Tabulations of various kinds, which have to be used in
astrology (as, for instance, in finding the positions of planets),

have had painstaking calculation and preparation, and have been given in the simplest possible form. Besides a gain in simplicity, there is an undoubted advantage because possession of these tabulations in the one work obviates the necessity for purchase of fairly costly books a student must normally use.

One could not talk in this way of simplification without making the warmest mention of research work which preceded the writing of the work. This was chiefly in consultations with Brigadier Roy Firebrace, one of the greatest research workers in this field, whose advices were quite invaluable. In fine, the author should not be credited with most of such merits at this work may contain. Researchers, together with experts in other related fields whose findings were consulted, deserve far more than mere acknowledgement.

Having said this, perhaps one may be permitted to say a little concerning the basics of astrology and what it is intended that the reader shall attempt.

Astrology has two principal functions. The first, and by far more important, is to give the life of mankind a meaning and purpose. This is very much an exercise in psychology. The idea is to find the main essentials of that which is brought into the world and to assess its potentialities.

The second function is to essay an interpretation of the future: by no means the dominant feature of the subject, despite the belief held by many people that astrology exists solely to "tell the future". It is true that this science alone has the means to predict with reasonable accuracy, but it must be underlined that it has *not* the means to offer finalized accuracy. Critics of the science like to fool their public with the suggestion that astrology claims some kind of omniscience. This it has never done, and these critics know that this is so, though nothing on earth will prevent them from continuing to make statements which they are well aware are blatant lies. They have the superb protection of the astrological philosophy, which discourages, so far as possible, returning bitterness with bitterness. It requires no courage to aim blows at people who are committed to avoidance of strife!

If one wished to assess the possibilities of accuracy, it might be reasonable to suggest that eighty to ninety per cent is achieved. In itself this is no mean claim, for where else can parallel accuracy be found? In astronomy? In physics? Not in these, nor in most of the works of men. Indeed, the great compliment paid to astrology by even its worst critics is the high expectation in excess of anything asked elsewhere which they demand of it. We try our best to live up to that expectation, but are aware of certain human failings.

As for the reader, he is asked only to know the basis of what he is to undertake. Beyond that he should not concern himself. He will be expected to begin work at once, going to it as an apprentice, and the first task will be to look over the author's shoulder as he sets up a map. This is not asking very much of the reader except patience. A quiet following of the various simple processes will instruct him far more easily and much more quickly than launching him on an ocean of words.

Now watch.

PART ONE

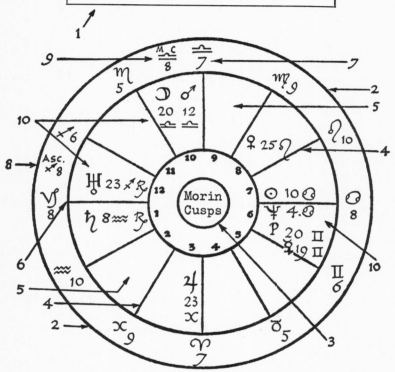

MAP OF AN IMPORTANT MAN
B. 2 July 1903 at 17h50   52 N 50—0 E 31
S.T. 12 : 30

1. Parts of the Map

(1) Description. This must always be given in closest possible detail.
(2) A circle representing the area round the earth in which Sun, Moon, and Planets appear to move because of the earth's rotation.
(3) A small circle representing the earth itself.
(4) Cusps. These are the spokes of the wheel design.
(5) Houses. The spaces enclosed by cusps.   (6) The East Point.
(7) The Mid-Equator.   (8) The Ascendant.   (9) The Midheaven.
(10) Sun, Moon, and Planets, showing signs and degrees.

WE SET UP A MAP

BE CONTENT AT FIRST to watch how this is done.

A specimen map is given on the opposite page. It is this map which we shall reconstruct, going through each process until the design is complete.

When this has been done, begin again with the first stage so that you are quite clear about the methods adopted.

Do not hurry this work. The more thoroughly you follow it through the more certainty you will feel as you start on your own map.

It would be a good idea to make a design like the one on the page opposite. You need not be worried about not having such a design at hand. Simply take some round object—a teacup would serve—and draw the outer circle. It is then not difficult to draw a line from top to bottom and from side to side to make a cross over the centre. Divide each quadrant in three and connect across to make the twelve divisions. Printed chart forms are easily obtainable if you prefer them.

Do not accept the author's statement that a certain table contains such-and-such a reading. Look it up for yourself and check all that he is doing. The constant use of the tabulations will become a habit and will make it easier for you when you come to make your own map.

I. WHAT THE MAP REPRESENTS

An event must occur at a certain place and at a certain time. We are able to fix it by using a map to show where it occurred and a clock to show when. Usually we have a map for a country and an ordinary clock.

There is another way of fixing place and time. We can use a sky map, showing the Solar System as it appeared above the place of the event, and a sky clock showing the time. This way is just as accurate.

Astrology uses this second method because it is concerned primarily with the associations between the Solar System and the event. The map which results is of the kind seen on page 2. Naturally, the time for the map is taken from the sky clock which measures the apparent movement of the sky as a whole. You will not need to be told that this movement is in reality caused by the earth's axial rotation.

Time told in this fashion is called Sidereal Time. Let us forget the formal name and call it Star Time, which is what is meant.

The map selected is for a birth which occurred at 5.50 p.m. (17 h. 50 m.) on a certain day. That is what the ordinary clock, set for Greenwich Mean Time, stated. Had another clock, set for Star Time, been used, it would have shown the time to be about 12.30 on its twenty-four-hour dial. (Such clocks exist and are used extensively by astronomers and astrologues.) The map shows how the sky above the birth place appeared at that precise moment.

We may be fairly sure that no Star Time clock was available there. A record of the birth time by the ordinary clock was, however, enough to enable us to calculate what the other kind of clock would have shown.

So the first step in preparing the map has to be the changing of the normal clock reading to a reading in terms of Star Time. This is not a complicated task. If you will look over my shoulder while I perform it you will see at once what has to be done.

Do not worry at this stage about problems of time. These can well be studied at your leisure when you know how to prepare maps. All you are invited to do is to trust yourself to the author for the time being.

You should take note of the parts of the map given here. Either learn them or refer to page 2 whenever they are mentioned. It is not necessary to delve into questions concerning them at this time.

See special remarks on maps drawn where birth time is unknown (page 25).

2. DRAWING THE MAP

First find its S.T. (Star Time)

Every map starts with the calculation of its S.T. This can be found with a simple formula devised for you. It is:

S plus T plus A plus or minus R. Or **S+T+A±R.**

S stands for the star clock time at 0 h. 0 m. (midnight) of a date. A list for the days of all the years from 1900–1960 is found in Table 2 on page 105, given to nearest minute.

Our specimen map is for 2 July 1903. Against 2 July in the table we find 18.36. As 1903 is not in the heading, we look below and find it requires a deduction of 1 minute. So we arrive at 18.36 minus 0.01. That is 18.35. We write this down.

T stands for the local time of the event. Such times are stated in ordinary clock times, which are based on the Zone Time for the country or state. (Great Britain uses the Greenwich Zone, New York uses the Zone called E.S.T. for Eastern Standard Time, and so forth.) The time of our specimen map is 5.50 p.m., which is 17 h. 50 m. after 0 h. 0 m. (midnight). So we write down 17.50, putting it beneath the 18.35.

Had Summer Time been in use, we should have needed to deduct 1 hour to bring the time to the Zone Time. Summer Time should always be taken into account when dealing with 1916 onwards.

A stands for acceleration on the given time. The difference between
Mean Time and Star Time acceleration is near enough 10
seconds for each hour after midnight. For 17 h. 50 m. this is
2 minutes 56 seconds but as we are working in whole minutes in
this work it will be sufficient to put down 3 minutes. Add this
to the figures already written down and be careful to put the
3 under minutes: 0.03, not 3.00.

In all maps this A quantity must be added to the given time.

R stands for rectification to Zone Time. This rectification has
to be made for many places because they lie east or west of
their Zones. It is calculated at 4 minutes per degree. For
example, the birth-place here was 0° 31 (about half a degree)
east of Greenwich. Add 0.02 to your calculation.

R (Rectification) is added at the rate of 4 minutes per degree if a
place is East of its Zone, but deducted at the same rate for places West
of their Zones. See Table 3 where corrections for many important
centres are given.

Now total the figures you have written down.

They come to 12.30. If you are uncertain, see the workings
beneath the specimen map opposite.

The S.T. for this specimen map is therefore 12.30 approx.

Writing in the Cusps

We now turn to the Morinus Table (Table 4) on page 111.
This gives us the signs and degrees for the cusps of the map.
First we must find the time we have already calculated: 12.30.

In the column headed " S.T." we see there are two times
close to this: 12.28 and 12.32. It is obvious that the amounts
we need will come between those against these two times.

Now look at column 1. This contains the amounts for the
First Cusp. Against 12.28 we see 7 37 and against 12.32 is
8 43. These are degrees and minutes. But of what sign?
Glance at the top of the column and you will see the sign ♑
(Capricorn). So we know that

at 12.28 the First Cusp will be 7♑37, and that
at 12.32 the First Cusp will be 8♑43.

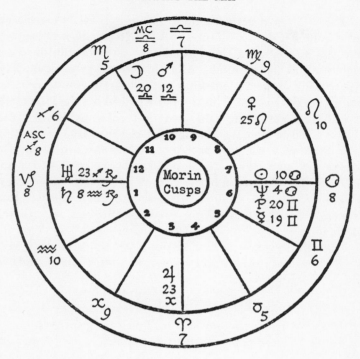

2. CALCULATION FOR THE S.T. OF THIS MAP

S	(Table 2, page 105) for 2 July	18.36
	1903 (see beneath Table 2) requires deduction of 1 minute	1
	S.T. for 0 h. 0 m. (midnight) on 2 July 1903	18.35
T	5.50 p.m. = 17 h. 50 m. after midnight	17.50
A	17 h. 50 m. is approximately 18 hours × 10 seconds =	
	180 seconds = ...	3
R	For 0 E 31 (about half a degree) at 4 mins. per degree ..	2
	Total	36.30

But there can only be statement of time in terms of 24 hours
and so we must deduct 24 hours from this total (and this
has always to be done where a total exceeds 24 hours) .. | 24.00

Therefore S.T. for this map (S + T + A + R) is ... .. | 12.30

The difference between these amounts is easily calculated: 1° 6′ (one degree six minutes). As 12.30 is half-way between the times, we halve this amount (1° 6′ = 66 minutes) and the result is 33 minutes. Add this to 7♑37 and we have 8♑10. But as we are working to the nearest minute we need only note down 8♑. This is what we need for the First Cusp.

Looking across the table we find columns headed 2–6. These contain the cusp amounts for the next five cusps.

In column 2 we have ♒ (Aquarius) at the top of the list. Beside the two times (12.28 and 12.32) we have 9♒24 and 10♒25. The difference between these is 1° 1′ (or 61 minutes). Half of this is 30½ minutes. Add this to 9♒24 and we have 9♒54½. As we are working to whole degrees we call this 10♒.

The same process is carried out with the other columns. We conclude this simple operation with these quantities:

S.T.	1	2	3	4	5	6
12.30	8♑	10♒	9♓	7♈	5♉	6♊

But what about the Seventh to Twelfth Cusps?

These have the same degrees but opposite signs. You have 8♑ for the First Cusp. Therefore (looking across the map) you have 8♋ for the Seventh. And so on.

Once the amounts for the cusps are found, we enter them in the map.

You will understand all this quite easily by studying the specimen.

Note on Checking the Cusps

It is sound astrological practice always to check the cusps of a map when they have been written in. You should note these points:

(1) The cusps go round the map in correct order. That is to say that you must have ♈ ♉ ♊ ♋ ♌ ♍ ♎ ♏ ♐ ♑ ♒ ♓.

If you start at the First Cusp (as in this map we are drawing) with ♑, then the next sign round must be ♒, and after that ♓, and so on to ♈ and the rest.

(2) The signs on opposite cusps must always be opposite signs. That

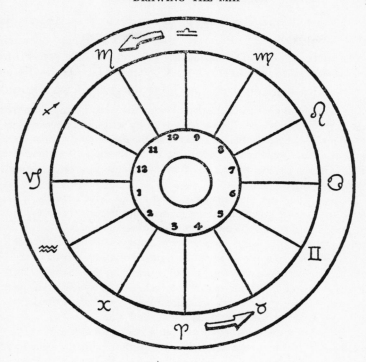

3. INSERTION OF SIGNS

Note carefully the anti-clockwise direction. The order of Signs as shown here has always to be preserved, the entire twelve having their correct places no matter what the requirements of the map. In every map drawn the fact that all twelve are entered should be checked.

Each Sign has an opposite. If at first uncertain, check back with the following listing:

ᛞ Aries   is opposite ♎ Libra
♉ Taurus   is opposite ♏ Scorpio
♊ Gemini   is opposite ♐ Sagittarius
♋ Cancer   is opposite ♑ Capricorn
♌ Leo   is opposite ♒ Aquarius
♍ Virgo   is opposite ♓ Pisces

is to say that ♑ must always have ♋ opposite to it, ♈ must always be opposite ♎, and so forth. The opposite pairs are repeated:

The Signs: ♈ ♉ ♊ ♋ ♌ ♍ ♎ ♏ ♐ ♑ ♒ ♓
Opposites: ♎ ♏ ♐ ♑ ♒ ♓ ♈ ♉ ♊ ♋ ♌ ♍

(3) The signs always go in an anti-clockwise direction. Occasionally a sign is not found in the Table, there being an apparent jump from one sign to the next-but-one. This is dealt with by writing the missing sign between the other two (half-way between the cusps involved), and the opposite of the missing sign is written in on the opposite side of the map. This completes the series ♈ to ♓. Signs so treated we call Intercepted Signs.

(4) In a little time the calculation of amounts which are for times between the times given in Table 4 (as with our present specimen) will be a mechanical process. You will be able to see at a glance which is the proper amount. But it is never a waste of time to look over this work a second time just to make sure that the right amounts have been used.

In this connection it might be worth mentioning that the times right through the table are at four-minute intervals. If you wished to calculate for 0.01 S.T. you would need, therefore, to take a quarter of the degrees and minutes between the amounts for 0.0 and 0.04.

(5) It does not matter whether you put 8 ♑ or ♑ 8 on the First Cusp and fill in the other cusps similarly. The author prefers to put ♑ 8. It is purely a matter of taste. Do whichever you find easier.

Inserting the Sun, Moon, and Planets

The positions these will hold on any given date are found in a day book, known as an ephemeris (pl. ephemerides), which is a Latin word derived from Greek meaning day-book or diary. Such a book is not a present necessity to you because you have in this work a tabulation of the planetary positions. If, however, you wish to deal with dates before 1900 or after 1960, you will need to possess yourself of the appropriate ephemerides. These you will find are published in single years and also in volumes containing two or more decades.

Positions given in ephemerides are usually in terms of Greenwich. A modern form of ephemeris like *Die Deutsche Ephemeride* has made it a practice to give positions for o h. o m.,

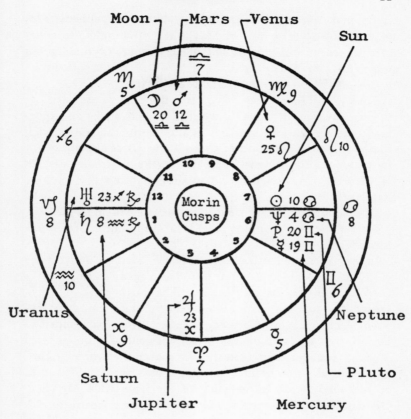

4. IDENTIFICATION OF BODIES

It is necessary to learn the various symbols. For quick reference:

⊙	Sun	♃	Jupiter
☽	Moon	♄	Saturn
☿	Mercury	♅	Uranus
♀	Venus	♆	Neptune
♂	Mars	♇	Pluto

Greenwich Mean Time (midnight) but other ephemerides tend to use 12 h. 0 m. (midday). If you should use ephemerides, therefore, you should make a point of finding out which notation is employed.

The tabulations given in this work are for 0 h. 0 m., G.M.T.

Now it will be obvious to you that if we are to use positions that are in terms of G.M.T., we shall have to make an adjustment where a location is distant from the Greenwich Meridian, using some other Zone Time. It is also necessary to make an adjustment even where the place lies east or west of the Greenwich Meridian though using it as a time standard.

This adjustment is simple but it must be made in all maps.

It is done by changing the local time into Greenwich Mean Time.

In our specimen no adjustment is needed. Can you see why? It is because the birth time has already been given in G.M.T. and not in local time. The birth took place in reality at a local time two minutes past the clock time at Greenwich. This made no difference because we are accustomed to British times being so given. A fact not generally remembered is that it was not until 1880 that by statute the word " time " was for legal purposes interpreted as always in Great Britain to be reckoned as the Mean Time of the Greenwich Meridian. Old data are often in sundial, railway, or other standards.

So long as you make sure that, whatever Zone is used, you have reduced the given time to G.M.T., you can feel safe about using either the tabulations here or those in other books based on G.M.T.

Finding the Sun Position

Nothing could be easier. In Table 6 on page 121, under SUN POSITIONS you will find the positions of the Sun for every day of the year.

This part of the tabulation is divided into two parts: the first is for ordinary years, the second for leap years.

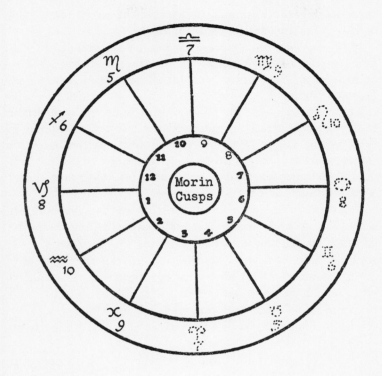

5. Insertion of Cusp Values

The method by which these values are ascertained has been described. You now see how they are entered on the map design. This is invariably the first stage in erecting a map. Double-check details before making entries. Note from dotting the opposites of signs.

Since 1903 was not a leap year we shall be concerned with the first table.

Under July, and opposite 2, we find the entry 10♋.

This is the Sun position for our map.

Note it down on a piece of paper. You will discover as you go forward with the work that it is a convenience to make a list of Sun, Moon, and the planets from Mercury to Pluto, beforehand.

There is a reason for this. The writing in of results can make the map very confusing unless all the bodies are entered in their proper order. Beginners often write in two or three only to find that they need to insert another body just where one of their entries stands! So make a list. Common sense? Yes, and much neater.

Another point: even in writing down the symbols for such a list, do make them clear! The circle for Sun should be decently round, not a sort of scribbled O. The symbol for Moon should be a true crescent and not something resembling a banana. Why give your eye any risks of confusion when you have so much else to think about? Yet it is not uncommon to find even experienced astrologues making symbols of appalling style. Keep clear of this bad habit from the start.

About the Sun tabulation it is necessary to direct your attention to the fact that it is to within one degree—an approximation. When you come to refinements of calculation approximations will not do; but you will come to no harm in using them for present purposes.

To show you the measure of approximation, it may be well to state that the correct position of the Sun in our specimen, as shown in an ephemeris, is 9° 39′ 11″ of ♋ (39 minutes 11 seconds past nine degrees of Cancer).

We are working to nearest whole degrees, and the nearest to true Sun position, as you can see, is precisely what we have found in our Sun tabulation: 10♋.

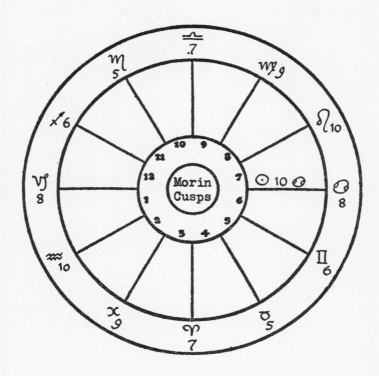

6. INSERTION OF THE SUN

This is done after the complete list of placements has been made (see page 23) and it is essential to see that the position is shown on the map between the appropriate cusp readings. On the cusp of the Seventh House we have 8°♋ and on the cusp of the Eighth House is 10°♌. The Sun's position is 10°♋ and this is between the readings on these two cusps, therefore the correct placement is in the Seventh House.

Finding the Moon Position

Just beyond the Sun tabulation there is a Moon Table, page 123.

This is a listing of Moon positions for every other day. You will find, if you turn to 1903, that the dates down go 1, 3, 5, etc.

Look at the entries for 1 and 3 July. The position we need comes between those dates, being for 2 July.

We find these entries:

        1 July 1903   ..   ..   27♍.
        3 July 1903   ..   ..   23♎.

From this we know that between 0 h. 0 m. (midnight) on 1 July and 0 h. 0 m. (midnight) on 3 July—a period of 48 hours, being two days—a total Moon movement of 26° has taken place. You can reckon this out. From 27♍ to the end of the sign is 3°. Add this to the 23° of ♎, and it is seen that 26° has to be taken.

How long has it taken Moon to move to the time of birth? That is what we need to know.

There was the whole of 1 July = 24 hours. Then there was to 17 h. 50 m., you will remember, of 2 July. So we have a total of 24 + 17.50 hours which equals 41 hours 50 minutes. This we can conveniently regard as 42 hours.

A little sum has then to be done:

Moon has moved   42
                  ——— × and gone 26°.
Out of a total   48 hours

Write this $\frac{42}{48}$ × 26.

42 × 26 = 1092. Divide this by 48 = 22¾°, which is the distance we are seeking.

Make this over into whole degrees and call it 23°.

Then add it to the Moon position on 1 July = 27♍ + 23°. That is 20°♎, and this is what we need to write into the list we are now making.

You can always do a rough check of any Moon position by remembering that this body moves at approximately ½° (half

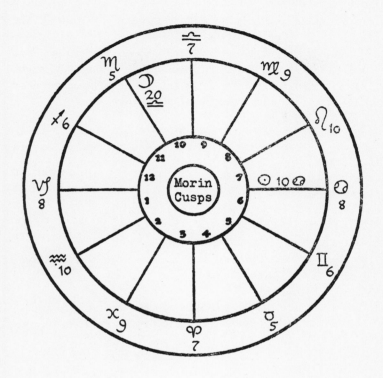

7. INSERTION OF THE MOON

It will be understood that this follows the same method as for insertion of the Sun. Here we have 7°♎ on the Tenth House cusp, and on the cusp of the Eleventh House is 5°♏. The Moon being in 20°♎ is obviously to be placed between these two cusps—in other words, in the Tenth House.

a degree) an hour. In the present instance, the time is about 6 hours before o h. o m. on 3 July. We would therefore expect Moon to make roughly 3° (six times half a degree). Take 3° from 23°♎︎ and we have the same result of 20°♎︎.

Go over this again. It is not complicated and amounts only to common sense reckoning.

Finding the Mercury, Venus, and Mars Positions

The process is similar to that used for the Moon. Turn to the tables for Mercury (page 151), Venus (page 165), and Mars (page 179), in turn. You will see that positions for these are given for each ten days, sometimes for shorter periods.

Taking Mercury as our example:

The nearest entry to 2 July 1903 is 30 June, which shows 15♊︎. The next entry is for 10 July, showing 29♊︎. So in the ten days Mercury has moved 14° (29 — 15).

In three days movement will be (30 June–2 July) three-tenths of 14°. One-tenth is 1·4°. Multiply by 3 and we have 4·2°.

As we are working to nearest degrees we therefore add 4° to the 15° for 30 June, giving the result 19♊︎. Add this to your list.

Looking now at the Venus table, we note that from 30 June to 10 July the planet moves from 22♌︎ to 2♍︎. This is 10°. In the three days to midnight of 2 July Venus therefore moves 3°.

Add this to 22 and we have 25♌︎. Add this to your list.

Similarly, for the Mars position. In the Mars table we find that in the period from midnight (o h. o m.) 30 June to 10 July the planet moves 5°. That is ½° a day. We must therefore take the movement to late on 2 July as having been about 1½°. Add this to 10♎︎ and we have 11½°♎︎; but as we are keeping to whole degrees we may call this 12♎︎. Add this to your list.

It is necessary to state here that it is quite impossible to give a consistent rendering for these three planets without taking

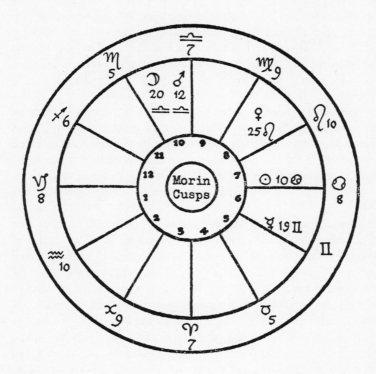

8. INSERTION OF MERCURY, VENUS, AND MARS

Entering of these between the correct cusps is done by following the same method described for the Sun and Moon. The symbols should be written very distinctly so that later examination of the map may be without error. Note particularly the difference between Mercury and Venus.

the day-to-day positions from an ephemeris, and this must be done where there is need for complete accuracy. The margin of inaccuracy using tabulations in this work will be under one degree in most instances. This is not serious, especially when one realizes that few birth times are known with complete accuracy. To strive after total accuracy in such matters is only justified where the original data can be verified.

You will discover when you come to the later stages of your study of this subject that there are methods whereby any birth map can have rectification. It is not considered practical or advisable for the beginner to attempt anything of this kind, hence omission from this work of the way it has to be done.

The symbol R in the Planetary Tables, and the following D

This indicates that the planet turns *retrograde* on the first date where R occurs. Following dates with an R marking show that the retrograde movement continues. On the date when the planet ceases to be retrograde appears the letter D, meaning *direct*.

Planets, due to the earth's motion, appear at times to move backwards (retrograde). This is because the earth appears to be overtaking another planet which, as observed from the earth, has all the appearance of moving backwards, much as a fast train passing in the same direction as a slow one makes the slow one appear to be going backwards to the passengers looking out.

Do not let this perplex you. For the time being it is enough if you realize that where the R makes its first appearance a planet is going backwards in the signs, and therefore instead of adding quantities for later dates they must be deducted. For example, on 22 May 1903 for Mercury we have the entry 16♊ R. On 31 May we have 14♊ R, and on 10 June we have 9♊ R. This means that Mercury was moving backwards, as it were, and so on 10 June it is 7° of ♊ *less* than on 22 May.

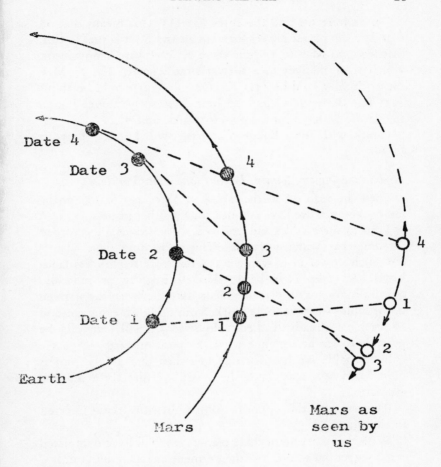

Date 4
Date 3
Date 2
Date 1
Earth
Mars

Mars as
seen by
us

9. RETROGRADE AND DIRECT MOTION (R. & D.)

The facts are here made clear enough. Dates when Mercury, Venus, and Mars are retrograde and those when they resume direct motion are shown in the tables by R. and D. after planetary positions. For other planets see lists which appear following their tables.

On 15 June we find the entry 8♊ D. This means that on that date the planet moves forward again. So it comes to this, that from 22 May to 15 June there is 'backward' movement, which then changes to a forward movement. On 27 May the position would be 15♊ R. On 5 June it would be about 12♊ R. Between 15 and 20 June it scarcely moves but in the period 20 to 30 June it goes forward some 7°.

Check with the tabulation and this will be clear to your mind.

Finding the Jupiter, Saturn, Uranus, and Pluto Positions

These are read off in the tables on pages 193 to 208 in the same manner as we have adopted for the other planets.

Turn to these tables and you will see positions are recorded at somewhat wider intervals. This is because these planets are much slower in movement and therefore require less tabulation. So they have been tabled fortnightly or monthly. Naturally, the exact placements on dates between those given in the table will have to be worked out using the same method as we have already studied. However, it will generally be possible to see at a glance what the positions are.

In the table we find for our specimen that 2 July 1903 is given. So we may take the positions directly from the tabulation.

Reference to the opposite page will show these inserted in the map.

With the insertion of these planets we shall have completed what we set out to do. For the moment put them on your list.

It is always wise, however, to check that all the positions are in fact correct.

Inserting Sun, Moon, and Planets in the Map

This has already been demonstrated as we went along. But this was a result of having made a preliminary list. With this list in hand, we looked to see which of the bodies were in the various signs and gave them a grouping mentally.

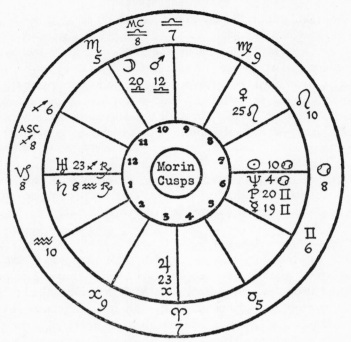

10. INSERTION OF OTHER PLANETS AND ASC AND MC

The map is now completed with the insertion of Jupiter, Saturn, Uranus, Neptune, Pluto, the true Ascendant and Midheaven.

How the completed list of bodies should look

The List		Order of Insertion		
☉ 10 ♋		(1) ☿ 19 ♊ ⎫		
☽ 20 ♎		(2) ♇ 20 ♊ ⎬ 6th House.		
☿ 19 ♊		(3) ♆ 4 ♋ ⎭		
♀ 25 ♌		(4) ☉ 10 ♋	7th House.	
♂ 12 ♎		(5) ♀ 25 ♌	8th House.	
♃ 23 ♓		(6) ♂ 12 ♎ ⎫		
♄ 8 ♒ R		(7) ☽ 20 ♎ ⎬ 10th House.		
♅ 23 ♐ R		(8) ♅ 23 ♐	12th House.	
♆ 4 ♋		(9) ♄ 8 ♒	1st House.	
♇ 20 ♊		(10) ♃ 23 ♓	3rd House.	

Thus, the first of the twelve signs which holds planets is Gemini, which has Mercury and Pluto. Then we come to Cancer, which has Neptune and Sun. We can see that Mercury and Pluto are beyond ♊ 6 and must therefore be placed in the Sixth House. Neptune is in a lower degree than the ♋ 8 on the Seventh Cusp, and so it must also go into the Sixth House. But Sun is beyond the degree on the Seventh Cusp, being in 10° of Cancer, and so it must go into the Seventh House. This you will observe clearly enough if you examine the specimen.

Finally, having inserted the various bodies in a map, be quite sure to check that there are ten entries: Sun, Moon, and eight planets. It is only too easy to miss one out!

Finding the ASC and MC Positions

This is the final stage in erecting the map. It is usual nowadays to indicate the positions of the true ASC (an abbreviation for Ascendant) and MC (Medium Coeli, or Midheaven) in Morinus maps though it is none too clear whether Morin himself intended this to be done. We know, however, from experience (and as will be discussed later) that these positions have strong relevance to individual trends. Even if this were not so, it would still seem to the author desirable to insert them so that people using other systems may make easy transposition of Morinus maps. Merely an act of courtesy, for many of them may have no Morinus Table handy.

Locating the positions is easy enough. You have only to turn to the table on page 117. There against the S.T. for the map you will find the proper MC in the second column and, under the necessary longitude, the proper ASC.

Having found these, write them in on the map as shown in our specimen.

Note, please, that the ASC in other systems is also the cusp of the First House, and the MC the cusp of the Tenth. Systems much in use are Placidus, found in most ephemerides (most inaccurate in usage), Natural Graduation, and Equal House Division.

Having dealt with the specimen, following the processes which the author has used, you are now ready to attempt a map of your own. It is suggested that you tackle your own. Do this unhurriedly. Where in doubt about a process, turn back to the equivalent stage in dealing with our specimen. Re-read the instructions and you will find how to continue.

Provided you follow the correct steps, and get your data right, it is possible for you to produce a map of very considerable accuracy.

As an *aide-mémoire* these steps are condensed on page 27.

3. WHERE THE TIME FACTOR IS UNCERTAIN

In some countries it is customary for the correct time of a birth to be recorded. Where this is not so there is often uncertainty, or even complete ignorance, about the time. In such instances there are three methods which can be adopted:

(1) The correct time can be arrived at by a process of rectification which is in regular use amongst practitioners. It is considered to be unsuited to the beginner because of its technicalities.

(2) The time of sunrise for the day of birth can be taken as an acceptable makeshift. It is true that the resultant map will not have as much individuality as one for the correct birth time; but it will yet be a map for those people born on that day, in the sense that the time of sunrise is the beginning of it and therefore a proper basis for a map covering the day. Certainly, the map so drawn has importance; but it has to be judged in realization that it lacks much individuality.

(3) A map can be drawn which shows merely the signs on the cusps, as shown on page 9. Such a map has the virtue of giving a secondary house-value to the planetary positions and it would probably be regarded as a good deal more individualistic than a sunrise map in that respect.

The author would recommend the use of the third method. However, as use of sunrise maps is fairly widespread the tabulation below will enable the reader to arrive at the correct sunrise time for drawing a personal map at 51 N 30.

Perhaps one should add here that it is the structural relationships, caused by their distances one from another, which hold dominant importance in studying the luminaries and planets in a map. It would be quite possible to dispense with a map altogether and still to achieve a very large understanding of an individual. Naturally, one wishes to have a more complete understanding than this. Yet it can be said, with little fear of contradiction, that (provided the Moon placements were not taken into judgement) much would be revealed merely from the positions of the various bodies at any time during a given day. People born in that day share many characteristics. This will be understood in the later stages of this study.

. . . . .

SUNRISE (51 N 30)

Jan.	1	8.06	Apr.	1	5.38	July	1	3.46	Oct.	1	5.59
	7	8.05		7	5.24		7	3.51		7	6.09
	14	8.01		14	5.08		14	3.58		14	6.20
	21	7.54		21	4.53		21	4.06		21	6.33
Feb.	1	7.40	May	1	4.34	Aug.	1	4.22	Nov.	1	6.52
	7	7.30		7	4.23		7	4.32		7	7.02
	14	7.18		14	4.11		14	4.42		14	7.15
	21	7.04		21	4.01		21	4.53		21	7.27
Mar.	1	6.47	June	1	3.49	Sep.	1	5.12	Dec.	1	7.42
	7	6.34		7	3.45		7	5.21		7	7.50
	14	6.19		14	3.43		14	5.32		14	7.57
	21	6.02		21	3.42		21	5.43		21	8.03

STAGES OF ERECTING A MAP
Giving pages where instructions appear

(1) Use formula S + T + A ± R to find S.T.*   ..   .. page 5
(2) Turn to Morinus Table (Table 4) to find cusps.   Insert .. page 6
(3) List Sun, Moon, and planet positions (Table 6)   .. pages 12 to 24
(4) After collation insert above in the map
(5) Find ASC and MC and insert in the map (Table 5)   .. page 24
(6) Check to see all necessary factors are entered

* Instead of (1) use method (2) or (3) if time is unknown

N.B.: Make sure that all the necessary data on which the map is founded is shown clearly above or below it. This information should include:

Name........ Date of Birth........ Time of Birth........
Place of Birth........ Latitude and Longitude of Place........
S.T. for the map........

In the centre of the map should be inserted the name of the system of map-construction which has been used.

It is also a convenience if the date on which the map was erected is noted. If the information on which it is based has been taken from a book, or provided in some other way, it is generally an advantage to make a note of the source.

Should the name not suffice to indicate sex, this should be noted and, of course, where the map is for a person already dead that fact should appear together with the date of death.

A Note on Circular Measure

Since degrees and minutes are having mention, it may be as well to remind you how calculation is done.

A circle contains 360° (360 degrees).

One degree equals 60 minutes.	$1° = 60'$.
One minute equals 60 seconds.	$1' = 60''$.

Also we have the division into signs.

One circle contains 12 signs.	1 circle = 12 S.
One sign contains 30 degrees.	1 S = 30°.
One degree equals 60 minutes.	1° = 60'.
One minute equals 60 seconds.	1' = 60''.

S + T + A ± R Calculations for some other places

(1) 5.50 p.m. G.M.T., 2 July 1903, Exeter, England. S.T. for date =
    18.35 at oo hours.

S	= 18.35	
T	= 17.50	This is G.M.T. and so the time for planets' places.
A	= 3	
	36.28	
	24.00	
	12.28	
R (minus) =	14	This is correction given in Table 3.
	12.14	This is the time consulted in Table 4.

(2) 5.50 p.m. Local Time, 2 July 1903, Washington, U.S.A.

S	= 18.35	
T	= 17.50	This is = G.M.T. 22.50, Zone Time being 5 hours behind G.M.T. Planets therefore are for 22.50.
A	= 3	
	12.28	(The 24 hours have been deducted. See above example.)
R (minus) =	8	This is correction given in Table 3.
	12.20	This is the time consulted in Table 4.

(3) 5.50 p.m. Local Time, 2 July 1903, Stockholm.

S	= 18.35	
T	= 17.50	This is 1 hour ahead of G.M.T. Planets' places at 16.50.
A	= 3	
	12.28	(The 24 hours have been deducted.)
R (plus) =	12	This is correction given in Table 3.
	12.40	This is the time consulted in Table 4.

PART TWO

MEANING IN THE MAP

LIKE ALL OTHER KINDS of maps, ours have special meaning. You will have realized already that placing the various bodies in the houses of the map must have meaning. That is so. It is one of several means for interpreting the map. Let us deal with this one first.

Each of the twelve houses represents a separate area of the individual's interests. Here is a brief statement of what is involved:

House 1: The personality and disposition of the person, and his outlook on the world.

House 2: The resources of the person, notably in terms of money and possessions, and also the strength of his ambition.

House 3: The intellectual qualities of the person: his capability of self-expression, his communication with the world at large (as where he writes, or travels, or communes), and his subconscious mind.

House 4: The original milieu of the individual, his home life, and all matters which bear upon these as in estate and inheritance, etc.

House 5: The person's generative powers (procreation chiefly), and those things in which he finds pleasure and amusement.

House 6: The service given by (and to) the person, and the question of physical resources in general.

House 7: The relationships of the person, in particular those which are brought about by partnership or marriage.

House 8: The regeneration of the person, including augmentation of his resources—especially through some form of partnership or as a result of some other person's volition (as in a legacy). This house is also associated with the decay of energies and death.

House 9: The ideology of the person and things which call for possession of a philosophy. We include here such varied subjects as religion, science, the presentation of views (as in publications), and the legalistic side of life. Also included here is foreign travel.

House 10: The vocation, the ability with which it can be pursued, and the status of the person together with the responsibilities and activities which it involves.

House 11: The effects of friendships and social life on the person, his interest in humanity, and in general his hopes and desires.

House 12: The limitations of the person, whether self-imposed or as imposed by others (enemies, critics, etc.), and intimate secrets.

Sun, Moon, and Planets in the Twelve Houses

Knowing what the twelve houses represent is interesting, but it is not sufficient to enable a judgement to be made. What we need to know is what happens as the various bodies are found to be in certain of the houses.

Primarily, we can say that the presence of Sun, Moon, or a Planet in any house gives additional importance to it.

This you will realize if one puts it in this manner. It is of very little use talking abstractly of some other person's relationships. A normal person has relationships but we need more precision if we are to say something positive about them.

We may, in the ordinary way of things, learn that he has a wife—perhaps a woman of imagination and drive—and this will lead us to recognize that in dealing with him we need to count in the influence of this partner. You see, he has a special relationship.

The same thing occurs in dealing with a map. We may find Venus is in the Seventh House. This would immediately

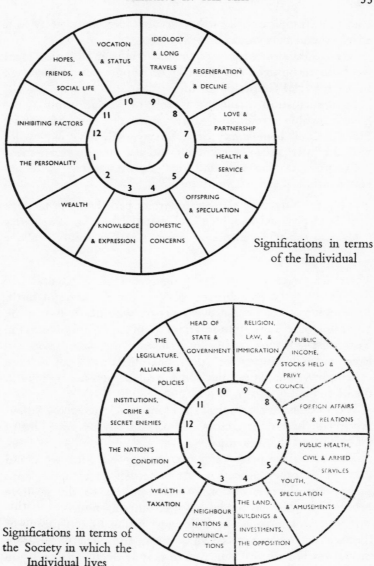

Significations in terms
of the Individual

Significations in terms of
the Society in which the
Individual lives

II. SIGNIFICANCE OF THE HOUSES

lead us to suppose that further inquiry into matrimony as it
affects the person would be advisable.

We would know, for instance, that Venus in that placement
has been recognized as indicative of importance of marriage
in the material factors of the life.

So that, instead of talking merely of " relationships " we
have been able at once to create a picture of a person in whose
life marriage, beneficially or adversely, will have had widespread effects on the personality and its outer expressions.

On page 38 you will find that this placement of Venus
conveys these general suggestions:

> Marriage tends to play an important part, being productive
> of both personal happiness and material benefit. Popularity
> helps in the achievement of success. Artistic ability is above
> average.

These are *suggestions* not final judgements. A good deal will
depend upon the conditioning of Venus at the time of birth.
You must not take it that every person who has Venus in the
Seventh House is happy in marriage, popular, artistic, and so on.
You *can* take it more or less for granted that such a person will
have much emphasis on questions affecting happiness in
matrimony, popularity, and some kind of artistic interests in
the life.

What you have here is the broad hint which will allow you to
investigate important factors. Also, you have a widening of
viewpoint on the individual.

This opens the personality out far beyond what we could
manage by other processes. At once we are brought from
the purely abstract notion of relationships to the positive
insight into their probable shape and directioning.

If you will look at the following listing of the meanings
that are accepted when the Sun, Moon, and planets are found
in various houses you will realize that with this in hand you
have a clue to much that any map can represent.

We will consider later how this information can be used.

THE SUN

(1) Ambition and a love of power tend to be well supported by good health and vitality.

(2) Extravagance and a love of ostentation and splendour fortunately tend to be counterbalanced by the ability to acquire money easily.

(3) Keen observation and eagerness for investigation increase the capacity for educational progress. Science and literature usually have a strong appeal.

(4) Filial sentiments and family ties are strong and inheritance through the parents is probable. Occupations connected with land or property have normally a strong appeal and ability for this kind of thing is marked.

(5) Love of pageantry and social occasions is usually well marked, with consequent attention to amusement and pleasure. Charm of personality tends to arouse the interest of the opposite sex. Music and drama have a strong appeal.

(6) Considerable administrative efficiency usually brings well-paid positions well within reach and success is promised in responsible posts, preferably under the direction of others. Liability to frequent changes of occupation.

(7) Marriage tends to assume considerable importance, usually bringing widening of social status.

(8) Probability of financial benefit by marriage, although this may be dissipated by the extravagance or generosity of the marriage partner. Gain by inheritance is likely.

(9) High ideals and lofty ambitions go hand in hand as a general rule with tolerance and depth of understanding. There is a love of travel and probably much attention to matters of a highly enterprising nature. Intellectual and scientific pursuits have a strong attraction.

(10) Success and the ability to hold positions of trust are probable, but the benevolent interest of superiors is likely to be another important factor. Public recognition may result.

(11) Friends and acquaintances, especially those in positions of responsibility, may contribute largely to early success and the realization of the ambitions.

(12) Possibility of conflict with those in authority or incompatibility in family life strengthen the inclination for seclusion and a quiet, retired life. Those in a superior position are likely to give assistance if necessary.

THE MOON

(1) Considerable restlessness is usually tempered by an easy-going disposition, but love of travel is likely to be strongly marked.

(2) There is likely to be considerable fluctuation in finances, although they tend to be on a satisfactory basis. The chief danger appears to reside in a marked love of opulence and general extravagance.

(3) Love of change and variety is likely to encourage travel and stimulate interest in those occupations, such as newspaper work, in which novelty is the dominant element.

(4) Family life tends to be an important factor in the development of personality and the major interests are usually centred round domestic questions. Frequent removals may occur, but gain can normally be expected from houses and land. Financial benefit may also come from inheritance.

(5) Inconstancy and unusually fickle affections are linked up with a love of gambling and speculation. There may be a rather exaggerated interest in amusement and social activities. Fondness for children is usually strongly marked.

(6) Service is likely to be the key to success and the greatest benefits tend to come from work in a subordinate capacity.

(7) Popularity tends to confer success in all dealings with the public at large and contributes to social success. Money or property may result from marriage and partnerships are likely to prove profitable.

(8) Possibility of money by legacy, or through mother, wife, or partner.

(9) Imagination is usually strong and tends to encourage mental changeability. The person often experiences dreams of unusual vividness. Much travel, especially by sea, is probable and is likely to be productive of gains.

(10) Popularity and prosperity are likely to come from success in public ventures. Feminine interest is likely to be aroused and success usually comes from occupations in connexion with the public at large. Thrift helps considerably in the accumulation of property.

(11) A wide range of friends brings popularity and success in connexion with societies, associations, and clubs. Women tend to play a large part in the life.

(12) Home life tends to be favoured or an occupation involving seclusion, such as nursing, prison work, or charitable work.

MERCURY

(1) Quickness of wit and mental ingenuity tend to be strongly marked. There is likely to be a vital love of knowledge, devotion to study and interest in literary pursuits. Adaptability is a striking feature.

(2) Gain is likeliest to come from a profession, or an occupation in which the person acts as go-between often proves highly lucrative. Considerable skill in the handling of money is another feature.

(3) Serenity and an optimistic outlook tend to enhance the mental faculties and encourage a love of study. There is likely to be considerable practical ability and success.

(4) Home conditions are likely to assume undue importance and environment may cause much mental disturbance.

(5) Refinement tends to be an important characteristic. Ability for drama or acting may be conferred. Children usually play a large part in the life and have a special fascination.

(6) Too much mental activity is likely to be a source of difficulty. There is a liability to overtax the physical resources. Trouble arising from dealings with subordinates tends to induce worry.

(7) Popularity in literary and scientific circles may lead to success. Partnership is likely to be an important factor in connexion with the occupation, especially an alliance with a younger person.

(8) Sedentary occupations in partnership, or some form of literary or scientific work, are the most promising sources of gain. Financial benefits may also come by marriage or by a legacy.

(9) Travel is likely to be an important factor and the occupation may be linked up with it in some way. The self-expression is strong.

(10) Resourcefulness and great mental activity are conducive to the necessary ability for coping with the contingencies of life. Success from the vivid self-expression is highly probable. Business ability is usually strong.

(11) Intellectual keenness tends to enhance the reputation in connexion with societies and associations, but there is a liability to drift into a hypercritical attitude and to indulge too freely in cynicism.

(12) Literary work or scientific research are likely to constitute the major interests. Worry and over-attention to trifles are grave menaces to peace of mind and latent mental ability may fail to be developed owing to lack of suitable practical opportunities.

VENUS

(1) Amiability and a cheerful temperament help popularity and there is a usually great love of companionship and social life.

(2) To natural ability in handling finance is usually added the necessary magnetism of personality which ensures the good will and assistance of others. There may be some tendency towards extravagance.

(3) Interest in literature, music, and painting is likely to be marked and gain may arise from these sources. Travel is another potential source of profit and pleasure. A sunny disposition.

(4) Domestic environment tends to play a large part in enriching the personality and there will be intense love of beautiful home surroundings. Home life usually creates much happiness, especially in later years.

(5) Social intercourse, pleasure, and amusements tend to be a centre of interest. Contact with others on terms of affection will contribute much to happiness and popularity is likely to be an extremely important feature. Interest in the arts and practical ability in those branches which encourage social intercourse is likely.

(6) Harmony tends to prevail in occupational matters and smooth co-operation with others is likely to facilitate the achievement of success. Health is likely to be good.

(7) Marriage tends to play an important part, being productive of both personal happiness and material benefit. Popularity helps in the achievement of success. Artistic ability is above average.

(8) Marriage, partnership, and inheritance are likely to be vital issues, being productive either of great benefits or of heavy losses.

(9) Idealism and sensitiveness to the poetry of life help to enhance the charm of personality. Good taste in artistic matters and an intense love of beauty tend to have as their complements sympathetic understanding for others and great generosity.

(10) Popularity, especially with the opposite sex, and a wide circle of acquaintances are usually indicative of harmonious contacts in both public and private life. Success is likely to be accelerated as a result of the benevolent interest of superiors.

(11) Friends tend to assume great importance and interest centres round social contacts. The interest and assistance of others is usually present in the endeavours.

(12) Some secluded occupation is likely to offer the maximum possibilities of gain, or work of a rather commonplace nature.

MARS

(1) Courage, self-confidence, enterprise, and industriousness are usually the salient attributes. Marked administrative ability and speedy execution of projects tend to ensure early success. Natural energy and physical endurance may have to be brought into play to counteract the effects of an inherent tendency to rashness.

(2) Individual effort is likely to be the greatest factor in the acquisition of wealth and money tends to be a big incentive to endeavour.

(3) Mental alertness and executive ability, backed by initiative and resourcefulness, facilitate early success. The argumentative disposition tends to be productive of frequent quarrels.

(4) Aggressive acquisitiveness is likely to stimulate efforts to accumulate wealth and possessions, but personal endeavour may be supplemented by inheritance or gain by marriage. Domestic disturbances are highly probable.

(5) Love of sport is likely to be well developed and there will be much attention to pleasure. Interest in the opposite sex will tend to be strong, but is balanced by a capacity for loyal companionship. Leadership is likely to be the dominant principle.

(6) Energy and industriousness facilitate promotion to responsible positions, but efforts should be in connexion with some large concern where they are under the control of a superior. Individual effort tends to have less chance of success.

(7) An impetuous temperament tends to precipitate strange domestic circumstances (sometimes an early marriage) but benefit usually results. The marriage partner is often a person of strong and forceful character, with great energy and a love of domination.

(8) Pecuniary gain by marriage, legacy, or partnership is probable.

(9) Mental alertness is stimulated by a love of change and there is likely to be considerable fondness for a roving existence. Excellent capacity for propaganda. A somewhat contentious nature.

(10) Ambition is usually backed by energy and vitality. A masterful temperament in alliance with exceptional executive ability permits surmounting of obstacles in the way of success. Courage and independence may result in social prominence.

(11) Capacity for social leadership and enthusiastic pursuit of pleasure usually help to attract a wide circle of friends, particularly among people interested in sports and energetic activities.

(12) Considerable administrative ability usually produces success.

JUPITER

(1) Urbanity and a generous, honourable disposition inspire respect, but there may be a tendency to self-righteousness. There is likely to be considerable love of pleasure, especially travel and outdoor pursuits. Executive ability is often found.

(2) Financial talent and the ability to accumulate wealth are frequently marked characteristics.

(3) An optimistic temperament and philosophical turn of mind often enable the maximum benefit to be derived from educational facilities. Popularity, especially with members of the family and neighbours, may also result. Travel and correspondence may be important factors in the development of personality.

(4) Domestic environment is frequently of great importance and home conditions will play an important part in shaping the character. Business affairs will tend to evolve on a sound basis with the prospect of material prosperity as life advances.

(5) Social success is highly probable and friends may bring not only pleasure but material benefits. Gain by speculation is possible.

(6) The ability to inspire respect and the willing co-operation of subordinates and fellow workers is an important factor in ensuring success. A capacity for loyal service. Health is normally good.

(7) Marriage and partnership are likely to confer great benefits and result in material gain. The assistance of friends and acquaintances is usually of great importance. Success in the profession is probable.

(8) Gains are most probable through marriage, legacy, or partnerships although the occupation will also produce material benefits.

(9) Natural benevolence and a philosophical outlook strengthen the principles. Tolerance and broadmindedness tend to inspire general respect. Travel is conducive to gain. There is ability to hold office.

(10) The occupation will tend to bring material prosperity and social prestige. Gain is also probable through inheritance. Great nobility of character tends to inspire universal esteem.

(11) Wealth and influential friends tend to facilitate the realization of the ambitions. There is likely to be much love of social life and consequent popularity.

(12) A philanthropic disposition and interest in schemes for the amelioration of troubles often result in success. Willingness to help others is often reciprocated by willingness on the part of others to offer assistance as required.

SATURN

(1) Industriousness allied with patient persistence and self-control is usually sufficiently marked to ensure success. Self-confidence is normally justified by sound, practical ability. A penetrating mind makes for shrewdness, while moral stability guarantees loyalty.

(2) Business acumen, thrift, and prudence contribute largely to the accumulation of wealth, but the process of acquisition may be slow. There is a possibility also of gain by inheritance.

(3) A serious and penetrating mind, well capable of concentration, usually induces the qualities of tact, justice, and honesty. Frequent disappointments may inculcate a habit of gloomy foreboding.

(4) There may be some gain through land or houses, but in the main home life tends to produce cares, deprivations, and a need for the imposition of strict discipline.

(5) Speculation, especially in houses, lands, and mines, tends to be favoured and there is a possibility of holding public office.

(6) Success is likely to come in a managerial capacity, for there is usually considerable ability for the tactful handling of people. Quiet discipline is normally a marked characteristic.

(7) Marriage is likely to be delayed and will probably be to someone older. Loyal co-operation is likely to characterize the union and material benefit may ensue.

(8) Marriage plays an important part in improving or reducing the chances of prosperity. The major gains, however, are likely to come from hard work and sustained effort. Where health is good, long life is usually likely.

(9) Strong opinions on philosophic questions usually make for the right temperament to hold an official position.

(10) Self-reliance and ambition, backed by determination and perseverance, tend to characterize the self-made man. Strong moral qualities and sound business capacity encourage the holding of prominent posts with great responsibility. Organizing ability is likely to be strong and is often spurred on for social prestige.

(11) A few and faithful friends are likely to give valuable assistance in the shape of sound advice based on experience. Older friends, possibly wealthy people, will materially assist in the realization of the ambitions.

(12) A secluded existence is likely. There is likely to be a craving for solitude.

URANUS

(1) Originality and independence of spirit are often the outstanding characteristics, even to the point of eccentricity. There is a love of freedom and hatred of control. Wilfulness is usually well marked and the manner may be brusque. Intellectual interests exercise fascination and there is a strong interest in new ideas.

(2) Restlessness and instability are perhaps the most striking characteristics. Fantastic expenditure and extravagance are likely to imperil the finances. The unexpected will always tend to enter in, and there is some danger of unforeseen losses.

(3) Intellectual and intuitional faculties tend to be good and to bestow ability for dealing with new ideas and inventions. Eccentricity may be a feature. Erratic conduct often interferes with stable education. A love of movement and travel is often also present.

(4) Frequent changes of residence are likely and there may be a strong love of unconventional methods of living. The occupation may bring worries, arising from trouble with superiors.

(5) Unconventional views on social relationships and interest in progressive ideas are likely to be strongly marked characteristics.

(6) Irritability and brusqueness of manner may be present. The temperament is highly strung.

(7) Incompatibility of temperament and inconstancy in matters of the affections are likely to create difficulties in marriage, with consequent estrangement. In any event, marriage tends to be hasty and the romantic element is often well to the fore.

(8) Sudden gains are probable through marriage or partnership.

(9) Independence of mind is well developed, but may tend to be somewhat iconoclastic. There is some liability to fanaticism. There are likely to be long journeys.

(10) A vital love of freedom and abhorrence of restraint intensify the independence and unconventionality of the personality, but often create difficulties with those in authority. Considerable ability, however, on original lines. There is much love of change.

(11) Friends are likely to belong to advanced circles and their originality and creative thought will often help in moulding the personality.

(12) Research work and private endeavour are likely to be the most productive lines of action. Treachery on the part of others, however, is likely to endanger the reputation. Sudden and unexpected misfortunes tend to occur.

NEPTUNE

(1) Aesthetic and psychic powers are likely to be well developed and the temperament may tend to be rather visionary and unpractical. Extreme sensitiveness tends to intensify latent mysticism. There is likely to be much devotion to the arts.

(2) A love of luxury tends to produce financial extravagance and there is often little practical ability in the handling of money matters. There is some danger of loss through fraud. Occupations associated with the sea, institutions, and diplomacy can lead to success.

(3) There is often a strong sense of companionship and possibilities of success in public contacts, especially through public speaking. Frequent journeys by sea may be undertaken. There may be some susceptibility to hallucinations, obsessions, and morbidity.

(4) Harmony tends to prevail in domestic matters and the ties linking the family are likely to be strong. Frequent changes of residence may take place and there will probably be considerable travel. Houses and land tend in the main to be productive of gain.

(5) Love of luxury and entertainment is likely to be a strong characteristic and there is a possibility of over-indulgence in pleasure. There are likely to be good returns from investments.

(6) There tends to be some love of solitude or secluded places. There will probably be considerable capacity for the service of humanity.

(7) Companionship is an important factor in marriage, but there is likely to be some danger from fickleness and inconstancy.

(8) There tends to be considerable fluctuation in financial prospects, but marriage usually brings gain. Money often comes from totally unexpected sources.

(9) The aesthetic sensibilities are exceptionally keen. Intuition and imagination are strong factors. There is usually a love of travel and much of it, but it may be productive of difficulties.

(10) High aspirations coupled with capacity for leadership may bring fame. Irresponsibility, however, and lack of method may make it difficult to secure permanency in any occupation.

(11) An attractive disposition tends to create a wide circle of friends, but many of these are often unstable and may even be actively treacherous. Too much susceptibility to the attractions of others may lead to deception and fraud.

(12) Success in quiet occupations is frequent. A love of seclusion, however, tends to encourage clandestine friendships.

PLUTO

The planet appears to be associated with changes in the matters involved in each of the Houses. Thus:

In the First House:	In early life.
In the Second House:	In financial position.
In the Third House:	In things concerning relatives or travel.
In the Fourth House:	In domestic concerns.
In the Fifth House:	In emotional considerations.
In the Sixth House:	In health or the occupation.
In the Seventh House:	In marriage or other partnerships.
In the Eighth House:	In partnered money matters.
In the Ninth House:	In psychological trends.
In the Tenth House:	In the vocation.
In the Eleventh House:	In friendships.
In the Twelfth House:	In intimate questions of a secret nature.

The Question of Aspects

We now come to a second operation which gives further information about the individual whose map is being studied. It is judgement from what are known as *aspects*.

Aspects are simply certain distances of Sun, Moon, and Planets from one another. In this work, because it is being used by beginners, only five of these measurements are described. There are more, but they are of far less significance, and, in some instances, are of questionable value.

The five aspects treated of here are:

The Conjunction. This is where two bodies are together in the map. If Sun and Moon are both located in 5° Aries we say they are in conjunction.

The Sextile. This is where two bodies are separated by 60°. If Sun is in 5° Aries and Moon is in 5° Gemini, they are 60° apart, so we say they are in sextile aspect.

The Square, or Quadrature. This is where two bodies are

separated by 90°. If the map shows Sun in 5° Aries and Moon in 5° Cancer they are 90° apart and are therefore said to be square one another.

The Trine. This is where two bodies are separated by 120°. If Sun is in 5° Aries and Moon in 5° Leo, they are 120° apart and are said to be trine one another.

The Opposition. This where two bodies are opposite one another in the map. As you will see from the diagram, page 47, to have Sun in 5° Aries and Moon in 5° Libra would be to have them in opposite sides of the map. They are then said to be in opposition.

Quite clearly one could have a sextile from Aries to Gemini, or from Aries to Aquarius. So with the other aspects, except the opposition. Look at the diagram on page 47 and you will see how the distances can be measured. Try one or two examples for yourself.

Put a pointer at 15° Taurus (just midway round the Taurus sector of the diagram). Now put another pointer at 15° Virgo. Count up the degrees between these. They are given in separate degrees and also in groups of 5°. You will find that your answer is 120°. So you will have measured off a trine. If you had measured the other way, so as to have your second pointer at 15° Capricorn, you would have the same result: 120°.

Until you have learned by experience how to make such calculations in your head, you can use this extremely easy method.

The positions which have been given are of *exact* aspects. In our work we allow a little latitude. Thus, it is general to allow for several degrees on either side of an aspect point.

This allowance is called an *orb*.

For the purposes of this book, and to simplify matters for readers without sacrificing accuracy, we shall consider all orbs as of 10°. This would be considered rather too much by the purists, but practical experience shows that it is a reasonable measure.

How do orbs work? If we take the positionings mentioned on the previous page we can say that if Sun is at 5° Aries it is *exactly* in conjunction with Moon at 5° Aries. But in fact we allow that it begins to be in conjunction when Moon is at 0° Aries and continues conjoined until Moon is at 10° Aries.

The aspect when forming (that is, from 0° Aries to 5° Aries) is considered more effective than the time when it is separating (that is, from 6° Aries to 10° Aries). This factor need not concern you too much at this stage because, in any event, the conjunction has great significance whether forming or separating.

Similarly with other aspects. Let Sun be at 5° Aries and Moon at 0° Leo and a trine aspect is forming. The trine will continue to be in force until the Moon is at 10° Leo. And so on.

Naturally, since we use a sort of shorthand for other matters, we do the same with aspects. There are special symbols, and these will need to be memorized. Here are those for the five aspects used in this work:

Conjunction ☌. Sextile ⚹. Square □. Trine △. Opposition ☍.

Thus, when we wish to write down the fact that Sun is in conjunction with Moon we put ☉ ☌ ☽. Sun sextile Moon would be ☉ ⚹ ☽. Sun square Moon would be ☉ □ ☽. Sun trine Moon would be ☉ △ ☽. Sun opposition Moon would be ☉ ☍ ☽.

It saves time and is much clearer to the eye. That is all.

From now on we shall often use the various symbols, not their names, so make sure you really do know them.

Meanings of Aspects

It is considered in astrology that the relationships between the various bodies are coincident with certain conditions in the individual. Do not take any notice of people who wish to tell you that aspects *cause* certain conditions. This is absolutely untrue. What happens is that at the time of birth

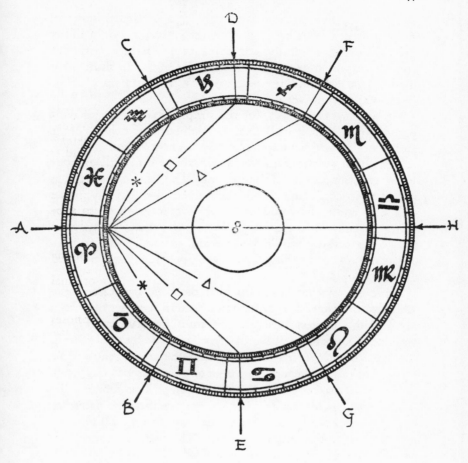

12. MEASURING ASPECTS

It will be seen that the arrow marked A is beside 5° Aries.
Arrow B shows where (at 5° Gemini) a sextile aspect is formed.
Arrow C shows where (at 5° Aquarius) another sextile forms.
Arrows D and E are set at points which are square to 5° Aries.
Arrows F and G are set at points which are trine to 5° Aries.
Arrow H is set at the point which is in opposition to 5° Aries.

all things in the entire universe are at a particular stage of development. Man being part of the universe, and a direct product of it, naturally conforms in his nature with the conditions which exist at the time of his birth. In short, he is made physically and temperamentally in conformity at his birth with the universe.

He will not remain so, for the simple reason that his will-power gives him a malleability. Influence of other people and of milieu will have some bearing on how he will develop, and his own reactions to the world about him will exercise other effects upon his development. The life of mankind is not lived in conformity with the universe—unhappily, some will say—and so it would be utterly preposterous to suppose that as an individual is at birth, so he will remain throughout life. Such a thing would be rare and generally due to sub-normality of some kind. We are speaking here only of normal people.

There is, however, no doubt that the basic structure of the individual remains. It is as though a pattern were set up which can undergo endless variation but must preserve its original outlines. This pattern, as we all know, is very powerful indeed. We have but to see its physical manifestations to know that. Most of us have a likeness to a parent or grandparent. Our noses or our eyes, maybe, have a certain shaping. This remains discernible through life but it also undergoes modification. How we live, the habits we form, what we eat, and so on, will all have some effects on that original pattern. The pattern is there, but we will have modified it—for good or ill.

We can say, for example, that a person born with a quick temper will always show some signs of rapid reaction to affronts. What we *cannot* say is that a child so shaped will *always* respond to those affronts with an explosion of anger. Acquired religious views, for example, may well cause him to control his anger so that it all but disappears. He uses his rapid reactions in a creative instead of a destructive manner.

What was in all probability violent anger in the original

make-up of a man like St. Thomas Aquinas (regarded as a bull of a man), becomes redirected as he lives into a new experience. There then emerges a great passion, in which common anger would be completely lost, and a driving force capable of impressing the world.

On the other hand, the unsuspected anger in a man like the early Hitler was untransformed by him and when the moment came he emerged as a person of unbridled violence. He had done nothing about the original pattern of his life in this respect. As a man, probably as a child, he tended to "eat the carpet". There was nothing in his birth chart to show that he just *had* to develop that way.

There was not, in either of these lives, any element of fatalism. These two men became what they were because of numerous factors, a good many of which were within their own control.

So in considering the placement of planets in a map, and the numerous modifications introduced by aspects, we must not be led into the error of thinking that the map will tell us all about the individual. It will only tell us all about *the original patterning of the individual*, which is a very different thing.

We have means, as will be shown later, of finding out how this original pattern will probably be modified as the life proceeds. At very least, we can estimate the various aids and stresses that are likely to play upon the individual as he lives his life from year to year. From this we can make estimates of how, being the man he is, he is likely to react. But there we come to an ending, for the man himself may, at a moment's notice, call up his will-power and defy even the universe itself in order to do something of entirely different type. He then becomes incalculable.

Aspects are regarded as showing good tendencies and traits, or adverse ones. The writer does not like the too positive naming of them in this respect. True, the word " good " is used in the sense of harmonious, helpful, favourable; " adverse " is used as meaning inharmonious, unhelpful, unfavourable. Such descriptions are approximations. None of us knows what is good or adverse when it comes to the long-term effects of

circumstances. What may seem good to us now may turn out
to be productive of great evil later on; what may appear a
terrible adversity may later on be seen as a blessing.

In using these terms, therefore, let it be understood that their
intention is to indicate what to the detached observer must
appear good or adverse at the given time.

Let us take an example. When Venus has a " good " aspect
with Sun it is generally recognized that the individual will tend
to enjoy the more luxurious things of life. Good? Yes, if he
knows where to draw the line. But what if he regards luxury
foods as desirable and spends many years indulging his appetites?
Is that good? It might be. Who knows? Yet it seems very
probable that it will be productive of physical conditions which
are anything but good.

Meanings of aspects must therefore be taken as informing us
of traits and tendencies, and if we call these good or adverse it
can only be in a relative sense. Perhaps in a *common*-sense
meaning. We must always bear that in mind.

But which aspects are good and which adverse amongst these
five?

The Conjunction varies. In the following list of aspects there
will be sufficient indication of the judgement that can be made.

The Sextile is good, and so is the Trine, the latter being maybe
of much greater intensity. Again, the list will show under " good
aspect ".

The Square and the Opposition are adverse aspects, the latter
of considerable intensity. The list shows these under " adverse ".

Your procedure is thus merely to note Conjunctions as listed,
to look under " good aspect " for Sextiles and Trines, and to look
under " adverse aspect " for Squares and Oppositions.

Now for the list of aspects.

THE SUN

SUN in good aspect with MOON

Success in the occupation. Skill in business affairs. Popularity in social life. Friendly relations with colleagues. Physical well-being. Parents or partners bring material benefits. Many openings for success.

SUN in conjunction with MOON

Intensifies the characteristics of the House involved. Some limitation likely to be imposed. Over-exertion reacts on the physical condition. Frustration may lead to periodic depression.

SUN in adverse aspect with MOON

Delays likely owing to interference by other people. Failure to persevere tends to limit the chances of success. Questions of employment could be troublesome. Relations with women often difficult. Powers of recuperation slow.

SUN in conjunction with MERCURY

Much ingenuity and resourcefulness. A marked capacity to learn with ease and rapidity. Considerable powers of self-expression. Skill in mechanical matters likely to be well developed. Complacency the biggest drawback.

The Sun and Mercury are never more than 28° apart.

SUN in conjunction or good aspect with VENUS

A cultured personality with a marked interest in the arts. Friendly relations make for success in social life. A liking for luxury and amusement, but good taste can be expected in these matters. Great personal popularity. Skill in handling money counteracts extravagance.

The Sun and Venus are never more than 48° apart.

SUN in good aspect with MARS

Superabundant energy and a strong constitution are big assets. Success comes usually through personal efforts. Obstacles are overcome by sheer will-power. Bluntness in handling others is offset by considerable capacity for leadership.

SUN in conjunction with MARS

Some liability to go to extremes. A conflict possible between the will and the desires and there is far too great a tendency to act on impulse. Over-excitement often reacts on health.

SUN in adverse aspect with MARS

A tendency to react too violently to situations. Extreme measures only create fresh difficulties. Recklessness responsible for setbacks and accidents. Quarrels make for strain in relations with colleagues. Restlessness checks progress at work and also affects health.

SUN in good aspect with JUPITER

Social popularity a prominent factor in achieving success. Sports prove attractive. Late in life, perhaps, philosophic or religious trends. Considerable executive ability. Plenty of vitality. Help likely to be forthcoming from people with influence.

SUN in conjunction with JUPITER

Co-operation with others plays a big part in achieving the ambitions. Prosperity can be expected. Benefits through superiors likely. Practical ability, plus generosity and good health, should bring success.

SUN in adverse aspect with JUPITER

Rash action produces difficulties both in the occupation and in money matters. The failure of ambitious schemes makes for strain in relations with others. Litigation, travel, correspondence, all need care. Over-indulgence would be likely to affect health.

SUN in good aspect with SATURN

Good management plays a big part in success. Capacity for organization and skill in handling others are big assets. The necessary ability to fill a responsible post or play a part in public life. Money comes through relatives or older people. Prospect of a good old age.

SUN in conjunction with SATURN

Losses occur chiefly through attempting too much. Thrift and perseverance in methods most likely to bring success. Opportunities missed on occasion through giving way to pessimism.

SUN in adverse aspect with SATURN

Other people create difficulties. An uncongenial environment often causes considerable frustration. Coldness towards others makes co-operation difficult. Excessive caution acts as a brake. Marriage may be delayed. Lowered resistance affects health.

SUN in good aspect with URANUS

Originality and organizing power are big factors in success. Considerable capacity for leadership. New methods bring prosperity. Gains are often sudden and may come through other people. Travel, new friendships, and romantic experiences, important.

SUN in conjunction with URANUS

An exceptional personality with some capacity for success in public life. Success depends on keeping the emotions under control. A highly strung temperament needs to be watched.

SUN in adverse aspect with URANUS

Too many experiments reduce the chances of success. Relations with others often stormy. Unconventionality and stubbornness could cause unpopularity. Sudden reversals of fortune possible. Tactlessness makes enemies. Chief drawback is the inability to concentrate.

SUN in conjunction or good aspect with NEPTUNE

Personal charm and intellectual capacity guarantee success. Ability to influence the public at large by no means improbable. Artistic tastes and creative interests prominent. Some gains through speculation.

SUN in adverse aspect with NEPTUNE

Unreliability reduces the chances of success. A risk of getting involved in shady business transactions. Personal irresponsibility and inability to choose the right friends could damage the reputation. Schemes proposed by other people may involve an element of deception.

THE MOON

MOON in conjunction or good aspect with MERCURY

More than average intelligence shown and intellectual interests are likely to produce benefit. An alert mind and good memory make for success. Charm of manner brings social success. An intense love of change often produces some inconstancy.

MOON in adverse aspect with MERCURY

Failure to concentrate reduces the chances of success. Worry and indecision also act as brakes on progress. Resentment of control can make relations with others difficult. Indiscretions are likely to arouse adverse criticism. Unpopularity and slander possible features.

MOON in conjunction or good aspect with VENUS

Great personal popularity can be expected. Artistic interests are likely to prove attractive. Social prestige above the average, thanks to many and loyal friends. Marriage a source of great happiness. Good expectations of prosperity.

MOON in adverse aspect with VENUS

Disappointments may occur in matters of the affections. Marriage, for instance, suffers through misunderstandings. Domestic friction and even estrangement possible. Extravagance makes for financial difficulties. Health could be affected.

MOON in good aspect with MARS

Personal initiative the best guarantee of success. A good constitution makes it possible to work hard in pursuit of the ambitions. Considerable ability for making money, but this is offset by a free-and-easy manner. There could be gains through marriage or a legacy.

MOON in conjunction with MARS

Strong powers of physical resistance. Difficulties spring chiefly from restlessness. The tendency to fly to extremes needs to be corrected. Irritability makes for strain in relations with others.

MOON in adverse aspect with MARS

Financial difficulties result from carelessness. The passions are easily roused and a hot temper leads to frequent quarrels. Marriage could involve financial difficulties. A domineering manner stirs up antagonism on the part of others, with resultant unpopularity.

MOON in conjunction or good aspect with JUPITER

Prosperity and social success give grounds for satisfaction. The environment is likely to be pleasant with home comforts well marked. Possible gain through speculation or the assistance of someone of a higher social status.

MOON in adverse aspect with JUPITER

Inefficiency over money a big factor. Speculation often results in losses and there is a liability to adopt somewhat doubtful business methods. Litigation a source of trouble. Disturbances likely at home. The unreliability of friends another possible feature.

MOON in good aspect with SATURN

The financial position is satisfactory, thanks largely to thrift and industry. Good management brings success in business affairs. The ability to hold responsible positions makes for considerable personal popularity. Co-operation with others valuable.

MOON in conjunction or adverse aspect with SATURN

The failure of business schemes adversely affects finances. Opportunities may be missed through lack of initiative. Trouble possible in connexion with the home or marriage. The tendency to look on the black side could affect health.

MOON in good aspect with URANUS

Inventiveness and imagination play a big part. Some psychic capacity possible. The power to attract others brings many friends. A possibility of romantic attachments.

MOON in conjunction with URANUS

Mental alertness makes it easier to realize the ambitions. Considerable personal popularity, but some risk of clandestine, or irregular, love affairs.

MOON in adverse aspect with URANUS

Eccentricity makes it difficult to concentrate on the ambitions. A Bohemian existence with much changeability. Relations with others made difficult by a spirit of rebelliousness. Touchiness on personal matters alienates friends. Accidents often caused by carelessness.

MOON in good aspect with NEPTUNE

Great personal popularity. Interest in artistic things and beautiful surroundings. Some creative capacity and great sensitiveness to outside influences. Travel may be a feature.

MOON in conjunction with NEPTUNE

Practical ability is often accompanied by psychic qualities and a tendency towards mysticism. More than average inventive gifts and there could be an interest in scientific research.

MOON in adverse aspect with NEPTUNE

A tendency to live in a make-believe world. Day-dreams and fantasy reduce the chances of success in practical matters. Extravagance and a love of luxury often deplete the financial resources. Wishful thinking a danger in business affairs, especially as associates are often unreliable. Will-power weak and there is great susceptibility to outside influences.

MERCURY

MERCURY in conjunction or good aspect with VENUS

Good powers of self-expression coupled with a keen interest in the arts. A cheerful temperament makes for easy relations with others and considerable personal popularity. The pursuit of pleasure could lead to some dislike of responsibility.

MERCURY in conjunction or good aspect with MARS

Mental energy is marked and there is considerable initiative in the handling of affairs. Swift analysis and a direct manner make for decisiveness. Enthusiasm and industry help to realize the ideals. The drawbacks are too much impulsiveness and a hypercritical attitude.

MERCURY in adverse aspect with MARS

Conclusions are reached far too quickly. Argumentativeness and a sarcastic manner often alienate others. Overwork could dull the mental faculties. Trouble may occur with relatives and there is a risk of treachery. Selfishness warps judgement and causes frequent quarrels.

MERCURY in conjunction or good aspect with JUPITER

Generosity and tolerance make for easy relations with others. Success promised in studies or intellectual pursuits. A cheerful disposition makes for courage in adverse circumstances. Travel helpful.

MERCURY in adverse aspect with JUPITER

Impatience leads to errors of judgement. Opportunities missed, too, through too great attachment to old-fashioned ideas or methods. Indiscretions make for strain in relations with others. Some risk of scandal through choosing the wrong associates. Vacillation causes further delays.

MERCURY in good aspect with SATURN

Ability to concentrate on the main issues helps success. A serious outlook, accuracy, and a sense of responsibility valuable assets. The capacity exists to hold public office. A sober temperament restricts social activities.

MERCURY in conjunction or adverse aspect with SATURN

Lack of foresight frequently delays ambitions. Other people also make difficulties and there seems to be a general lack of opportunity. Misplaced caution often causes delays. An unduly suspicious attitude reduces the number of friendships.

MERCURY in conjunction or good aspect with URANUS

Success comes through personal initiative. Originality of method valuable. Sympathy and honesty of purpose win many friends. Travel usually profitable. Success promised in literary, artistic, scientific, and social pursuits.

MERCURY in adverse aspect with URANUS

Relations with others difficult owing to extreme views amounting almost to eccentricity. Too many changes reduce the chances of success. Some risk of social ostracism through quarrels and the championing of unpopular opinions.

MERCURY in good aspect with NEPTUNE

Refinement is the key to the personality. Varied intellectual interests and considerable powers of intuition. Success promised in the arts, including broadcasting, and activities requiring plenty of imagination.

MERCURY in conjunction or adverse aspect with NEPTUNE

Unreliability creates difficulties in both private and business affairs. Muddled thinking and a love of intrigue spoil relations with others. Schemes are impractical and vague fears cramp initiative. Sensationalism interferes with sound judgement.

VENUS

VENUS in good aspect with MARS

An affectionate personality with a strong love of society. The passions are strong. Gaiety and love of sport prominent features. Marriage could be expected to bring social and financial benefits. Business acumen and skill in handling money probable.

VENUS in conjunction with MARS

Strong likes and dislikes probable. The emotions are easily roused and impulsiveness may lead to difficulties in connexion with the affections. Plenty of optimism and self-confidence.

VENUS in adverse aspect with MARS

Carelessness over money and love of pleasure soon create difficulties. Indiscretions likely in love affairs. Disappointments likely, too, in social life. Partnerships often involve losses. An element of violence makes for strain.

VENUS in conjunction or good aspect with JUPITER

Charm of personality makes for considerable personal popularity. A refined temperament, loving beauty and the arts. Material benefits even may come through artistic interests or travel. Marriage usually happy and prosperous.

VENUS in adverse aspect with JUPITER

Social life frequently made difficult by extravagance or insincerity. Bad taste shows itself in the excessive love of finery. Emotions are unstable and there is a tendency to exaggerate. Quarrels likely to affect married life. Some difficulty, too, in keeping friends.

VENUS in good aspect with SATURN

Stability a marked feature of marriage and social relationships. Loyalty makes for permanency in most associations. Business capacity often above average and benefits come from sound investment. Wealth likely to be accumulated through sound administration of resources. Tastes are simple and there is likely to be a strong sense of responsibility.

VENUS in conjunction or adverse aspect with SATURN

Emotional difficulties and financial worries often occur. The affections are liable to be thwarted and there may be estrangement or bereavement. Some risk, too, of scandal in connexion with love affairs. Jealousy further complicates relations with others. In business affairs there is likely to be opposition from associates, causing delays and losses.

VENUS in conjunction or good aspect with URANUS

Great personal popularity. A romantic temperament with a love of new faces. Easily stimulated emotions and great enthusiasm for new ideas. Good taste in artistic matters and a quick intellect. Brilliant gifts often bring early success. Sudden financial gains possible and frequent travel or removals.

VENUS in adverse aspect with URANUS

Emotional difficulties probable, largely owing to a changeable disposition and lack of tact in dealing with others. A hasty marriage could result in estrangement. Divorce or separation possible. Unconventional views attract criticism. In financial matters there could be sudden losses or difficulties through speculation.

VENUS in conjunction or good aspect with NEPTUNE

A highly emotional and romantic temperament with a keen interest in the arts. Many friendships and numerous love affairs. Other people strongly attracted and there is likely to be considerable success in social life. Artistic talent above the average, especially in music, poetry, or drama.

VENUS in adverse aspect with NEPTUNE

Undesirable friendships could damage the reputation. Far too great a susceptibility to the influence of others. Self-deception also creates difficulties and there is too marked a tendency to live in a world of make-believe. Imprudence and fraud can make for money worries. Faulty speculation and the treachery of associates have to be guarded against.

MARS

MARS in good aspect with JUPITER

A vital personality, enjoying robust health. An adventurous spirit adds zest and there is usually militant championship of causes which appeal. A love of display, colour, ceremony, and movement. Strong powers of leadership. A capacity to make money easily, but gains are usually quickly spent. A love of sport, action, and outdoor activities.

MARS in conjunction with JUPITER

Wealth easily accumulated, but there may be some lack of scruple in the choice of methods. A robust constitution with a keen love of activity. Recklessness, however, makes for unreliability and affairs are often unduly complicated.

MARS in adverse aspect with JUPITER

Too great a tendency to fly to extremes. Boastfulness, recklessness, prodigality common defects. A swaggering attitude reduces the chances of social success. Losses result from over-optimism, gambling, and sometimes the employment of dishonest methods. Errors of judgement likely owing to the strongly biased opinions held.

MARS in good aspect with SATURN

Sound judgement, thoroughness, and perseverance play a big part in achieving success. The necessary qualities exist for holding positions of authority. Only drawback a streak of hardness in the make-up which alienates the sympathy of others. A rather severe temperament with strongly materialistic values.

MARS in conjunction or adverse aspect with SATURN

A malicious temperament with even a possibility of sadism. An explosive temper often creates nervous strain. Mishaps result from recklessness. Violent separations and hostility on the part of others are often associated with an atmosphere of suspicion and mistrust. Sudden misfortunes possible and even disgrace.

MARS in good aspect with URANUS

Success usually comes from boldness in the conception of schemes and energy in their execution. A well-marked inventive faculty, backed by sound practical ability. Confidence, self-reliance, and tolerance other valuable assets. Some recklessness, but absolute fearlessness usually overcomes the obstacles.

MARS in conjunction or adverse aspect with URANUS

An unstable character, highly excitable and with erratic habits. A violent temper frequently causes nervous strain. Strong reactions to even the slightest restraint make for stubborn persistence in a wrong course of action. A liability to accidents and even sudden catastrophes.

MARS in good aspect with NEPTUNE

A generous nature with plenty of enthusiasm guarantees a high degree of personal popularity. Powerful emotions likely, but usually well controlled and the whole personality is dominant and forceful. Plenty of executive ability and there may be special skill in surgery or things to do with the sea.

MARS in conjunction or adverse aspect with NEPTUNE

Grave defects of personality could exist, especially conceit, hatred, and self-indulgence. A self-centred attitude alienates others. The desire for self-glorification appears to be strong. A liability to make enemies easily and to be slow to forgive. Some risk of obsessions and even a persecution complex. Conflict with authority probable.

JUPITER

JUPITER in conjunction or good aspect with SATURN

A strong character, marked by common sense, benevolence, and honesty. Marked practical ability allied with prudence and a liking for the golden mean. Some conservatism. The capacity to win the confidence of others. Success is frequently associated with gains by investment, land or property, and legacies. Great social prestige. Happiness and prosperity increase as life advances.

JUPITER in adverse aspect with SATURN

Ambitions are liable to be thwarted and personal dishonesty could be a factor. Bigotry often makes relations with others difficult. Initiative seems to be lacking, or failure to persist, and vacillation holds up progress. A materialistic outlook with far too much mistrust of others. A liability to make false or libellous statements could create enemies.

JUPITER in conjunction or good aspect with URANUS

Philosophic interests are a marked feature with considerable originality in the opinions held. The religious instinct is well developed and there is usually an attachment to social work and philanthropic ventures. The readiness to help others, allied with real administrative capacity, plays a big part in success. Help from superiors can be expected.

JUPITER in adverse aspect with URANUS

The temperament appears to be headstrong and there is a risk of conflict with authority. Some lack of practical ability together with considerable inconsistency in ideas. Stubborn adherence to misguided opinions, plus a rebellious attitude, makes relations with others difficult. Losses are often due to faulty speculation, litigation, or even travel.

JUPITER in conjunction or good aspect with NEPTUNE

A sympathetic personality, hospitable, humanitarian, and loving beauty. The spiritual side is usually well developed and there may be a tendency towards mysticism. Considerable financial ability, nevertheless, although this may be coupled with rather extravagant tastes.

JUPITER in adverse aspect with NEPTUNE

Certain instability of character with far too much emotionalism. Great attention to ritual and ceremony. Some hypocrisy even and the views held are often extreme. Irresponsibility in financial matters makes for complications. Will-power is weak and there is exceptional sensitiveness to outside influence. Hysterical outbursts possible.

Saturn

SATURN in good aspect with URANUS
Ambition is well marked and there is the necessary capacity to exercise authority in public life. A strong will and serious temperament encourage the holding of responsible positions. Keen devotion to the truth and admirable intellectual powers. Concentration seems to be allied with inventiveness and mechanical skill.

SATURN in conjunction or adverse aspect with URANUS
Success is limited by eccentricity and indolence. Little capacity for concentrating on the practical problems of everyday life. Energy is often wasted on worthless objectives, due to an obsession with vague philosophic ideas. Inhibitions are strong and there may be a deep sense of frustration.

SATURN in good aspect with NEPTUNE
A subtle intellect with keen intuition. Self-reliance well in evidence and determination plays a big part in ensuring success. Considerable skill in wordly affairs. Ideals are usually practical and sound organization makes it possible to realize them.

SATURN in conjunction or adverse aspect with NEPTUNE
An inferiority complex makes it difficult to realize ambitions. The situation can be complicated by scandal or treachery. Fraud often a feature. Initiative is weak and mistakes are liable to be made in dealing with investments, speculation, or property.

Uranus

URANUS in good aspect with NEPTUNE
A strong will is matched with excellent executive ability. Other features are intuition and even some psychic capacity. Love of travel is well marked and there may be many unusual experiences.

URANUS in conjunction or adverse aspect with NEPTUNE
Restlessness and instability the chief source of disappointments. Many strange experiences and there is a liability to suffer from scandal. Some risk of delusions, presentiments, or forebodings. The reputation could be affected by sudden reverses, especially in social life.

Pluto aspects, pending results of research, have been omitted.

There are other forms of judgement which are used, but it is the author's view that the beginner should confine himself to the two procedures described in this Part. Otherwise it is likely that he will find himself hopelessly involved in a maze of intricacies. What will be produced by only these two procedures will be less than is desirable; but not so as to make judgements lacking in utility. In fact, a good many of the more intricate methods employed are found to serve little purpose in increasing sound judgement.

A word more on calculation

Always work in orderly fashion. Start with Sun to Moon, then to Mercury, Venus, Mars, and so on. Then take Moon to Mercury, Venus, Mars, etc. Next take Mercury to Venus, Mars, etc. So through all of the bodies.

Begin by making a list like the one on the opposite page. This ensures that you cover all the likely aspects.

Taking our specimen map we can begin to calculate thus: ⊙ 10 ♋ to ☽ 20 ♎. Using the method already described this is found to be 100°. The orb of the Sun extends forwards to 15♋ and that of the Moon backwards to 15 ♎. This is therefore a square, □.

Next we take ⊙ 10 ♋ to ☿ 18 ♊. This does not give a result in our calculations here.

So on to ⊙ 10 ♋ to ♀ 25 ♌. Again, no result.

Next, ⊙ 10 ♋ to ♂ 12 ♎. This we find is 92°. It is within orbs of square. So we write against ⊙ in our list □ ♂. (See how this has been done opposite.)

You can now try ⊙ to ♃, ♄, and ♅, for yourself; but you will find that there are no aspects such as are required by us here.

Forward then to ⊙ 10 ♋ to ♆ 4 ♋. This is only a distance of 6°, and it is, therefore, a conjunction. We write ☌ ♆ against ⊙. (Check with the list opposite to see how this has been done.)

Now take aspects of Moon to the planets. Start with ☽ to ☿, then to ♀, then ♂, and so on.

After that take aspects of Mercury to the planets.

So right through the list.

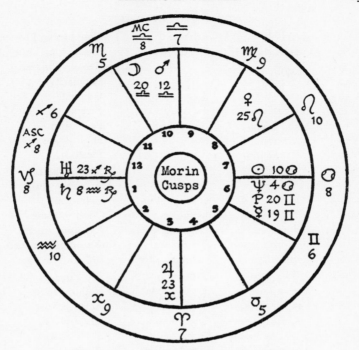

13. Specimen Map Complete with Aspects

ASPECTS

☉	10	♋		☉ □ ☽ □ ♂ ☌ ♆.
☽	20	♎		☽ △ ☿ ✱ ♀ ☌ ♂ ✱ ♅ △ ♇.
☿	19	♊		☿ ✱ ♀ △ ♂ □ ♃ △ ♄ ☍ ♅ ☌ ♇.
♀	25	♌		♀ △ ♅ ✱ ♇.
♂	12	♎		♂ △ ♄ □ ♆ △ ♇.
♃	23	♓		♃ □ ♅ □ ♇.
♄	8	♒ R		♄ –.
♅	23	♐ R		♅ ☍ ♇.
♆	4	♋		♆ –.
♇	20	♊		♇ –.

CONDENSED LIST OF ASPECTS

	Good (✳ or △)	Adverse (□ or ☍)	Conjunct (☌)
☉ to ☽	Beneficial.	Frustration.	Limitation.
☉ to ☿	—	—	Resourcefulness.
☉ to ♀	Refinement.	—	Popularity.
☉ to ♂	Invigoration.	Aggressiveness.	Conflict.
☉ to ♃	Expansion.	Extravagance.	Prosperity.
☉ to ♄	Stabilization.	Obstruction.	Pessimism.
☉ to ♅	Successes.	Misfortunes.	High success.
☉ to ♆	Creativeness.	Deceptiveness.	Idealism.
☽ to ☿	Animation.	Indecision.	Intuitiveness.
☽ to ♀	Harmony.	Friction.	Attractiveness.
☽ to ♂	Initiative.	Unpopularity.	Extremism.
☽ to ♃	Advancement.	Inefficiency.	Good fortune.
☽ to ♄	Industriousness.	Destructiveness.	Disappointment.
☽ to ♅	Imaginativeness.	Erratic action.	Ambitions succeed.
☽ to ♆	Popularity.	Impracticality.	Other-worldly.
☿ to ♀	Self-expression.	Indiscretions.	Joviality.
☿ to ♂	Enthusiasm.	Argumentativeness.	Impulsiveness.
☿ to ♃	Discrimination.	Impetuosity.	Achievement.
☿ to ♄	Logicality.	Overcaution.	Gravity.
☿ to ♅	Inventiveness.	Eccentricity.	Studiousness.
☿ to ♆	Intellectualism.	Unreliability.	Aestheticism.
♀ to ♂	Strong emotions.	Discord.	Emotionalism.
♀ to ♃	Geniality.	Instability.	Sociability.
♀ to ♄	Constancy.	Exaction.	Shrewdness.
♀ to ♅	Romanticism.	Estrangements.	Artistry.
♀ to ♆	Attractiveness.	Self-deceptiveness.	Exaltation mentally.
♂ to ♃	Self-reliance.	Recklessness.	Prodigality.
♂ to ♄	Bold perseverance.	Inhibitions.	Unsettlement.
♂ to ♅	Progressiveness.	Wrongheadedness.	Overimpressionable.
♂ to ♆	Organization.	Overventuresome.	Adventurousness.
♃ to ♄	Success-winning.	Mistrustfulness.	Cautiousness.
♃ to ♅	Originality.	Inconsistency.	Resourcefulness.
♃ to ♆	Humanitarianism.	Unstable character.	Idealism.
♄ to ♅	Ambitiousness.	Deep inhibitions.	Determination.
♄ to ♆	Perseverance.	Inferiority complex.	Restrictions.
♅ to ♆	Uplifting ideas.	Delusiveness.	Restlessness.

PART THREE

JUDGEMENT OF THE MAP

IN ALL WALKS OF LIFE judgement presents difficulties. For one thing, it depends much on the mental equipment and outlook of the judge. For another, it rests upon the possession of a sufficient array of facts. For yet another, it calls for the assembling of facts in such a way that synthesis is possible.

It would be preposterous to expect the beginner in any subject to know enough to form anything like a perfect judgement, though a good many books which have been written on this particular one assume that this is possible. In consequence learners are disappointed and come to the erroneous conclusion that they are minus some special gift. The truth is that in most subjects even those regarded as experts fail often to form perfect judgements and are hag-ridden by the human factor in their efforts.

We must learn to be patient in these matters, remembering that in all the things in which we have to exercise judgement of one kind or another we made innumerable failures before we reached a point of modest competence. Even the tying of shoe-laces demands a judgement of just where to cross one lace over another to form a bow. We perform this task unconsciously every day of our lives, but there was a time when we fumbled it badly and made, at best, a lop-sided bow which positively refused to stay tied for long.

Judgement comes with use. It comes more quickly for people with swift appreciation of facts. Some see how a thing may be done in minutes, while others require hours to find the way. On balance, it often turns out that the person who learns slowly avoids many of the pitfalls of the swifter learner. Doing the task patiently (failing time and time again, perhaps) a deftness is acquired and this gradually becomes a painstaking habit of judgement. However it may be with the reader, the achievement of a high standard of judgement cannot—and, indeed, should not—be too hurried. Take your time.

Synthesis is another story altogether. Whether it can be taught is difficult to say. Some people have a natural gift for piecing the jigsaw puzzles of varied subjects together so as to produce a neat consensus of facts. Some have a hard time learning how. In some instances there is total absence of the ability to succeed.

Some people are better at synthesis in one subject than in another. A doctor will have the ability to assemble the facts of an illness so as to form a synthesis on which to base treatment; but he may be completely at sea if his car breaks down and the varied symptoms of trouble have to be synthesized so as to know what to do to get it started. The garage hand will be able to perform the task, which seems to him child's play. But then, he would never know how to judge his own symptoms, if ill, so as to provide the synthesis necessary for curing them. He goes to the doctor!

No author can legislate for this side-play in readers' minds. He can only hope that a sufficiency of necessary qualifications will be present, or can be acquired.

Synthesis is, one feels, more a matter of use of previous experience. Everybody has to make a synthesis in some activity or other. The reader will be aware of this and he is recommended to put his experience in some other direction to work on this subject.

For example: a motor mechanic will have found in himself a capability for relating a certain noise to certain causes. When he is confronted with an engine he has a previously settled way of looking into it. He goes from one major point to another, watches how various parts are functioning, listens, and so on. In two or three minutes his brain will have assembled the factors, formed a number of judgements of possible troubles, and as if by a miracle he reduces the whole to a synthesis. He inserts a screw-driver at a certain point and, hey presto!—there, he says, is the point at which trouble is being caused.

To the uninitiated this is almost magical. The mechanic thinks it the most ordinary thing in the world. Yet there was a time not very distant when he also thought the person who taught him was all but a magician. He had in himself the means to synthesize but it had to be called out and trained by hard experience. This is precisely what happens (except where born geniuses are at work, a very small percentage of human beings) in everything.

It is precisely what, if the reader will be patient, will happen in his handling of astrology.

In this spirit, let us see what factors we have at our disposal in trying to judge the specimen map.

First, we have the map itself, which is a picture of an individual. Everything we need is concentrated there.

Secondly, we have discovered that the placement of Sun, Moon, and planets in the various houses has meaning. We have a list giving the meaning for each possible positioning.

Thirdly, we have found that the distances measured between the Sun, Moon, and planets convey meaning. We have a list giving the meaning for each of the possible measurements— aspects—of which the present work treats.

This is a tremendous quantity of material to start us off. How are we to use it?

A first step is to go over the map, seeing what the various positions of bodies means. That is easily done by checking against the list on pages 35 to 44.

Then we can take the aspects we have worked out (page 65) and study their meanings in the list on pages 51 to 63.

This is just about where the motor mechanic is when he looks at an engine for the first time. He could, if he wished, write down all the numerous factors he sees. It would be a cumbersome task, but it would only be what (with long experience) his mind does, anyhow.

In other words, when you look at a map in this manner, you

are receiving a great deal of assorted information. It is useful and it does not matter how cumbersome the task may seem, you will not fail to conclude with some clear impressions of an all-over meaning.

Do this with the specimen map.

Saturn is in the First House. What does that mean? Look at page 41. And so with the other bodies.

Then go back over your tracks. Saturn, you will say, is trined by Mercury. What does this fact mean? Look at pages 37 and 57 and you will see.

Makes notes as you go along.

When we have looked into everything we shall have reached these points of information:

We have found Saturn in the First House.

By looking at our list of aspects we know that it has

a trine from Mercury, which is in the Sixth House—as explained, we are ignoring Pluto here.

Saturn in the First House: that shows industriousness, self-confidence, shrewdness. (This is a condensation of the material on page 41.)

Mercury is in the Sixth House: that shows intensification of mental energy and possible overtaxing of resources.

Saturn is trine Mercury: this is a good aspect. It shows ability to concentrate and to exercise logicality.

So we would conclude, at any rate as a preliminary judgement of this part of the map, that the person concerned is likely to put much hard work, backed by self-confidence and shrewdness, into the logical treatment of intellectual questions.

You see, what we have done is to examine the Saturn placement—to add to this the Mercury placement's meaning—and then, seeing that the two planets are well aspected one to the other, we have formed a conclusion about the individual.

This is the method which has to be adopted with all the bodies, taking each in turn.

In order to help judgement, the author has given on page

66 a useful condensation of aspects. This is the kind of rough guide which can be carried in the mind and will be found helpful when a judgement is being formed. Nobody can hope to carry the full interpretation of every aspect in his head. Use this condensed list in your work.

Thus: Saturn in First—Industry. Mercury in Sixth—Intensive mental drive, perhaps overdone. Saturn trine Mercury— Logicality. Therefore a person capable of hard mental work based upon a sound logicality.

This is by no means difficult to carry through.

Do not be afraid to go at this procedure boldly. What you need to do is to wander around the specimen, as it were, just as you would explore an unfamiliar garden. You will not see everything, nor is it really desirable that you should try to do so. Be content to wander, picking up bits of information as you go.

One thing is certain, and you should not be disappointed at it: after a time you will find there is a sense of confusion. Well, who can describe in any accuracy a garden which has been wandered around? It would require almost unnatural observation, unless it were an expert landscape gardener who did the wandering.

After all, nobody is hurrying you. Take your time. Go from one planet to another in the manner shown. Make a few notes, if you like. You will not be wasting time, for this is an exercise in how to begin an assessment of the various factors.

Look again.

Venus ... Eighth House. Meaning: Marriage an important factor in the life, for good or ill.

Venus is trine Uranus.

Uranus ... Twelfth House. Meaning: Among other things we can find (list on page 42) sudden and unexpected misfortunes, but also that certain productive work is made possible.

The trine is very helpful. Meaning: Romance (list on page 66).

So we can say that marriage, important, will be based on quite romantic lines, giving help in productive work, but possibly not without some sudden misfortune despite the helpful aspect. That would be a reasonable snap judgement. You can see how it is made.

There is need, however, to reduce the quantity of confusion any map can involve. This, in the author's view, is best done by the drawing up of a kind of skeleton of the main aspects. One can by that means have a compact structure which can be studied without so many interlacing factors bound to exist in such maps.

On the opposite page is shown how the most important aspects of the specimen map might be drawn. One has taken the conjunctions, trines, squares, and oppositions. The result is the picturing of the largest effects which would be likely to influence the life.

Such a drawing is in reality a simplification of the map. It is not all the map, but the skeleton which holds it together.

In suggesting this treatment of the specimen, and all the other maps you may erect, the author is specifically limiting the area of judgement to meet the requirements of the learner. *He is not saying that this is the only method, nor is he suggesting that it provides a sufficient basis for, shall we say, interpreting some friend's map.* It is only the basic method used by the astrologue for preliminary inspection of the various bodies in a map. There is a great deal more beyond this and it is recommended that when the learner has done plenty of " wandering " he shall extend his reading so as to learn the finesse of judgement. Obviously, this is not the kind of material with which this work is concerned. It is something which must follow perfecting of the methods that are here described.

It will, however, be instructive to know of one of the ways in which the practised astrologue deals with a map. This can be tried out by the reader when he feels sufficient confidence. Do not be in too great a hurry to make the effort. Far more important will be to get thoroughly familiar with the appearance of a map and to do the " wandering " which has been suggested. Fear of the unfamiliar can be damaging in learning anything. Get rid of this first by a leisurely progress with the specimen.

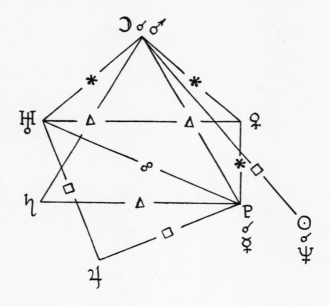

14. The " Skeleton " of the Map

Here we have the principal aspects removed from the body of the map to form a kind of " skeleton ". Doing this allows a clearer viewpoint on their associations and probable interactions.

This is a method which at a later stage can be followed:

Having decided to study the map for some particular side of the individual's life, turn first to the list (page 31) showing which house is connected with it.

Let us suppose you wish to consider marriage. The list will show that the Seventh House deals with this matter.

Now turn the map round so that the cusp of the Seventh House is where the cusp of the First is.

The Seventh House now becomes the First for the time being. The Eighth House becomes the Second, showing the financial effects of marriage. The Ninth House becomes the Third, showing how mental trends will be affected by marriage. So through the whole map.

You may find it easier if you redraw the map to suit this purpose. It is not easy to read a map when it is upside down. Make a new map and you will reduce possibilities of error.

Such a redrawing of the specimen map is shown on the opposite page.

What has happened to our specimen?

It has been moved so that we may form judgement of the concerns of the Seventh House primarily, and the chief of those concerns is the type of partnership of which marriage is the most important.

We now judge in this manner:

Sun in First House: see list of positionings on page 35.

Aspects to Sun, as previously described.

Venus in Second House, and its aspects.

So through the whole map, treating each body as though it were of the new house position instead of its original one. In fact, follow the procedures given for the original map.

Naturally, the practised eye will be attracted to the placement of Saturn in the Seventh House. This is interesting. It has the meaning that matrimony may be delayed rather and be concluded with an older person.

You may ask whether this was so in the life of the individual of our specimen. Indeed it was. He married on 21 March 1929.

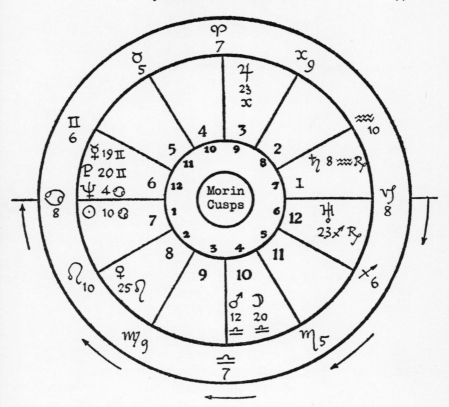

15. THE MAP TURNED ROUND FOR INSPECTION

This is one possible positioning of the map so as to cause the Seventh House effects to be studied. The same can be done with all the other houses in turn. In this example the Seventh House has been given the position of the First House and shows how relationships by marriage or other partnership may affect the individual. The Eighth House now becomes the Second, showing the possible financial effects of such relationships. The Ninth House becomes the Third, showing possible effects upon the individual's mind. And so on.

That is somewhat later than average. His wife was born on 28 March 1901, being more than two years older. The interpretation given on page 73 is confirmed, even to the marriage bringing benefits of a material nature.

Suppose we turn the map round so that the Tenth House is placed where the First was originally, thus examining the vocation of the individual..

We now find that Mars is in the First House conjoining the cusp and that Sun is in the Tenth House conjoining the cusp. Mars so placed is indicative of courage and administrative abilities. Sun so placed is indicative of power.

Do the facts of the life confirm this? Yes, they do. The man concerned (though of a markedly seafaring nation) has given most of his life to military activities, including sportsmanship on an impressive scale, and eventually achieved a position of very great power.

Examination of the aspects gives amplification of this very bold statement, but you can see that a long way can be travelled towards forming a preliminary judgement merely by turning the map round in this manner.

In many maps it will be found that one or more of the houses are unoccupied. For example, in our specimen map the Fourth House has nothing in it. We do not conclude from this that the individual has no indications associated with Fourth House matters, i.e. the home environment. Instead, we make use of a very old device.

We take the sign on the cusp of the house and use the planet associated with that sign as operative. Thus, in our specimen the sign on the Fourth Cusp is Aries. The planet associated with that sign is Mars. Mars is in the Tenth House of this map. Therefore in studying the home environment we look to the Tenth House and in particular to the condition of Mars from aspects.

As you can see from the list on page 39, Mars is known to be representative of social prominence, as well as concerned with a militaristic and administrative set-up, when in the Tenth House.

In the present instance, it is quite correct as an interpretation, for the person of the map has lived continuously in such a social setting and surrounded by people engaged in administration and military concerns.

If we turn the map so that the Fourth House becomes First, then we realize that Mars is placed in a Seventh House position. Our list mentions strange domestic circumstances and refers to impetuosity. It happens that the person of this map was actually compelled to act with great impetuosity, leaving his home and being away from it for several years. You will read that benefits are not uncommonly derived in spite of this kind of situation. So in this instance. The return to his home brought enhanced popularity.

You will note further that in the turned map we now have Sun in a Fourth House position. This is invariably associated with large questions of family ties and inheritance. The man of the map has an unusual consideration of family ties and certainly came into a handsome inheritance.

For this purpose of judging unoccupied houses it is necessary to give you the planetary associations of signs. These are:

Aries (♈)	♂ Mars.	Libra (♎)	♀ Venus.
Taurus (♉)	♀ Venus.	Scorpio (♏)	♂ Mars.
Gemini (♊)	☿ Mercury.	Sagittarius (♐)	♃ Jupiter.
Cancer (♋)	☽ Moon.	Capricorn (♑)	♄ Saturn.
Leo (♌)	☉ Sun.	Aquarius (♒)	♅ Uranus.*
Virgo (♍)	☿ Mercury.	Pisces (♓)	♆ Neptune.*

When you find an unoccupied house, turn to this statement to find which planet is involved. Gradually you will learn this list.

At this point let us summarize the possible procedures:

(1) You can begin by examining the meanings of placements in the map.

(2) You can go on to examine the meanings of the various aspects formed between the various bodies.

This will have given you an all-over impression of the map.

* Some astrologues continue the older usage of assigning Saturn to Aquarius and Jupiter to Pisces. Experience endorses the new usage.

(3) You can take each house separately and note which planets or other bodies aspect the planet occupying it. This will enable you to see how matters affecting the house are given beneficial or adverse tendencies from other houses. A planet in the Second may have a beneficial aspect from a planet in the Tenth. The Second House concerns financial resources. The Tenth concerns the vocation. According to the nature of the planets we know that in the vocational life there will be certain financial advantages. And so on.

(4) You can simplify the map by drawing a skeleton of the major aspects, as has been shown.

(5) You can then turn the map so that whichever house you desire to study forms an artificial First House, proceeding to judge it as if it were, indeed, the First.

Do not imagine that this is the entirety of judgement. It is a useful beginning only. More needs to be learned. Nevertheless, in normal practice many astrologues use little beyond what has been given here—and that chiefly in small refinements. As to making an exhaustive interpretation of a map, that is almost beyond the human capability. The map, like the individual it pictures, is an inexhaustible story the telling of which would require more time than most of us are ever likely to afford. A man is a whole book in himself.

·   ·   ·   ·   ·

A Note on Conjunctions

The Harmonious Conjunctions are:

Sun with Mercury, Venus, Jupiter. Moon also with reservations.

Moon with Mercury, Venus, Jupiter. Sun also with reservations.

Mercury with Sun, Moon, Venus, Jupiter.

Venus with Sun, Moon, Mercury, Jupiter.

Jupiter with Sun, Moon, Mercury, Venus, Saturn.

Saturn with Jupiter.

The Inharmonious Conjunctions are:

Sun with Mars, Saturn.

Moon with Mars, Saturn.

Mercury with Mars, Saturn.

Venus with Saturn.

Mars with Sun, Moon, Mercury, Saturn, Uranus, Neptune.

Saturn with Sun, Moon, Mercury, Venus, Mars, Uranus, Neptune.

Uranus with Mars, Saturn.

Neptune with Mars, Saturn.

Of mixed quality and sometimes adverse are:

Sun with Uranus, Neptune.

Moon with Uranus, Neptune.

Mercury with Uranus, Neptune.

Venus with Mars, Uranus, Neptune.

Mars with Jupiter.

Jupiter with Mars, Uranus, Neptune.

Uranus with Sun, Moon, Mercury, Venus, Jupiter, Neptune.

Neptune with Sun, Moon, Mercury, Venus, Jupiter, Uranus.

It must be realized that the nature of many conjunctions depends on the condition of the bodies forming them. If, for example, one finds a Sun-Moon conjunction in which Moon is undergoing several adverse aspects, the already dubiously harmonious effects will be reduced, if not eliminated altogether.

Another point which needs to be made is that nobody knows altogether precisely how far harmonious conjunctions will operate with beneficial results when viewing them in the birth map. By that is meant that there are people who utterly abuse their good fortune—or transmute their ill fortune—and so miss the effects which are intended. It is never easy to see from the birth map how this may happen. One should therefore be wary about estimating that favourable or unfavourable effects must inevitably follow.

Much the same applies to the other aspects. We have to remember all the time that the birth map is the seedling, as it were, of a growing plant. The plant itself will not be seen for some considerable time after. We are occupied at this stage only with potentialities and trends.

The truth about the individual's use of conjunctions and all the other aspects will only be revealed as we study the progression, as it is called, of the map.

This is dealt with in the next Part.

PART FOUR

The techniques of this Part are based upon the original work by E. H. Troinski in which he gave a description of Tertiary Directions: Das Welt-schicksalsjahr 1959, *published by* Verlag Baumgartner, Warpke-Billerbeck, Hannover. *Subsequent works by the same author are* Tertiar-Direktionen II, Das Horoskop des Atom-Zeitalters, *and the monumental* 1001 Welt-politische Horoskope. *The author wishes to acknowledge most gratefully Herr Troinski's permission* (carte blanche, *indeed*) *to make use of his works in the present book. Table 7 is taken directly from Troinski.*

THE PAUL MASTERS COMPLETE ANALYSIS REFERENCE CHART

ARIES ♈
Cardinal
Fire
Positive
Impulsive
Leaps in
Overly careless
runs in tangents
Self-expressive
Energetic
Assertive
Objective Attitude
Expresses urgency
Self-assertive
Restless
Pioneering
Adventurous
Frank
Direct
Go-getter
Freedom-lover
Quick-thinking
Quick-witted
Overlooks details
Selfish
Impatient
Argumentative
Quick tempered
Foolhardy
Agressive
Brusque
Rude

SCORPIO ♏
Fixed
Water
Negative
Self-repressive
Passive
Emotional
Intuitive
Intensity
Steadfast
Penetrating
Strength of will
Magnetic
Penetrating eyes
Convictions
Restrained
Energtic
Intimate
Mystically inclined
Regenerative
Subtle
Secretive
Purposeful
Experiences deeply
Strong in silence
Ice-cold self-control
Strong reasoning
Imaginative
Skillful
Analytical
Keenly perceptive
Passionate
Extremely jealous
Brooding
Resentment
Destructive
Stubborn
Vindictive
Deliberate cruelty
Hidden

TAURUS ♉
Fixed
Earth
Negative
Restrained
Self-repressive
Passive
Intense
Practical
Steadfast
Productive attitude
Expresses endurance
Security
Material sustinance
Reliable
Conserves
Withholds
Needs to possess
Sense of material values
Art
Beauty
Harmony
Love of good food
Luxuries
Comfort
Productive
Industrious
Cautious nature
Fixed ways
Strong feelings
Stable
Methodical
Deliberate
Constructive
Unoriginal
Possessive
Sensual
Too possessive
Self-indulgent
Stubborn
Rut
Stodgy
Self-centered
Grasping
Resentful
Organized

SAGITTARIUS ♐
Mutable
Fire
Positive
Self-expressive
Energetic
Assertive
Adaptability
Variableness
Spontaneity
Extensive attitude
Freedom
Exploration
Opportunity
Optimistic
Sincere
Frank
Versatile
Mentally active
Sporty
Nature loving
Adventurous
Idealistic
Foresighted
Jovial
Benevolent
Religious
Moralizing tendencies
intellectually inclined
Open minded
Deep thinker
Good judgement
Outspoken
Interpreter
Ardent
Conventional
Extremist

Extravagant
Tactless
Boastful
Inconsiderate
Exaggerating
Careless
Restless

GEMINI ♊
Mutable
Air
Positive
Essentially communicative
Self-expressive
Mentally active
Adaptability
Variability
Spontaneity
Dual
Adjusts
Incessantly on the go
Restless
Inquisitive
Variety
Change
Transmitting
Nervously excitable
Inconsistant
Witty
Chatty
Never dull
Agile
Intelligent
Light-hearted
Fickle
Cooly-affectionate
Flirtations
Unemotional
Superficiality
Lack of continuity
Two-faced
Indefinite
Cunning
Dissipates
Nervous energy

CAPRICORN ♑
Cardinal
Earth
Negative
Self-repressive
Passive
Restrained
Enterprising
Practical
Rational
Prudence
Disciplined
Patient
Persevering
Cautious
Methodical
Resourceful
Bears hardships
Frustration
Self-containment
Serious
Responsible
Careful
Cool
Deliberate
Ambitious
Conscientious
Dutiful
Concentration
Calculating
Exacting
Rationalizing
Severe
Conservative
Modist
Faithful
Selfish
Narrow-minded
Cruel
Unfeeling
Critical
Miserly
Pessimistic
Worrisome
Too conventional
Ambitious

CANCER ♋
Cardinal
Water
Negative
Emotional
Intuitive
Self-repressive
Passive
Defensive attitude
Expressing sensitiveness
Urge to protect
Nourish
Sensitive
Easily hurt within
Outwardly tough
Resourceful
Tenaciously protective
Loyal to Family
Clannishness
Patriotism
Sympathetic
Imaginative
Sentimental
Moody
Reserved
Collects things
Shrewd
Receptive
Retentive
Good memory
Romantic
Very clinging
Tender
Touchy
Inclined to pity
Timid
Untidy
Unstable
Easily flattered
Harbours slights
Sensuous
Jealous

AQUARIUS ♒
Fixed
Air
Positive
Expressive
Communicative
Mentally active
Intenseness
Steadfastness
Spontaneity
Detached attitude
Unconventionality
Progressive
Strong ideals
Humanitarian
Originality
Progressive thinker
Intense energy
Revolutionary
Unorthodox
Scientifically inclined
Artistic
Unpredictable
Friendly
Attracted to unusual
Intuitive
Intelligent
Reforming ideas
Imaginative
Broad-minded
Inventive
Ability to synthetize
Independent
Dispassionate
Detached
Perverse
Eccentric
Touchy
Rebellious
Rude-tactless
Lacks principle

LEO ♌
Fixed
Fire
Positive
Self-expressive
Energetic
Assertive
Intenseness
Steadfastness
Spontaneity
Powerful
Impressive
Pride
Authority
Generous
Warm-hearted
Born leader
Enthusiastic
Dignified
Broad-minded
Outspoken
Good organizer
Dramatic
Self-assured
Loves pleasure
Forthright expression
Overbearing
Fixed opinions
Intolerant
Autocratic
Conceited
Pompous
Bombastic
Touchy
Snobbish
Self-appraising
Patronizing

PISCES ♓
Mutable
Water
Negative
Self-repressive
Passive
Emotional
Intuitiveness
Adaptability
Variableness
Nebulous attitude
Impressionable
Transcend the material
Dual
Compassionate
Emotionally sensitive
Kindly
Sympathetic
Easy-going
Moved to tears easily
Cannot bear to witness suffering
Unworldly
Fluid nature
Impossible to confine
Psychic
Mediumistic
Receptive
Intuitive
Sensitive
Lovable
Submissive
Impractical
Over-emotional
Too-soft
Careless
Indecisive
Touchy
Secretive
Incomprehensible
Confused
Gullible
Extravagant
Tempermental
Dependent
Quiet

VIRGO ♍
Mutable
Earth
Negative
Self-repressive
Passive
Restrained
Practical
Adaptability
Variableness
Analytical
Critical
Efficency
Perfectionist
Discriminating
Detail-conscious
Purity
Thorough
Methodical
Precise
Conscientious
Hygenic
Cleanliness
Reserved
Intelligent
Shrewd
Discerning
Critical
Conventional
Modest
Love of techniques
Hypercritical
Pedantic
Fastidious
Interferring
Too-modest
Suppression of emotion
Over-specialization
Worrying

SUN ☉
Masculine
Positive
Leadership
Superior
Proud - Regal
Dominant
Powerful
Vitality
Expressive
Affectionate
Ambitious
Generous
Honorable
Sense of self
Life-giving
Frank
Forcefull
Arrogant
Extravagant
Impulsiveness
Creator
Aristocratic
Magnetic
Salesmanship
Public contact

MERCURY ☿
Communication
Speed
Wisdom
Neutral
Intellect - Mentality
Changes
Adjustments
Interpreter
Transmitter
Messenger
Perceptive
Observative
Quick to discern
Aquire knowledge
Research
Adaptability
Dexterity
Mental skill
Quick wit
Imagination
Methodical
Systematic
Worry
Haste
Mental irritability
Forgetfulness
Controversy
Reasoning
Written
Spoken
Mental tension

LIBRA ♎
Cardinal
Air
Positive
Self-expressive
Communicative
Mentally active
Enterprising
Spontaneity
Relatedness
Harmony
Wit
Unity
Charming
Kind
Easy-going
Diplomatic
Cooperative
Idealistic
Lazy
Intelligent
Balanced judgement
Inclined to indecision
Influenced by opinions
Optimistic
Compromising
Romantic
Sentimental
Indecisive
Too easy-going
Un-tidy
Frivolous
Changeable
Lack of confidence
Too-soft

MOON ☽
Rythem
Emotional nature
Instinct
Memory
Assimilation
Minor changes
Sensitive
Psychic
Maternal
Sympathetic
Fertility
Imagination
Receptive
Self-gratification
Over-indulgence
Changeable
Uncertain
Feminine
Negative
Fruitful
Convertible
Curious
Reflective
Personality
Desire
Habits
Nagging
Anxiety
Moodiness
Vague imaginings
Hypersensitivity
Touchiness

VENUS ♀
Unity
Love nature
Sympathy
Feeling
Beauty
Love
Warm
Productive
Generous
Kind
Good humoured
Gentleness
Social
Harmony
Attraction
Joy
Expression
Artistic expression
Creativity
Desire
Music
Appreciation
Fantasy
Disharmony
Unbalance
Unstable

MARS ♂
Activity
Energy
Self-assertion
Sex nature
Drive
Identifies with healing
Mechanical
Ability to probe
Probing
Masculine
Strength
Force
Courage
Creative
Power
Work
Strife
Death
Self-confident
Ambitious
Positive
Inventive
Domineering
Passion
Vitality
Accepts challenges
Quarrelsomeness
Argumentativeness
Carelessness
Over-excitability
Extreme sensuality

JUPITER ♃
Expansiveness
Benefits
Generosity
Social
Masculine
Positive
Fortune
Hope
Benevolence
Compassion
Justice
Honesty
Spirituality
Logical
Self-confidence
Development
Wisdom
Higher mind
Jovial
Advancement
Easy-going
Bluntness
Tactless
Exaggeration
Extremes
Losses

SATURN ♄
Stability
Loyalty
Longevity
Conservatism
Paternal
Organizing
Ambition
Positive self-image
Formative
Responsible
Restriction
Discipline
Ridgity
Delays
Denials
Frustrations
Negative
Tester
Barren
Constructive
Isolated
Domineering
Indifference
Negative self-image
Dis-organized
Fulfilled or
Unfulfilled

URANUS ♅
Sudden gains
Unexpected gains
Sudden insights
Genius
Inventiveness
Deviation
Independence
Drastic change
Originality
Inventive ideas
Inspiration
Sudden losses
Over-excitability
Extremism
Rebellious
Anti-social
Anti-custom
Stress

NEPTUNE ♆
Deep emotions
Refinement
Depth of feelings
Drastic changes
Imagination
Sentiment
Mystical
Intuitive
Persuasive
Dramatic
Idealistic
Confusion
Fantasies
Alcholism
Drug addiction
Self-deception

PLUTO ♇
Sex
Drastic Positive Changes
Regenerative powers
Transforming ability
Elimination
Renewal
Children
Chaotic
Violent
Destructive

Erratic
Impulsive
Idealism
Extreme

(Wheel chart labels)

Occupation / Career
Ideology-Religion / Long Travels
Social Life / Groups-Friends
Later Years / Financial Security / Legacies / Stocks Held / Regeneration
Marriage
Business / Partnerships
Health
Work / Relations
Employment
Limitations / Inhibitions / Institutions / Spiritual / Service / Secrets
Outer Personality / Appearance To Others
Wealth / Income / Financial / Resources / Ambition / Possessions
Knowledge / Expression / Education - Arts / Communication
Family-Property / Domestic Life / Inheritance
Romance / Children / Speculation / Amusement / Sex

1970 paul leon masters

TERTIARY DIRECTIONS

THE MAKING OF ESTIMATES of the future of an individual is through what is known as progression of the birth map. There are numbers of processes but all depend upon using dates subsequent to the date of birth as measuring to various years in the life.

This is not too easy to comprehend. Perhaps the best way of describing it would be by taking a parallel in map construction. On a scale map, as you know, distances are reduced. We know we could not use a map the same size as a piece of country and so we say " Let an inch represent one mile " (or some other such measure). By this means we produce something which can be handled easily and which gives us the same information that we would find in exploring the real land area itself.

There is no valid reason why time, as well as distance, should not be represented by a scale. We do, indeed, contrive something of the sort in producing diaries. Nobody pretends that the length of page from one day to another would take as long to fill as a page which we began to write on at midnight one day and continued writing upon until the following midnight, but both represent the same time.

In astrology we say, " Let such-and-such a period represent a year of life ". This may appear very odd to you, but the facts of research prove that the measure adopted for the purposes of this work shows absolute validity when this process is carried out. (Claims are made for other systems, but the author has felt obliged to abandon them as lacking in anything like the same accuracy.)

The system used here is known as Tertiary Direction. By direction we mean the act of progressing a map in this manner. This system is the product of many years of research conducted by the German astrologue E. H. Troinski and first appeared in 1951.

Troinski decided to divide the year (a little more than 365 days) by the Sidereal month (a little more than twenty-seven days). This sum gives a result which is between thirteen and fourteen days.

He then experimented on the basis of taking each thirteen-plus days after birth as representing a year of life. Thus, approximately thirteen days after birth was taken as representing the start of the second year of life; in practice the odd amount is taken as fourteen days. Then twenty-seven days after birth represents the start of the third year of life, and so on.

In my view he overlooked a fact which is fundamental to the whole concept of Tertiary Directions. It is a fact which intimately concerns every one of us because it dominated the possibility of our births. The conception which began our lives was dependent upon a certain periodicity, and this periodicity, in my belief, is by far the greatest and most influential factor in all our lives.

I refer, of course, to periodicity in woman. This may be regarded as continuing *for approximately the same number of years as the number of days occupied by the Moon in one lunation.* Individual variations occur, but I have been guided by a world average which had medical confirmation.

The number of periods likely is therefore about the same as the number of days in a year.

Now this is a remarkable fact, and it looks as if Troinski more or less stumbled upon a measure which exactly fits the same scheme, it being a scale reduction in terms of time. However this may be, none of the experts who have conducted research into his system has been able to break it. Under the most rigorous tests it has proved conclusively correct.

If you will turn to Table 7 you will see a list of years with the appropriate number of days against them. This is the basis for work in Tertiary Directions. You will be able to see how the work is carried out using our specimen map.

Here, perhaps, I should make a confession. I have refrained from giving the name of the individual of the specimen because I wished you to study it without prejudgement. Nothing is easier than to get all kinds of ideas about maps when one knows a good deal about the person represented.

The specimen map is, in fact, the birth map of King Olav V of Norway. Data on which it is founded was from official sources.

It is now possible to show how this specimen has responded in the past to Tertiary Directions.

But first let us see how a typical tertiary calculation is made.

One would regard it as only fair that the claims made here on behalf of Tertiary Directions should call for a rigorous test. Let us therefore pit the system against the two most tragic events in the King's life so far: the invasion of Norway, and the death of Kronprinsesse Märtha, his wife. Both events occurred when he was heir to the throne.

(1) *The Invasion of Norway.* This was on 9 April 1940, when the King was thirty-six years old.

The procedure for setting up the progressed map is as follows:

(*a*) Having ascertained the years which have elapsed, turn to page 212 and find the appropriate entry.

In this instance it will be against 36. There we find 482.

(*b*) Next the equivalent of the birth date is found in the table on page 212.

In this instance, looking against 2 July we find 183.

(*c*) The number of months which have elapsed from the date of birth to the date of the event is noted and a day a month allowed. Where the period exceeds 9 months allow for 10 months 11 days, 11 months 12 days.

In this instance we shall take nine months. The equivalent is 9.

(*d*) The above figures are added together and if they exceed multiples of a year such multiples are subtracted.

In this instance the total is 674. This is more than one year but less than two, so 365 is subtracted, leaving a total of 309.

(e) The total so found is looked for in the Table on page 212.

In this instance this number is against 5 November.
Here we must deduct one day because 1904 is a Leap Year and has a 29 day February. This leaves us with 4 November.

(f) Finally, we take the addition of the year of (d) above to the year of birth and consider 4 November 1904 as the date for the map we require. The map is then set up for the same time of day as the time of birth.

This calculation is set out in detail on the next page.

(2) *The Death of Kronprinsesse Märtha.* This sad event occurred on 5 April 1954. The King was then fifty years of age.

We set up the tertiary map as before:

Years elapsed = 50. From Table 7	..	..	..	..	669
Equivalent of 2 July from Table 7	..	..	..	..	183
Equivalent of 9 months ..	..	..	..	..	9
					861
This being more than 2 years deduct ..	..	..	..	730
					131

In Day Table: 131 = 11 May. Minus 1 day for Leap Year = 10 May. That gives 10 May 1905. Add 2 years to 1903 = 1905.

We proceed to erect the map in the usual manner:

S (10 May 1905) in Table 2 (Part I) 15.07 + 1 minute	=	15.08
T (as before)	=	17.50
A (as before)	=	3
R (as before)	=	2
		33.03
less		24.00
S.T. for Tertiary Map	=	9.03

CALCULATION OF A TERTIARY MAP

Details of the Map for the Invasion of Norway:
9 April 1940

(a) From 1903 (2 July) to 1939 (2 July) = 36 years.
In Table 7 we find against 36 years   482
(b) In Table 7 the equivalent of birth date (2 July)   183
(c) Months from 2 July 1939 to date of event   9

————
674
(d) This being in excess of one year,   deduct   365
————

(e) In Day Table 7 we must now look for the equivalent of 5
November. This is   309
But 1904 is a Leap Year and we therefore deduct 1 day, making
the required date 4 November.

N.B.: In all calculations which overlap a 29 day February you
must make this deduction of 1 day.

(f) 1903 + the year deducted in (d) = 1904.

Result: The date required for the tertiary map is 4 November 1904.
This date is the tertiary equivalent of 36 years 8 months and 20 days
from the date of birth. That is where the Increment comes in.

Add 36 years 8 months to 2 July 1903 and you get 2 March 1940 and
the further addition of 20 days gives you 22 March 1940. In short,
4 November 1904 = 22 March 1940.

This date is considered an operative point: the beginning of a month
in the life and therefore of a period about which judgement may begin.

As to the tertiary map, the calculation as shown earlier applies:

S   (4 November 1904) in Table 2 (Part II) = 2.52, deduct 1 minute for
1904 as it is a Leap Year. ∴.   S =   2.51

T   (as before)   = 17.50
A   (as before)   = 3
R   (as before)   = 2
————
S.T. for Tertiary Map   = 20.46
————

We now have two very important maps covering events in the King's life. These are given on the next page so that you may check your own working out of them, which one hopes you will have attempted.

It should be understood that these maps showing Tertiary Direction are judged in precisely the same manner as any others. All that has to be borne in mind is that the conclusions drawn will have a forward look, instead of the rather static statements given in earlier parts of this work. What we are trying to do is to stand, as it were, at the month-beginnings prior to these events to see what we would have judged as likely to happen during those months.

All tertiary maps need to be looked at in this manner. Obviously, you will be erecting maps for future events (and not with benefit—as here—of knowledge of what actually happened). Interpretations, therefore, must be couched in terms of the future. Once this has been understood, you can make free use of the lists given earlier.

Now let us look at each of these maps to see the main structures. The one for the Invasion shows Venus opposing the Ascendant. Mars is square to both Venus and Uranus, on the one side, and to Pluto on the other. Moon is square Neptune. But above everything, Saturn is right on the Mid-Equator!— while Sun and Mercury are opposite the East Point! More than that, Saturn and the Sun-Mercury conjunction form a square aspect!!

If you did no more than look at the statements already listed you would realize at once what a terrible map this is. Take just the factors mentioned above:

Venus adverse to Mars. The statement mentions an element of violence which makes for strain.

Venus adverse Uranus. The statement gives a picture of the type of events when translated into terms of political events.

Moon adverse Neptune. The statement stresses exterior influences.

Sun adverse Saturn. The statement mentions difficulties created by other people, plus an uncongenial environment.

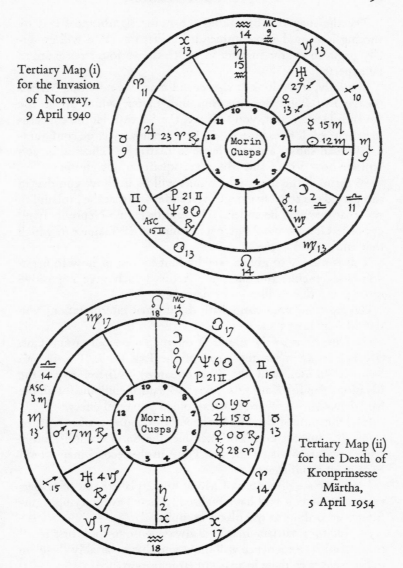

Tertiary Map (i) for the Invasion of Norway, 9 April 1940

Tertiary Map (ii) for the Death of Kronprinsesse Märtha, 5 April 1954

16. EXAMPLES OF TERTIARY MAPS

Try the map out by taking the house significances and by turning it around as recommended earlier on. You will gradually begin to see the manner in which the various stresses are to be expected.

Similarly, if we look at the second map, we note that Mars is on the East Point opposite Sun and Jupiter, which are in the Seventh House. But, you will say, the Seventh House concerns matrimony! It does indeed. So here is one very large configuration which shows a direct threat to marriage. Then, also, you will see how Venus and Moon are square to one another.

So through the map. The results will be to show you that in this period the royal marriage must suffer and that the probability was that it would be ended. The Eighth House Neptune, lying opposite Uranus, would give a fair hint of the manner in which that end would come.

This is merely to give a sketchy hint to you of how to begin your judgement. But there are factors which give a positive toning, and these will now be described.

Having tried your hand with the normal interpretations you should now note these facts:

(1) Directions to the angles of the map are vitally important. (By angles we mean the cusps of the East Point, Fourth and Seventh Houses, and the Mid-Equator.) Where, as in the Invasion Map for King Olav, we find Saturn conjoined with the Mid-Equator, we regard it as exerting a powerful effect.

(2) Direction of the Sun to the various bodies is also regarded as of vital importance. For example, the Sun (Seventh House) lying opposite Mars on the East Point in the second map would have great significance.

(3) There are directions of Moon to the planets and of planets to planets, as you will have realized. These have varying significance according to the places occupied.

In judging a tertiary map it is always wise to look first of all to the angles. Experience will show you that invariably there are major aspects to these in maps of large importance.

Another point which needs mention is that the true Midheaven and true Ascendant of the maps have importance parallel with that of the angles.

In dealing with maps of this kind you may find it very helpful to draw up skeletons of the aspects, as has been shown you earlier. It certainly clarifies the major effects.

You should not, however, attempt too much at this stage. There is room for a book of a thousand pages to describe all the possibilities indicated in maps and nobody should expect that you should be able to compass the entire art of judgement here and now. What you should aim at is a handling of the main factors.

Once you have isolated these, you can then make use of the list of interpretations which follows. One would wish to make it clear that this list is not to be taken as the final word on any of the matters mentioned. It is merely a guide to your own judgement. That it should be used as an " authority " is quite out of the question.

Besides, you must realize that the interpretations given must depend upon the actual positioning of the various bodies in the map you are judging.

1. DIRECTIONS TO ANGLES

Favourable Aspect from Sun

Beneficial effects upon the health and upon the general status. Gains are felt from outside influences—for instance, help from people in a better position. Reactions upon the finances are consequently probable. Marriage often takes place under this aspect. Women are strongly affected and child-birth is known to take place with great frequency when this aspect appears in their charts.

Conjunction of Sun

Usually an intensification of the effects noted above.

Unfavourable Aspect from Sun

Occupational interests suffer. Position lost. Adversities brought about by influential people. Health questions raised in the chart need special study at these times. Anxiety concerning the father of the individual.

Favourable Aspect from Moon

Important changes are made. Often more travel than normally. Projects come to success more easily than at other times. Links with other people are formed. This aspect also coincides frequently with marriage or child-birth.

Conjunction of Moon

Makes for similar events and possibilities.

Unfavourable Aspect from Moon

Misjudged changes take place. Other effects similar to those for the unfavourable aspect of the Sun.

Favourable Aspect from Mercury

Practically always indicates travel. Much mental activity at the time. Changes of a minor order take place, such as removals. Profitable period for intellectual pursuits.

Conjunction of Mercury

Much more movement in the general affairs, changes, and far more travel than usual. Residential changes. Very favourable for such pursuits as writing or teaching.

Unfavourable Aspect from Mercury

Much mental anxiety and a general attitude of apprehension. Nervous complaints often coincide. Care has to be used to avoid deception, especially in business matters. A most unfavourable time for anything in the nature of intellectual work.

Favourable Aspect from Venus

This aspect, like those of the Sun and the Moon, is frequently found to coincide with marriage or the birth of a child. This especially in women's charts. The aspect denotes a pleasurable period, some success with financial matters, constructive developments of home life, and gains through artistic pursuits.

Conjunction of Venus

A time of great happiness in domestic life. Financial possibilities become increasingly good. Marriages or engagements are often coincident, especially in women's charts, with this aspect.

Unfavourable Aspect from Venus

Women and matrimonial matters generally cause anxieties when the aspect is found in men's charts. In a woman's chart it usually denotes domestic difficulties and anxiety regarding women relations. The period is one of extravagance or actual financial loss, and there are often health troubles as well.

Favourable Aspect from Mars

Intense activity in all departments of life. The occupation is the centre of most of this. Plans are hurried forward and the whole tempo of the life takes on a feverish tone.

Unfavourable Aspect from Mars

Note that the Conjunction is an unfavourable aspect. Overwork or feverish ailments. Accidents often coincide. Danger of loss of parents. Quarrels, enmity, and litigation are often features of this period.

Favourable Aspect from Jupiter

Similar effects to those felt under the favourable aspect of the Sun, with emphasis on the social side of affairs. Expansion.

Conjunction of Jupiter

Expansion in business, promotions, financial success. Sometimes the birth of a child takes place under this aspect.

Unfavourable Aspect from Jupiter

Effects are mainly on the health usually. Losses financially occur. Litigation possible with loss of action.

Favourable Aspect from Saturn

Gains mainly through inheritance. Benefits are also obtained from older, or more influential, people.

Unfavourable Aspect from Saturn

Illness probable. Disappointments in connexion with plans. Old people cause much anxiety. So also do matters relating to land and property. Accidents often coincide with the aspect. The Conjunction is an unfavourable aspect.

Favourable Aspect from Uranus

Events of an unexpected order producing benefits. Fortunate deals. Travel undertaken. Major changes carried through. In some charts the aspect indicates romance.

Conjunction of Uranus

Generally speaking reverses the above observations.

Unfavourable Aspect from Uranus

Illness comes suddenly. May be through an accident or nerve derangement. Losses, financially and otherwise, take place with great suddenness.

Favourable Aspect from Neptune

Good period financially. Travel to distant places. But the Neptunian aspects nearly always come with strange experiences and should be treated with reserve.

The Conjunction is variable.

Unfavourable Aspect from Neptune

Affects the nervous system adversely. Losses occur in connexion with travel and business at some distance.

II. SUN TO PLANETS

The effects are similar to those given in the List of Aspects (pages 51–53) but should be taken, of course, as referring to *the future*.

III. MOON TO PLANETS

Taking the major effects produced, the following hints will be helpful in assessing these if you couple them with the lunar aspects already noted in the List of Aspects (pages 53–56).

Favourable Aspect to the Sun

Happiness and success. Time for expansion. More peaceful atmosphere generally. Improvements in position with financial benefits.

Unfavourable Aspect to the Sun

Estrangements and separations. Anxiety over a parent. Some danger of damage to the reputation. Health troubles.

Favourable Aspect to Mercury

Development of talents. Writing, trading, and studying well favoured. Intellectual pursuits generally productive of success. A good time for travelling and for the less vital changes in the individual's plans.

Unfavourable Aspect to Mercury

Not a good time for beginning undertakings, or for signing agreements or other documents. Negotiations fail or come to small success. Nervous tension leading to actual illness very often occurs.

Favourable Aspect to Venus

Affects the social departments of life mostly. Partnerships of any kind can be formed. Marriage or engagement possible—favourable, anyway, if carried out at this period. Contentment. Financial betterment and general diminishing of problems.

Unfavourable Aspect to Venus

Emotional upsets. Unsatisfactory arrangements and ill fortune over link-ups with others. Domestic difficulties occur. A very disappointing atmosphere is produced by this aspect.

Favourable Aspect to Mars

Produces an enterprising spirit. Ambitious schemes move along more freely. Problems attacked and settled. Vitality good and health improved. But, as with all aspects of the Moon to Mars, there is danger of rashness and high passions.

Unfavourable Aspect to Mars

Necessity for much caution in all things. Over-rash moves often made. No binding arrangements should, if possible, be entered into. Sickness, or accidents, generally take place under the unfavourable aspect.

Favourable Aspect to Jupiter

One of the best of aspects, bringing widened opportunities, chances for occupational and social betterment, increases financially, and general good fortune. New undertakings. Practical advancement of the individual's ambitions.

Unfavourable Aspect to Jupiter

Produces the precise opposites of the things yielded during a favourable aspect. This especially in connexion with finance.

Favourable Aspect to Saturn

Consolidation and settlement mainly. Steady progress. Movement, though slow, on lines of conservative advancement. Often coincident with benefits through inheritance.

Unfavourable Aspects to Saturn

Disappointments. A slowing down of activities. Plans go completely awry. Depression. Illness frequently accompanies the aspect. A heavy—possibly sad—period.

Favourable Aspect to Uranus

Changes take place. New enterprises. New contacts with beneficial reactions on the finances. All events tend to be sudden and unexpected. Much stimulation and good fortune in all departments of the life.

Unfavourable Aspect to Uranus

Produces the opposite of these effects of the favourable aspects.

Favourable Aspect to Neptune and Unfavourable Aspect to Neptune

Affect the mental processes variously. The favourable aspects help all idealistic thinking and planning; the unfavourable ones lead to a kind of psychic depression. Difficult to describe, the effects are always variable and at this time caution against deception, whether from himself or from others, should be exercised by the individual.

IV. PLANETS TO PLANETS

The effects are similar to those given in the List of Aspects (pages 56–63) but must be read in terms of *the future*.

By way of an example, look at the interpretation given for an adverse aspect from Saturn to an angle. In the Invasion map we find Saturn conjoined with the Mid-Equator. This is certainly adverse, since no conjunction of Saturn to an angle is likely to give other than unfortunate events.

The interpretation speaks of disappointments—and how heavy these were for the King as the enemy troops entered! It goes on to speak of anxiety about older people (the safety of King Haakon was a grave anxiety), and about land and property. You see, there are the solid facts of the situation and in case it occurs to the reader that, after the event, it was easy for an appropriate interpretation to be inserted here, let it be mentioned that the interpretations given above were taken from a work published by me in 1938—long before the actual events! There has been no "cooking of the books", nor would Tertiaries have need of any.

A final point needs to be underlined. In general it will be found that both beneficial and adverse directions given in the list above will be strengthened much if the birth map has some similar conditioning. If, say, the birth map has Sun trine to Jupiter, and Sun and Jupiter are in very good aspect in a tertiary map, the benefits expectable would be increased. This is understandable enough since the tertiaries are an extension of the life of the individual depicted in the birth map.

STAGES OF ERECTING A MAP
Giving pages where instructions appear

(1) Use formula S + T + A $\pm$ R to find S.T.*   ..   .. page 5
(2) Turn to Morinus Table (Table 4) to find cusps. Insert   .. page 6
(3) List Sun, Moon, and planet positions (Table 6)   ..   pages 12 to 24
(4) After collation insert above in the map
(5) Find ASC and MC and insert in the map (Table 5)   .. page 24
(6) Check to see all necessary factors are entered

       * Instead of (1) use method (2) or (3) if time is unknown

N.B.:   Make sure that all the necessary data on which the map is founded is shown clearly above or below it. This information should include:

Name........ Date of Birth........ Time of Birth........
Place of Birth........ Latitude and Longitude of Place........
S.T. for the map........

In the centre of the map should be inserted the name of the system of map-construction which has been used.

It is also a convenience if the date on which the map was erected is noted. If the information on which it is based has been taken from a book, or provided in some other way, it is generally an advantage to make a note of the source.

Should the name not suffice to indicate sex, this should be noted and, of course, where the map is for a person already dead that fact should appear together with the date of death.

PART FIVE

TABULATIONS

1. Elements of the Solar System, together with Reminder List of Symbols.
2. Sidereal Time Table: (I) for ordinary years, (II) for leap years.
3. Latitude and Longitude of (i) World Capitals, (ii) a selection of Cities and Towns in Great Britain, and (iii) a selection of Cities and Towns in the United States of America and Canada.
4. Morinus Table of Houses.
5. Ascendant and Midheaven for Nine Important Latitudes.
6. Condensed Ephemeris for the years 1900–1975.
7. Tertiary Direction Tables: (I) Year Equivalents, and (II) Date Equivalents.

INDEX OF TABULATIONS

ELEMENTS OF THE SOLAR SYSTEM

Object	Mean distance from Sun. *Millions of Miles*	Sidereal Period		Diameter (*Circa*)	Mass compared with Earth (*Circa*)	Period of Rotation on Axis		
		Yrs.	Days	Miles		d.	h.	m.
Sun ☉ ..	—	–	–	864,000	332,000	25	7	48
Mercury ☿	36	0	88	3,000	0·05	88	0	0
Venus ♀ ..	67	0	225	7,600	0·82	247	(?)	
Earth ..	93	1	0	7,900	1·00		23	56
Mars ♂ ..	142	1	322	4,200	0·11		24	38
Jupiter ♃ ..	483	11	315	90,000eq.	} 318		9	50
				84,000p.			9	56
Saturn ♄	886	29	167	75,100	} 95		10	14
				67,200			10	38
Uranus ♅	1,783	84	6	31,900	15		10	49
Neptune ♆	2,793	164	288	32,900	17		15	40
Pluto ♇ ..	3,666	247	255	3,600	★	6	9	17(?)

★ In doubt (1969).

REMINDER LIST

♈ Aries		♎ Libra
♉ Taurus		♏ Scorpio
♊ Gemini	In drawing maps are	♐ Sagittarius
♋ Cancer	inserted on opposite	♑ Capricorn
♌ Leo	cusps to	♒ Aquarius
♍ Virgo		♓ Pisces

☉ Sun	☽ Moon	☿ Mercury	♀ Venus
♂ Mars	♃ Jupiter	♄ Saturn	♅ Uranus
	♆ Neptune	♇ Pluto	

☌ Conjunction   ☍ Opposition (see above)

Square □

♈ Aries	♉ Taurus	♊ Gemini
♋ Cancer	♌ Leo	♍ Virgo *my*
♎ Libra	♏ Scorpio	♐ Sagittarius
♑ Capricorn	♒ Aquarius	♓ Pisces

Trine △

♈ Aries	♉ Taurus	♊ Gemini	♋ Cancer
♌ Leo	♍ Virgo	♎ Libra	♏ Scorpio
♐ Sagittarius	♑ Capricorn	♒ Aquarius	♓ Pisces

SIDEREAL TIME TABLE (I)

(0 h. 0 m. Greenwich Mean Time)

For 1902, 1906, 1910, 1914, 1918, 1922, 1927, 1931, 1935, 1939, 1943, 1947, 1951, 1955.

	Jan.	Feb.	Mar.	April	May	June	July	Aug.	Sept.	Oct.	Nov.	Dec.
1	6 39	8 41	10 31	12 34	14 32	16 34	18 32	20 35	22 37	0 35	2 37	4 36
2	6 43	8 45	10 35	12 37	14 36	16 38	18 36	20 38	22 41	0 39	2 41	4 39
3	6 47	8 49	10 39	12 41	14 40	16 42	18 40	20 42	22 45	0 43	2 45	4 43
4	6 51	8 53	10 43	12 45	14 44	16 46	18 44	20 46	22 49	0 47	2 49	4 47
5	6 54	8 57	10 47	12 49	14 48	16 50	18 48	20 50	22 53	0 51	2 53	4 51
6	6 58	9 1	10 51	12 53	14 52	16 54	18 52	20 54	22 56	0 55	2 57	4 55
7	7 2	9 5	10 55	12 57	14 55	16 58	18 56	20 58	23 0	0 59	3 1	4 59
8	7 6	9 9	10 59	13 1	14 59	17 2	19 0	21 2	23 4	1 3	3 5	5 3
9	7 10	9 12	11 3	13 5	15 3	17 6	19 4	21 6	23 8	1 7	3 9	5 7
10	7 14	9 16	11 7	13 9	15 7	17 10	19 8	21 10	23 12	1 11	3 13	5 11
11	7 18	9 20	11 11	13 13	15 11	17 13	19 12	21 14	23 16	1 14	3 17	5 15
12	7 22	9 24	11 15	13 17	15 15	17 17	19 16	21 18	23 20	1 18	3 21	5 19
13	7 26	9 28	11 19	13 21	15 19	17 21	19 20	21 22	23 24	1 22	3 25	5 23
14	7 30	9 32	11 23	13 25	15 23	17 25	19 24	21 26	23 28	1 26	3 29	5 27
15	7 34	9 36	11 27	13 29	15 27	17 29	19 28	21 30	23 32	1 30	3 32	5 31
16	7 38	9 40	11 30	13 33	15 31	17 33	19 31	21 34	23 36	1 34	3 36	5 35
17	7 42	9 44	11 34	13 37	15 35	17 37	19 35	21 38	23 40	1 38	3 40	5 39
18	7 46	9 48	11 38	13 41	15 39	17 41	19 39	21 42	23 44	1 42	3 44	5 43
19	7 50	9 52	11 42	13 45	15 43	17 45	19 43	21 46	23 48	1 46	3 48	5 47
20	7 54	9 56	11 46	13 48	15 47	17 49	19 47	21 49	23 52	1 50	3 52	5 50
21	7 58	10 0	11 50	13 52	15 51	17 53	19 51	21 53	23 56	1 54	3 56	5 54
22	8 2	10 4	11 54	13 56	15 55	17 57	19 55	21 57	24 0	1 58	4 0	5 58
23	8 5	10 8	11 58	14 0	15 59	18 1	19 59	22 1	0 4	2 2	4 4	6 2
24	8 9	10 12	12 2	14 4	16 3	18 5	20 3	22 5	0 7	2 6	4 8	6 6
25	8 13	10 16	12 6	14 8	16 6	18 9	20 7	22 9	0 11	2 10	4 12	6 10
26	8 17	10 20	12 10	14 12	16 10	18 13	20 11	22 13	0 15	2 14	4 16	6 14
27	8 21	10 23	12 14	14 16	16 14	18 17	20 15	22 17	0 19	2 18	4 20	6 18
28	8 25	10 27	12 18	14 20	16 18	18 21	20 19	22 21	0 23	2 21	4 24	6 22
29	8 29		12 22	14 24	16 22	18 24	20 23	22 25	0 27	2 25	4 28	6 26
30	8 33		12 26	14 28	16 26	18 28	20 27	22 29	0 31	2 29	4 32	6 30
31	8 37		12 30		16 30		20 31	22 33		2 33		6 34

For 1903, 1907, 1911, 1915, 1919, 1923   Deduct 1 minute from above table.

For 1901, 1905, 1909, 1913, 1917, 1921, 1925, 1926, 1930, 1934, 1938, 1942, 1946, 1950, 1954, 1959, 1963, 1967, 1971, 1975 } Add 1 minute to above table.

For 1900, 1929, 1933, 1937, 1941, 1945, 1949, 1953, 1957, 1958, 1962, 1966, 1970, 1974 } Add 2 minutes to above table.

For 1961, 1965, 1969, 1973 Add 3 minutes to above table.

SIDEREAL TIME TABLE (II)

(0 h. 0 m. Greenwich Mean Time)

For 1924, 1928, 1932, 1936, 1940, 1944, 1948, 1952—All Leap Years

	Jan.	Feb.	Mar.	April	May	June	July	Aug.	Sept.	Oct.	Nov.	Dec.
1	6 38	8 40	10 34	12 37	14 35	16 37	18 35	20 38	22 40	0 38	2 40	4 39
2	6 42	8 44	10 38	12 40	14 39	16 41	18 39	20 41	22 44	0 42	2 44	4 42
3	6 46	8 48	10 42	12 44	14 43	16 45	18 43	20 45	22 48	0 46	2 48	4 46
4	6 50	8 52	10 46	12 48	14 47	16 49	18 47	20 49	22 52	0 50	2 52	4 50
5	6 54	8 56	10 50	12 52	14 51	16 53	18 51	20 53	22 56	0 54	2 56	4 54
6	6 57	9 0	10 54	12 56	14 55	16 57	18 55	20 57	22 59	0 58	3 0	4 58
7	7 1	9 4	10 58	13 0	14 58	17 1	18 59	21 1	23 3	1 2	3 4	5 2
8	7 5	9 8	11 2	13 4	15 2	17 5	19 3	21 5	23 7	1 6	3 8	5 6
9	7 9	9 12	11 6	13 8	15 6	17 9	19 7	21 9	23 11	1 10	3 12	5 10
10	7 13	9 15	11 10	13 12	15 10	17 13	19 11	21 13	23 15	1 14	3 16	5 14
11	7 17	9 19	11 14	13 16	15 14	17 16	19 15	21 17	23 19	1 17	3 20	5 18
12	7 21	9 23	11 18	13 20	15 18	17 20	19 19	21 21	23 23	1 21	3 24	5 22
13	7 25	9 27	11 22	13 24	15 22	17 24	19 23	21 25	23 27	1 25	3 28	5 26
14	7 29	9 31	11 26	13 28	15 26	17 28	19 27	21 29	23 31	1 29	3 32	5 30
15	7 33	9 35	11 30	13 32	15 30	17 32	19 31	21 33	23 35	1 33	3 35	5 34
16	7 37	9 39	11 33	13 36	15 34	17 36	19 34	21 37	23 39	1 37	3 39	5 38
17	7 41	9 43	11 37	13 40	15 38	17 40	19 38	21 41	23 43	1 41	3 43	5 42
18	7 45	9 47	11 41	13 44	15 42	17 44	19 42	21 45	23 47	1 45	3 47	5 46
19	7 49	9 51	11 45	13 48	15 46	17 48	19 46	21 49	23 51	1 49	3 51	5 50
20	7 53	9 55	11 49	13 51	15 50	17 52	19 50	21 52	23 55	1 53	3 55	5 53
21	7 57	9 59	11 53	13 55	15 54	17 56	19 54	21 56	23 59	1 57	3 59	5 57
22	8 1	10 3	11 57	13 59	15 58	18 0	19 58	22 0	0 3	2 1	4 3	6 1
23	8 5	10 7	12 1	14 3	16 2	18 4	20 2	22 4	0 7	2 5	4 7	6 5
24	8 8	10 11	12 5	14 7	16 6	18 8	20 6	22 8	0 10	2 9	4 11	6 9
25	8 12	10 15	12 9	14 11	16 9	18 12	20 10	22 12	0 14	2 13	4 15	6 13
26	8 16	10 19	12 13	14 15	16 13	18 16	20 14	22 16	0 18	2 17	4 19	6 17
27	8 20	10 22	12 17	14 19	16 17	18 20	20 18	22 20	0 22	2 21	4 23	6 21
28	8 24	10 26	12 21	14 23	16 21	18 23	20 22	22 24	0 26	2 24	4 27	6 25
29	8 28	10 30	12 25	14 27	16 25	18 27	20 26	22 28	0 30	2 28	4 31	6 29
30	8 32		12 29	14 31	16 29	18 31	20 30	22 32	0 34	2 32	4 35	6 33
31	8 36		12 33		16 33		20 34	22 36		2 36		6 37

For 1904, 1908, 1912, 1916, 1920 Deduct 1 minute from above table.

For 1956, 1960, 1964, 1968, 1972 Add 1 minute to above table.

TABLES OF WORLD CAPITALS, AND BRITISH AND NORTH AMERICAN CITIES AND TOWNS

Showing Corrections on the Zone Times

Variations of Zone Times over the years should be studied from official references

★ ★

WORLD CAPITALS—A SELECTION

City	State	Latitude	Longitude	Longitude as Time h. m.	Zone hours	Correction Mins.
Algiers	Algeria	36 N 50	3 E 0	0.12	0	+12
Amsterdam	Netherlands	52 N 22	4 E 56	0.20	+ 1	−40
Ankara	Turkey	39 N 55	32 E 55	2.12	+ 2	+12
Asuncion	Paraguay	25 S 15	57 W 40	3.51	− 4	+ 9
Athens	Greece	37 N 54	23 E 52	1.35	+ 2	−25
Baghdad	Iraq	33 N 15	44 E 30	2.58	+ 3	− 2
Belfast	N. Ireland	54 N 42	6 W 15	0.25	1	−25
Belgrade	Yugoslavia	44 N 52	20 E 32	1.22	+ 1	+22
Berlin	Germany	52 N 30	13 E 25	0.54	+ 1	− 6
Berne	Switzerland	46 N 56	7 E 23	0.30	+ 1	−30
Bogota	Colombia	4 N 32	74 W 15	4.57	− 5	+ 3
Bonn	Germany	50 N 45	7 E 6	0.28	+ 1	−32
Brussels	Belgium	50 N 52	4 E 22	0.17	1	+17
Bucharest	Rumania	44 N 25	26 E 7	1.44	+ 2	−16
Budapest	Hungary	47 N 30	19 E 5	1.16	+ 1	+16
Buenos Aires	Argentine	34 S 35	58 W 22	3.53	− 4	+ 7
Cairo	Egypt	30 N 2	31 E 21	2.05	+ 2	+ 5
Canberra	Australia	35 S 28	149 E 9	9.57	+10	− 3
Cape Town	South Africa	33 S 55	18 E 22	1.13	+ 2	−47
Caracas	Venezuela	10 N 30	66 W 58	4.28	− 4½	+ 2
Copenhagen	Denmark	55 N 40	12 E 34	0.50	+ 1	−10
Delhi	India	28 N 29	77 E 15	5.09	+ 5½	−21
Dublin	Ireland	53 N 20	6 W 15	0.25	1	−25
Helsinki	Finland	60 N 10	23 E 58	1.36	+ 2	−24
Jerusalem	Israel	31 N 46	35 E 14	2.21	+ 2	+21
La Paz	Bolivia	16 S 29	68 W 3	4.32	− 4	−32
Lima	Peru	12 S 0	77 W 0	5.08	− 5	− 8
Lisbon	Portugal	38 N 44	9 W 9	0.37	1	−37
London	Great Britain	51 N 32	0 W 5	0.00	1	0
Madrid	Spain	40 N 26	3 W 42	0.15	1	−15
Mexico City	Mexico	19 N 26	99 W 7	6.36	− 6°	−36
Montevideo	Uruguay	34 S 40	56 W 15	3.45	− 3½	−15
Moscow	U.S.S.R.	55 N 45	37 E 36	2.30	+ 2	+30
Oslo	Norway	59 N 57	10 E 42	0.43	+ 1	−17
Ottawa	Canada	45 N 30	75 W 44	5.03	− 5	− 3
Paris	France	48 N 52	2 E 20	0.09	1	+ 9
Peiping (Pekin)	China	39 N 55	116 E 25	7.46	+ 8	−14
Prague	Czechoslovakia	50 N 5	14 E 26	0.58	+ 1	− 2
Quito	Ecuador	0 S 10	78 W 30	5.14	− 5	−14
Riga	Latvia	56 N 58	24 E 5	1.36	+ 2	−24
Rio de Janeiro	Brazil	23 S 0	43 W 20	2.53	− 3	+ 7
Rome	Italy	41 N 45	12 E 15	0.49	+ 1	−11
Santiago	Chili	33 S 28	70 W 45	4.43	− 4	−43
Singapore	Malaya	1 N 14	103 E 55	6.56	+ 7½	−34
Sofia	Bulgaria	42 N 40	23 E 20	1.33	+ 2	−27
Stockholm	Sweden	59 N 20	18 E 0	1.12	+ 1	+12
Teheran	Iran	35 N 45	51 E 45	3.27	+ 3½	+27
Tokyo	Japan	35 N 40	139 E 45	9.19	+ 9	+19
Vienna	Austria	48 N 14	16 E 20	1.05	+ 1	+ 5
Warsaw	Poland	52 N 14	21 E 0	1.24	+ 1	+24
Washington	U.S.A.	38 N 53	77 W 1	5.08	− 5	− 8
Wellington	New Zealand	41 S 17	174 E 47	11.39	+12	−21

BRITISH COUNTY TOWNS

ENGLAND	Latitude	Correction (Mins.)	WALES	Latitude	Correction (Mins.)
Aylesbury	51 N 50	− 3	Mold	53 N 10	−13
Bedford	52 N 12	− 2	Newport	51 N 34	−12
Beverley	53 N 48	− 2	Ruthin	53 N 07	−13
Boston	53 N 00	0	Welshpool	52 N 52	−12
Bury St. Edmunds	52 N 12	+ 3			
Cambridge	52 N 12	0			
Carlisle	54 N 55	−12	**SCOTLAND**		
Chelmsford	51 N 45	+ 2	Aberdeen	57 N 09	− 9
Chester	53 N 12	−12	Alloa	56 N 05	−15
Chichester	50 N 50	− 3	Ayr	55 N 25	−18
Derby	52 N 55	− 6	Banff	57 N 40	−10
Dorchester	50 N 45	−10	Cupar	56 N 19	−12
Durham	54 N 45	− 7	Dingwall	57 N 36	−18
Exeter	50 N 45	−14	Dumbarton	55 N 55	−18
Gloucester	51 N 55	− 9	Dumfries	55 N 05	−14
Hereford	52 N 05	−11	Duns	55 N 46	− 9
Hertford	51 N 50	− 1	Edinburgh	55 N 55	−13
Huntingdon	52 N 20	− 1	Elgin	57 N 40	−13
Ipswich	52 N 05	+ 5	Forfar	56 N 35	−11
Kendal	54 N 20	−11	Glasgow	55 N 50	−17
Kingston-on-Th.	51 N 25	− 1	Golspie	57 N 58	−16
Leicester	52 N 40	− 5	Haddington	55 N 57	−11
Lewes	50 N 55	0	Inverness	57 N 30	−17
Lincoln	53 N 15	− 2	Kinross	56 N 17	−14
London	51 N 32	0	Kirkcudbright	54 N 50	−16
Maidstone	51 N 15	+ 2	Kirkwall	59 N 00	−12
March	52 N 33	0	Lerwick	60 N 10	− 5
Newcastle-on-T.	54 N 55	− 6	Linlithgow	55 N 58	−14
Newport	51 N 35	−12	Lochgilphead	56 N 02	−22
Northallerton	54 N 20	− 6	Nairn	57 N 33	−16
Northampton	52 N 15	− 4	Newtown St. B.	55 N 34	−11
Norwich	52 N 40	+ 5	Paisley	55 N 50	−18
Nottingham	52 N 55	− 5	Peebles	55 N 39	−13
Oakham	52 N 40	− 3	Perth	56 N 25	−14
Oxford	51 N 45	− 5	Rothesay	55 N 50	−20
Peterborough	52 N 35	− 1	Selkirk	55 N 35	−12
Preston	53 N 45	−11	Stirling	56 N 05	−16
Reading	51 N 25	− 4	Stonehaven	56 N 58	− 9
Shrewsbury	52 N 42	−11	Stranraer	54 N 54	−20
Sleaford	52 N 59	− 2	Wick	58 N 25	−13
Stafford	52 N 50	− 9			
Taunton	51 N 00	−13			
Trowbridge	51 N 15	− 9	**N. IRELAND**		
Truro	50 N 15	−20	Armagh	54 N 21	−27
Wakefield	53 N 40	− 6	Belfast	54 N 42	−25
Warwick	52 N 15	− 7	Downpatrick	54 N 20	−23
Winchester	51 N 05	− 5	Enniskillen	54 N 20	−31
Worcester	52 N 10	− 9	Londonderry	55 N 00	−29
			Omagh	54 N 35	−30
WALES					
Aberystwyth	52 N 25	−16	**ISLE OF MAN**		
Brecon	51 N 57	−14	Douglas	54 N 10	−18
Caernarvon	53 N 08	−18			
Cardiff	51 N 30	−13			
Carmarthen	51 N 50	−17			
Dolgelley	52 N 45	−16	**CHANNEL IS.**		
Haverfordwest	51 N 48	−20	St. Anne's	49 N 41	− 9
Llandrindod W.	52 N 15	−14	St. Helier	49 N 11	− 8
Llangefni	53 N 16	−19	St. Peter Port	49 N 27	−10

UNITED STATES OF AMERICA AND CANADA

Place	Latitude ° '	Longitude ° '	Longitude as Time h. m.	Zone hours	Correction Mins.
Albany, N.Y.	42 N 42	73 W 46	4.55	5	+ 5
Amarillo, Tex.	35 N 13	101 W 49	6.47	6	−47
Atlanta, Ga.	33 N 45	84 W 25	5.38	6	+22
Atlantic City, N.J.	39 N 21	74 W 27	4.58	5	+ 2
Austin, Nev.	32 N 39	117 W 4	7.48	8	+12
Baker, Ore.	44 N 47	117 W 50	7.51	8	+ 9
Baltimore, Md.	39 N 18	76 W 38	5.07	5	− 7
Bangor, Me.	44 N 47	68 W 47	4.35	5	+25
Birmingham, Ala.	33 N 30	86 W 50	5.47	6	+13
Bismarck, N.D.	46 N 49	100 W 46	6.43	6	−43
Boise, Ida.	43 N 38	116 W 12	7.45	7	−45
Boston, Mass.	42 N 15	71 W 7	4.44	5	+16
Buffalo, N.Y.	42 N 55	78 W 55	5.16	5	−16
Calgary, Can.	51 N 1	114 W 1	7.36	7	−36
Carlsbad, N. Mex.	32 N 36	104 W 15	6.57	7	+ 3
Charleston, S.C.	32 N 42	79 W 53	5.20	5	−20
Charleston, W.Va.	38 N 22	81 W 38	5.27	5	−27
Charlotte, N.C.	35 N 14	80 W 50	5.23	5	−23
Cheyenne, Wyo.	41 N 9	104 W 48	6.59	7	+ 1
Chicago, Ill.	41 N 52	87 W 39	5.51	6	+ 9
Cincinnati, Ohio	39 N 6	84 W 30	5.38	5	−38
Cleveland, Ohio	41 N 30	81 W 42	5.27	5	−27
Columbia, S.C.	34 N 0	81 W 2	5.24	5	−24
Columbus, Ohio	39 N 58	83 W 1	5.32	5	−32
Dallas, Tex.	32 N 47	96 W 47	6.27	6	−27
Denver, Colo.	39 N 45	104 W 59	7.00	7	0
Des Moines, Iowa	41 N 36	93 W 38	6.15	6	−15
Detroit, Mich.	42 N 20	83 W 3	5.32	5	−32
Dubuque, Iowa	42 N 30	90 W 40	6.03	6	− 3
Duluth, Minn.	46 N 47	92 W 6	6.08	6	− 8
Eastport, Maine	44 N 54	67 W 0	4.28	5	+32
El Centro, Calif.	32 N 47	115 W 34	7.42	8	+18
El Paso, Tex.	31 N 46	106 W 28	7.06	7	− 6
Eugene, Ore.	44 N 3	123 W 6	8.12	8	−12
Fargo, N.D.	46 N 53	96 W 47	6.27	6	−27
Fresno, Calif.	36 N 44	119 W 48	7.59	8	+ 1
Garden City, Kan.	37 N 58	100 W 52	6.43	7	+17
Grand Junction, Colo.	39 N 3	108 W 34	7.14	7	−14
Grand Rapids, Mich.	42 N 58	85 W 40	5.43	6	+17
Havre, Mont.	48 N 33	109 W 40	7.19	7	−19
Helena, Mont.	46 N 35	112 W 2	7.28	7	−28
Honolulu, Haw.	21 N 18	157 W 51	10.31	10	−31
Hoquiam, Wash.	46 N 58	123 W 53	8.16	8	−16
Hot Springs, Ark.	34 N 31	93 W 3	6.12	6	−12
Idaho Falls, Ida.	43 N 30	112 W 2	7.28	7	−28
Indianapolis, Ind.	39 N 46	86 W 10	5.45	6	+15
Jackson, Miss.	32 N 18	90 W 11	6. 1	6	− 1
Jacksonville, Fla.	30 N 20	81 W 39	5.27	5	−27
Kansas City, Mo.	39 N 7	94 W 38	6.19	6	−19
Key West, Fla.	24 N 33	81 W 48	5.27	5	−27
Kingston, Can.	44 N 10	76 W 44	5.07	5	− 7
Klamath Falls, Ore.	42 N 13	121 W 47	8.08	8	− 7
Knoxville, Tenn.	35 N 58	83 W 55	5.36	6	+24
Las Vegas, Nev.	36 N 10	115 W 8	7.41	8	+19
Lewiston, Ida.	46 N 25	117 W 1	7.48	8	+12
Lincoln, Neb.	40 N 49	96 W 42	6.27	6	−27
London, Can.	43 N 2	81 W 30	5.26	5	+34
Los Angeles, Calif.	34 N 3	118 W 15	7.53	8	+ 7
Louisville, Ky.	38 N 15	85 W 45	5.43	6	+17
Manchester, N.H.	43 N 0	71 W 28	4.46	5	+14

UNITED STATES OF AMERICA AND CANADA

Place	Latitude ° '	Longitude ° '	Longitude as Time h. m.	Zone hours	Correction Mins.
Memphis, Tenn.	35 N 9	90 W 3	6.00	6	0
Miami, Fla.	25 N 46	80 W 12	5.21	5	−21
Milwaukee, Wis.	43 N 2	87 W 55	5.52	6	+ 8
Minneapolis, Minn.	44 N 59	93 W 16	6.13	6	−13
Mobile, Ala.	30 N 42	88 W 2	5.52	6	+ 8
Montgomery, Ala.	32 N 21	86 W 18	5.45	6	+15
Montpelier, Vt.	44 N 16	72 W 35	4.50	5	+10
Montreal, Can.	45 N 33	73 W 35	4.54	5	+ 6
Moose Jaw, Can.	50 N 28	105 W 35	7.02	7	− 2
Nashville, Tenn.	36 N 10	86 W 47	5.47	6	+13
Nelson, Can.	49 N 30	117 W 2	7.48	8	+12
New Haven, Conn.	41 N 18	72 W 55	4.52	5	+ 8
New Orleans, La.	29 N 57	90 W 4	6.00	6	0
New York, N.Y.	40 N 45	73 W 57	4.56	5	+ 4
Nome, Alsk.	64 N 30	165 W 30	11.02	11	− 2
North Platte, Neb.	41 N 8	100 W 46	6.43	6	−43
Oklahoma City, Okla.	35 N 28	97 W 31	6.30	6	−30
Ottawa, Can.	45 N 30	74 W 44	5.03	5	− 3
Philadelphia, Pa.	39 N 57	75 W 11	5.01	5	− 1
Phoenix, Ariz.	33 N 27	112 W 4	7.28	7	−28
Pierre, S.D.	44 N 22	100 W 20	6.41	6	−41
Pittsburgh, Pa.	40 N 27	80 W 0	5.20	5	−20
Port Arthur, Can.	48 N 30	89 W 10	5.57	5	−57
Portland, Me.	43 N 39	70 W 16	4.41	5	+19
Portland, Ore.	45 N 31	122 W 41	8.11	8	−11
Providence, R.I.	41 N 49	71 W 25	4.46	5	+14
Quebec, Can.	46 N 53	71 W 20	4.45	5	+15
Raleigh, N.C.	35 N 47	78 W 38	5.15	5	−15
Reno, Nev.	39 N 32	119 W 48	7.59	8	+ 1
Richmond, Va.	37 N 32	77 W 26	5.10	5	−10
Roanoke, Va.	37 N 16	79 W 57	5.20	5	−20
Sacramento, Calif.	38 N 35	121 W 30	8.06	8	− 6
St. John, N.B.	45 N 18	66 W 10	4.25	4	−25
St. Louis, Mo.	38 N 38	90 W 12	6.01	6	− 1
Salt Lake City, Utah.	40 N 46	111 W 54	7.28	7	−28
San Antonio, Tex.	29 N 25	98 W 29	6.34	6	−34
San Diego, Calif.	32 N 43	117 W 10	7.49	8	+11
San Francisco, Calif.	37 N 47	122 W 26	8.10	8	−10
Santa Fe, N.M.	35 N 41	105 W 57	7.04	7	− 4
Sault Ste. Marie, Mich.	46 N 36	84 W 21	5.37	6	+23
Savannah, Ga.	32 N 4	81 W 5	5.24	5	−24
Scranton, Pa.	41 N 25	75 W 40	5.03	5	− 3
Seattle, Wash.	47 N 37	122 W 20	8.09	8	− 9
Shreveport, La.	32 N 31	93 W 45	6.15	6	−15
Sioux Falls, S.D.	43 N 33	96 W 44	6.27	6	−27
Spokane, Wash.	47 N 40	117 W 25	7.50	8	+10
Springfield, Ill.	39 N 49	89 W 39	5.59	6	+ 1
Springfield, Mass.	42 N 6	72 W 36	4.50	5	+10
Springfield, Mo.	37 N 14	93 W 17	6.13	6	−13
Syracuse, N.Y.	43 N 2	76 W 9	5.05	5	− 5
Tampa, Fla.	27 N 57	82 W 27	5.30	5	−30
Toronto, Can.	43 N 38	79 W 27	5.18	5	−18
Trinidad, Colo.	37 N 10	104 W 30	6.58	7	+ 2
Victoria, Can.	48 N 25	123 W 21	8.13	8	−13
Washington, D.C.	38 N 53	77 W 0	5.08	5	− 8
Watertown, N.Y.	43 N 58	75 W 55	5.04	5	− 4
Wichita, Kan.	37 N 42	97 W 20	6.29	6	−29
Wilmington, N.C.	34 N 14	77 W 57	5.12	5	−12
Winnipeg, Can.	49 N 47	97 W 15	6.29	6	−29
Yakima, Wash.	46 N 36	120 W 30	8.02	8	− 2

MORINUS TABLE OF HOUSES

S.T.	1	2	3	4	5	6
0 0	0 ♋ 0	2 ♌ 11	2 ♍ 5	0 ♎ 0	27 ♎ 55	27 ♏ 49
0 4	1 5	3 13	3 3	0 55	28 53	28 52
0 8	2 11	4 16	4 0	1 50	29 49	29 54
0 12	3 16	5 18	4 57	2 45	0 ♏ 47	0 ♐ 57
0 16	4 22	6 20	5 54	3 40	1 45	2 0
0 20	5 27	7 21	6 50	4 35	2 43	3 3
0 24	6 32	8 23	7 47	5 31	3 41	4 7
0 28	7 37	9 24	8 43	6 26	4 39	5 10
0 32	8 43	10 25	9 40	7 21	5 38	6 14
0 36	9 48	11 26	10 36	8 16	6 36	7 18
0 40	10 53	12 27	11 33	9 11	7 35	8 22
0 44	11 58	13 27	12 28	10 7	8 34	9 26
0 48	13 3	14 28	13 24	11 2	9 33	10 30
0 52	14 7	15 28	14 20	11 57	10 33	11 34
0 56	15 12	16 28	15 16	12 53	11 32	12 39
1 0	16 17	17 28	16 11	13 49	12 32	13 43
1 4	17 21	18 28	17 7	14 44	13 32	14 48
1 8	18 26	19 27	18 3	15 40	14 32	15 52
1 12	19 30	20 27	18 58	16 36	15 32	16 57
1 16	20 34	21 26	19 53	17 32	16 33	18 2
1 20	21 38	22 25	20 49	18 27	17 33	19 7
1 24	22 42	23 24	21 43	19 24	18 34	20 12
1 28	23 46	24 22	22 39	20 20	19 35	21 17
1 32	24 50	25 21	23 34	21 17	20 36	22 23
1 36	25 53	26 19	24 29	22 13	21 37	23 28
1 40	26 57	27 17	25 25	23 10	22 39	24 33
1 44	28 0	28 15	26 20	24 6	23 40	25 38
1 48	29 3	29 13	27 15	25 3	24 42	26 44
1 52	0 ♌ 6	0 ♍ 11	28 10	26 0	25 44	27 49
1 56	1 8	1 7	29 5	26 57	26 47	28 55
2 0	2 ♌ 11	2 ♍ 5	0 ♎ 0	27 ♎ 55	27 ♏ 49	0 ♑ 0
2 4	3 13	3 3	0 55	28 53	28 52	1 5
2 8	4 16	4 0	1 50	29 49	29 54	2 11
2 12	5 18	4 57	2 45	0 ♏ 47	0 ♐ 57	3 16
2 16	6 20	5 54	3 40	1 45	2 0	4 22
2 20	7 21	6 50	4 35	2 43	3 3	5 27
2 24	8 23	7 47	5 31	3 41	4 7	6 32
2 28	9 24	8 43	6 26	4 39	5 10	7 37
2 32	10 25	9 40	7 21	5 38	6 14	8 43
2 36	11 26	10 36	8 16	6 36	7 18	9 48
2 40	12 27	11 33	9 11	7 35	8 22	10 53
2 44	13 27	12 28	10 7	8 34	9 26	11 58
2 48	14 28	13 24	11 2	9 33	10 30	13 3
2 52	15 28	14 20	11 57	10 33	11 34	14 7
2 56	16 28	15 16	12 53	11 32	12 39	15 12
3 0	17 28	16 11	13 49	12 32	13 43	16 17
3 4	18 28	17 7	14 44	13 32	14 48	17 21
3 8	19 27	18 3	15 40	14 32	15 52	18 26
3 12	20 27	18 58	16 36	15 32	16 57	19 30
3 16	21 26	19 53	17 32	16 33	18 2	20 34
3 20	22 25	20 49	18 27	17 33	19 7	21 38
3 24	23 24	21 43	19 24	18 34	20 12	22 42
3 28	24 22	22 39	20 20	19 35	21 17	23 46
3 32	25 21	23 34	21 17	20 36	22 23	24 50
3 36	26 19	24 29	22 13	21 37	23 28	25 53
3 40	27 17	25 25	23 10	22 39	24 33	26 57
3 44	28 15	26 20	24 6	23 40	25 38	28 0
3 48	29 13	27 15	25 3	24 42	26 44	29 3
3 52	0 ♍ 11	28 10	26 0	25 44	27 49	0 ♋ 6
3 56	1 7	29 5	26 57	26 47	28 55	1 8

MORINUS TABLE OF HOUSES

S.T.	1	2	3	4	5	6
4 0	2 ♍ 5	0 ♎ 0	27 ♎ 55	27 ♏ 49	0 ♑ 0	2 ♒ 11
4 4	3 3	0 55	28 53	28 52	1 5	3 13
4 8	4 0	1 50	29 49	29 54	2 11	4 16
4 12	4 57	2 45	0 ♏ 47	0 ♐ 57	3 16	5 18
4 16	5 54	3 40	1 45	2 0	4 22	6 20
4 20	6 50	4 35	2 43	3 3	5 27	7 21
4 24	7 47	5 31	3 41	4 7	6 32	8 23
4 28	8 43	6 26	4 39	5 10	7 37	9 24
4 32	9 40	7 21	5 38	6 14	8 43	10 25
4 36	10 36	8 16	6 36	7 18	9 48	11 26
4 40	11 33	9 11	7 35	8 22	10 53	12 27
4 44	12 28	10 7	8 34	9 26	11 58	13 27
4 48	13 24	11 2	9 33	10 30	13 3	14 28
4 52	14 20	11 57	10 33	11 34	14 7	15 28
4 56	15 16	12 53	11 32	12 39	15 12	16 28
5 0	16 11	13 49	12 32	13 43	16 17	17 28
5 4	17 7	14 44	13 32	14 48	17 21	18 28
5 8	18 3	15 40	14 32	15 52	18 26	19 27
5 12	18 58	16 36	15 32	16 57	19 30	20 27
5 16	19 53	17 32	16 33	18 2	20 34	21 26
5 20	20 49	18 27	17 33	19 7	21 38	22 25
5 24	21 43	19 24	18 34	20 12	22 42	23 24
5 28	22 39	20 20	19 35	21 17	23 46	24 22
5 32	23 34	21 17	20 36	22 23	24 50	25 21
5 36	24 29	22 13	21 37	23 28	25 53	26 19
5 40	25 25	23 10	22 39	24 33	26 57	27 17
5 44	26 20	24 6	23 40	25 38	28 0	28 15
5 48	27 15	25 3	24 42	26 44	29 3	29 13
5 52	28 10	26 0	25 44	27 49	0 ♒ 6	0 ♓ 11
5 56	29 5	26 57	26 47	28 55	1 8	1 7
6 0	0 ♎ 0	27 ♎ 55	27 ♏ 49	0 ♑ 0	2 ♒ 11	2 ♓ 5
6 4	0 55	28 53	28 52	1 5	3 13	3 3
6 8	1 50	29 49	29 54	2 11	4 16	4 0
6 12	2 45	0 ♏ 47	0 ♐ 57	3 16	5 18	4 57
6 16	3 40	1 45	2 0	4 22	6 20	5 54
6 20	4 35	2 43	3 3	5 27	7 21	6 50
6 24	5 31	3 41	4 7	6 32	8 23	7 47
6 28	6 26	4 39	5 10	7 37	9 24	8 43
6 32	7 21	5 38	6 14	8 43	10 25	9 40
6 36	8 16	6 36	7 18	9 48	11 26	10 36
6 40	9 11	7 35	8 22	10 53	12 27	11 33
6 44	10 7	8 34	9 26	11 58	13 27	12 28
6 48	11 2	9 33	10 30	13 3	14 28	13 24
6 52	11 57	10 33	11 34	14 7	15 28	14 20
6 56	12 53	11 32	12 39	15 12	16 28	15 16
7 0	13 49	12 32	13 43	16 17	17 28	16 11
7 4	14 44	13 32	14 48	17 21	18 28	17 7
7 8	15 40	14 32	15 52	18 26	19 27	18 3
7 12	16 36	15 32	16 57	19 30	20 27	18 58
7 16	17 32	16 33	18 2	20 34	21 26	19 53
7 20	18 27	17 33	19 7	21 38	22 25	20 49
7 24	19 24	18 34	20 12	22 42	23 24	21 43
7 28	20 20	19 35	21 17	23 46	24 22	22 39
7 32	21 17	20 36	22 23	24 50	25 21	23 34
7 36	22 13	21 37	23 28	25 53	26 19	24 29
7 40	23 10	22 39	24 33	26 57	27 17	25 25
7 44	24 6	23 40	25 38	28 0	28 15	26 20
7 48	25 3	24 42	26 44	29 3	29 13	27 15
7 52	26 0	25 44	27 49	0 ♒ 6	0 ♓ 11	28 10
7 56	26 57	26 47	28 55	1 8	1 7	29 5

MORINUS TABLE OF HOUSES

S.T.	1	2	3	4	5	6
8 0	27 ♎ 55	27 ♏ 49	0 ♑ 0	2 ♒ 11	2 ♓ 5	0 ♈ 0
8 4	28 53	28 52	1 5	3 13	3 3	0 55
8 8	29 49	29 54	2 11	4 16	4 0	1 50
8 12	0 ♏ 47	0 ♐ 57	3 16	5 18	4 57	2 45
8 16	1 45	2 0	4 22	6 20	5 54	3 40
8 20	2 43	3 3	5 27	7 21	6 50	4 35
8 24	3 41	4 7	6 32	8 23	7 47	5 31
8 28	4 39	5 10	7 37	9 24	8 43	6 26
8 32	5 38	6 14	8 43	10 25	9 40	7 21
8 36	6 36	7 18	9 48	11 26	10 36	8 16
8 40	7 35	8 22	10 53	12 27	11 33	9 11
8 44	8 34	9 26	11 58	13 27	12 28	10 7
8 48	9 33	10 30	13 3	14 28	13 24	11 2
8 52	10 33	11 34	14 7	15 28	14 20	11 57
8 56	11 32	12 39	15 12	16 28	15 16	12 53
9 0	12 32	13 43	16 17	17 28	16 11	13 49
9 4	13 32	14 48	17 21	18 28	17 7	14 44
9 8	14 32	15 52	18 26	19 27	18 3	15 40
9 12	15 32	16 57	19 30	20 27	18 58	16 36
9 16	16 33	18 2	20 34	21 26	19 53	17 32
9 20	17 33	19 7	21 38	22 25	20 49	18 27
9 24	18 34	20 12	22 42	23 24	21 43	19 24
9 28	19 35	21 17	23 46	24 22	22 39	20 20
9 32	20 36	22 23	24 50	25 21	23 34	21 17
9 36	21 37	23 28	25 53	26 19	24 29	22 13
9 40	22 39	24 33	26 57	27 17	25 25	23 10
9 44	23 40	25 38	28 0	28 15	26 20	24 6
9 48	24 42	26 44	29 3	29 13	27 15	25 3
9 52	25 44	27 49	0 ♒ 6	0 ♓ 11	28 10	26 0
9 56	26 47	28 55	1 8	1 7	29 5	26 57
10 0	27 ♏ 49	0 ♑ 0	2 ♒ 11	2 ♓ 5	0 ♈ 0	27 ♈ 55
10 4	28 52	1 5	3 13	3 3	0 55	28 53
10 8	29 54	2 11	4 16	4 0	1 50	29 49
10 12	0 ♐ 57	3 16	5 18	4 57	2 45	0 ♉ 47
10 16	2 0	4 22	6 20	5 54	3 40	1 45
10 20	3 3	5 27	7 21	6 50	4 35	2 43
10 24	4 7	6 32	8 23	7 47	5 31	3 41
10 28	5 10	7 37	9 24	8 43	6 26	4 39
10 32	6 14	8 43	10 25	9 40	7 21	5 38
10 36	7 18	9 48	11 26	10 36	8 16	6 36
10 40	8 22	10 53	12 27	11 33	9 11	7 35
10 44	9 26	11 58	13 27	12 28	10 7	8 34
10 48	10 30	13 3	14 28	13 24	11 2	9 33
10 52	11 34	14 7	15 28	14 20	11 57	10 33
10 56	12 39	15 12	16 28	15 16	12 53	11 32
11 0	13 43	16 17	17 28	16 11	13 49	12 32
11 4	14 48	17 21	18 28	17 7	14 44	13 32
11 8	15 52	18 26	19 27	18 3	15 40	14 32
11 12	16 57	19 30	20 27	18 58	16 36	15 32
11 16	18 2	20 34	21 26	19 53	17 32	16 33
11 20	19 7	21 38	22 25	20 49	18 27	17 33
11 24	20 12	22 42	23 24	21 43	19 24	18 34
11 28	21 17	23 46	24 22	22 39	20 20	19 35
11 32	22 23	24 50	25 21	23 34	21 17	20 36
11 36	23 28	25 53	26 19	24 29	22 13	21 37
11 40	24 33	26 57	27 17	25 25	23 10	22 39
11 44	25 38	28 0	28 15	26 20	24 6	23 40
11 48	26 44	29 3	29 13	27 15	25 3	24 42
11 52	27 49	0 ♒ 6	0 ♓ 11	28 10	26 0	25 44
11 56	28 55	1 8	1 7	29 5	26 57	26 47

MORINUS TABLE OF HOUSES

S.T.	1	2	3	4	5	6
12 0	0 ♑ 0	2 ♒ 11	2 ♓ 5	0 ♈ 0	27 ♈ 55	27 ♉ 49
12 4	1 5	3 13	3 3	0 55	28 53	28 52
12 8	2 11	4 16	4 0	1 50	29 49	29 54
12 12	3 16	5 18	4 57	2 45	0 ♉ 47	0 ♊ 57
12 16	4 22	6 20	5 54	3 40	1 45	2 0
12 20	5 27	7 21	6 50	4 35	2 43	3 3
12 24	6 32	8 23	7 47	5 31	3 41	4 7
12 28	7 37	9 24	8 43	6 26	4 39	5 10
12 32	8 43	10 25	9 40	7 21	5 38	6 14
12 36	9 48	11 26	10 36	8 16	6 36	7 18
12 40	10 53	12 27	11 33	9 11	7 35	8 22
12 44	11 58	13 27	12 28	10 7	8 34	9 26
12 48	13 3	14 28	13 24	11 2	9 33	10 30
12 52	14 7	15 28	14 20	11 57	10 33	11 34
12 56	15 12	16 28	15 16	12 53	11 32	12 39
13 0	16 17	17 28	16 11	13 49	12 32	13 43
13 4	17 21	18 28	17 7	14 44	13 32	14 48
13 8	18 26	19 27	18 3	15 40	14 32	15 52
13 12	19 30	20 27	18 58	16 36	15 32	16 57
13 16	20 34	21 26	19 53	17 32	16 33	18 2
13 20	21 38	22 25	20 49	18 27	17 33	19 7
13 24	22 42	23 24	21 43	19 24	18 34	20 12
13 28	23 46	24 22	22 39	20 20	19 35	21 17
13 32	24 50	25 21	23 34	21 17	20 36	22 23
13 36	25 53	26 19	24 29	22 13	21 37	23 28
13 40	26 57	27 17	25 25	23 10	22 39	24 33
13 44	28 0	28 15	26 20	24 6	23 40	25 38
13 48	29 3	29 13	27 15	25 3	24 42	26 44
13 52	0 ♒ 6	0 ♓ 11	28 10	26 0	25 44	27 49
13 56	1 8	1 7	29 5	26 57	26 47	28 55
14 0	2 ♒ 11	2 ♓ 5	0 ♈ 0	27 ♈ 55	27 ♉ 49	0 ♋ 0
14 4	3 13	3 3	0 55	28 53	28 52	1 5
14 8	4 16	4 0	1 50	29 49	29 54	2 11
14 12	5 18	4 57	2 45	0 ♉ 47	0 ♊ 57	3 16
14 16	6 20	5 54	3 40	1 45	2 0	4 22
14 20	7 21	6 50	4 35	2 43	3 3	5 27
14 24	8 23	7 47	5 31	3 41	4 7	6 32
14 28	9 24	8 43	6 26	4 39	5 10	7 37
14 32	10 25	9 40	7 21	5 38	6 14	8 43
14 36	11 26	10 36	8 16	6 36	7 18	9 48
14 40	12 27	11 33	9 11	7 35	8 22	10 53
14 44	13 27	12 28	10 7	8 34	9 26	11 58
14 48	14 28	13 24	11 2	9 33	10 30	13 3
14 52	15 28	14 20	11 57	10 33	11 34	14 7
14 56	16 28	15 16	12 53	11 32	12 39	15 12
15 0	17 28	16 11	13 49	12 32	13 43	16 17
15 4	18 28	17 7	14 44	13 32	14 48	17 21
15 8	19 27	18 3	15 40	14 32	15 52	18 26
15 12	20 27	18 58	16 36	15 32	16 57	19 30
15 16	21 26	19 53	17 32	16 33	18 2	20 34
15 20	22 25	20 49	18 27	17 33	19 7	21 38
15 24	23 24	21 43	19 24	18 34	20 12	22 42
15 28	24 22	22 39	20 20	19 35	21 17	23 46
15 32	25 21	23 34	21 17	20 36	22 23	24 50
15 36	26 19	24 29	22 13	21 37	23 28	25 53
15 40	27 17	25 25	23 10	22 39	24 33	26 57
15 44	28 15	26 20	24 6	23 40	25 38	28 0
15 48	29 13	27 15	25 3	24 42	26 44	29 3
15 52	0 ♓ 11	28 10	26 0	25 44	27 49	0 ♌ 6
15 56	1 7	29 5	26 57	26 47	28 55	1 8

MORINUS TABLE OF HOUSES

S.T.	1	2	3	4	5	6
16 0	2 ♓ 5	0 ♈ 0	27 ♈ 55	27 ♉ 49	0 ♋ 0	2 ♌ 11
16 4	3 3	0 55	28 53	28 52	1 5	3 13
16 8	4 0	1 50	29 49	29 54	2 11	4 16
16 12	4 57	2 45	0 ♉ 47	0 ♊ 57	3 16	5 18
16 16	5 54	3 40	1 45	2 0	4 22	6 20
16 20	6 50	4 35	2 43	3 3	5 27	7 21
16 24	7 47	5 31	3 41	4 7	6 32	8 23
16 28	8 43	6 26	4 39	5 10	7 37	9 24
16 32	9 40	7 21	5 38	6 14	8 43	10 25
16 36	10 36	8 16	6 36	7 18	9 48	11 26
16 40	11 33	9 11	7 35	8 22	10 53	12 27
16 44	12 28	10 7	8 34	9 26	11 58	13 27
16 48	13 24	11 2	9 33	10 30	13 3	14 28
16 52	14 20	11 57	10 33	11 34	14 7	15 28
16 56	15 16	12 52	11 32	12 39	15 12	16 28
17 0	16 11	13 49	12 32	13 43	16 17	17 28
17 4	17 7	14 44	13 32	14 48	17 21	18 28
17 8	18 3	15 40	14 32	15 52	18 26	19 27
17 12	18 58	16 36	15 32	16 57	19 30	20 27
17 16	19 53	17 32	16 33	18 2	20 34	21 26
17 20	20 49	18 27	17 33	19 7	21 38	22 25
17 24	21 43	19 24	18 34	20 12	22 42	23 24
17 28	22 39	20 20	19 35	21 17	23 46	24 22
17 32	23 34	21 17	20 36	22 23	24 50	25 21
17 36	24 29	22 13	21 37	23 28	25 53	26 19
17 40	25 25	23 10	22 39	24 33	26 57	27 17
17 44	26 20	24 6	23 40	25 38	28 0	28 15
17 48	27 15	25 3	24 42	26 44	29 3	29 13
17 52	28 10	26 0	25 44	27 49	0 ♌ 6	0 ♍ 11
17 56	29 5	26 57	26 47	28 55	1 8	1 7
18 0	0 ♈ 0	27 ♈ 55	27 ♉ 49	0 ♋ 0	2 ♌ 11	2 ♍ 5
18 4	0 55	28 53	28 52	1 5	3 13	3 3
18 8	1 50	29 49	29 54	2 11	4 16	4 0
18 12	2 45	0 ♉ 47	0 ♊ 57	3 16	5 18	4 57
18 16	3 40	1 45	2 0	4 22	6 20	5 54
18 20	4 35	2 43	3 3	5 27	7 21	6 50
18 24	5 31	3 41	4 7	6 32	8 23	7 47
18 28	6 26	4 39	5 10	7 37	9 24	8 43
18 32	7 21	5 38	6 14	8 43	10 25	9 40
18 36	8 16	6 36	7 18	9 48	11 26	10 36
18 40	9 11	7 35	8 22	10 53	12 27	11 33
18 44	10 7	8 34	9 26	11 58	13 27	12 28
18 48	11 2	9 33	10 30	13 3	14 28	13 24
18 52	11 57	10 33	11 34	14 7	15 28	14 20
18 56	12 53	11 32	12 39	15 12	16 28	15 16
19 0	13 49	12 32	13 43	16 17	17 28	16 11
19 4	14 44	13 32	14 48	17 21	18 28	17 7
19 8	15 40	14 32	15 52	18 26	19 27	18 3
19 12	16 36	15 32	16 57	19 30	20 27	18 58
19 16	17 32	16 33	18 2	20 34	21 26	19 53
19 20	18 27	17 33	19 7	21 38	22 25	20 49
19 24	19 24	18 34	20 12	22 42	23 24	21 43
19 28	20 20	19 35	21 17	23 46	24 22	22 39
19 32	21 17	20 36	22 23	24 50	25 21	23 34
19 36	22 13	21 37	23 28	25 53	26 19	24 29
19 40	23 10	22 39	24 33	26 57	27 17	25 25
19 44	24 6	23 40	25 38	28 0	28 15	26 20
19 48	25 3	24 42	26 44	29 3	29 13	27 15
19 52	26 0	25 44	27 49	0 ♌ 6	0 ♍ 11	28 10
19 56	26 57	26 47	28 55	1 8	1 7	29 5

MORINUS TABLE OF HOUSES*

S.T.	1	2	3	4	5	6
20 0	27 ♈ 55	27 ♉ 49	0 ♋ 0	2 ♌ 11	2 ♍ 5	0 ♎ 0
20 4	28 53	28 52	1 5	3 13	3 3	0 55
20 8	29 49	29 54	2 11	4 16	4 0	1 50
20 12	0 ♉ 47	0 ♊ 57	3 16	5 18	4 57	2 45
20 16	1 45	2 0	4 22	6 20	5 54	3 40
20 20	2 43	3 3	5 27	7 21	6 50	4 35
20 24	3 41	4 7	6 32	8 23	7 47	5 31
20 28	4 39	5 10	7 37	9 24	8 43	6 26
20 32	5 38	6 14	8 43	10 25	9 40	7 21
20 36	6 36	7 18	9 48	11 26	10 36	8 16
20 40	7 35	8 22	10 53	12 27	11 33	9 11
20 44	8 34	9 26	11 58	13 27	12 28	10 7
20 48	9 33	10 30	13 3	14 28	13 24	11 2
20 52	10 33	11 34	14 7	15 28	14 20	11 57
20 56	11 32	12 39	15 12	16 28	15 16	12 52
21 0	12 32	13 43	16 17	17 28	16 11	13 49
21 4	13 32	14 48	17 21	18 28	17 7	14 44
21 8	14 32	15 52	18 26	19 27	18 3	15 40
21 12	15 32	16 57	19 30	20 27	18 58	16 36
21 16	16 33	18 2	20 34	21 26	19 53	17 32
21 20	17 33	19 7	21 38	22 25	20 49	18 27
21 24	18 34	20 12	22 42	23 24	21 43	19 24
21 28	19 35	21 17	23 46	24 22	22 39	20 20
21 32	20 36	22 23	24 50	25 21	23 34	21 17
21 36	21 37	23 28	25 53	26 19	24 29	22 13
21 40	22 39	24 33	26 57	27 17	25 25	23 10
21 44	23 40	25 38	28 0	28 15	26 20	24 6
21 48	24 42	26 44	29 3	29 13	27 15	25 3
21 52	25 44	27 49	0 ♌ 6	0 ♍ 11	28 10	26 0
21 56	26 47	28 55	1 8	1 7	29 5	26 57
22 0	27 ♉ 49	0 ♋ 0	2 ♌ 11	2 ♍ 5	0 ♎ 0	27 ♎ 55
22 4	28 52	1 5	3 13	3 3	0 55	28 53
22 8	29 54	2 11	4 16	4 0	1 50	29 49
22 12	0 ♊ 57	3 16	5 18	4 57	2 45	0 ♏ 47
22 16	2 0	4 22	6 20	5 54	3 40	1 45
22 20	3 3	5 27	7 21	6 50	4 35	2 43
22 24	4 7	6 32	8 23	7 47	5 31	3 41
22 28	5 10	7 37	9 24	8 43	6 26	4 39
22 32	6 14	8 43	10 25	9 40	7 21	5 38
22 36	7 18	9 48	11 26	10 36	8 16	6 36
22 40	8 22	10 53	12 27	11 33	9 11	7 35
22 44	9 26	11 58	13 27	12 28	10 7	8 34
22 48	10 30	13 3	14 28	13 24	11 2	9 33
22 52	11 34	14 7	15 28	14 20	11 57	10 33
22 56	12 39	15 12	16 28	15 16	12 53	11 32
23 0	13 43	16 17	17 28	16 11	13 49	12 32
23 4	14 48	17 21	18 28	17 7	14 44	13 32
23 8	15 52	18 26	19 27	18 3	15 40	14 32
23 12	16 57	19 30	20 27	18 58	16 36	15 32
23 16	18 2	20 34	21 26	19 53	17 32	16 33
23 20	19 7	21 38	22 25	20 49	18 27	17 33
23 24	20 12	22 42	23 24	21 43	19 24	18 34
23 28	21 17	23 46	24 22	22 39	20 20	19 35
23 32	22 23	24 50	25 21	23 34	21 17	20 36
23 36	23 28	25 53	26 19	24 29	22 13	21 37
23 40	24 33	26 57	27 17	25 25	23 10	22 39
23 44	25 38	28 0	28 15	26 20	24 6	23 40
23 48	26 44	29 3	29 13	27 15	25 3	24 42
23 52	27 49	0 ♌ 6	0 ♍ 11	28 10	26 0	25 44
23 56	28 55	1 8	1 7	29 5	26 57	26 47
24 0	0 ♋ 0	2 11	2 5	0 ♎ 0	27 55	27 49

ASCENDANT AND MIDHEAVEN FOR NINE IMPORTANT LATITUDES*

S.T. h. m.	M.C. °	13 N 0	19 N 0	31 N 46	39 N 54	45 N 0	48 N 50	53 N 25	55 N 53	60 N 0
0 00	0 ♈ 0	5 ♋ 15	7 ♋ 48	13 ♋ 50	18 ♋ 24	21 ♋ 42	25 ♋ 28	28 ♋ 12	0 ♌ 25	4 ♌ 34
0 08	2 11	7 4	9 35	15 33	20 3	23 16	26 58	29 37	1 47	5 49
0 20	5 27	9 47	12 17	18 8	22 30	25 37	29 13	1 ♌ 44	3 49	7 40
0 40	10 53	14 18	16 45	22 23	26 33	29 30	1 ♌ 56	4 28	7 10	10 45
0 52	14 7	17 1	19 25	24 54	28 58	1 ♌ 48	4 9	6 39	9 10	12 35
1 00	16 17	18 49	21 11	26 35	0 ♌ 33	3 20	5 37	8 0	10 30	13 48
1 08	18 26	20 38	22 58	28 16	2 8	4 51	7 5	10 4	11 48	15 2
1 20	21 38	23 21	25 38	0 ♌ 48	4 31	7 8	9 16	12 13	13 48	16 52
1 40	26 57	27 53	0 ♌ 4	4 58	8 38	10 55	12 55	15 39	17 5	19 55
1 52	0 ♉ 6	0 ♌ 37	2 44	7 41	10 50	13 11	14 10	16 49	19 4	21 45
2 00	2 11	2 27	4 31	9 8	12 25	14 41	16 33	19 2	20 23	22 58
2 08	4 16	4 17	6 19	10 48	13 59	16 11	17 59	20 19	21 40	24 11
2 20	7 21	7 2	9 0	13 19	16 21	18 27	20 9	22 22	23 39	26 1
2 40	12 27	11 40	13 29	17 30	20 17	22 12	23 45	25 4	26 57	29 5
2 52	15 28	14 27	16 12	20 0	22 39	24 27	25 55	27 49	28 53	0 ♍ 55
3 00	17 28	16 19	18 1	21 42	23 26	25 57	27 21	28 46	0 ♍ 16	2 8
3 08	19 27	18 12	19 50	23 22	25 48	27 27	28 48	0 ♍ 32	1 33	3 22
3 20	22 25	21 2	22 24	25 43	28 10	29 43	0 ♍ 58	2 34	3 31	5 13
3 40	27 17	25 47	27 9	0 ♍ 7	2 ♍ 7	3 ♍ 29	4 34	5 59	6 50	8 17
3 52	0 ♊ 11	28 39	29 35	2 41	4 29	5 44	6 44	8 1	8 51	10 8
4 00	2 5	0 ♍ 34	1 ♍ 46	4 17	6 5	7 15	8 11	9 25	9 59	11 23
4 08	3 59	2 30	3 38	6 2	7 40	8 46	9 39	10 47	11 26	12 37
4 20	6 50	5 24	6 25	8 35	10 3	11 2	11 48	12 50	13 26	14 28
4 40	11 32	10 17	11 6	12 51	14 1	14 49	15 27	16 15	16 44	17 34
4 52	14 20	13 13	13 55	15 24	16 25	17 5	17 38	18 17	18 44	19 26
5 00	16 11	15 11	15 48	17 8	18 0	18 36	19 5	19 41	20 1	20 40
5 08	18 2	17 9	17 41	18 50	19 36	20 7	20 31	21 3	21 27	21 55
5 20	20 49	20 6	20 32	21 25	22 0	22 24	22 43	23 7	23 24	23 47
5 40	25 25	25 3	25 16	25 43	26 0	26 12	26 21	26 34	26 36	26 53
5 52	28 10	28 1	28 1	28 17	28 24	28 29	28 33	28 37	28 43	28 45
6 00	0 ♋ 0	0 ♎ 0	0 ♎ 0	0 ♎ 0	0 ♎ 0	0 ♎ 0	0 ♎ 0	0 ♎ 0	0 ♎ 0	0 ♎ 0
6 08	1 50	1 59	1 54	1 43	1 36	1 31	1 27	1 23	1 17	1 15
6 20	4 35	4 57	4 44	4 17	4 0	3 48	3 39	3 26	3 24	3 7
6 40	9 11	9 54	9 28	8 35	7 59	7 36	7 17	6 53	6 39	6 13
6 52	11 58	12 51	12 18	11 9	10 24	9 53	9 29	8 57	8 33	8 5
7 00	13 49	14 49	14 12	12 53	12 0	11 24	10 55	10 19	9 59	9 20
7 08	15 40	16 47	16 5	14 35	13 35	12 55	12 22	11 43	11 16	10 34
7 20	18 28	19 43	18 54	17 9	15 58	15 11	14 33	13 45	13 16	12 26
7 40	23 10	24 36	23 34	21 25	19 57	18 58	18 12	17 10	16 35	15 32
7 52	26 0	27 30	26 22	23 58	22 20	21 34	20 21	19 13	18 34	17 23
8 00	27 55	29 26	28 13	25 43	23 55	22 45	21 49	20 35	20 1	18 37
8 08	29 50	1 ♏ 21	0 ♏ 25	27 19	25 31	24 16	23 16	21 59	21 9	19 52
8 20	2 ♌ 43	4 13	2 51	29 53	27 53	26 31	25 26	24 1	23 10	21 43
8 40	7 35	8 58	7 36	4 ♏ 17	1 ♏ 50	0 ♏ 17	29 2	27 26	26 29	24 47
8 52	10 33	11 48	10 10	6 38	4 2	2 33	1 ♏ 29	29 28	28 27	26 38
9 00	12 32	13 41	11 59	8 18	6 34	4 3	2 39	1 ♏ 14	29 44	27 52
9 08	14 32	15 33	13 48	10 0	7 21	5 33	4 5	2 11	1 ♏ 7	29 5
9 20	17 33	18 20	16 31	12 30	9 43	7 48	6 15	4 13	3 3	0 ♏ 55
9 40	22 39	23 41	21 9	16 41	13 39	11 38	9 51	7 38	6 21	3 59
9 52	25 44	25 43	23 41	19 12	16 1	13 49	12 1	9 41	8 20	5 49

* This table departs from the whole-degree renderings of the rest of this work so as to meet requirements of practitioners. To reduce to whole degrees regard any amount above 30' as a whole degree (e.g. 9° 41' — 10° 0')

ASCENDANT AND MIDHEAVEN FOR NINE IMPORTANT LATITUDES*

S.T. h. m.	M.C. ° ,	13 N 0	19 N 0	31 N 46	39 N.54	45 N 0	48 N 50	53 N 25	55 N 53	60 N 0
10 00	27 ♌ 49	27 ♍ 33	25 ♍ 29	20 ♍ 52	17 ♍ 35	15 ♍ 19	13 ♍ 27	10 ♍ 58	9 ♍ 37	7 ♍ 2
10 08	29 54	29 23	27 16	22 32	19 10	16 49	15 50	13 11	10 56	8 15
10 20	3 ♍ 3	2 ♎ 7	29 56	25 2	21 22	19 5	17 5	14 21	12 55	10 5
10 40	8 22	6 39	4 ♎ 22	29 12	25 29	22 52	20 44	17 47	16 12	13 8
10 52	11 34	9 22	7 2	1 ♎ 44	27 52	25 9	22 55	19 56	18 12	14 58
11 00	13 43	11 11	8 49	3 25	29 27	26 40	24 23	22 0	19 30	16 12
11 08	15 53	12 59	10 35	5 6	1 ♎ 2	28 12	25 51	23 21	20 50	17 25
11 20	19 7	15 42	13 15	7 37	3 27	0 ♎ 30	28 4	25 32	22 50	19 15
11 40	24 33	20 13	17 43	11 52	7 30	4 23	0 ♎ 47	28 16	26 11	22 20
11 52	27 49	22 56	20 25	14 27	9 57	6 44	3 2	0 ♎ 23	28 13	24 11
12 00	0 ♎ 0	24 45	22 12	16 10	11 36	8 18	4 32	1 45	29 35	25 26
12 08	2 11	26 34	24 0	17 54	13 15	9 54	7 4	3 14	0 ♎ 57	26 41
12 20	5 27	0 ♏ 29	29 26	20 32	15 46	12 18	9 22	5 24	3 1	28 33
12 40	10 53	3 55	0 ♏ 51	24 57	20 1	16 23	13 17	9 4	6 30	1 ♎ 43
12 52	14 7	6 52	4 4	27 40	22 37	18 53	15 41	11 20	8 39	3 49
13 00	16 17	8 34	5 56	29 29	24 22	20 34	17 18	12 46	10 5	4 56
13 08	18 26	10 27	7 49	1 ♐ 19	26 15	22 17	18 58	14 20	11 33	6 15
13 20	21 38	13 17	10 39	4 7	28 57	24 53	20 29	16 41	13 45	8 14
13 40	26 57	18 5	15 28	8 51	3 ♐ 34	29 22	25 45	20 42	17 35	11 36
13 52	0 ♏ 6	21 0	18 24	11 48	6 27	2 ♐ 8	28 25	23 16	19 56	13 41
14 00	2 11	22 57	19 23	14 47	8 24	4 1	0 ♐ 14	24 53	21 33	15 6
14 08	4 16	24 56	22 23	15 48	10 25	5 57	2 6	26 38	23 12	16 33
14 20	7 21	27 56	25 25	18 52	13 24	8 54	4 58	29 14	24 9	18 45
14 40	12 27	3 ♐ 1	0 ♐ 35	24 9	18 40	14 4	9 58	4 ♑ 1	0 ♑ 10	22 36
14 52	15 28	6 8	3 45	27 25	21 57	17 18	13 8	7 0	3 0	25 3
15 00	17 28	8 13	5 54	29 39	24 12	19 32	15 19	9 3	4 58	26 44
15 08	19 27	10 20	8 4	1 ♑ 55	26 30	21 49	17 34	11 38	6 59	29 27
15 20	22 25	13 33	11 21	5 4	0 ♑ 3	25 23	21 4	14 32	10 11	1 ♑ 13
15 40	27 17	19 0	16 58	11 6	6 15	1 ♑ 39	27 20	20 35	15 58	6 13
15 52	0 ♐ 11	22 19	20 25	15 6	10 9	5 39	1 ♑ 21	24 33	19 47	9 32
16 00	2 5	24 42	22 45	17 38	12 47	8 26	4 10	27 21	22 31	11 54
16 08	3 59	26 50	25 6	20 13	15 29	11 17	7 6	0 ♑ 15	25 22	14 27
16 20	6 50	0 ♒ 15	28 41	24 10	19 44	15 44	11 41	4 56	0 ♒ 1	18 37
16 40	11 32	6 3	4 ♒ 45	0 ♒ 57	27 8	23 37	19 58	13 37	8 46	26 0
16 52	14 20	9 35	8 27	5 9	1 ♒ 46	28 38	25 18	19 24	14 46	2 ♒ 47
17 00	16 11	11 27	10 56	7 59	4 56	2 ♒ 5	29 1	23 30	19 6	7 17
17 08	18 2	14 7	13 27	10 15	8 5	5 36	2 ♒ 52	29 10	23 43	12 19
17 20	20 49	17 55	17 14	14 59	13 5	11 3	8 50	5 ♒ 49	1 ♒ 13	21 0
17 40	25 25	23 57	23 36	22 34	21 20	20 25	19 14	17 31	15 3	8 ♓ 49
17 52	28 10	24 38	27 26	27 2	26 34	26 9	25 46	25 0	23 56	21 17
18 00	0 ♑ 0	0 ♈ 0	0 ♈ 0	0 ♈ 0	0 ♈ 0	0 ♈ 0	0 ♈ 0	0 ♈ 0	0 ♈ 0	0 ♈ 0
18 08	1 50	5 22	2 34	2 58	3 26	3 51	4 14	5 0	6 4	8 43
18 20	4 35	6 3	6 24	7 26	8 32	9 35	10 46	12 29	14 57	21 11
18 40	9 11	12 5	12 46	15 1	16 55	18 57	21 10	24 11	28 47	9 ♉ 0
18 52	11 58	15 53	16 33	19 9	21 50	24 24	27 8	0 ♉ 50	6 ♉ 17	17 41
19 00	13 49	18 33	19 4	22 0	25 4	27 55	0 ♉ 59	6 30	10 54	22 43
19 08	15 40	20 25	21 33	24 51	28 14	1 ♉ 22	4 42	10 36	15 14	27 13
19 20	18 28	23 57	25 15	29 3	2 ♉ 52	6 23	10 2	16 23	21 14	3 ♊ 10
19 40	22 10	29 45	1 ♉ 19	5 50	10 16	14 6	18 19	25 29	0 ♊ 59	11 23
19 52	26 0	3 ♉ 10	4 54	9 47	14 31	18 43	22 54	29 45	4 ♊ 38	15 33

* This table departs from the whole-degree renderings of the rest of this work so as to meet requirements of practitioners. To reduce to whole degrees regard any amount above 30' as a whole degree (e.g. 9° 41' — 10° 0').

ASCENDANT AND MIDHEAVEN FOR NINE IMPORTANT LATITUDES*

S.T. h. m.	M.C. ° '	13 N 0	19 N 0	31 N 46	39 N 54	45 N 0	48 N 50	53 N 25	55 N 53	60 N 0
20 00	27 ♑ 55	5 ♉ 26	7 ♉ 15	12 ♉ 22	17 ♉ 13	21 ♉ 34	25 ♉ 50	2 ♊ 39	7 ♊ 29	18 ♊ 6
20 08	29 50	7 41	9 35	14 54	19 51	24 21	28 39	5 27	11 13	20 28
20 20	2 ♒ 43	11 0	13 2	18 54	23 45	28 21	2 ♊ 40	9 25	14 2	23 47
20 40	7 35	16 27	18 39	24 56	29 57	4 ♊ 37	8 56	15 28	20 11	28 33
20 52	10 33	19 40	21 56	28 5	3 ♊ 0	8 11	12 26	18 22	24 1	1 ♋ 13
21 00	12 32	21 47	24 6	0 ♊ 21	5 48	10 28	14 41	21 57	26 2	3 6
21 08	14 32	23 52	26 15	2 35	8 3	12 42	16 52	23 0	27 0	4 57
21 20	17 33	26 59	29 25	5 51	11 20	15 56	20 2	25 59	29 50	7 24
21 40	22 39	27 56	4 ♊ 35	11 8	16 35	21 6	25 2	0 ♋ 46	5 ♋ 51	11 15
21 52	25 44	5 ♊ 4	7 37	14 12	19 35	24 3	27 54	4 22	6 48	13 27
22 00	27 49	7 3	10 37	15 13	21 36	25 59	29 46	5 7	8 27	14 54
22 08	29 54	9 0	11 36	18 12	23 33	27 52	1 ♋ 35	6 44	10 4	16 19
22 20	3 ♓ 3	11 55	14 32	21 9	27 26	0 ♋ 38	4 15	9 18	12 25	18 24
22 40	8 22	16 43	19 21	25 53	1 ♋ 3	5 7	9 31	13 19	16 15	21 46
22 52	11 34	19 33	22 11	29 41	3 45	7 43	11 2	15 40	18 27	23 45
23 00	13 43	21 26	24 4	0 ♋ 31	5 38	9 26	12 42	17 14	19 55	25 4
23 08	15 53	23 8	25 56	2 20	7 23	11 7	14 19	18 40	21 27	27 11
23 20	19 7	26 5	29 9	5 3	9 59	13 37	16 43	20 56	23 30	28 17
23 40	24 33	29 31	0 ♋ 34	9 28	14 17	17 42	20 38	24 36	26 59	1 ♌ 27
23 52	27 49	3 ♋ 26	6 0	11 6	16 45	20 6	22 56	26 46	29 3	3 19
24 00	0 ♈ 0	5 ♋ 15	7 ♋ 48	13 ♋ 50	18 ♋ 24	21 ♋ 42	25 ♋ 28	28 ♋ 12	0 ♌ 25	4 ♌ 34

* This table departs from the whole-degree renderings of the rest of this work so as to meet requirements of practitioners. To reduce to whole degrees regard any amount above 30' as a whole degree (e.g. 9° 41' — 10° 0').

ASC. AND M.C. FOR SOUTHERN BRITAIN (51 N 30).

(Calculated to nearest degree for each quarter hour).

S.T.	M.C.	ASC.	S.T.	M.C.	ASC.	S.T.	M.C.	ASC.	S.T.	M.C.	ASC.
00 00	0 ♈	27 ♋	06 00	0 ♋	0 ♎	12 00	0 ♎	3 ♐	18 00	0 ♑	0 ♈
00 15	4	29	06 15	4	3	12 15	4	6	18 15	4	10
00 30	8	2 ♌	06 30	7	5	12 30	8	9	18 30	7	18
00 45	12	5	06 45	10	8	12 45	12	12	18 45	10	26
01 00	16	7	07 00	14	11	13 00	16	15	19 00	14	4 ♉
01 15	21	10	07 15	18	13	13 15	21	18	19 15	18	12
01 30	25	13	07 30	21	16	13 30	25	21	19 30	21	18
01 45	28	15	07 45	24	18	13 45	28	24	19 45	24	24
02 00	2 ♉	18	08 00	28	21	14 00	2 ♏	27	20 00	28	0 ♊
02 15	6	21	08 15	2 ♌	24	14 15	6	1 ♑	20 15	2 ♒	5
02 30	10	23	08 30	5	26	14 30	10	4	20 30	5	9
02 45	14	26	08 45	9	29	14 45	14	8	20 45	9	14
03 00	17	28	09 00	13	2 ♏	15 00	17	12	21 00	13	18
03 15	21	1 ♍	09 15	17	4	15 15	21	16	21 15	17	22
03 30	25	4	09 30	20	7	15 30	25	20	21 30	20	26
03 45	28	6	09 45	24	10	15 45	28	24	21 45	24	29
04 00	2 ♊	9	10 00	28	12	16 00	2 ♐	0 ♒	22 00	28	3 ♋
04 15	6	12	10 15	2 ♍	15	16 15	6	6	22 15	2 ♓	6
04 30	9	14	10 30	6	17	16 30	9	12	22 30	6	9
04 45	13	17	10 45	10	20	16 45	13	19	22 45	10	12
05 00	16	19	11 00	14	23	17 00	16	26	23 00	14	15
05 15	20	22	11 15	18	25	17 15	20	4 ♓	23 15	18	18
05 30	23	25	11 30	22	28	17 30	23	12	23 30	22	21
05 45	27	27	11 45	26	1 ♐	17 45	27	22	23 45	26	24
06 00	0 ♋	0 ♎	12 00	0 ♎	3	18 00	0 ♑	0 ♈	24 00	0 ♈	27

CONDENSED EPHEMERIS FOR THE YEARS
1900 TO 1975

Calculated throughout for o h. o m.
(midnight)

for the Meridian of Greenwich,
nearest whole degrees being taken.

★   ★

These Tables being highly condensed will grant accuracy to within one degree. Their inclusion is designed to obviate the necessity for obtaining full tabulations and to give more portability than would otherwise be possible. In view of the fact that few people have their birth data in any accuracy (*i.e.* to the exact minute) the method here employed gives results as near as could be obtained without specialist rectification of the birth map. Where greater accuracy is desired it will be necessary to consult full ephemerides as in the volumes of *Das Deutsche Ephemeride* or in annual publications of the country concerned. It is highly probable that these can be consulted in a public library.

Where a calculation from these tables shows an excess of a whole degree, it may usually be taken for granted that the next whole degree may be used.

SUN POSITIONS

(Given to within 1° for every day of the year. Note the Table overleaf for Leap Years)

	Jan.	Feb.	Mar.	April	May	June	July	Aug.	Sep.	Oct.	Nov.	Dec.
	°	°	°	°	°	°	°	°	°	°	°	°
1	10♑	12♒	10♓	11♈	10♉	11♊	9♋	8♌	8♍	7♎	8♏	9♐
2	11	13	11	12	11	11	10	9	9	8	9	10
3	12	14	12	13	12	12	11	10	10	9	10	11
4	13	15	13	14	13	13	12	11	11	10	11	12
5	14	16	14	15	14	14	13	12	12	11	12	13
6	15	17	15	16	15	15	14	13	13	12	13	14
7	16	18	16	17	16	16	14	14	14	13	14	15
8	17	19	17	18	17	17	15	15	15	14	15	16
9	18	20	18	19	18	18	16	16	16	15	16	17
10	20	21	19	20	19	19	17	17	17	16	17	18
11	21	22	20	21	20	20	18	18	18	17	18	19
12	22	23	21	22	21	21	19	19	19	18	19	20
13	23	24	22	23	22	22	20	20	20	19	20	21
14	24	25	23	24	23	23	21	21	21	20	21	22
15	25	26	24	25	24	23	22	22	22	21	22	23
16	26	27	25	26	25	24	23	23	23	22	23	24
17	27	28	26	27	26	25	24	24	24	23	24	25
18	28	29	27	28	27	26	25	25	25	24	25	26
19	29	0♓	28	29	28	27	26	26	26	25	26	27
20	0♒	1	29	0♉	29	28	27	27	27	26	27	28
21	1	2	0♈	1	0♊	29	28	28	28	27	28	29
22	2	3	1	2	1	0♋	29	29	29	28	29	0♑
23	3	4	2	3	2	1	0♌	0♍	0♎	29	0♐	1
24	4	5	3	4	3	2	1	1	1	0♏	1	2
25	5	6	4	5	4	3	2	2	2	1	2	3
26	6	7	5	6	5	4	3	3	3	2	3	4
27	7	8	6	7	6	5	4	4	4	3	4	5
28	8	9	7	8	7	6	5	5	5	4	5	6
29	9		8	9	8	7	6	6	6	5	7	7
30	10		9	10	9	8	7	6	6	6	8	8
31	11		10		9		8	7		7		9

SUN POSITIONS (Leap Years)

(Given to within 1° for every day of the year)

	Jan.	Feb.	Mar.	April	May	June	July	Aug.	Sep.	Oct.	Nov.	Dec.
	°	°	°	°	°	°	°	°	°	°	°	°
1	10♑	11♒	11♓	11♈	11♉	11♊	9♋	9♌	9♍	8♎	9♏	9♐
2	11	12	12	12	12	12	10	10	10	9	10	10
3	12	13	13	13	13	12	11	11	11	10	11	11
4	13	14	14	14	14	13	12	12	12	11	12	12
5	14	15	15	15	15	14	13	13	13	12	13	13
6	15	16	16	16	16	15	14	14	14	13	14	14
7	16	17	17	17	17	16	15	15	14	14	15	15
8	17	18	18	18	18	17	16	16	15	15	16	16
9	18	19	19	19	18	18	17	16	16	16	17	17
10	19	20	20	20	19	19	18	17	17	17	18	18
11	20	21	21	21	20	20	19	18	18	18	19	19
12	21	22	22	22	21	21	20	19	19	19	20	20
13	22	24	23	23	22	22	21	20	20	20	21	21
14	23	25	24	24	23	23	22	21	21	21	22	22
15	24	26	25	25	24	24	23	22	22	22	23	23
16	25	27	26	26	25	25	24	23	23	23	24	24
17	26	28	27	27	26	26	24	24	24	24	25	25
18	27	29	28	28	27	27	25	25	25	25	26	26
19	28	0♓	29	29	28	28	26	26	26	26	27	27
20	29	1	0♈	0♉	29	29	27	27	27	27	28	28
21	0♒	2	1	1	0♊	0♋	28	28	28	28	29	29
22	1	3	2	2	1	1	29	29	29	29	0♐	0♑
23	2	4	3	3	2	2	0♌	0♍	0♎	0♏	1	1
24	3	5	4	4	3	3	1	1	1	1	2	2
25	4	6	5	5	4	4	2	2	2	2	3	3
26	5	7	6	6	5	4	3	3	3	3	4	4
27	6	8	6	7	6	5	4	4	4	4	5	5
28	7	9	7	8	7	6	5	5	5	5	6	7
29	8	10	8	9	8	7	6	6	6	6	7	8
30	9		9	10	9	8	7	7	7	7	8	9
31	10		10		10		8	8		8		10

MOON   Greenwich Mean Midnight (0 h. 0 m.)   1900–1902

1900	Jan.	Feb.	Mar.	April	May	June	July	Aug.	Sep.	Oct.	Nov.	Dec.
1	2♑	25♒	3♓	27♈	4♊	22♋	25♌	9♎	23♏	27♐	16♒	25♓
3	2♒	25♓	4♈	26♉	1♋	17♌	19♍	2♏	18♐	23♑	15♓	23♈
5	1♓	24♈	2♉	23♊	26♋	11♍	12♎	27♏	14♑	21♒	15♈	23♉
7	0♈	22♉	1♊	18♋	21♌	5♎	7♏	23♐	13♒	21♓	15♉	23♊
9	28♈	18♊	27♊	12♌	15♍	29♎	2♐	20♑	13♓	22♈	14♊	22♋
11	25♉	12♋	22♋	6♍	8♎	24♏	28♐	19♒	13♈	22♉	11♋	19♌
13	21♊	7♌	16♌	0♎	3♏	20♐	26♑	19♓	11♉	20♊	8♌	15♍
15	15♋	1♍	9♍	24♎	28♏	17♑	25♒	19♈	8♊	16♋	2♍	10♎
17	10♌	24♍	3♎	19♏	24♐	15♒	23♓	17♉	4♋	11♌	26♍	4♏
19	4♍	18♎	27♎	14♐	21♑	13♓	23♈	14♊	29♋	6♍	20♎	28♏
21	27♍	12♏	22♏	10♑	18♒	12♈	21♉	10♋	23♌	29♍	14♏	22♐
23	21♎	8♐	17♐	7♒	17♓	10♉	17♊	5♌	17♍	23♎	8♐	17♑
25	16♏	4♑	14♑	6♓	15♈	7♊	13♋	0♍	11♎	17♏	4♑	13♒
27	12♐	3♒	12♒	6♈	14♉	4♋	8♌	23♍	5♏	11♐	0♒	10♓
29	10♑		11♓	5♉	12♊	0♌	3♍	17♎	29♏	6♑	27♒	8♈
31	10♒		12♈		12♋		27♍	11♏		3♒		6♉

1901	Jan.	Feb.	Mar.	April	May	June	July	Aug.	Sep.	Oct.	Nov.	Dec.
1	18♉	10♋	20♋	7♍	10♎	24♏	27♐	15♒	7♈	16♉	7♋	15♌
3	16♊	6♌	15♌	1♎	4♏	18♐	23♑	13♓	6♉	15♊	3♌	11♍
5	14♋	1♍	10♍	25♎	27♏	13♑	19♒	11♈	4♊	13♋	28♌	6♎
7	10♌	26♍	4♎	18♏	21♐	9♒	16♓	9♉	2♋	9♌	24♍	0♏
9	6♍	20♎	28♎	12♐	16♑	6♓	14♈	8♊	29♋	5♍	19♎	24♏
11	0♎	13♏	22♏	7♑	12♒	4♈	13♉	6♋	25♌	0♎	13♏	17♐
13	24♎	7♐	16♐	3♒	9♓	2♉	11♊	5♌	21♍	24♎	7♐	11♑
15	17♏	3♑	11♑	1♓	8♈	1♊	10♋	2♍	16♎	18♏	1♑	6♒
17	12♐	0♒	7♒	0♈	8♉	29♊	7♌	29♍	11♏	11♐	26♑	2♓
19	8♑	28♒	6♓	0♉	7♊	26♋	4♍	25♎	5♐	5♑	21♒	0♈
21	5♒	28♓	6♈	0♊	5♋	23♌	0♎	19♏	29♐	0♒	18♓	0♉
23	4♓	27♈	6♉	29♊	2♌	19♍	25♎	13♐	23♑	26♒	16♈	0♊
25	4♈	26♉	4♊	26♋	28♌	15♎	19♏	7♑	18♒	24♓	15♉	29♊
27	1♉	23♊	3♋	22♌	23♍	8♏	13♐	1♒	14♓	22♈	15♊	26♋
29	29♉		29♋	16♍	16♎	2♐	6♑	27♒	11♈	24♉	13♋	23♌
31	26♊		25♌		12♏		2♒	22♓		24♊		20♍

1902	Jan.	Feb.	Mar.	April	May	June	July	Aug.	Sep.	Oct.	Nov.	Dec.
1	2♎	16♏	24♏	7♑	10♒	28♓	5♉	28♊	22♌	28♍	15♎	18♐
3	26♎	10♐	18♐	2♒	6♓	26♈	4♊	28♋	20♍	24♎	9♏	12♑
5	20♏	4♑	12♑	28♒	3♈	25♉	4♋	27♌	16♎	19♏	3♐	5♒
7	14♐	29♑	7♒	24♓	0♉	24♊	3♌	25♍	11♏	13♐	27♐	29♒
9	8♑	25♒	3♓	22♈	29♉	23♋	1♍	21♎	5♐	7♑	21♑	25♓
11	3♒	22♓	0♈	20♉	28♊	21♌	28♍	16♏	29♐	1♒	16♒	21♈
13	29♒	19♈	29♈	20♊	27♋	19♍	25♎	11♐	23♑	26♒	12♓	20♉
15	25♓	17♉	28♉	18♋	25♌	15♎	20♏	5♑	17♒	21♓	9♈	20♊
17	22♈	15♊	26♊	16♌	22♍	10♏	14♐	29♑	12♓	18♈	8♉	20♋
19	21♉	14♋	24♋	13♍	18♎	4♐	8♑	23♒	8♈	16♉	8♊	20♌
21	19♊	12♌	21♌	10♎	13♏	28♐	2♒	18♓	4♉	16♊	8♋	18♍
23	17♋	9♍	18♍	5♏	7♐	22♑	26♒	14♈	2♊	16♋	8♌	14♎
25	14♌	5♎	13♎	29♏	1♑	16♒	21♓	11♉	1♋	15♌	6♍	9♏
27	10♍	0♏	8♏	22♐	25♑	11♓	18♈	10♊	1♌	13♍	3♎	3♐
29	4♎		2♐	16♑	19♒	7♈	15♉	9♋	1♍	10♎	28♎	27♐
31	28♎		25♐		15♓		14♊	7♌		7♏		20♑

MOON   Greenwich Mean Midnight (0 h. 0 m.)   1903-1905

1903	Jan.	Feb.	Mar.	April	May	June	July	Aug.	Sep.	Oct.	Nov.	Dec.
1	2 ♒	18 ♓	27 ♓	17 ♉	25 ♊	19 ♌	27 ♍	16 ♏	1 ♑	3 ♒	17 ♉	20 ♈
3	26 ♒	13 ♈	23 ♈	15 ♊	24 ♋	17 ♍	23 ♎	11 ♐	11 ♒	27 ♒	12 ♊	17 ♉
5	21 ♓	10 ♉	20 ♉	13 ♋	22 ♌	14 ♎	19 ♏	5 ♑	25 ♒	22 ♓	9 ♋	15 ♊
7	17 ♈	7 ♊	18 ♊	11 ♌	20 ♍	9 ♏	13 ♐	28 ♑	19 ♓	17 ♈	6 ♌	14 ♋
9	14 ♉	7 ♋	16 ♋	10 ♍	17 ♎	4 ♐	8 ♑	22 ♒	13 ♈	13 ♉	4 ♍	13 ♌
11	13 ♊	7 ♌	16 ♌	7 ♎	13 ♏	29 ♐	1 ♒	16 ♓	8 ♉	10 ♊	3 ♎	12 ♍
13	13 ♋	6 ♍	15 ♌	4 ♏	8 ♐	23 ♑	25 ♒	11 ♈	3 ♊	8 ♋	1 ♏	9 ♎
15	14 ♌	5 ♎	12 ♎	0 ♐	2 ♑	16 ♒	19 ♓	6 ♉	29 ♊	6 ♌	29 ♏	6 ♏
17	13 ♍	1 ♏	9 ♏	24 ♐	26 ♑	10 ♓	14 ♈	1 ♊	27 ♋	5 ♍	26 ♐	2 ♐
19	10 ♎	26 ♏	4 ♐	18 ♑	20 ♒	5 ♈	10 ♉	1 ♋	25 ♌	3 ♎	23 ♑	27 ♐
21	6 ♏	20 ♐	28 ♐	12 ♒	14 ♓	1 ♉	7 ♊	1 ♌	24 ♍	1 ♏	19 ♒	22 ♑
23	0 ♐	14 ♑	22 ♑	6 ♓	10 ♈	29 ♉	7 ♋	1 ♍	23 ♎	28 ♏	13 ♓	15 ♒
25	24 ♐	8 ♒	16 ♒	2 ♈	7 ♉	29 ♊	8 ♌	28 ♍	20 ♏	23 ♐	7 ♈	9 ♓
27	17 ♑	2 ♓	11 ♓	28 ♈	5 ♊	29 ♋	6 ♍	25 ♎	15 ♐	18 ♑	1 ♉	3 ♈
29	11 ♒		6 ♈	26 ♉	5 ♋		3 ♏	19 ♏	10 ♑	11 ♒	25 ♉	28 ♈
31	6 ♓		3 ♉		4 ♌					5 ♓		24 ♉

1904	Jan.	Feb.	Mar.	April	May	June	July	Aug.	Sep.	Oct.	Nov.	Dec.
1	9 ♊	1 ♌	24 ♌	17 ♎	24 ♏	12 ♑	15 ♒	29 ♓	13 ♉	18 ♊	9 ♌	17 ♍
3	8 ♋	1 ♍	24 ♍	16 ♏	21 ♐	6 ♒	8 ♓	22 ♈	9 ♊	15 ♋	7 ♍	16 ♎
5	8 ♌	1 ♎	24 ♎	13 ♐	16 ♑	0 ♓	2 ♈	17 ♉	5 ♋	13 ♌	6 ♎	14 ♏
7	8 ♍	29 ♎	22 ♏	8 ♑	11 ♒	24 ♓	26 ♈	13 ♊	4 ♌	12 ♍	5 ♏	12 ♐
9	6 ♎	26 ♏	18 ♐	3 ♒	4 ♓	18 ♈	21 ♉	11 ♋	4 ♍	12 ♎	2 ♐	10 ♑
11	3 ♏	21 ♐	12 ♑	26 ♒	28 ♓	13 ♉	18 ♊	10 ♌	4 ♎	10 ♏	29 ♐	5 ♒
13	29 ♏	15 ♑	6 ♒	20 ♓	23 ♈	8 ♊	14 ♋	10 ♍	2 ♏	7 ♐	24 ♑	29 ♒
15	24 ♐	9 ♒	0 ♓	14 ♈	18 ♉	5 ♋	12 ♌	10 ♎	28 ♏	2 ♑	18 ♒	23 ♓
17	18 ♑	3 ♓	23 ♓	9 ♉	13 ♊	3 ♌	10 ♍	9 ♏	23 ♐	26 ♑	11 ♓	17 ♈
19	12 ♒	26 ♓	18 ♈	5 ♊	10 ♋	2 ♍	10 ♎	6 ♐	17 ♑	20 ♒	4 ♈	12 ♉
21	6 ♓	21 ♈	12 ♉	2 ♋	8 ♌	1 ♎	9 ♏	1 ♑	11 ♒	13 ♓	29 ♈	7 ♊
23	29 ♓	15 ♉	8 ♊	0 ♍	7 ♍	29 ♎	7 ♐	26 ♑	4 ♓	7 ♈	25 ♉	4 ♋
25	24 ♈	12 ♊	5 ♋	28 ♍	6 ♎	25 ♏	4 ♑	20 ♒	28 ♓	1 ♉	22 ♊	2 ♌
27	19 ♉	11 ♋	3 ♌	27 ♎	5 ♏	20 ♐	0 ♒	14 ♓	22 ♈	26 ♉	20 ♋	0 ♍
29	17 ♊	9 ♌	3 ♍	26 ♏	3 ♐	14 ♑	25 ♒	7 ♈	25 ♉	22 ♊	19 ♌	28 ♍
31	16 ♋		3 ♎		29 ♐		17 ♓	1 ♉		18 ♋		26 ♎

1905	Jan.	Feb.	Mar.	April	May	June	July	Aug.	Sep.	Oct.	Nov.	Dec.
1	10 ♏	1 ♑	11 ♑	27 ♒	0 ♈	14 ♉	18 ♊	6 ♌	28 ♍	7 ♏	0 ♑	6 ♒
3	8 ♐	27 ♑	6 ♒	21 ♓	24 ♈	9 ♊	14 ♋	4 ♍	27 ♎	6 ♐	27 ♑	1 ♓
5	5 ♑	22 ♒	0 ♓	15 ♈	18 ♉	4 ♋	11 ♌	3 ♎	26 ♏	4 ♑	23 ♒	26 ♓
7	1 ♒	16 ♓	24 ♓	9 ♉	12 ♊	1 ♌	9 ♍	2 ♏	24 ♐	1 ♒	17 ♓	20 ♈
9	25 ♒	9 ♈	18 ♈	3 ♊	7 ♋	28 ♌	8 ♎	0 ♐	21 ♑	26 ♒	11 ♈	13 ♉
11	19 ♓	3 ♉	12 ♉	28 ♊	1 ♌	26 ♍	6 ♏	27 ♐	16 ♒	20 ♓	5 ♉	7 ♊
13	13 ♈	27 ♉	6 ♊	24 ♋	29 ♌	24 ♎	3 ♐	24 ♑	10 ♓	14 ♈	28 ♉	2 ♋
15	7 ♉	22 ♊	1 ♋	20 ♌	27 ♍	22 ♏	0 ♑	19 ♒	4 ♈	8 ♉	23 ♊	27 ♋
17	2 ♊	20 ♋	28 ♋	20 ♍	28 ♎	22 ♐	26 ♑	15 ♓	29 ♈	2 ♊	21 ♋	23 ♌
19	28 ♊	19 ♌	28 ♌	20 ♎	29 ♏	16 ♑	23 ♒	9 ♈	23 ♉	26 ♊	18 ♌	20 ♍
21	26 ♋	19 ♍	27 ♍	20 ♏	28 ♐	11 ♒	16 ♓	2 ♉	17 ♊	21 ♋	14 ♍	18 ♎
23	25 ♌	19 ♎	27 ♎	20 ♐	25 ♑	5 ♓	11 ♈	26 ♉	12 ♋	17 ♌	10 ♎	17 ♏
25	24 ♎	18 ♏	25 ♐	17 ♑	19 ♒	28 ♓	5 ♉	22 ♊	8 ♌	15 ♍	8 ♏	17 ♐
27	23 ♎	15 ♐	21 ♑	12 ♒	15 ♓	22 ♈	28 ♉	17 ♋	6 ♍	14 ♎	8 ♐	16 ♑
29	21 ♏		15 ♒	6 ♓	8 ♉	23 ♉	26 ♊	14 ♌	5 ♎	15 ♏	8 ♑	13 ♒
31	18 ♐		15 ♓		2 ♊		22 ♋	13 ♍		15 ♐		9 ♓

MOON   Greenwich Mean Midnight (0 h. 0 m.)   1906–1908

1906	Jan.	Feb.	Mar.	April	May	June	July	Aug.	Sep.	Oct.	Nov.	Dec.
1	22 ♓	6 ♉	13 ♉	27 ♊	0 ♌	19 ♍	27 ♎	20 ♐	13 ♒	19 ♓	5 ♉	8 ♊
3	16 ♈	29 ♉	7 ♊	22 ♋	26 ♌	17 ♎	26 ♏	19 ♑	10 ♓	14 ♈	0 ♊	2 ♋
5	10 ♉	24 ♊	1 ♋	18 ♌	24 ♍	17 ♏	25 ♐	18 ♒	6 ♈	9 ♉	23 ♊	26 ♋
7	4 ♊	19 ♋	27 ♋	15 ♍	23 ♎	17 ♐	25 ♑	15 ♓	4 ♉	3 ♊	17 ♋	20 ♌
9	28 ♊	15 ♌	23 ♌	15 ♎	23 ♏	17 ♑	23 ♒	11 ♈	25 ♉	27 ♊	11 ♌	15 ♍
11	24 ♋	13 ♍	15 ♍	15 ♏	23 ♐	15 ♒	20 ♓	5 ♉	19 ♊	21 ♋	6 ♍	11 ♎
13	20 ♌	11 ♎	21 ♍	15 ♐	20 ♑	12 ♓	15 ♈	29 ♉	13 ♋	15 ♌	4 ♎	11 ♏
15	17 ♍	10 ♏	19 ♎	10 ♑	15 ♒	6 ♈	9 ♉	23 ♊	7 ♌	12 ♍	3 ♏	11 ♐
17	15 ♎	8 ♐	17 ♏	6 ♒	10 ♓	1 ♉	3 ♊	17 ♋	4 ♍	10 ♎	3 ♐	11 ♑
19	13 ♏	6 ♑	13 ♐	0 ♓	4 ♈	24 ♉	27 ♊	12 ♌	0 ♎	9 ♏	2 ♑	9 ♒
21	12 ♐	3 ♒	9 ♑	25 ♓	27 ♈	18 ♊	21 ♋	6 ♍	29 ♎	9 ♐	2 ♒	5 ♓
23	10 ♑	0 ♓	4 ♒	18 ♈	21 ♉	12 ♋	16 ♌	4 ♎	28 ♏	8 ♑	29 ♒	0 ♈
25	8 ♒	25 ♓	28 ♒	12 ♉	15 ♊	7 ♌	9 ♍	2 ♐	25 ♐	6 ♒	25 ♓	23 ♈
27	4 ♓	20 ♈	22 ♓	6 ♊	10 ♋	2 ♍	7 ♎	1 ♑	23 ♑	3 ♓	20 ♈	17 ♉
29	29 ♓		15 ♈		5 ♌	29 ♍	7 ♏	1 ♒		28 ♓	14 ♉	11 ♊
31	24 ♈		15 ♉		5 ♍		6 ♐	29 ♒		23 ♈		11 ♋

1907	Jan.	Feb.	Mar.	April	May	June	July	Aug.	Sep.	Oct.	Nov.	Dec.
1	23 ♋	9 ♍	18 ♍	9 ♏	17 ♐	11 ♒	18 ♓	6 ♉	21 ♊	23 ♋	7 ♍	10 ♎
3	17 ♌	5 ♎	15 ♎	7 ♐	15 ♑	8 ♓	15 ♈	1 ♊	15 ♋	17 ♌	2 ♎	6 ♏
5	12 ♍	2 ♏	12 ♏	6 ♑	14 ♒	5 ♈	10 ♉	25 ♊	9 ♌	12 ♍	29 ♎	5 ♐
7	8 ♎	0 ♐	11 ♐	4 ♒	12 ♓	0 ♉	4 ♊	18 ♋	3 ♍	7 ♎	27 ♏	5 ♑
9	5 ♏	28 ♐	9 ♑	1 ♓	8 ♈	25 ♉	28 ♊	12 ♌	28 ♍	4 ♏	26 ♐	4 ♒
11	4 ♐	28 ♑	7 ♒	28 ♓	3 ♉	19 ♊	21 ♋	7 ♍	24 ♎	2 ♐	25 ♑	4 ♓
13	4 ♑	27 ♒	5 ♓	24 ♈	28 ♉	13 ♋	15 ♌	1 ♎	23 ♏	0 ♑	23 ♒	1 ♈
15	4 ♒	25 ♓	3 ♈	20 ♉	22 ♊	6 ♌	9 ♍	27 ♎	21 ♐	29 ♑	21 ♓	28 ♈
17	3 ♓	21 ♈	29 ♈	14 ♊	16 ♋	0 ♍	4 ♎	25 ♏	20 ♑	28 ♒	18 ♈	23 ♉
19	0 ♈	16 ♉	24 ♉	8 ♋	9 ♌	25 ♍	1 ♏	23 ♐	18 ♒	26 ♓	14 ♉	18 ♊
21	26 ♈	10 ♊	18 ♊	1 ♌	3 ♍	20 ♎	28 ♏	23 ♑	15 ♓	22 ♈	9 ♊	12 ♋
23	20 ♉	4 ♋	12 ♋	26 ♌	28 ♍	17 ♏	28 ♐	21 ♒	13 ♈	18 ♉	3 ♋	5 ♌
25	14 ♊	28 ♋	6 ♌	21 ♍	26 ♎	16 ♐	28 ♑	21 ♓	10 ♉	13 ♊	27 ♋	29 ♌
27	7 ♋	22 ♌	0 ♍	19 ♎	26 ♏	18 ♑	28 ♒	19 ♈	5 ♊	7 ♋	21 ♌	23 ♍
29	2 ♌		27 ♍	18 ♏	26 ♐	20 ♒	27 ♓	15 ♉	29 ♊	1 ♌	15 ♍	18 ♎
31	26 ♌		24 ♎		26 ♑		24 ♈	9 ♊		25 ♌		15 ♏

1908	Jan.	Feb.	Mar.	April	May	June	July	Aug.	Sep.	Oct.	Nov.	Dec.
1	29 ♏	21 ♑	15 ♒	8 ♈	15 ♉	2 ♋	4 ♌	19 ♍	4 ♏	9 ♐	0 ♒	10 ♓
3	28 ♐	22 ♒	15 ♓	6 ♉	11 ♊	26 ♋	28 ♌	13 ♎	0 ♐	6 ♑	29 ♒	8 ♈
5	29 ♑	22 ♓	14 ♈	3 ♊	6 ♋	20 ♌	22 ♍	7 ♏	26 ♐	4 ♒	28 ♓	6 ♉
7	29 ♒	20 ♈	12 ♉	28 ♊	0 ♌	14 ♍	16 ♎	3 ♐	24 ♑	3 ♓	27 ♈	3 ♊
9	29 ♓	17 ♉	8 ♊	22 ♋	24 ♌	8 ♎	11 ♏	1 ♑	24 ♒	3 ♈	25 ♉	0 ♋
11	25 ♈	12 ♊	2 ♋	16 ♌	18 ♍	4 ♏	9 ♐	1 ♒	24 ♓	1 ♉	22 ♊	25 ♋
13	20 ♉	6 ♋	26 ♋	10 ♍	13 ♎	1 ♐	8 ♑	1 ♓	23 ♈	0 ♊	17 ♋	19 ♌
15	15 ♊	29 ♋	19 ♌	4 ♎	9 ♏	1 ♑	7 ♒	0 ♈	19 ♉	27 ♊	11 ♌	13 ♎
17	9 ♋	23 ♌	14 ♍	0 ♏	6 ♐	0 ♒	8 ♓	27 ♈	14 ♊	22 ♋	5 ♍	7 ♏
19	2 ♌	17 ♍	8 ♎	27 ♏	4 ♑	0 ♓	7 ♈	22 ♉	7 ♋	15 ♌	29 ♍	1 ♐
21	26 ♌	11 ♎	4 ♏	24 ♐	3 ♒	0 ♈	4 ♉	16 ♊	0 ♌	9 ♍	24 ♎	27 ♐
23	20 ♍	7 ♏	0 ♐	23 ♑	1 ♓	26 ♈	0 ♊	10 ♋	25 ♌	3 ♎	19 ♏	24 ♑
25	14 ♎	3 ♐	27 ♐	22 ♒	29 ♓	20 ♉	25 ♊	4 ♌	19 ♍	28 ♎	16 ♐	23 ♒
27	10 ♏	1 ♑	25 ♑	19 ♓	27 ♈	16 ♊	19 ♋	28 ♌	14 ♎	23 ♏	13 ♑	22 ♓
29	7 ♐	0 ♒	24 ♒	17 ♈	24 ♉	10 ♋	13 ♌	22 ♍		20 ♐	11 ♒	21 ♈
31	6 ♑		24 ♓		19 ♊		7 ♍	22 ♎		19 ♑		19 ♈

MOON   Greenwich Mean Midnight (o h. o m.)   1909-1911

1909	Jan.	Feb.	Mar.	April	May	June	July	Aug.	Sep.	Oct.	Nov.	Dec.
1	3 ♉	22 ♊	2 ♋	18 ♌	20 ♍	4 ♏	7 ♐	26 ♑	19 ♓	28 ♈	20 ♊	25 ♋
3	0 ♊	17 ♋	27 ♋	11 ♍	14 ♎	29 ♏	4 ♑	25 ♒	19 ♈	28 ♉	17 ♋	21 ♌
5	26 ♊	12 ♌	21 ♌	5 ♎	8 ♏	25 ♐	2 ♒	25 ♓	18 ♉	25 ♊	13 ♌	16 ♍
7	21 ♋	6 ♍	14 ♍	29 ♎	3 ♐	22 ♑	0 ♓	24 ♈	16 ♊	22 ♋	8 ♍	10 ♎
9	15 ♌	29 ♍	8 ♎	24 ♏	29 ♐	20 ♒	29 ♓	22 ♉	12 ♋	17 ♌	1 ♎	3 ♏
11	9 ♍	23 ♎	2 ♏	19 ♐	25 ♑	18 ♓	27 ♈	19 ♊	7 ♌	11 ♍	25 ♎	27 ♏
13	3 ♎	18 ♏	27 ♏	15 ♑	23 ♒	16 ♈	25 ♉	15 ♋	2 ♍	4 ♎	19 ♏	22 ♐
15	27 ♎	13 ♐	22 ♐	12 ♒	21 ♓	15 ♉	22 ♊	10 ♌	26 ♍	28 ♎	13 ♐	18 ♑
17	22 ♏	10 ♑	19 ♑	11 ♓	21 ♈	13 ♊	18 ♋	5 ♍	19 ♎	22 ♏	8 ♑	15 ♒
19	18 ♐	9 ♒	17 ♒	11 ♈	20 ♉	10 ♋	14 ♌	29 ♍	13 ♏	16 ♐	4 ♒	12 ♓
21	17 ♑	10 ♓	18 ♓	11 ♉	18 ♊	6 ♌	8 ♍	22 ♎	7 ♐	11 ♑	2 ♓	10 ♈
23	16 ♒	10 ♈	18 ♈	10 ♊	15 ♋	0 ♍	2 ♎	16 ♏	2 ♑	8 ♒	0 ♈	9 ♉
25	16 ♓	9 ♉	18 ♉	10 ♋	10 ♌	24 ♍	26 ♎	11 ♐	29 ♑	6 ♓	29 ♈	8 ♊
27	15 ♈	6 ♊	15 ♊	7 ♌	4 ♍	18 ♎	20 ♏	7 ♑	27 ♒	6 ♈	29 ♉	6 ♋
29	13 ♉		11 ♋	2 ♍	28 ♍	12 ♏	15 ♐	7 ♒	27 ♓	6 ♉	28 ♊	3 ♌
31	10 ♊		6 ♌		22 ♎		12 ♑	4 ♓		6 ♊		29 ♌

1910	Jan.	Feb.	Mar.	April	May	June	July	Aug.	Sep.	Oct.	Nov.	Dec.
1	12 ♍	25 ♎	3 ♏	17 ♐	21 ♑	10 ♓	19 ♈	12 ♊	4 ♌	10 ♍	26 ♎	28 ♏
3	6 ♎	19 ♏	27 ♏	12 ♑	17 ♒	9 ♈	18 ♉	10 ♋	1 ♍	5 ♎	20 ♏	22 ♐
5	29 ♎	13 ♐	21 ♐	9 ♒	15 ♓	8 ♉	17 ♊	8 ♌	26 ♍	29 ♎	13 ♐	16 ♑
7	23 ♏	9 ♑	16 ♑	6 ♓	14 ♈	8 ♊	16 ♋	5 ♍	21 ♎	23 ♏	7 ♑	11 ♒
9	18 ♐	6 ♒	14 ♒	6 ♈	14 ♉	7 ♋	13 ♌	0 ♎	15 ♏	16 ♐	1 ♒	6 ♓
11	14 ♑	4 ♓	13 ♓	6 ♉	14 ♊	5 ♌	10 ♍	25 ♎	8 ♐	10 ♑	27 ♒	3 ♈
13	11 ♒	3 ♈	12 ♈	6 ♊	13 ♋	2 ♍	5 ♎	18 ♏	2 ♑	5 ♒	24 ♓	2 ♉
15	9 ♓	2 ♉	12 ♉	4 ♋	10 ♌	27 ♍	29 ♎	12 ♐	27 ♑	2 ♓	23 ♈	1 ♊
17	7 ♈	0 ♊	11 ♊	0 ♌	6 ♍	22 ♎	22 ♏	7 ♑	22 ♒	0 ♈	24 ♉	1 ♋
19	6 ♉	28 ♊	8 ♋	27 ♌	0 ♎	16 ♏	16 ♐	2 ♒	20 ♓	28 ♈	23 ♊	29 ♋
21	4 ♊	24 ♋	4 ♌	22 ♍	24 ♎	10 ♐	11 ♑	0 ♓	19 ♈	28 ♉	21 ♋	25 ♌
23	1 ♋	20 ♌	0 ♍	15 ♎	17 ♏	4 ♑	6 ♒	28 ♓	17 ♉	24 ♊	16 ♌	20 ♍
25	28 ♋	15 ♍	24 ♍	9 ♏	11 ♐	28 ♑	4 ♓	26 ♈	14 ♊	19 ♋	11 ♍	13 ♎
27	24 ♌	10 ♎	18 ♎	2 ♐	6 ♑	23 ♒	2 ♈	25 ♉	10 ♋	14 ♌	5 ♎	7 ♏
29	19 ♍		12 ♏	26 ♐	1 ♒	21 ♓	0 ♉	23 ♊	6 ♌	10 ♍	29 ♎	1 ♐
31	13 ♎		5 ♐		27 ♒		28 ♉	20 ♋		5 ♎		25 ♐

1911	Jan.	Feb.	Mar.	April	May	June	July	Aug.	Sep.	Oct.	Nov.	Dec.
1	13 ♑	0 ♓	9 ♓	0 ♉	8 ♊	2 ♌	9 ♍	27 ♎	11 ♐	13 ♑	27 ♒	0 ♈
3	8 ♒	27 ♓	6 ♈	29 ♉	8 ♋	0 ♍	5 ♎	21 ♏	5 ♑	7 ♒	22 ♓	27 ♈
5	3 ♓	24 ♈	4 ♉	28 ♊	6 ♌	26 ♍	1 ♏	15 ♐	29 ♑	2 ♓	19 ♈	26 ♉
7	0 ♈	22 ♉	3 ♊	26 ♋	3 ♍	21 ♎	24 ♏	8 ♑	24 ♒	28 ♓	18 ♉	26 ♊
9	27 ♈	20 ♊	1 ♋	23 ♌	29 ♍	16 ♏	18 ♐	3 ♒	19 ♓	24 ♈	18 ♊	24 ♋
11	26 ♉	19 ♋	29 ♋	19 ♍	24 ♎	9 ♐	12 ♑	27 ♒	16 ♈	22 ♉	17 ♋	21 ♌
13	25 ♊	17 ♌	27 ♌	15 ♎	18 ♏	3 ♑	6 ♒	23 ♓	13 ♉	21 ♊	16 ♌	16 ♍
15	25 ♋	15 ♍	23 ♍	10 ♏	12 ♐	26 ♑	0 ♓	21 ♈	11 ♊	20 ♋	13 ♍	11 ♎
17	23 ♌	11 ♎	19 ♎	4 ♐	6 ♑	20 ♒	26 ♓	19 ♉	11 ♋	19 ♌	9 ♎	5 ♏
19	20 ♍	6 ♏	14 ♏	28 ♐	0 ♒	16 ♓	22 ♈	19 ♊	10 ♌	16 ♍	4 ♏	29 ♏
21	16 ♎	0 ♐	7 ♐	21 ♑	24 ♒	13 ♈	20 ♉	14 ♋	8 ♍	13 ♎	29 ♏	23 ♐
23	10 ♏	23 ♐	1 ♑	15 ♒	20 ♓	11 ♉	20 ♊	9 ♌	4 ♎	8 ♏	23 ♐	17 ♑
25	3 ♐	17 ♑	25 ♑	12 ♓	18 ♈	10 ♊	19 ♋	5 ♍	0 ♏	3 ♐	17 ♑	11 ♒
27	27 ♐	13 ♒	19 ♒	9 ♈	17 ♉	11 ♋	17 ♌	2 ♎	25 ♏	27 ♐	11 ♒	6 ♓
29	22 ♑		17 ♓	8 ♉	17 ♊	11 ♌	14 ♎	26 ♎	19 ♐	20 ♑	5 ♓	1 ♈
31	17 ♒		15 ♈		17 ♋		10 ♏	19 ♏		14 ♒		27 ♈

MOON Greenwich Mean Midnight (o h. o m.) — 1912–1914

1912

1912	Jan.	Feb.	Mar.	April	May	June	July	Aug.	Sep.	Oct.	Nov.	Dec.
1	19 ♉	12 ♋	6 ♌	29 ♍	5 ♏	22 ♐	25 ♑	14 ♓	3 ♉	9 ♊	28 ♋	3 ♍
3	19 ♊	13 ♌	6 ♍	27 ♎	1 ♐	16 ♑	21 ♒	10 ♈	29 ♉	5 ♋	24 ♌	29 ♍
5	20 ♋	13 ♍	5 ♎	23 ♏	26 ♐	10 ♒	18 ♓	6 ♉	26 ♊	2 ♌	21 ♍	26 ♎
7	20 ♌	11 ♎	2 ♏	18 ♐	20 ♑	4 ♓	14 ♈	3 ♊	22 ♋	28 ♌	17 ♎	22 ♏
9	19 ♍	8 ♏	28 ♏	12 ♑	13 ♒	28 ♓	11 ♉	29 ♊	18 ♌	25 ♍	13 ♏	18 ♐
11	16 ♎	2 ♐	22 ♐	6 ♒	8 ♓	23 ♈	7 ♊	26 ♋	15 ♍	21 ♎	10 ♐	15 ♑
13	11 ♏	26 ♐	16 ♑	0 ♓	2 ♈	21 ♉	3 ♋	22 ♌	11 ♎	17 ♏	6 ♑	11 ♒
15	5 ♐	20 ♑	10 ♒	25 ♓	29 ♈	20 ♊	0 ♌	19 ♍	8 ♏	14 ♐	2 ♒	7 ♓
17	29 ♐	13 ♒	4 ♓	21 ♈	27 ♉	20 ♋	26 ♌	15 ♎	4 ♐	10 ♑	29 ♒	4 ♈
19	23 ♑	8 ♓	29 ♓	18 ♉	25 ♊	20 ♌	22 ♍	11 ♏	0 ♑	6 ♒	25 ♓	0 ♉
21	16 ♒	4 ♈	25 ♈	16 ♊	24 ♋	18 ♍	19 ♎	8 ♐	27 ♑	3 ♓	21 ♈	26 ♉
23	11 ♓	0 ♉	19 ♉	14 ♋	22 ♌	15 ♎	15 ♏	4 ♑	23 ♒	29 ♓	17 ♉	23 ♊
25	5 ♈	28 ♉	18 ♊	13 ♌	22 ♍	11 ♏	11 ♐	0 ♒	20 ♓	25 ♈	14 ♊	19 ♋
27	1 ♉	25 ♊	18 ♋	11 ♍	18 ♎	6 ♐	8 ♑	27 ♒	16 ♈	22 ♉	10 ♋	15 ♌
29	28 ♉	22 ♋	16 ♌	8 ♎	14 ♏	1 ♑	4 ♒	23 ♓	13 ♉	18 ♊	7 ♌	12 ♍
31	27 ♊		15 ♍		9 ♐		1 ♓	20 ♈		15 ♋		9 ♎

1913

1913	Jan.	Feb.	Mar.	April	May	June	July	Aug.	Sep.	Oct.	Nov.	Dec.
1	25 ♎	13 ♐	22 ♐	8 ♒	10 ♓	24 ♈	27 ♉	17 ♋	6 ♍	7 ♎	26 ♏	2 ♑
3	21 ♏	8 ♑	17 ♑	2 ♓	4 ♈	19 ♉	24 ♊	13 ♌	3 ♎	3 ♏	22 ♐	28 ♑
5	16 ♐	2 ♒	11 ♒	26 ♓	28 ♈	14 ♊	20 ♋	10 ♍	0 ♏	0 ♐	19 ♑	25 ♒
7	11 ♑	26 ♒	5 ♓	19 ♈	22 ♉	10 ♋	16 ♌	6 ♎	27 ♏	26 ♐	15 ♒	21 ♓
9	5 ♒	20 ♓	29 ♓	14 ♉	16 ♊	7 ♌	14 ♍	3 ♏	23 ♐	22 ♑	11 ♓	18 ♈
11	29 ♒	13 ♈	23 ♈	10 ♊	12 ♋	4 ♍	10 ♎	29 ♏	19 ♑	19 ♒	8 ♈	14 ♉
13	23 ♓	8 ♉	18 ♉	7 ♋	10 ♌	4 ♎	7 ♏	25 ♐	15 ♒	15 ♓	4 ♉	10 ♊
15	17 ♈	4 ♊	13 ♊	4 ♌	8 ♍	2 ♏	4 ♐	22 ♑	10 ♓	11 ♈	0 ♊	7 ♋
17	12 ♉	0 ♋	10 ♋	2 ♍	7 ♎	0 ♐	1 ♑	18 ♒	5 ♈	7 ♉	26 ♊	3 ♌
19	8 ♊	27 ♋	8 ♌	2 ♎	6 ♏	26 ♐	27 ♑	14 ♓	0 ♉	4 ♊	23 ♋	29 ♌
21	7 ♋	26 ♌	7 ♍	0 ♏	4 ♐	22 ♑	23 ♒	11 ♈	25 ♉	0 ♋	19 ♌	26 ♍
23	8 ♌	27 ♍	9 ♎	28 ♏	0 ♑	17 ♒	18 ♓	7 ♉	21 ♊	26 ♋	16 ♍	22 ♎
25	7 ♍	27 ♎	8 ♏	27 ♐	26 ♑	12 ♓	12 ♈	4 ♊	17 ♋	23 ♌	12 ♎	18 ♏
27	7 ♎	26 ♏	6 ♐	22 ♑	20 ♒	6 ♈	5 ♉	0 ♋	14 ♌	19 ♍	9 ♏	15 ♐
29	5 ♏		2 ♑	16 ♒	14 ♓	0 ♉	29 ♉	26 ♋	11 ♍	16 ♎	6 ♐	11 ♑
31	1 ♐		26 ♑		7 ♈		25 ♊	23 ♌		13 ♏		8 ♒

1914

1914	Jan.	Feb.	Mar.	April	May	June	July	Aug.	Sep.	Oct.	Nov.	Dec.
1	1 ♓	15 ♈	23 ♈	8 ♊	12 ♋	2 ♍	11 ♎	4 ♐	26 ♑	1 ♓	16 ♈	19 ♉
3	25 ♓	11 ♉	19 ♉	4 ♋	8 ♌	28 ♍	7 ♏	0 ♑	22 ♒	27 ♓	12 ♉	15 ♊
5	19 ♈	8 ♊	16 ♊	1 ♌	5 ♍	25 ♎	4 ♐	27 ♑	19 ♓	24 ♈	9 ♊	12 ♋
7	13 ♉	4 ♋	12 ♋	27 ♌	1 ♎	21 ♏	0 ♑	23 ♒	15 ♈	20 ♉	5 ♋	8 ♌
9	8 ♊	1 ♌	9 ♌	23 ♍	27 ♎	17 ♐	26 ♑	19 ♓	11 ♉	17 ♊	1 ♌	5 ♍
11	4 ♋	27 ♌	5 ♍	20 ♎	24 ♏	14 ♑	23 ♒	16 ♈	8 ♊	13 ♋	28 ♌	1 ♎
13	2 ♌	24 ♍	1 ♎	16 ♏	20 ♐	10 ♒	19 ♓	12 ♉	4 ♋	9 ♌	24 ♍	27 ♎
15	1 ♍	20 ♎	28 ♎	12 ♐	16 ♑	6 ♓	15 ♈	8 ♊	0 ♌	6 ♍	20 ♎	24 ♏
17	29 ♍	16 ♏	24 ♏	9 ♑	13 ♒	3 ♈	12 ♉	5 ♋	27 ♌	2 ♎	17 ♏	20 ♐
19	28 ♎	13 ♐	20 ♐	5 ♒	9 ♓	29 ♈	8 ♊	1 ♌	23 ♍	28 ♎	13 ♐	16 ♑
21	26 ♏	9 ♑	17 ♑	1 ♓	5 ♈	25 ♉	4 ♋	27 ♌	19 ♎	25 ♏	9 ♑	13 ♒
23	23 ♐	6 ♒	13 ♒	27 ♓	1 ♉	22 ♊	1 ♌	24 ♍	16 ♏	21 ♐	6 ♒	9 ♓
25	19 ♑	2 ♓	9 ♓	24 ♈	28 ♉	18 ♋	27 ♌	20 ♎	12 ♐	17 ♑	2 ♓	5 ♈
27	15 ♒	28 ♓	6 ♈	20 ♉	24 ♊	15 ♌	24 ♍	16 ♏	9 ♑	14 ♒	28 ♓	2 ♉
29	9 ♓		2 ♉	18 ♊	21 ♋	12 ♍	20 ♎	13 ♐	6 ♒	10 ♓	26 ♈	28 ♉
31	3 ♈		29 ♉		18 ♌		17 ♏	10 ♑		7 ♈		25 ♊

MOON Greenwich Mean Midnight (o h. o m.)

1915-1917

1915	Jan.	Feb.	Mar.	April	May	June	July	Aug.	Sep.	Oct.	Nov.	Dec.
1	4 ♋	21 ♌	29 ♌	21 ♎	0 ♐	23 ♑	29 ♒	16 ♈	1 ♊	2 ♋	17 ♌	20 ♍
3	29 ♋	18 ♍	27 ♍	21 ♏	0 ♑	21 ♒	26 ♓	11 ♉	24 ♊	26 ♋	12 ♍	18 ♎
5	25 ♌	16 ♎	26 ♎	20 ♐	28 ♑	17 ♓	20 ♈	5 ♊	21 ♋	21 ♌	10 ♎	17 ♏
7	22 ♍	14 ♏	25 ♏	18 ♑	25 ♒	12 ♈	14 ♉	28 ♊	13 ♌	18 ♍	9 ♏	17 ♐
9	19 ♎	13 ♐	24 ♐	15 ♒	20 ♓	6 ♉	8 ♊	23 ♋	10 ♍	16 ♎	9 ♐	18 ♑
11	18 ♏	11 ♑	21 ♑	11 ♓	15 ♈	29 ♉	2 ♋	18 ♌	7 ♎	15 ♏	9 ♑	17 ♒
13	17 ♐	8 ♒	18 ♒	5 ♈	9 ♉	23 ♊	26 ♋	14 ♍	5 ♏	14 ♐	7 ♒	14 ♓
15	16 ♑	5 ♓	14 ♓	0 ♉	2 ♊	17 ♋	21 ♌	11 ♎	7 ♐	13 ♑	4 ♓	10 ♈
17	14 ♒	1 ♈	9 ♈	24 ♉	26 ♊	12 ♌	17 ♍	9 ♏	11 ♒	11 ♒	0 ♈	4 ♉
19	10 ♓	25 ♈	27 ♈	17 ♊	20 ♋	7 ♍	14 ♎	6 ♐	0 ♑	7 ♓	25 ♈	28 ♉
21	5 ♈	19 ♉	27 ♉	11 ♋	15 ♌	4 ♎	12 ♏	4 ♑	27 ♒	3 ♈	20 ♉	22 ♊
23	29 ♈	13 ♊	21 ♊	6 ♌	11 ♍	2 ♏	11 ♐	4 ♒	24 ♓	28 ♈	13 ♊	16 ♋
25	23 ♉	7 ♋	15 ♋	2 ♍	8 ♎	1 ♐	10 ♑	2 ♓	20 ♈	23 ♉	7 ♋	10 ♌
27	17 ♊	3 ♌	10 ♌	0 ♎	7 ♏	1 ♑	9 ♒	29 ♓	15 ♉	17 ♊	2 ♌	4 ♍
29	12 ♋		7 ♍	29 ♎	8 ♐	1 ♒	7 ♓	24 ♈	10 ♋	10 ♋	25 ♌	0 ♎
31	8 ♌		6 ♎		8 ♑		4 ♈	19 ♉		4 ♌		27 ♎

1916	Jan.	Feb.	Mar.	April	May	June	July	Aug.	Sep.	Oct.	Nov.	Dec.
1	11 ♏	4 ♑	28 ♑	20 ♓	26 ♈	12 ♊	15 ♋	29 ♋	16 ♎	23 ♏	15 ♑	24 ♒
3	10 ♐	4 ♒	27 ♑	17 ♈	21 ♉	6 ♋	8 ♌	24 ♌	12 ♏	20 ♐	14 ♒	22 ♓
5	11 ♑	3 ♓	25 ♒	13 ♉	16 ♊	0 ♌	2 ♍	19 ♎	10 ♐	19 ♑	12 ♓	19 ♈
7	11 ♒	1 ♈	22 ♓	7 ♊	9 ♋	23 ♌	27 ♍	16 ♏	8 ♑	17 ♒	9 ♈	15 ♉
9	9 ♓	27 ♈	17 ♈	1 ♋	3 ♌	18 ♍	23 ♎	14 ♐	7 ♒	15 ♓	6 ♉	11 ♊
11	6 ♈	22 ♉	12 ♉	25 ♋	27 ♌	14 ♎	19 ♏	13 ♑	6 ♓	14 ♈	2 ♊	5 ♋
13	1 ♉	16 ♊	5 ♊	19 ♌	22 ♍	11 ♏	19 ♐	13 ♒	3 ♈	11 ♉	27 ♊	29 ♋
15	25 ♉	9 ♋	29 ♋	14 ♍	19 ♎	11 ♐	19 ♑	13 ♓	3 ♉	7 ♊	21 ♋	22 ♌
17	19 ♊	3 ♌	24 ♌	11 ♎	18 ♏	11 ♑	20 ♒	8 ♈	23 ♉	7 ♋	14 ♌	16 ♍
19	13 ♋	28 ♌	19 ♍	9 ♏	17 ♐	11 ♒	19 ♓	8 ♉	23 ♊	25 ♋	8 ♍	11 ♎
21	7 ♌	23 ♍	16 ♎	8 ♐	17 ♑	9 ♓	18 ♈	6 ♊	21 ♋	17 ♌	3 ♎	7 ♏
23	1 ♍	20 ♎	14 ♏	7 ♑	16 ♒	7 ♈	16 ♉	2 ♋	16 ♌	13 ♍	27 ♎	5 ♐
25	27 ♍	17 ♏	12 ♐	5 ♒	13 ♓	4 ♉	12 ♊	27 ♋	11 ♍	8 ♎	27 ♏	5 ♑
27	23 ♎	15 ♐	10 ♑	3 ♓	10 ♈	27 ♉	6 ♋	20 ♌	5 ♎	5 ♏	26 ♐	5 ♒
29	20 ♏	14 ♑	8 ♒	0 ♈	5 ♉	21 ♊	0 ♌	14 ♍	0 ♏	3 ♐	26 ♑	4 ♓
31	19 ♐		6 ♓		0 ♊		24 ♌	8 ♎		1 ♐		3 ♈
							17 ♌	3 ♎		26 ♎		

1917	Jan.	Feb.	Mar.	April	May	June	July	Aug.	Sep.	Oct.	Nov.	Dec.
1	16 ♈	4 ♊	13 ♊	28 ♋	29 ♌	14 ♎	18 ♏	7 ♑	1 ♓	9 ♈	1 ♊	6 ♋
3	12 ♉	29 ♊	8 ♋	21 ♌	23 ♍	10 ♏	15 ♐	7 ♒	1 ♈	9 ♉	28 ♊	1 ♌
5	7 ♊	22 ♋	1 ♌	15 ♍	18 ♎	7 ♐	14 ♑	7 ♓	1 ♉	7 ♊	23 ♋	25 ♌
7	2 ♋	16 ♌	25 ♌	10 ♎	14 ♏	5 ♑	13 ♒	7 ♈	28 ♉	3 ♋	17 ♌	19 ♍
9	26 ♋	10 ♍	19 ♍	5 ♏	12 ♐	4 ♒	13 ♓	5 ♉	24 ♊	21 ♋	11 ♍	13 ♎
11	19 ♌	4 ♎	13 ♎	2 ♐	9 ♑	3 ♓	12 ♈	2 ♊	18 ♋	15 ♌	5 ♎	7 ♏
13	13 ♍	29 ♎	9 ♏	29 ♐	7 ♒	1 ♈	9 ♉	27 ♊	12 ♍	9 ♎	29 ♎	3 ♐
15	7 ♎	24 ♏	5 ♐	27 ♑	6 ♓	28 ♈	5 ♊	21 ♋	6 ♎	4 ♏	25 ♏	1 ♑
17	2 ♏	22 ♐	2 ♑	25 ♒	4 ♈	25 ♉	0 ♋	15 ♌	0 ♏	2 ♐	21 ♐	28 ♑
19	29 ♏	21 ♑	0 ♒	24 ♓	2 ♉	22 ♊	25 ♋	9 ♍	24 ♏	28 ♐	18 ♑	25 ♒
21	28 ♐	21 ♒	0 ♓	23 ♈	29 ♉	16 ♋	18 ♌	3 ♎	19 ♐	24 ♑	16 ♒	25 ♓
23	28 ♑	21 ♓	29 ♓	20 ♉	25 ♊	10 ♌	12 ♍	27 ♎	14 ♑	19 ♒	23 ♓	21 ♈
25	28 ♒	20 ♈	28 ♈	17 ♊	20 ♋	3 ♍	6 ♎	22 ♏	11 ♒	19 ♓	28 ♈	21 ♉
27	26 ♓	18 ♉	26 ♉	12 ♋	14 ♌	0 ♎	1 ♏	18 ♐	9 ♓	18 ♈	27 ♉	18 ♊
29	26 ♈		22 ♊	6 ♌	7 ♍	26 ♎	26 ♏	16 ♑	9 ♈	18 ♉	25 ♊	14 ♋
31	22 ♉		16 ♋		1 ♎		23 ♐	15 ♒		17 ♉		9 ♌

MOON

1915-1917

MOON Greenwich Mean Midnight (0 h. 0 m.)   1918–1920

1918	Jan.	Feb.	Mar.	April	May	June	July	Aug.	Sep.	Oct.	Nov.	Dec.
1	21 ♌	5 ♎	13 ♎	29 ♏	3 ♑	24 ♒	4 ♈	27 ♉	17 ♋	21 ♌	7 ♎	9 ♏
3	15 ♍	29 ♎	7 ♏	24 ♐	0 ♒	22 ♓	0 ♉	24 ♊	12 ♌	16 ♍	0 ♏	3 ♐
5	8 ♎	23 ♏	2 ♐	20 ♑	28 ♒	21 ♈	0 ♊	20 ♋	7 ♍	10 ♎	24 ♏	28 ♐
7	3 ♏	19 ♐	27 ♐	18 ♒	27 ♓	20 ♉	28 ♊	15 ♌	1 ♎	3 ♏	18 ♐	23 ♑
9	28 ♏	16 ♑	24 ♑	17 ♓	26 ♈	18 ♊	24 ♋	10 ♍	24 ♎	27 ♏	13 ♑	19 ♒
11	25 ♐	16 ♒	24 ♒	18 ♈	26 ♉	16 ♋	19 ♌	4 ♎	18 ♏	21 ♐	9 ♒	17 ♓
13	23 ♑	16 ♓	24 ♓	18 ♉	24 ♊	11 ♌	14 ♍	28 ♎	12 ♐	16 ♑	6 ♓	15 ♈
15	22 ♒	16 ♈	25 ♈	16 ♊	21 ♋	6 ♍	8 ♎	22 ♏	7 ♑	13 ♒	5 ♈	14 ♉
17	21 ♓	14 ♉	24 ♉	13 ♋	16 ♌	0 ♎	2 ♏	16 ♐	4 ♒	12 ♓	5 ♉	13 ♊
19	20 ♈	11 ♊	21 ♊	8 ♌	10 ♍	24 ♎	26 ♏	13 ♑	3 ♓	12 ♈	5 ♊	12 ♋
21	18 ♉	7 ♋	16 ♋	2 ♍	4 ♎	18 ♏	21 ♐	11 ♒	4 ♈	12 ♉	4 ♋	9 ♌
23	14 ♊	2 ♌	11 ♌	25 ♍	28 ♎	13 ♐	18 ♑	10 ♓	4 ♉	12 ♊	1 ♌	5 ♍
25	10 ♋	26 ♌	5 ♍	19 ♎	22 ♏	11 ♑	16 ♒	10 ♈	3 ♊	10 ♋	27 ♌	29 ♍
27	5 ♌	20 ♍	28 ♍	13 ♏	17 ♐	7 ♒	15 ♓	9 ♉	27 ♋	6 ♌	21 ♍	23 ♎
29	29 ♌		22 ♎	8 ♐	13 ♑	5 ♓	14 ♈	7 ♊		1 ♍	15 ♎	17 ♏
31	23 ♍		16 ♏		10 ♒		13 ♉	4 ♋		25 ♍		11 ♐

1919	Jan.	Feb.	Mar.	April	May	June	July	Aug.	Sep.	Oct.	Nov.	Dec.
1	24 ♐	12 ♒	20 ♒	12 ♈	21 ♉	13 ♋	19 ♌	6 ♎	20 ♏	22 ♐	7 ♒	11 ♓
3	19 ♑	10 ♓	19 ♓	12 ♉	20 ♊	11 ♌	16 ♍	0 ♏	14 ♐	16 ♑	3 ♓	9 ♈
5	16 ♒	8 ♈	18 ♈	12 ♊	20 ♋	7 ♍	10 ♎	24 ♏	8 ♑	11 ♒	0 ♈	8 ♉
7	14 ♓	7 ♉	17 ♉	10 ♋	16 ♌	2 ♎	4 ♏	18 ♐	3 ♒	8 ♓	0 ♉	8 ♊
9	12 ♈	5 ♊	16 ♊	6 ♌	11 ♍	26 ♎	28 ♏	12 ♑	0 ♓	7 ♈	0 ♊	8 ♋
11	10 ♉	2 ♋	13 ♋	1 ♍	3 ♎	20 ♏	22 ♐	8 ♒	28 ♓	6 ♉	29 ♊	7 ♌
13	8 ♊	29 ♋	9 ♌	26 ♍	27 ♎	13 ♐	16 ♑	5 ♓	27 ♈	6 ♊	26 ♋	5 ♍
15	7 ♋	25 ♌	4 ♍	20 ♎	21 ♏	8 ♑	9 ♒	3 ♈	26 ♉	5 ♋	21 ♌	1 ♎
17	4 ♌	21 ♍	29 ♍	14 ♏	16 ♐	3 ♒	6 ♓	1 ♉	24 ♊	3 ♌	16 ♍	25 ♎
19	0 ♍	15 ♎	23 ♎	7 ♐	11 ♑	29 ♒	6 ♈	0 ♊	22 ♋	0 ♍	10 ♎	19 ♏
21	25 ♍	9 ♏	17 ♏	1 ♑	6 ♒	26 ♓	4 ♉	28 ♊	19 ♌	29 ♍	4 ♏	12 ♐
23	19 ♎	3 ♐	11 ♐	26 ♑	2 ♓	24 ♈	3 ♊	25 ♋	15 ♍	19 ♎	27 ♏	6 ♑
25	13 ♏	27 ♐	5 ♑	22 ♒	0 ♈	23 ♉	2 ♋	23 ♌	10 ♎	13 ♏	21 ♐	0 ♒
27	7 ♐	22 ♑	0 ♒	20 ♓	29 ♈	22 ♊	28 ♋	19 ♍	5 ♏	7 ♐	16 ♑	25 ♒
29	2 ♑		28 ♒	20 ♈	29 ♉	20 ♋	24 ♌	14 ♎	28 ♏	0 ♑		21 ♓
31	28 ♑		27 ♓		29 ♊			8 ♏		24 ♑		18 ♈

1920	Jan.	Feb.	Mar.	April	May	June	July	Aug.	Sep.	Oct.	Nov.	Dec.
1	2 ♉	25 ♊	20 ♋	11 ♍	17 ♎	2 ♐	5 ♐	20 ♒	8 ♈	13 ♉	7 ♋	17 ♌
3	1 ♊	24 ♋	18 ♌	8 ♎	11 ♏	26 ♐	29 ♐	15 ♓	4 ♉	11 ♊	6 ♌	14 ♍
5	1 ♋	23 ♌	16 ♍	3 ♏	5 ♐	20 ♑	23 ♑	11 ♈	2 ♊	11 ♋	4 ♍	11 ♎
7	1 ♌	21 ♍	12 ♎	27 ♏	29 ♐	14 ♒	18 ♒	7 ♉	0 ♋	9 ♌	1 ♎	6 ♏
9	0 ♍	17 ♎	7 ♏	21 ♐	23 ♑	9 ♓	14 ♓	5 ♊	29 ♋	7 ♍	27 ♎	1 ♐
11	26 ♍	11 ♏	1 ♐	15 ♑	17 ♒	4 ♈	10 ♈	4 ♋	28 ♌	5 ♎	22 ♏	25 ♐
13	21 ♎	5 ♐	25 ♐	9 ♒	13 ♓	2 ♉	8 ♉	4 ♌	26 ♍	1 ♏	16 ♐	19 ♑
15	15 ♏	29 ♐	19 ♑	4 ♓	10 ♈	1 ♊	8 ♊	3 ♍	23 ♎	26 ♏	10 ♑	13 ♒
17	9 ♐	23 ♑	14 ♒	1 ♈	8 ♉	1 ♋	8 ♋	1 ♎	18 ♏	20 ♐	4 ♒	7 ♓
19	3 ♑	18 ♒	10 ♓	29 ♈	8 ♊	2 ♌	9 ♌	28 ♎	13 ♐	14 ♑	28 ♒	3 ♈
21	27 ♑	15 ♓	7 ♈	29 ♉	7 ♋	2 ♍	7 ♍	23 ♏	6 ♑	8 ♒	23 ♓	28 ♈
23	22 ♒	12 ♈	5 ♉	29 ♊	7 ♌	28 ♍	2 ♎	17 ♐	0 ♒	3 ♓	20 ♈	25 ♉
25	18 ♓	11 ♉	4 ♊	27 ♋	5 ♍	26 ♎	26 ♎	10 ♑	25 ♒	28 ♓	18 ♉	26 ♊
27	15 ♈	9 ♊	2 ♋	25 ♌	1 ♎	20 ♏	20 ♏	5 ♒	20 ♓	24 ♈	17 ♊	26 ♋
29	12 ♉	6 ♋	0 ♌	21 ♍	26 ♎	11 ♐	14 ♐	29 ♒	17 ♈	24 ♉		26 ♌
31	11 ♊		28 ♌		20 ♏		8 ♑	25 ♓		23 ♊		24 ♍

TABLE SIX—*continued*

MOON Greenwich Mean Midnight (0 h. 0 m.) 1921-1923

1921	Jan.	Feb.	Mar.	April	May	June	July	Aug.	Sep.	Oct.	Nov.	Dec.
1	8♎	25♏	3♐	17♑	19♒	4♈	8♉	28♊	22♌	0♎	21♏	25♐
3	3♏	19♐	27♐	11♒	13♓	29♈	5♊	28♋	22♍	29♎	17♐	21♑
5	28♏	13♑	21♑	5♓	8♈	27♉	4♋	29♌	21♎	26♏	13♑	15♒
7	22♐	6♒	15♒	0♈	5♉	26♊	5♌	28♍	18♏	22♐	7♒	8♓
9	16♑	0♓	9♓	26♈	2♊	25♋	5♍	26♎	14♐	17♑	2♓	2♈
11	9♒	25♓	4♈	23♉	1♋	25♌	3♎	23♏	9♑	11♒	24♓	27♈
13	3♓	20♈	0♉	21♊	0♌	23♍	0♏	18♐	2♒	5♓	19♈	23♉
15	28♓	16♉	26♉	19♋	28♌	20♎	26♏	12♑	26♒	29♓	15♉	21♊
17	23♈	13♊	24♊	17♌	26♍	16♏	21♐	6♒	20♓	24♈	12♊	20♋
19	20♉	12♋	22♋	16♍	23♎	11♐	15♑	29♒	15♈	19♉	10♋	19♌
21	18♊	12♌	21♌	14♎	19♏	6♑	9♒	23♓	10♉	16♊	9♌	18♍
23	19♋	12♍	21♍	11♏	15♐	0♒	2♓	18♈	6♊	14♋	7♍	16♎
25	19♌	11♎	19♎	6♐	9♑	24♒	26♓	13♉	3♋	12♌	5♎	12♏
27	19♍	8♏	16♏	1♑	3♒	17♓	21♈	9♊	1♌	12♍	2♏	9♐
29	17♎		11♐	25♑	27♒	12♈	16♉	7♋	1♍	10♎	29♏	4♑
31	12♏		6♑		21♓		14♊	7♌		7♏		29♑

1922	Jan.	Feb.	Mar.	April	May	June	July	Aug.	Sep.	Oct.	Nov.	Dec.
1	11♒	25♓	4♈	19♉	25♊	17♌	26♍	18♏	8♑	12♒	27♓	28♈
3	5♓	19♈	28♈	15♊	22♋	15♍	24♎	15♐	3♒	6♓	20♈	23♉
5	28♓	13♉	22♉	11♋	20♌	13♎	21♏	11♑	27♒	0♈	14♉	18♊
7	22♈	9♊	18♊	9♌	18♍	11♏	18♐	6♒	21♓	23♈	9♊	15♋
9	18♉	7♋	15♋	9♍	17♎	8♐	14♑	0♓	14♈	17♉	5♋	12♌
11	15♊	7♌	15♌	8♎	14♏	4♑	10♒	24♓	8♉	12♊	2♌	9♍
13	14♋	7♍	15♍	6♏	11♐	29♑	4♓	18♈	4♊	8♋	28♌	7♎
15	14♌	6♎	14♎	3♐	6♑	23♒	28♓	12♉	3♋	5♌	26♍	6♏
17	13♍	2♏	11♏	28♐	0♒	17♓	23♈	8♊	3♌	3♍	26♎	4♐
19	12♎	28♏	7♐	22♑	23♒	13♈	19♉	3♋	3♍	3♎	26♏	3♑
21	9♏	22♐	1♑	15♒	17♓	9♉	16♊	2♌	3♎	3♏	24♐	29♑
23	6♐	16♑	25♑	9♓	12♈	8♊	14♋	1♍	2♏	2♐	22♑	25♒
25	1♑	10♒	19♒	4♈	8♉	8♋	13♌	1♎	0♐	0♑	17♒	19♓
27	25♑	4♓	13♓	29♈	5♊	7♌	11♍	1♏	26♐	26♑	11♓	13♈
29	19♒		13♈	23♉	3♋	6♍	8♎	29♏	21♑	21♒	5♈	6♉
31	13♓		7♉		2♌		5♏	25♐		15♓		1♊

1923	Jan.	Feb.	Mar.	April	May	June	July	Aug.	Sep.	Oct.	Nov.	Dec.
1	14♊	2♌	10♌	2♎	11♏	6♑	6♒	26♓	10♉	12♊	27♋	3♍
3	10♋	1♍	9♍	3♏	11♐	1♒	1♓	20♈	4♊	6♋	23♌	0♎
5	8♌	0♎	9♎	3♐	10♑	26♒	25♓	14♉	0♋	1♌	21♍	28♎
7	6♍	28♎	9♏	1♑	6♒	20♓	20♈	8♊	26♋	27♌	20♎	27♏
9	4♎	27♏	8♐	27♑	1♓	14♈	14♉	3♋	23♌	24♍	20♏	25♐
11	2♏	24♐	5♑	22♒	25♓	8♉	9♊	28♋	20♍	21♎	18♐	22♑
13	0♐	21♑	1♒	17♓	19♈	2♊	4♋	26♌	18♎	20♏	15♑	18♒
15	28♐	16♒	25♒	10♈	13♉	26♊	1♌	23♍	17♏	18♐	12♒	13♓
17	25♑	11♓	20♓	4♉	7♊	23♋	28♌	21♎	14♐	15♑	6♓	7♈
19	20♒	5♈	13♈	28♉	2♋	20♌	26♍	19♏	11♑	10♒	0♈	1♉
21	15♓	28♈	7♉	24♊	28♋	18♍	24♎	17♐	6♒	5♓	24♈	25♉
23	9♈	22♉	1♊	22♋	26♌	17♎	22♏	14♑	0♓	29♓	18♉	20♊
25	2♉	17♊	25♊	20♌	24♍	15♏	20♐	10♒	24♓	24♈	12♊	15♋
27	26♉	13♋	21♋	18♍	22♎	14♐	17♑	5♓	18♈	18♉	6♋	11♌
29	22♊		18♌	11♎	20♏	12♑	13♒	29♓	12♉	12♊	2♌	7♍
31	18♋		17♍		18♐		6♓	22♈		6♋		4♎

MOON   Greenwich Mean Midnight (o h. o m.)   1924-1926

1924	Jan.	Feb.	Mar.	April	May	June	July	Aug.	Sep.	Oct.	Nov.	Dec.
1	24 ♎	17 ♐	12 ♑	3 ♓	7 ♈	23 ♉	25 ♊	11 ♌	29 ♍	6 ♏	0 ♐	8 ♑
3	23 ♏	16 ♑	10 ♒	28 ♓	2 ♉	16 ♊	19 ♋	6 ♍	26 ♎	5 ♐	28 ♑	6 ♒
5	22 ♐	14 ♒	6 ♓	23 ♈	26 ♉	10 ♋	14 ♌	2 ♎	24 ♏	4 ♑	26 ♒	2 ♓
7	21 ♑	11 ♓	2 ♈	17 ♉	19 ♊	4 ♌	9 ♍	29 ♎	23 ♐	2 ♒	22 ♓	27 ♓
9	20 ♒	6 ♈	27 ♈	11 ♊	12 ♋	29 ♌	5 ♎	27 ♏	21 ♑	29 ♒	18 ♈	22 ♈
11	16 ♓	1 ♉	21 ♉	5 ♋	7 ♌	25 ♍	3 ♏	26 ♐	19 ♒	25 ♓	12 ♉	15 ♉
13	11 ♈	25 ♉	14 ♊	29 ♋	2 ♍	23 ♎	2 ♐	25 ♑	16 ♓	21 ♈	7 ♊	7 ♊
15	5 ♉	19 ♊	9 ♋	24 ♋	0 ♎	23 ♏	1 ♑	24 ♒	13 ♈	16 ♉	1 ♋	1 ♋
17	29 ♉	13 ♋	3 ♌	21 ♍	29 ♎	23 ♐	0 ♒	21 ♓	8 ♉	10 ♊	24 ♋	27 ♋
19	23 ♊	9 ♌	0 ♍	20 ♎	29 ♏	22 ♑	27 ♒	17 ♈	2 ♊	4 ♋	18 ♌	22 ♌
21	18 ♋	5 ♎	28 ♍	21 ♏	29 ♐	18 ♒	22 ♓	12 ♉	26 ♊	28 ♋	13 ♍	18 ♍
23	13 ♌	3 ♏	27 ♎	21 ♐	26 ♑	14 ♓	16 ♈	6 ♊	20 ♋	22 ♌	10 ♎	16 ♎
25	10 ♎	1 ♐	25 ♐	19 ♑	22 ♒	8 ♈	10 ♉	0 ♋	15 ♌	18 ♍	8 ♏	17 ♏
27	7 ♏	0 ♑	23 ♑	17 ♒	17 ♓	2 ♉	4 ♊	24 ♋	10 ♍	16 ♎	8 ♐	17 ♐
29	5 ♐	28 ♐	23 ♒	12 ♓	11 ♈		28 ♊	19 ♌	8 ♎	15 ♏	9 ♑	17 ♑
31	3 ♐		20 ♒		11 ♉			15 ♍		15 ♐		15 ♓

1925	Jan.	Feb.	Mar.	April	May	June	July	Aug.	Sep.	Oct.	Nov.	Dec.
1	28 ♓	15 ♉	23 ♉	7 ♋	9 ♌	23 ♍	28 ♍	19 ♐	13 ♒	21 ♓	12 ♉	16 ♊
3	24 ♈	9 ♊	17 ♊	1 ♌	3 ♍	20 ♎	26 ♎	19 ♑	12 ♓	19 ♈	8 ♊	10 ♋
5	19 ♉	3 ♋	11 ♋	25 ♌	28 ♍	18 ♏	25 ♏	19 ♒	11 ♈	17 ♉	2 ♋	4 ♌
7	12 ♊	27 ♋	5 ♌	20 ♍	25 ♎	17 ♐	26 ♐	19 ♓	9 ♉	15 ♊	26 ♋	28 ♌
9	6 ♋	21 ♌	29 ♌	17 ♎	24 ♏	17 ♑	26 ♑	17 ♈	6 ♊	11 ♋	20 ♌	22 ♍
11	0 ♌	16 ♍	25 ♍	15 ♏	23 ♐	15 ♒	24 ♒	13 ♉	1 ♋	7 ♌	14 ♍	17 ♎
13	24 ♌	11 ♎	21 ♎	13 ♐	22 ♑	12 ♓	21 ♓	8 ♊	26 ♋	0 ♍	9 ♎	13 ♏
15	19 ♍	8 ♏	19 ♏	12 ♑	18 ♒	7 ♈	17 ♈	2 ♋	22 ♌	16 ♎	4 ♏	11 ♐
17	14 ♎	6 ♐	16 ♐	10 ♒	15 ♓	2 ♉	11 ♉	26 ♋	16 ♍	10 ♏	1 ♐	11 ♑
19	11 ♏	4 ♑	15 ♑	7 ♓	10 ♈	26 ♉	5 ♊	19 ♌	10 ♎	5 ♐	29 ♐	7 ♒
21	10 ♐	3 ♒	13 ♒	5 ♈	5 ♉	20 ♊	29 ♊	14 ♍	5 ♏	1 ♑	27 ♑	4 ♓
23	10 ♑	1 ♓	11 ♓	1 ♉	0 ♊	13 ♋	22 ♋	8 ♎	1 ♐	4 ♒	27 ♒	0 ♈
25	10 ♒	28 ♓	9 ♈	27 ♉	29 ♊	8 ♌	16 ♌	4 ♏	28 ♐	2 ♓	24 ♓	25 ♈
27	9 ♓		6 ♉	21 ♊	23 ♋	2 ♍	11 ♍	1 ♐	25 ♑	0 ♈	20 ♈	19 ♉
29	7 ♈		1 ♊	15 ♋	17 ♌		7 ♎	29 ♐	22 ♒	28 ♈		25 ♉
31	3 ♉		25 ♊		11 ♍		5 ♏	28 ♑				19 ♊

1926	Jan.	Feb.	Mar.	April	May	June	July	Aug.	Sep.	Oct.	Nov.	Dec.
1	1 ♌	15 ♍	24 ♍	10 ♏	17 ♐	9 ♒	18 ♓	10 ♉	29 ♊	2 ♌	16 ♍	18 ♎
3	24 ♌	9 ♎	18 ♎	7 ♐	14 ♑	7 ♓	16 ♈	7 ♊	23 ♋	26 ♌	10 ♎	13 ♏
5	18 ♍	4 ♏	13 ♏	3 ♑	12 ♒	7 ♈	14 ♉	2 ♋	17 ♌	20 ♍	5 ♏	9 ♐
7	12 ♎	1 ♐	9 ♐	1 ♒	10 ♓	3 ♉	10 ♊	26 ♋	11 ♍	14 ♎	0 ♐	6 ♑
9	8 ♏	28 ♐	7 ♑	0 ♓	9 ♈	0 ♊	5 ♋	20 ♌	5 ♎	8 ♏	26 ♐	3 ♒
11	5 ♐	27 ♑	7 ♒	29 ♓	7 ♉	26 ♊	0 ♌	14 ♍	29 ♎	3 ♐	23 ♑	1 ♓
13	4 ♑	27 ♒	6 ♓	28 ♈	5 ♊	21 ♋	24 ♌	8 ♎	26 ♏	19 ♐	20 ♒	0 ♈
15	4 ♒	28 ♓	6 ♈	26 ♉	1 ♋	15 ♌	17 ♍	4 ♏	24 ♐	24 ♑	18 ♓	28 ♈
17	4 ♓	27 ♈	5 ♉	23 ♊	25 ♋	9 ♍	11 ♎	1 ♐	24 ♑	24 ♈	17 ♈	26 ♉
19	4 ♈	23 ♉	2 ♊	17 ♋	19 ♌	3 ♎	6 ♏	2 ♑	22 ♒	23 ♉	17 ♉	24 ♊
21	1 ♉	19 ♊	27 ♊	11 ♌	13 ♍	28 ♎	2 ♐	29 ♑	21 ♓	21 ♊	15 ♊	19 ♋
23	27 ♉	13 ♋	21 ♋	5 ♍	7 ♎	24 ♏	29 ♐	28 ♒	21 ♈	18 ♋	11 ♋	14 ♌
25	22 ♊	6 ♌	15 ♌	29 ♍	2 ♏	21 ♐	28 ♑	26 ♓	21 ♉	16 ♌	7 ♌	8 ♍
27	16 ♋	0 ♍	9 ♍	24 ♎	29 ♏	20 ♑	27 ♒	25 ♈	20 ♊	10 ♍	1 ♍	2 ♎
29	9 ♌		3 ♎	20 ♏	26 ♐	19 ♒	28 ♓	22 ♉	16 ♋	5 ♎	24 ♍	26 ♎
31	3 ♍		28 ♎		24 ♑		27 ♈	16 ♊		5 ♏		21 ♏

MOON   Greenwich Mean Midnight (o h. o m.)   1927–1929

1927	Jan.	Feb.	Mar.	April	May	June	July	Aug.	Sep.	Oct.	Nov.	Dec.
1	4 ♐	23 ♑	0 ♒	23 ♓	2 ♉	24 ♊	0 ♌	16 ♍	0 ♏	2 ♐	18 ♑	24 ♒
3	1 ♑	22 ♒	0 ♓	24 ♈	2 ♊	21 ♋	25 ♌	10 ♎	23 ♏	26 ♐	14 ♒	22 ♓
5	29 ♑	22 ♓	0 ♈	24 ♉	0 ♋	17 ♌	20 ♍	3 ♏	18 ♐	22 ♑	12 ♓	20 ♈
7	28 ♒	21 ♈	1 ♉	22 ♊	26 ♋	12 ♍	13 ♎	27 ♏	13 ♑	19 ♒	11 ♈	20 ♉
9	26 ♓	19 ♉	29 ♉	18 ♋	21 ♌	6 ♎	7 ♏	22 ♐	11 ♒	18 ♓	12 ♉	20 ♊
11	25 ♈	16 ♊	26 ♊	13 ♌	15 ♍	29 ♎	1 ♐	19 ♑	10 ♓	18 ♈	12 ♊	18 ♋
13	22 ♉	12 ♋	21 ♋	7 ♍	9 ♎	24 ♏	27 ♐	17 ♒	10 ♈	18 ♉	10 ♋	15 ♌
15	19 ♊	7 ♌	16 ♌	1 ♎	3 ♏	19 ♐	24 ♑	15 ♓	10 ♉	19 ♊	7 ♌	11 ♍
17	15 ♋	1 ♍	10 ♍	24 ♎	27 ♏	15 ♑	19 ♒	14 ♈	8 ♊	18 ♋	2 ♍	5 ♎
19	10 ♌	25 ♍	4 ♎	18 ♏	22 ♐	12 ♒	15 ♓	14 ♉	6 ♋	15 ♌	27 ♍	29 ♎
21	4 ♍	19 ♎	27 ♎	13 ♐	18 ♑	10 ♓	12 ♈	12 ♊	1 ♌	9 ♍	20 ♎	23 ♏
23	28 ♍	12 ♏	21 ♏	8 ♑	15 ♒	8 ♈	10 ♉	9 ♋	26 ♌	3 ♎	14 ♏	17 ♐
25	22 ♎	7 ♐	16 ♐	5 ♒	13 ♓	8 ♉	8 ♊	4 ♌	21 ♍	26 ♎	8 ♐	12 ♑
27	16 ♏	3 ♑	12 ♑	3 ♓	12 ♈	5 ♊	5 ♋	0 ♍	15 ♎	20 ♏	3 ♑	8 ♒
29	12 ♐		9 ♒	2 ♈	11 ♉	3 ♋	8 ♌	24 ♍	8 ♏	14 ♐	28 ♑	5 ♓
31	8 ♑		8 ♓		10 ♊		3 ♍	18 ♎		8 ♑		2 ♈

1928	Jan.	Feb.	Mar.	April	May	June	July	Aug.	Sep.	Oct.	Nov.	Dec.
1	16 ♈	9 ♊	4 ♋	24 ♌	28 ♍	13 ♏	15 ♐	1 ♒	20 ♓	28 ♈	21 ♊	29 ♋
3	15 ♉	7 ♋	29 ♋	19 ♍	22 ♎	7 ♐	9 ♑	27 ♒	18 ♈	27 ♉	20 ♋	27 ♌
5	14 ♊	5 ♌	25 ♌	13 ♎	16 ♏	1 ♑	4 ♒	24 ♓	17 ♉	25 ♊	17 ♌	23 ♍
7	12 ♋	1 ♍	20 ♍	7 ♏	10 ♐	25 ♑	0 ♓	22 ♈	15 ♊	21 ♋	14 ♍	18 ♎
9	10 ♌	26 ♍	15 ♎	1 ♐	4 ♑	20 ♒	27 ♓	20 ♉	10 ♋	18 ♌	9 ♎	12 ♏
11	6 ♍	21 ♎	9 ♏	25 ♐	28 ♑	16 ♓	25 ♈	18 ♊	7 ♌	13 ♍	3 ♏	6 ♐
13	1 ♎	14 ♏	3 ♐	19 ♑	23 ♒	14 ♈	23 ♉	15 ♋	2 ♍	7 ♎	27 ♏	0 ♑
15	25 ♎	8 ♐	27 ♐	14 ♒	20 ♓	13 ♉	22 ♊	11 ♌	28 ♍	1 ♏	21 ♐	24 ♑
17	19 ♏	3 ♑	21 ♑	11 ♓	17 ♈	11 ♊	20 ♋	7 ♍	22 ♎	25 ♏	15 ♑	18 ♒
19	13 ♐	26 ♑	16 ♒	9 ♈	15 ♉	7 ♋	17 ♌	2 ♎	16 ♏	19 ♐	9 ♒	13 ♓
21	7 ♑	24 ♒	12 ♓	8 ♉	13 ♊	2 ♌	13 ♍	26 ♎	10 ♐	13 ♑	4 ♓	9 ♈
23	4 ♒	24 ♓	10 ♈	7 ♊	10 ♋	27 ♌	8 ♎	20 ♏	4 ♑	7 ♒	0 ♈	7 ♉
25	1 ♓	22 ♈	9 ♉	4 ♋	5 ♌	21 ♍	2 ♏	14 ♐	28 ♑	2 ♓	28 ♈	6 ♊
27	29 ♓	20 ♉	8 ♊	0 ♌	1 ♍	15 ♎	26 ♏	8 ♑	23 ♒	29 ♓	26 ♉	4 ♋
29	27 ♈	18 ♊	6 ♋	26 ♌	25 ♍	9 ♏	20 ♐	2 ♒	19 ♓	27 ♈	24 ♊	1 ♌
31	25 ♉		3 ♌		19 ♎		14 ♑	28 ♒		25 ♉		27 ♌

1929	Jan.	Feb.	Mar.	April	May	June	July	Aug.	Sep.	Oct.	Nov.	Dec.
1	19 ♍	5 ♏	13 ♏	27 ♐	28 ♑	14 ♓	19 ♈	10 ♊	4 ♌	12 ♍	2 ♏	6 ♐
3	15 ♎	29 ♏	7 ♐	21 ♑	23 ♒	10 ♈	17 ♉	10 ♋	3 ♍	7 ♎	26 ♏	0 ♑
5	9 ♏	23 ♐	1 ♑	15 ♒	18 ♓	8 ♉	16 ♊	7 ♌	28 ♍	1 ♏	20 ♐	24 ♑
7	3 ♐	17 ♑	25 ♑	10 ♓	14 ♈	6 ♊	13 ♋	3 ♍	22 ♎	25 ♏	14 ♑	18 ♒
9	26 ♐	11 ♒	19 ♒	6 ♈	12 ♉	3 ♋	9 ♌	28 ♍	17 ♏	19 ♐	8 ♒	12 ♓
11	20 ♑	7 ♓	15 ♓	4 ♉	11 ♊	0 ♌	4 ♍	23 ♎	11 ♐	13 ♑	3 ♓	8 ♈
13	15 ♒	3 ♈	11 ♈	2 ♊	8 ♋	25 ♌	29 ♍	17 ♏	5 ♑	7 ♒	29 ♓	4 ♉
15	10 ♓	0 ♉	9 ♉	0 ♋	4 ♌	21 ♍	23 ♎	11 ♐	29 ♑	2 ♓	25 ♈	2 ♊
17	6 ♈	28 ♉	7 ♊	27 ♋	0 ♍	16 ♎	17 ♏	5 ♑	24 ♒	28 ♓	23 ♉	2 ♋
19	3 ♉	26 ♊	5 ♋	23 ♌	25 ♍	10 ♏	11 ♐	29 ♑	19 ♓	24 ♈	21 ♊	2 ♌
21	1 ♊	24 ♋	2 ♌	19 ♍	20 ♎	4 ♐	5 ♑	24 ♒	15 ♈	21 ♉	18 ♋	2 ♍
23	1 ♋	21 ♌	28 ♌	13 ♎	14 ♏	28 ♐	29 ♑	19 ♓	11 ♉	19 ♊	14 ♌	28 ♍
25	0 ♌	18 ♍	23 ♍	7 ♏	8 ♐	22 ♑	24 ♒	15 ♈	9 ♊	16 ♋	10 ♍	21 ♎
27	27 ♌	12 ♎	17 ♎	1 ♐	2 ♑	17 ♒	20 ♓	13 ♉	6 ♋	12 ♌	4 ♎	16 ♏
29	23 ♍		11 ♏	25 ♐	26 ♑	13 ♓	17 ♈	11 ♊	2 ♌	8 ♍	28 ♎	11 ♐
31	18 ♎		5 ♐		21 ♒		15 ♉	9 ♋		2 ♎		9 ♑

MOON   Greenwich Mean Midnight (0 h. 0 m.)   1930–1932

1930	Jan.	Feb.	Mar.	April	May	June	July	Aug.	Sep.	Oct.	Nov.	Dec.
1	21 ♑	6 ♓	15 ♓	1 ♉	8 ♊	1 ♌	10 ♍	2 ♏	19 ♐	22 ♑	6 ♓	8 ♈
3	15 ♒	0 ♈	9 ♈	28 ♉	6 ♋	0 ♍	8 ♎	28 ♏	14 ♑	16 ♒	0 ♈	3 ♉
5	8 ♓	25 ♈	5 ♉	25 ♊	4 ♌	28 ♍	5 ♏	23 ♐	8 ♒	10 ♓	25 ♈	29 ♉
7	3 ♈	21 ♉	1 ♊	23 ♋	3 ♍	25 ♎	1 ♐	17 ♑	1 ♓	4 ♈	21 ♉	27 ♊
9	28 ♈	19 ♊	28 ♊	22 ♌	1 ♎	21 ♏	25 ♐	11 ♒	25 ♓	29 ♈	17 ♊	25 ♋
11	26 ♉	18 ♋	27 ♋	19 ♍	28 ♎	16 ♐	20 ♑	4 ♓	20 ♈	24 ♉	15 ♋	24 ♌
13	25 ♊	18 ♌	27 ♌	16 ♎	25 ♏	11 ♑	14 ♒	28 ♓	14 ♉	21 ♊	13 ♌	22 ♍
15	25 ♋	19 ♍	27 ♍	12 ♏	20 ♐	5 ♒	7 ♓	22 ♈	10 ♊	18 ♋	11 ♍	20 ♎
17	26 ♌	17 ♎	25 ♎	12 ♐	15 ♑	29 ♒	1 ♈	18 ♉	8 ♋	16 ♌	10 ♎	17 ♏
19	25 ♍	14 ♏	22 ♏	7 ♑	9 ♒	23 ♓	26 ♈	14 ♊	7 ♌	16 ♍	8 ♏	14 ♐
21	22 ♎	9 ♐	17 ♐	1 ♒	3 ♓	17 ♈	22 ♉	13 ♋	6 ♍	15 ♎	5 ♐	9 ♑
23	18 ♏	3 ♑	11 ♑	25 ♒	27 ♓	13 ♉	19 ♊	13 ♌	6 ♎	13 ♏	1 ♑	4 ♒
25	12 ♐	27 ♑	5 ♒	19 ♓	22 ♈	11 ♊	18 ♋	13 ♍	5 ♏	10 ♐	26 ♑	28 ♒
27	6 ♑	20 ♒	29 ♒	14 ♈	19 ♉	11 ♋	20 ♌	13 ♎	2 ♐	6 ♑	20 ♒	22 ♓
29	0 ♒		23 ♓	10 ♉	17 ♊	11 ♌	20 ♍	11 ♏	28 ♐	1 ♒	14 ♓	16 ♈
31	24 ♒		18 ♈		16 ♋		18 ♎	7 ♐		24 ♒		11 ♉

1931	Jan.	Feb.	Mar.	April	May	June	July	Aug.	Sep.	Oct.	Nov.	Dec.
1	24 ♉	13 ♋	21 ♋	14 ♍	23 ♎	15 ♐	20 ♑	6 ♓	20 ♈	22 ♉	9 ♋	16 ♌
3	21 ♊	13 ♌	21 ♌	14 ♍	22 ♏	12 ♑	15 ♒	29 ♓	13 ♉	20 ♊	6 ♌	14 ♍
5	20 ♋	13 ♍	21 ♍	14 ♎	20 ♐	7 ♒	9 ♓	23 ♈	8 ♊	13 ♋	3 ♍	12 ♎
7	19 ♌	13 ♎	21 ♎	12 ♏	17 ♑	1 ♓	3 ♈	17 ♉	4 ♋	10 ♌	2 ♎	11 ♏
9	19 ♍	11 ♏	20 ♏	8 ♐	11 ♒	25 ♓	27 ♈	12 ♊	1 ♌	9 ♍	2 ♏	10 ♐
11	17 ♎	7 ♐	17 ♐	3 ♑	5 ♓	19 ♈	21 ♉	9 ♋	1 ♍	9 ♎	2 ♐	9 ♑
13	14 ♏	1 ♑	12 ♑	27 ♑	29 ♓	13 ♉	17 ♊	8 ♌	1 ♎	9 ♏	1 ♑	5 ♒
15	10 ♐	27 ♑	6 ♒	21 ♒	23 ♈	9 ♊	15 ♋	7 ♍	1 ♏	8 ♐	29 ♑	1 ♓
17	6 ♑	21 ♒	0 ♓	14 ♓	18 ♉	6 ♋	13 ♌	7 ♎	0 ♐	6 ♑	25 ♒	25 ♓
19	0 ♒	15 ♓	24 ♓	9 ♈	13 ♊	4 ♌	13 ♍	6 ♏	27 ♐	2 ♒	17 ♓	18 ♈
21	25 ♒	9 ♈	18 ♈	4 ♉	10 ♋	2 ♍	11 ♎	4 ♐	23 ♑	26 ♒	10 ♈	12 ♉
23	18 ♓	3 ♉	12 ♉	28 ♉	7 ♌	0 ♎	9 ♏	0 ♑	17 ♒	20 ♓	4 ♉	7 ♊
25	12 ♈	27 ♉	7 ♊	22 ♊	5 ♍	28 ♎	6 ♐	26 ♑	11 ♓	14 ♈	28 ♉	3 ♋
27	6 ♉	23 ♊	1 ♋	25 ♋	4 ♎	26 ♏	1 ♑	20 ♒	5 ♈	7 ♉	24 ♊	29 ♋
29	1 ♊		0 ♌	29 ♋	2 ♏	24 ♐	29 ♑	14 ♓	2 ♉	2 ♊	19 ♋	27 ♌
31	29 ♊		29 ♌		1 ♐		24 ♒	8 ♈		27 ♊		25 ♍

1932	Jan.	Feb.	Mar.	April	May	June	July	Aug.	Sep.	Oct.	Nov.	Dec.
1	9 ♎	2 ♐	26 ♐	15 ♒	19 ♓	3 ♉	5 ♊	21 ♋	11 ♍	18 ♎	12 ♐	20 ♑
3	7 ♏	29 ♐	22 ♑	10 ♓	12 ♈	27 ♉	0 ♋	18 ♌	9 ♎	18 ♏	11 ♑	18 ♒
5	5 ♐	26 ♑	18 ♒	4 ♈	6 ♉	21 ♊	26 ♋	15 ♍	8 ♏	18 ♐	9 ♒	14 ♓
7	3 ♑	22 ♒	12 ♓	27 ♈	0 ♊	16 ♋	22 ♌	14 ♎	7 ♐	16 ♑	5 ♓	8 ♈
9	0 ♒	16 ♓	7 ♈	20 ♉	24 ♊	12 ♌	19 ♍	12 ♏	5 ♑	12 ♒	29 ♓	2 ♉
11	26 ♒	10 ♈	0 ♉	15 ♊	19 ♋	8 ♍	17 ♎	10 ♐	2 ♒	8 ♓	23 ♈	26 ♉
13	20 ♓	4 ♉	24 ♉	9 ♋	15 ♌	6 ♎	15 ♏	8 ♑	28 ♒	2 ♈	17 ♉	20 ♊
15	14 ♈	28 ♉	18 ♊	5 ♌	12 ♍	5 ♏	14 ♐	6 ♒	23 ♓	26 ♈	11 ♊	14 ♋
17	8 ♉	23 ♊	13 ♋	2 ♍	11 ♎	4 ♐	13 ♑	2 ♓	18 ♈	20 ♉	5 ♋	9 ♌
19	2 ♊	19 ♋	9 ♌	0 ♎	11 ♏	4 ♑	10 ♒	27 ♓	12 ♉	14 ♊	29 ♋	4 ♍
21	28 ♊	17 ♌	9 ♍	0 ♏	11 ♐	2 ♒	7 ♓	22 ♈	5 ♊	8 ♋	24 ♌	1 ♎
23	24 ♋	16 ♍	9 ♎	0 ♐	10 ♑	29 ♒	2 ♈	16 ♉	29 ♊	3 ♌	21 ♍	29 ♎
25	22 ♌	15 ♎	8 ♏	29 ♐	8 ♒	24 ♓	26 ♈	9 ♊	24 ♋	29 ♌	20 ♎	28 ♏
27	21 ♍	14 ♏	7 ♐	25 ♑	3 ♓	18 ♈	19 ♉	3 ♋	21 ♌	27 ♍	20 ♏	28 ♐
29	20 ♎	12 ♐	6 ♑	20 ♒	27 ♓	11 ♉	13 ♊	29 ♋	19 ♍	27 ♎	20 ♐	28 ♑
31	18 ♏		2 ♒		21 ♈		8 ♋	27 ♌		27 ♏		26 ♒

MOON Greenwich Mean Midnight (o h. o m.) 1933-1935

1933	Jan.	Feb.	Mar.	April	May	June	July	Aug.	Sep.	Oct.	Nov.	Dec.
1	9 ♓	25 ♈	2 ♉	16 ♊	18 ♋	4 ♍	10 ♎	2 ♐	26 ♑	4 ♓	23 ♎	27 ♉
3	5 ♈	19 ♉	26 ♉	10 ♋	13 ♌	0 ♎	8 ♏	1 ♑	24 ♒	1 ♈	18 ♉	21 ♊
5	29 ♈	12 ♊	20 ♊	5 ♌	8 ♍	29 ♎	7 ♐	1 ♒	22 ♓	27 ♈	12 ♊	14 ♋
7	22 ♉	7 ♋	14 ♋	0 ♍	6 ♎	28 ♏	7 ♑	0 ♓	19 ♈	22 ♉	6 ♋	8 ♌
9	16 ♊	1 ♌	9 ♌	28 ♍	5 ♏	29 ♐	7 ♒	27 ♓	14 ♉	16 ♊	0 ♌	2 ♍
11	11 ♋	27 ♌	6 ♍	27 ♎	5 ♐	27 ♑	6 ♓	23 ♈	8 ♊	10 ♋	24 ♌	27 ♍
13	6 ♌	24 ♍	3 ♎	26 ♏	5 ♑	27 ♒	2 ♈	18 ♉	2 ♋	4 ♌	19 ♍	24 ♎
15	1 ♍	22 ♎	2 ♏	26 ♐	4 ♒	24 ♓	28 ♈	12 ♊	26 ♋	28 ♌	15 ♎	23 ♏
17	28 ♍	20 ♏	1 ♐	24 ♑	1 ♓	19 ♈	23 ♉	6 ♋	20 ♌	24 ♍	13 ♏	23 ♐
19	25 ♎	19 ♐	0 ♑	21 ♒	27 ♈	13 ♉	18 ♊	0 ♌	16 ♍	22 ♎	12 ♐	23 ♑
21	23 ♏	17 ♑	27 ♑	17 ♓	22 ♉	7 ♊	12 ♋	25 ♌	13 ♎	21 ♏	11 ♑	23 ♒
23	23 ♐	15 ♒	24 ♒	12 ♈	16 ♊	0 ♋	6 ♌	20 ♍	11 ♏	20 ♐	11 ♒	21 ♓
25	22 ♑	12 ♓	20 ♓	7 ♉	10 ♋	24 ♋	0 ♍	17 ♎	10 ♐	19 ♑	8 ♓	17 ♈
27	20 ♒	8 ♈	16 ♈	1 ♊	3 ♌	18 ♌	24 ♍	15 ♏	10 ♑	17 ♒	6 ♈	11 ♉
29	17 ♓		10 ♉	25 ♊	27 ♌	14 ♍	19 ♎	13 ♐	10 ♒	14 ♓	1 ♉	6 ♊
31	12 ♈		4 ♊		22 ♌		13 ♏	11 ♑		10 ♈		29 ♊

1934	Jan.	Feb.	Mar.	April	May	June	July	Aug.	Sep.	Oct.	Nov.	Dec.
1	11 ♋	26 ♌	5 ♍	22 ♎	29 ♏	23 ♑	1 ♓	23 ♈	10 ♊	12 ♋	26 ♌	28 ♍
3	5 ♌	21 ♍	0 ♎	20 ♏	28 ♐	22 ♒	0 ♈	19 ♉	4 ♋	6 ♌	20 ♍	23 ♎
5	29 ♌	16 ♎	26 ♎	18 ♐	27 ♑	20 ♓	26 ♈	13 ♊	28 ♋	0 ♍	15 ♎	20 ♏
7	24 ♍	13 ♏	23 ♏	16 ♑	25 ♒	16 ♈	22 ♉	7 ♋	21 ♌	24 ♍	11 ♏	18 ♐
9	19 ♎	10 ♐	21 ♐	14 ♒	23 ♓	12 ♉	16 ♊	1 ♌	15 ♍	19 ♎	9 ♐	16 ♑
11	17 ♏	10 ♑	19 ♑	12 ♓	21 ♈	7 ♊	10 ♋	25 ♌	10 ♎	16 ♏	7 ♑	14 ♒
13	16 ♐	9 ♒	18 ♒	10 ♈	19 ♉	1 ♋	4 ♌	19 ♍	6 ♏	13 ♐	5 ♒	12 ♓
15	16 ♑	9 ♓	17 ♓	7 ♉	15 ♊	25 ♋	27 ♌	13 ♎	2 ♐	11 ♑	4 ♓	9 ♈
17	16 ♒	7 ♈	15 ♈	4 ♊	11 ♋	19 ♌	21 ♍	6 ♏	0 ♑	10 ♒	1 ♈	5 ♉
19	15 ♓	4 ♉	12 ♉	29 ♊	7 ♌	13 ♍	16 ♎	6 ♐	28 ♑	9 ♓	29 ♈	0 ♊
21	13 ♈	29 ♉	8 ♊	24 ♋	1 ♍	7 ♎	12 ♏	4 ♑	27 ♒	8 ♈	26 ♉	24 ♊
23	8 ♉	23 ♊	4 ♋	18 ♌	25 ♍	2 ♏	10 ♐	4 ♒	27 ♓	6 ♉	21 ♊	18 ♋
25	3 ♊	17 ♋	28 ♋	12 ♍	19 ♎	28 ♏	10 ♑	4 ♓	25 ♈	2 ♊	16 ♋	12 ♌
27	27 ♊	10 ♌	22 ♌	6 ♎	13 ♏	24 ♐	10 ♒	3 ♈	23 ♉	27 ♊	10 ♌	6 ♍
29	20 ♋		16 ♍	1 ♏	11 ♐	20 ♑	9 ♓	1 ♉	18 ♊	21 ♋	4 ♍	1 ♎
31	14 ♌		10 ♎		10 ♑		9 ♈	27 ♉		15 ♌		26 ♎

1935	Jan.	Feb.	Mar.	April	May	June	July	Aug.	Sep.	Oct.	Nov.	Dec.
1	28 ♏	15 ♑	24 ♑	14 ♓	14 ♈	6 ♊	10 ♋	25 ♌	10 ♎	13 ♏	1 ♐	8 ♑
3	24 ♐	13 ♒	22 ♒	12 ♈	13 ♉	2 ♋	5 ♌	19 ♍	4 ♏	8 ♐	27 ♐	6 ♒
5	22 ♑	12 ♓	21 ♓	10 ♉	10 ♊	27 ♋	29 ♌	13 ♎	29 ♏	4 ♑	25 ♑	4 ♓
7	20 ♒	11 ♈	20 ♈	7 ♊	6 ♋	21 ♌	23 ♍	7 ♏	24 ♐	1 ♒	24 ♒	4 ♈
9	19 ♓	10 ♉	17 ♉	3 ♋	1 ♌	15 ♍	17 ♎	2 ♐	19 ♑	0 ♓	24 ♓	1 ♉
11	18 ♈	7 ♊	13 ♊	28 ♋	25 ♌	9 ♎	11 ♏	29 ♐	16 ♒	0 ♈	24 ♈	29 ♉
13	16 ♉	3 ♋	8 ♋	22 ♌	19 ♍	3 ♏	7 ♐	28 ♑	15 ♓	0 ♉	21 ♉	25 ♊
15	12 ♊	28 ♋	2 ♌	16 ♍	13 ♎	29 ♏	4 ♑	28 ♒	15 ♈	29 ♉	17 ♊	20 ♋
17	7 ♋	22 ♌	26 ♌	10 ♎	8 ♏	25 ♐	1 ♒	28 ♓	13 ♉	25 ♊	12 ♋	14 ♌
19	2 ♌	16 ♍	20 ♍	4 ♏	4 ♐	22 ♑	29 ♒	28 ♈	8 ♊	20 ♋	6 ♌	8 ♍
21	26 ♌	10 ♎	14 ♎	29 ♏	2 ♑	21 ♒	28 ♓	25 ♉	3 ♋	14 ♌	0 ♍	2 ♎
23	20 ♍	4 ♏	10 ♏	25 ♐	29 ♑	21 ♓	27 ♈	21 ♊	27 ♋	8 ♍	24 ♍	27 ♎
25	14 ♎	0 ♐	6 ♐	22 ♑	28 ♒	21 ♈	25 ♉	16 ♋	21 ♌	2 ♎	19 ♎	23 ♏
27	9 ♏	26 ♐	4 ♑	20 ♒	26 ♓	19 ♉	22 ♊	10 ♌	16 ♍	26 ♎	14 ♏	20 ♐
29	5 ♐		2 ♒	18 ♓	24 ♈	15 ♊	18 ♋	4 ♍	10 ♎	21 ♏	11 ♐	18 ♑
31	2 ♑		1 ♓		22 ♉		12 ♌	28 ♍		16 ♐		17 ♒

MOON Greenwich Mean Midnight (o h. o m.) 1936-1938

1936	Jan.	Feb.	Mar.	April	May	June	July	Aug.	Sep.	Oct.	Nov.	Dec.
1	1 ♈	24 ♉	18 ♊	6 ♌	9 ♍	23 ♎	25 ♏	11 ♐	1 ♓	9 ♈	3 ♊	10 ♋
3	29 ♈	21 ♊	14 ♋	0 ♍	3 ♎	17 ♏	20 ♐	8 ♑	10 ♉	0 ♉	2 ♋	8 ♌
5	27 ♉	17 ♋	9 ♌	24 ♍	26 ♎	12 ♐	16 ♑	7 ♓	1 ♉	9 ♉	0 ♌	4 ♍
7	24 ♊	12 ♌	3 ♍	18 ♎	20 ♏	7 ♑	13 ♒	6 ♈	29 ♉	7 ♊	25 ♌	29 ♍
9	20 ♋	6 ♍	27 ♍	11 ♏	15 ♐	3 ♒	11 ♓	5 ♉	27 ♊	3 ♋	20 ♍	22 ♎
11	16 ♌	0 ♎	21 ♎	6 ♐	10 ♑	0 ♓	9 ♈	3 ♊	23 ♋	28 ♋	14 ♎	16 ♏
13	10 ♍	24 ♎	14 ♏	1 ♑	4 ♒	28 ♓	8 ♉	0 ♋	19 ♌	23 ♌	7 ♏	11 ♐
15	4 ♎	18 ♏	9 ♐	26 ♑	27 ♒	27 ♈	6 ♊	27 ♋	14 ♍	17 ♎	1 ♐	4 ♑
17	28 ♎	13 ♐	3 ♑	23 ♒	2 ♈	2 ♉	4 ♋	22 ♌	8 ♎	10 ♏	25 ♐	0 ♒
19	22 ♏	9 ♑	1 ♒	23 ♓	2 ♉	25 ♉	1 ♌	17 ♍	2 ♏	4 ♐	20 ♑	26 ♒
21	18 ♐	7 ♒	29 ♒	23 ♈	2 ♊	20 ♋	26 ♌	11 ♎	25 ♐	28 ♐	16 ♒	23 ♓
23	15 ♑	6 ♓	0 ♈	23 ♉	0 ♋	18 ♌	21 ♍	5 ♏	19 ♑	23 ♑	13 ♓	21 ♈
25	13 ♒	7 ♈	0 ♉	22 ♊	27 ♋	13 ♍	15 ♎	29 ♏	14 ♒	19 ♒	11 ♈	20 ♉
27	13 ♓	6 ♉	0 ♊	19 ♋	23 ♌	7 ♎	9 ♏	23 ♐	11 ♓	18 ♓	11 ♉	19 ♊
29	12 ♈	4 ♊	27 ♊	15 ♌	17 ♍	1 ♏	3 ♐	19 ♑	9 ♈	18 ♈	11 ♊	18 ♋
31	10 ♉		23 ♋		11 ♎		28 ♐	17 ♒		18 ♉		16 ♌

1937	Jan.	Feb.	Mar.	April	May	June	July	Aug.	Sep.	Oct.	Nov.	Dec.
1	29 ♌	14 ♎	22 ♎	6 ♐	9 ♑	25 ♒	2 ♈	24 ♉	18 ♋	25 ♌	14 ♎	17 ♏
3	24 ♍	8 ♏	16 ♏	0 ♑	3 ♒	22 ♓	0 ♉	23 ♊	15 ♌	22 ♍	8 ♏	11 ♐
5	19 ♎	2 ♐	9 ♐	24 ♑	29 ♒	20 ♈	29 ♉	22 ♋	13 ♍	17 ♎	2 ♐	4 ♑
7	12 ♏	26 ♐	4 ♑	20 ♒	27 ♓	19 ♉	28 ♊	20 ♌	9 ♎	12 ♏	26 ♐	28 ♑
9	6 ♐	21 ♑	29 ♑	18 ♓	26 ♈	20 ♊	28 ♋	17 ♍	4 ♏	6 ♐	19 ♑	23 ♒
11	1 ♑	18 ♒	26 ♒	18 ♈	26 ♉	18 ♋	26 ♌	13 ♎	28 ♏	1 ♑	14 ♒	18 ♓
13	26 ♑	16 ♓	25 ♓	18 ♉	26 ♊	18 ♌	23 ♍	8 ♏	21 ♑	23 ♑	9 ♓	15 ♈
15	22 ♒	14 ♈	24 ♈	17 ♊	25 ♋	14 ♍	18 ♎	1 ♐	15 ♒	18 ♒	6 ♈	13 ♉
17	20 ♓	13 ♉	23 ♉	16 ♋	22 ♌	9 ♎	12 ♏	25 ♐	10 ♓	15 ♓	5 ♉	13 ♊
19	18 ♈	11 ♊	22 ♊	13 ♌	18 ♍	3 ♏	5 ♐	20 ♑	7 ♈	13 ♈	6 ♊	14 ♋
21	16 ♉	9 ♋	19 ♋	8 ♍	12 ♎	27 ♏	29 ♐	15 ♒	4 ♉	12 ♉	6 ♋	14 ♌
23	14 ♊	6 ♌	15 ♌	3 ♎	6 ♏	21 ♐	24 ♑	12 ♓	3 ♊	11 ♊	5 ♌	11 ♍
25	13 ♋	2 ♍	11 ♍	27 ♎	0 ♐	15 ♑	19 ♒	9 ♈	2 ♋	11 ♋	2 ♍	7 ♎
27	10 ♌	28 ♍	6 ♎	21 ♏	24 ♐	9 ♒	15 ♓	7 ♉	28 ♋	9 ♌	28 ♍	2 ♏
29	7 ♍		1 ♏	15 ♐	18 ♑	5 ♓	12 ♈	5 ♊	28 ♌	5 ♎	23 ♎	26 ♏
31	2 ♎		24 ♏		12 ♒		10 ♉	3 ♋		1 ♏		20 ♐

1938	Jan.	Feb.	Mar.	April	May	June	July	Aug.	Sep.	Oct.	Nov.	Dec.
1	1 ♑	16 ♒	25 ♒	13 ♈	20 ♉	14 ♋	23 ♌	13 ♎	0 ♐	2 ♑	15 ♒	17 ♓
3	25 ♑	12 ♓	21 ♓	11 ♉	20 ♊	13 ♌	21 ♍	9 ♏	24 ♐	26 ♑	10 ♓	13 ♈
5	20 ♒	8 ♈	18 ♈	10 ♊	19 ♋	14 ♍	17 ♎	3 ♐	18 ♑	20 ♒	5 ♈	10 ♉
7	15 ♓	5 ♉	15 ♉	8 ♋	17 ♌	8 ♎	12 ♏	27 ♐	11 ♒	14 ♓	2 ♉	8 ♊
9	11 ♈	2 ♊	13 ♊	6 ♌	15 ♍	3 ♏	7 ♐	21 ♑	6 ♓	10 ♈	0 ♊	8 ♋
11	8 ♉	1 ♋	11 ♋	4 ♍	11 ♎	28 ♏	0 ♑	15 ♒	2 ♈	7 ♉	29 ♊	8 ♌
13	7 ♊	0 ♌	10 ♌	1 ♎	6 ♏	21 ♐	24 ♑	9 ♓	0 ♉	5 ♊	28 ♋	7 ♍
15	7 ♋	29 ♌	8 ♍	27 ♎	1 ♐	15 ♑	18 ♒	4 ♈	0 ♊	5 ♋	24 ♌	4 ♎
17	7 ♌	27 ♍	6 ♎	22 ♏	25 ♐	9 ♒	12 ♓	0 ♉	0 ♋	4 ♌	21 ♍	0 ♏
19	3 ♍	24 ♎	2 ♏	16 ♐	18 ♑	3 ♓	7 ♈	27 ♉	0 ♌	2 ♍	16 ♎	26 ♏
21	6 ♍	19 ♏	26 ♏	10 ♑	12 ♒	28 ♓	4 ♉	25 ♊	27 ♌	27 ♍	11 ♏	20 ♐
23	29 ♎	14 ♐	20 ♐	5 ♒	7 ♓	24 ♈	1 ♊	25 ♋	24 ♍	21 ♎	6 ♐	14 ♑
25	23 ♏	6 ♑	14 ♑	28 ♒	2 ♈	22 ♉	1 ♋	25 ♌	21 ♎	16 ♏	1 ♑	8 ♒
27	16 ♐	0 ♒	8 ♒	24 ♓	0 ♉	22 ♊	1 ♌	24 ♍	17 ♏	10 ♐	0 ♒	2 ♓
29	10 ♑		3 ♓	22 ♈	0 ♊	23 ♋	1 ♍	21 ♎	12 ♐	10 ♑	23 ♒	26 ♓
31	4 ♒		0 ♈		29 ♊		0 ♎	17 ♏		3 ♒		21 ♈

MOON Greenwich Mean Midnight (o h. o m.)   1939-1941

1939	Jan.	Feb.	Mar.	April	May	June	July	Aug.	Sep.	Oct.	Nov.	Dec.
1	4 ♉	24 ♊	3 ♋	27 ♌	6 ♎	26 ♏	1 ♑	16 ♒	0 ♈	4 ♉	22 ♊	0 ♌
3	2 ♊	24 ♋	3 ♌	26 ♍	4 ♏	22 ♐	25 ♑	10 ♓	24 ♈	29 ♉	20 ♋	29 ♌
5	1 ♋	25 ♌	3 ♍	25 ♎	0 ♐	17 ♑	19 ♒	3 ♈	19 ♉	25 ♊	18 ♌	27 ♍
7	2 ♌	25 ♍	3 ♎	22 ♏	26 ♐	11 ♒	13 ♓	28 ♈	15 ♊	23 ♋	16 ♍	25 ♎
9	2 ♍	23 ♎	1 ♏	18 ♐	21 ♑	4 ♓	7 ♈	23 ♉	13 ♋	22 ♌	15 ♎	22 ♏
11	0 ♎	19 ♏	28 ♏	13 ♑	15 ♒	28 ♓	1 ♉	20 ♊	12 ♌	21 ♍	13 ♏	19 ♐
13	27 ♎	14 ♐	23 ♐	7 ♒	8 ♈	23 ♈	28 ♉	19 ♋	13 ♍	21 ♎	11 ♐	15 ♑
15	23 ♏	8 ♑	17 ♑	0 ♓	3 ♈	19 ♉	26 ♊	19 ♌	13 ♎	19 ♏	7 ♑	10 ♒
17	17 ♐	2 ♒	10 ♒	25 ♓	28 ♈	17 ♊	25 ♋	19 ♍	11 ♏	16 ♐	2 ♒	4 ♓
19	11 ♑	26 ♒	4 ♓	20 ♈	25 ♉	16 ♋	26 ♌	19 ♎	8 ♐	12 ♑	26 ♒	28 ♓
21	5 ♒	20 ♓	29 ♓	16 ♉	23 ♊	16 ♌	25 ♍	16 ♏	4 ♑	6 ♒	20 ♓	22 ♈
23	29 ♒	14 ♈	24 ♈	13 ♊	21 ♋	15 ♍	23 ♎	12 ♐	28 ♑	0 ♓	14 ♈	17 ♉
25	23 ♓	9 ♉	19 ♉	11 ♋	20 ♌	13 ♎	20 ♏	7 ♑	22 ♒	24 ♓	9 ♉	13 ♊
27	17 ♈	6 ♊	16 ♊	9 ♌	18 ♍	10 ♏	15 ♐	1 ♒	15 ♈	18 ♈	5 ♊	11 ♋
29	13 ♉		14 ♋	7 ♍	16 ♎	6 ♐	10 ♑	25 ♒	9 ♈	13 ♉	2 ♋	10 ♌
31	10 ♊		13 ♍		13 ♏		4 ♒	18 ♓		9 ♊		9 ♍

1940	Jan.	Feb.	Mar.	April	May	June	July	Aug.	Sep.	Oct.	Nov.	Dec.
1	24 ♍	16 ♏	9 ♐	26 ♑	29 ♒	13 ♈	15 ♉	1 ♋	22 ♌	0 ♎	24 ♏	1 ♑
3	22 ♎	12 ♐	5 ♑	21 ♒	23 ♓	7 ♉	10 ♊	29 ♋	22 ♍	1 ♏	23 ♐	28 ♑
5	19 ♏	8 ♑	29 ♑	14 ♓	16 ♈	2 ♊	7 ♋	28 ♌	22 ♎	0 ♐	20 ♑	24 ♒
7	15 ♐	2 ♒	23 ♒	8 ♈	11 ♉	28 ♊	28 ♋	28 ♍	21 ♏	28 ♐	16 ♒	18 ♓
9	11 ♑	27 ♒	17 ♓	2 ♉	5 ♊	25 ♋	3 ♍	25 ♎	18 ♐	24 ♑	10 ♓	12 ♈
11	6 ♒	20 ♓	11 ♈	26 ♉	1 ♋	23 ♌	2 ♎	25 ♏	15 ♑	19 ♒	4 ♈	6 ♉
13	0 ♓	14 ♈	5 ♉	21 ♊	28 ♋	21 ♍	0 ♏	22 ♐	10 ♒	13 ♓	27 ♈	0 ♊
15	24 ♓	8 ♉	29 ♉	18 ♋	26 ♌	19 ♎	28 ♏	18 ♑	4 ♓	7 ♈	21 ♉	25 ♊
17	17 ♈	3 ♊	25 ♊	15 ♌	24 ♍	17 ♏	25 ♐	13 ♒	28 ♓	1 ♉	16 ♊	21 ♋
19	12 ♉	29 ♊	22 ♋	14 ♍	23 ♎	15 ♐	21 ♑	7 ♓	22 ♈	24 ♉	11 ♋	18 ♌
21	7 ♊	27 ♋	20 ♌	14 ♎	22 ♏	12 ♑	17 ♒	1 ♈	15 ♉	19 ♊	7 ♌	15 ♍
23	5 ♋	27 ♌	21 ♍	14 ♏	21 ♐	8 ♒	11 ♓	25 ♈	10 ♊	15 ♋	4 ♍	13 ♎
25	4 ♌	28 ♍	21 ♎	12 ♐	17 ♑	3 ♓	5 ♈	19 ♉	5 ♋	11 ♌	2 ♎	10 ♐
27	4 ♍	27 ♎	20 ♏	9 ♑	13 ♒	27 ♓	29 ♈	13 ♊	2 ♌	9 ♍	2 ♏	9 ♑
29	4 ♎	26 ♏	18 ♐	5 ♒	7 ♈	21 ♈	23 ♉	10 ♋	0 ♍	8 ♎	2 ♐	6 ♒
31	2 ♏		14 ♑		1 ♈		18 ♊	7 ♌		9 ♏		6 ♓

1941	Jan.	Feb.	Mar.	April	May	June	July	Aug.	Sep.	Oct.	Nov.	Dec.
1	19 ♒	4 ♈	12 ♈	26 ♉	29 ♊	16 ♌	24 ♍	16 ♏	10 ♑	17 ♒	4 ♈	7 ♉
3	14 ♓	28 ♈	6 ♉	20 ♊	24 ♋	13 ♍	21 ♎	15 ♐	7 ♒	13 ♓	28 ♈	1 ♊
5	8 ♈	21 ♉	29 ♉	15 ♋	20 ♌	11 ♎	20 ♏	13 ♑	3 ♓	7 ♈	22 ♉	25 ♊
7	2 ♉	16 ♊	24 ♊	11 ♌	17 ♍	10 ♏	19 ♐	8 ♒	29 ♓	2 ♉	16 ♊	19 ♋
9	26 ♉	11 ♋	19 ♋	9 ♍	16 ♎	10 ♐	18 ♑	3 ♓	23 ♈	25 ♉	10 ♋	14 ♌
11	21 ♊	9 ♌	16 ♌	8 ♎	17 ♏	10 ♑	15 ♒	27 ♈	11 ♉	19 ♊	4 ♌	9 ♍
13	17 ♋	7 ♍	15 ♍	8 ♏	17 ♐	8 ♒	13 ♓	21 ♈	11 ♊	13 ♋	0 ♎	6 ♎
15	14 ♌	6 ♎	15 ♎	9 ♐	16 ♑	4 ♓	7 ♈	21 ♉	5 ♋	8 ♌	27 ♎	4 ♏
17	12 ♍	5 ♏	15 ♏	11 ♑	13 ♒	29 ♓	0 ♉	15 ♊	3 ♌	5 ♎	26 ♏	4 ♐
19	10 ♎	3 ♐	14 ♐	4 ♒	9 ♈	23 ♈	25 ♉	10 ♋	0 ♍	3 ♏	26 ♐	5 ♑
21	8 ♏	1 ♑	11 ♑	29 ♒	3 ♈	17 ♉	24 ♊	14 ♌	27 ♍	3 ♐	27 ♑	4 ♒
23	6 ♐	27 ♑	7 ♒	24 ♓	26 ♈	11 ♊	20 ♋	13 ♍	24 ♎	3 ♑	26 ♒	2 ♓
25	4 ♑	23 ♒	2 ♓	18 ♈	22 ♉	8 ♋	20 ♌	13 ♎	23 ♏	3 ♒	23 ♓	28 ♓
27	1 ♒	18 ♓	27 ♓	11 ♉	14 ♊	5 ♌	20 ♍	13 ♏	23 ♐	1 ♓	19 ♈	22 ♈
29	27 ♒		21 ♈	5 ♊	8 ♋	27 ♍	4 ♎	28 ♏	20 ♑	27 ♈	13 ♈	16 ♉
31	22 ♓		14 ♉		4 ♌		2 ♏	26 ♐		22 ♓		10 ♊

MOON   Greenwich Mean Midnight (o h. o m.)   1942–1944

1942	Jan.	Feb.	Mar.	April	May	June	July	Aug.	Sep.	Oct.	Nov.	Dec.
1	22 ♊	7 ♌	15 ♌	4 ♎	11 ♏	5 ♑	13 ♒	3 ♈	20 ♉	22 ♊	5 ♌	7 ♍
3	16 ♋	3 ♍	12 ♍	2 ♏	11 ♐	5 ♒	12 ♓	29 ♈	14 ♊	15 ♋	29 ♌	3 ♏
5	11 ♌	29 ♍	9 ♎	2 ♐	11 ♑	3 ♓	7 ♈	24 ♉	7 ♋	9 ♌	25 ♍	0 ♏
7	6 ♍	27 ♎	7 ♏	1 ♑	9 ♒	29 ♈	17 ♉	17 ♊	4 ♌	4 ♍	22 ♎	29 ♏
9	2 ♎	25 ♏	6 ♐	29 ♑	6 ♓	24 ♈	27 ♉	11 ♋	26 ♌	0 ♎	21 ♏	29 ♐
11	0 ♏	23 ♐	4 ♑	26 ♒	6 ♈	18 ♉	21 ♊	5 ♌	22 ♍	28 ♎	21 ♐	29 ♑
13	28 ♏	22 ♑	2 ♒	22 ♓	27 ♈	12 ♊	14 ♋	0 ♍	18 ♎	26 ♏	20 ♑	28 ♒
15	28 ♐	20 ♒	0 ♓	17 ♈	21 ♉	6 ♋	8 ♌	25 ♍	16 ♏	25 ♐	18 ♒	26 ♈
17	28 ♑	18 ♓	26 ♓	12 ♉	15 ♊	29 ♋	3 ♍	22 ♎	14 ♐	24 ♑	15 ♓	21 ♈
19	26 ♒	13 ♈	21 ♈	6 ♊	8 ♋	24 ♌	28 ♍	19 ♏	13 ♑	21 ♒	12 ♈	16 ♉
21	23 ♓	8 ♉	16 ♉	0 ♋	2 ♌	19 ♍	25 ♎	17 ♐	11 ♒	19 ♓	7 ♉	11 ♊
23	18 ♈	2 ♊	10 ♊	24 ♋	27 ♌	15 ♎	23 ♏	17 ♑	9 ♓	15 ♈	2 ♊	5 ♋
25	12 ♉	26 ♊	4 ♋	18 ♌	23 ♍	13 ♏	22 ♐	16 ♒	6 ♈	11 ♉	26 ♊	28 ♋
27	6 ♊	20 ♋	28 ♋	14 ♍	20 ♎	13 ♐	22 ♑	14 ♓	2 ♉	5 ♊	20 ♋	22 ♌
29	0 ♋		23 ♌	12 ♎	19 ♏	14 ♑	22 ♒	11 ♈	27 ♉	0 ♋	13 ♌	16 ♍
31	24 ♋		20 ♍		20 ♐		20 ♓	7 ♉		23 ♋		11 ♎

1943	Jan.	Feb.	Mar.	April	May	June	July	Aug.	Sep.	Oct.	Nov.	Dec.
1	25 ♎	16 ♐	26 ♐	19 ♒	27 ♓	17 ♉	21 ♊	6 ♌	21 ♍	25 ♎	14 ♐	22 ♑
3	22 ♏	15 ♑	25 ♑	24 ♓	21 ♈	12 ♊	15 ♋	20 ♍	15 ♏	21 ♏	12 ♑	21 ♒
5	22 ♐	16 ♒	16 ♒	15 ♈	21 ♉	7 ♋	9 ♌	24 ♍	11 ♏	17 ♐	10 ♒	19 ♓
7	23 ♑	15 ♓	23 ♓	12 ♉	16 ♊	0 ♌	3 ♍	18 ♎	7 ♐	15 ♑	8 ♓	17 ♈
9	23 ♒	13 ♈	21 ♈	8 ♊	10 ♋	24 ♌	27 ♍	14 ♏	5 ♑	13 ♒	6 ♈	14 ♉
11	21 ♓	10 ♉	18 ♉	2 ♋	4 ♌	18 ♍	22 ♎	11 ♐	3 ♒	12 ♈	4 ♉	10 ♊
13	18 ♈	4 ♊	13 ♊	26 ♋	28 ♌	13 ♎	16 ♏	10 ♑	3 ♓	11 ♈	1 ♊	5 ♋
15	13 ♉	28 ♊	7 ♋	20 ♌	22 ♍	10 ♏	16 ♐	9 ♒	1 ♈	10 ♉	27 ♊	0 ♌
17	8 ♊	22 ♋	0 ♌	14 ♍	18 ♎	8 ♐	16 ♑	9 ♓	0 ♉	7 ♊	22 ♋	23 ♌
19	2 ♋	16 ♌	24 ♌	10 ♎	15 ♏	8 ♑	16 ♒	7 ♈	29 ♉	2 ♋	16 ♌	17 ♍
21	25 ♋	10 ♍	19 ♍	7 ♏	14 ♐	8 ♒	16 ♓	7 ♉	24 ♊	26 ♋	9 ♍	11 ♎
23	19 ♌	5 ♎	14 ♎	5 ♐	12 ♑	7 ♈	11 ♉	3 ♊	18 ♋	20 ♌	3 ♎	7 ♏
25	13 ♍	1 ♏	11 ♏	3 ♑	12 ♒	5 ♈	8 ♉	27 ♊	13 ♌	13 ♍	29 ♎	4 ♐
27	8 ♎	28 ♏	8 ♐	2 ♒	10 ♓	1 ♉	6 ♊	21 ♋	5 ♍	8 ♎	26 ♏	2 ♑
29	4 ♏		6 ♑	0 ♓	9 ♈	0 ♊	0 ♋	15 ♌	2 ♎	4 ♏	24 ♐	2 ♒
31	1 ♐		5 ♒		4 ♉		24 ♋	9 ♍		0 ♐		1 ♓

1944	Jan.	Feb.	Mar.	April	May	June	July	Aug.	Sep.	Oct.	Nov.	Dec.
1	15 ♓	7 ♉	0 ♊	17 ♋	19 ♌	2 ♎	5 ♏	22 ♐	12 ♒	21 ♓	14 ♉	21 ♊
3	14 ♈	4 ♊	26 ♊	10 ♌	12 ♍	27 ♎	0 ♐	20 ♑	13 ♓	21 ♈	13 ♊	18 ♋
5	11 ♉	29 ♊	20 ♋	4 ♍	6 ♎	22 ♏	27 ♐	19 ♒	13 ♈	21 ♉	10 ♋	14 ♌
7	7 ♊	23 ♋	14 ♌	28 ♍	1 ♏	19 ♐	19 ♑	18 ♓	12 ♉	19 ♊	6 ♌	8 ♍
9	2 ♋	17 ♌	7 ♍	22 ♎	27 ♏	16 ♑	25 ♒	18 ♈	10 ♊	15 ♋	0 ♍	2 ♎
11	26 ♋	10 ♍	1 ♎	15 ♏	23 ♐	13 ♒	24 ♓	17 ♉	6 ♋	10 ♌	24 ♍	26 ♎
13	20 ♌	4 ♎	25 ♎	13 ♐	20 ♑	13 ♓	22 ♈	13 ♊	1 ♌	3 ♍	18 ♎	20 ♏
15	13 ♍	28 ♎	10 ♏	10 ♑	18 ♒	11 ♈	20 ♉	9 ♋	25 ♌	27 ♍	12 ♏	16 ♐
17	7 ♎	23 ♏	16 ♐	7 ♒	16 ♓	9 ♉	16 ♊	3 ♌	18 ♍	21 ♎	7 ♐	12 ♑
19	2 ♏	20 ♐	13 ♑	6 ♓	15 ♈	7 ♊	12 ♋	28 ♌	12 ♎	15 ♏	3 ♑	9 ♒
21	28 ♏	18 ♑	12 ♒	5 ♈	13 ♉	4 ♋	8 ♌	22 ♍	6 ♏	10 ♐	29 ♑	7 ♓
23	26 ♐	18 ♒	11 ♓	5 ♉	11 ♊	28 ♋	2 ♍	15 ♎	0 ♐	6 ♑	26 ♒	5 ♈
25	25 ♑	18 ♓	11 ♈	3 ♊	8 ♋	22 ♌	26 ♍	9 ♏	26 ♐	2 ♒	25 ♈	4 ♉
27	25 ♒	18 ♈	11 ♉	0 ♋	3 ♌	16 ♍	18 ♎	4 ♐	22 ♑	0 ♈	24 ♉	2 ♊
29	25 ♓	17 ♉	8 ♊	25 ♋	27 ♌	10 ♎	13 ♏	0 ♑	29 ♑	29 ♓	23 ♉	0 ♋
31	24 ♈		4 ♋		20 ♍		8 ♐	28 ♒		0 ♉		26 ♋

MOON   Greenwich Mean Midnight (o h. o m.)   1945–1947

1945	Jan.	Feb.	Mar.	April	May	June	July	Aug.	Sep.	Oct.	Nov.	Dec.
1	9 ♌	24 ♍	2 ♎	16 ♍	20 ♐	8 ♒	16 ♓	9 ♉	2 ♋	8 ♌	25 ♍	28 ♎
3	4 ♍	17 ♎	26 ♎	11 ♐	15 ♑	5 ♓	14 ♈	7 ♊	28 ♋	3 ♍	19 ♎	21 ♏
5	28 ♍	11 ♏	20 ♏	5 ♑	11 ♒	3 ♈	12 ♉	5 ♋	24 ♌	28 ♍	13 ♏	15 ♐
7	21 ♎	6 ♐	14 ♐	1 ♒	9 ♓	2 ♉	11 ♊	2 ♌	19 ♍	22 ♎	6 ♐	9 ♑
9	16 ♏	1 ♑	9 ♑	29 ♒	8 ♈	2 ♊	9 ♋	28 ♌	13 ♎	16 ♏	0 ♑	4 ♒
11	11 ♐	29 ♑	7 ♒	29 ♓	8 ♉	6 ♋	6 ♌	23 ♍	7 ♏	9 ♐	25 ♑	0 ♓
13	7 ♑	28 ♒	6 ♓	0 ♉	8 ♊	28 ♋	2 ♍	17 ♎	1 ♐	3 ♑	20 ♒	28 ♓
15	5 ♒	27 ♓	6 ♈	0 ♊	6 ♋	24 ♌	27 ♍	11 ♏	25 ♐	28 ♑	18 ♓	26 ♈
17	3 ♓	27 ♈	6 ♉	28 ♊	3 ♌	19 ♍	21 ♎	5 ♐	20 ♑	25 ♒	17 ♈	26 ♉
19	2 ♈	25 ♉	5 ♊	25 ♋	28 ♌	13 ♎	15 ♏	29 ♐	17 ♒	24 ♓	17 ♉	25 ♊
21	1 ♉	22 ♊	2 ♋	20 ♌	23 ♍	7 ♏	9 ♐	25 ♑	16 ♓	24 ♈	18 ♊	24 ♋
23	29 ♉	18 ♋	28 ♋	14 ♍	16 ♎	1 ♐	4 ♑	23 ♒	16 ♈	24 ♉	17 ♋	22 ♌
25	26 ♊	14 ♌	23 ♌	8 ♎	10 ♏	26 ♐	0 ♒	22 ♓	16 ♉	24 ♊	14 ♌	18 ♍
27	22 ♋	8 ♍	17 ♍	2 ♏	4 ♐	21 ♑	28 ♒	21 ♈	15 ♊	22 ♋	9 ♍	12 ♎
29	17 ♌		11 ♎	26 ♏	29 ♐	18 ♒	26 ♓	20 ♉	12 ♋	18 ♌	4 ♎	6 ♏
31	12 ♍		5 ♏		25 ♑		25 ♈	18 ♊		13 ♍		0 ♐

1946	Jan.	Feb.	Mar.	April	May	June	July	Aug.	Sep.	Oct.	Nov.	Dec.
1	12 ♐	27 ♑	5 ♒	24 ♓	2 ♉	26 ♊	4 ♌	23 ♍	9 ♏	11 ♐	25 ♑	28 ♒
3	6 ♑	23 ♒	2 ♓	24 ♈	2 ♊	25 ♋	29 ♌	19 ♎	3 ♐	5 ♑	19 ♒	23 ♓
5	1 ♒	21 ♓	0 ♈	24 ♉	2 ♋	23 ♌	28 ♍	13 ♏	27 ♐	29 ♑	15 ♓	21 ♈
7	27 ♒	19 ♈	29 ♈	23 ♊	1 ♌	20 ♍	7 ♏	7 ♐	21 ♑	24 ♒	13 ♈	20 ♉
9	24 ♓	17 ♉	28 ♉	21 ♋	27 ♌	14 ♎	11 ♐	16 ♑	16 ♓	21 ♈	12 ♉	20 ♊
11	22 ♈	15 ♊	26 ♊	17 ♌	23 ♍	8 ♏	11 ♐	25 ♑	12 ♈	19 ♉	12 ♊	20 ♋
13	21 ♉	13 ♋	24 ♋	13 ♍	17 ♎	2 ♐	4 ♑	20 ♒	10 ♉	18 ♊	11 ♋	19 ♌
15	19 ♊	11 ♌	20 ♌	8 ♎	11 ♏	26 ♐	29 ♑	17 ♓	8 ♊	17 ♋	10 ♌	17 ♍
17	18 ♋	8 ♍	16 ♍	2 ♏	5 ♐	20 ♑	24 ♒	14 ♈	7 ♋	15 ♌	8 ♍	13 ♎
19	16 ♌	3 ♎	12 ♎	26 ♏	29 ♐	14 ♒	17 ♓	12 ♉	6 ♌	13 ♍	3 ♎	7 ♏
21	13 ♍	28 ♎	6 ♏	20 ♐	23 ♑	10 ♓	17 ♈	10 ♊	3 ♍	10 ♎	28 ♎	1 ♐
23	8 ♎	22 ♏	0 ♐	14 ♑	17 ♒	7 ♈	15 ♉	8 ♋	0 ♎	6 ♏	22 ♏	25 ♐
25	2 ♏	15 ♐	23 ♐	8 ♒	13 ♓	5 ♉	14 ♊	7 ♌	27 ♎	1 ♐	16 ♐	18 ♑
27	26 ♏	10 ♑	18 ♑	5 ♓	11 ♈	4 ♊	13 ♋	5 ♍	23 ♏	25 ♐	9 ♑	12 ♒
29	20 ♐		13 ♒	3 ♈	11 ♉	4 ♋	12 ♌	2 ♎	19 ♐	19 ♑	3 ♒	7 ♓
31	14 ♑		10 ♓		11 ♊		10 ♍	27 ♎		13 ♒		2 ♈

1947	Jan.	Feb.	Mar.	April	May	June	July	Aug.	Sep.	Oct.	Nov.	Dec.
1	16 ♈	7 ♊	18 ♊	11 ♌	19 ♍	8 ♏	12 ♐	26 ♑	11 ♓	16 ♈	5 ♊	14 ♋
3	13 ♉	6 ♋	16 ♋	9 ♍	16 ♎	3 ♐	5 ♑	20 ♒	6 ♈	12 ♉	4 ♋	13 ♌
5	13 ♊	6 ♌	15 ♌	6 ♎	11 ♏	29 ♐	29 ♑	14 ♓	2 ♉	9 ♊	2 ♌	12 ♍
7	13 ♋	6 ♍	14 ♍	3 ♏	6 ♐	23 ♑	23 ♒	9 ♈	29 ♉	7 ♋	1 ♍	9 ♎
9	13 ♌	4 ♎	11 ♎	28 ♏	0 ♑	17 ♒	17 ♓	5 ♉	26 ♊	6 ♌	28 ♍	5 ♏
11	12 ♍	0 ♏	8 ♏	22 ♐	24 ♑	12 ♓	12 ♈	2 ♊	25 ♋	4 ♍	26 ♎	1 ♐
13	9 ♎	24 ♏	2 ♐	16 ♑	18 ♒	8 ♈	9 ♉	1 ♋	25 ♌	3 ♎	22 ♏	25 ♐
15	4 ♏	18 ♐	26 ♐	10 ♒	13 ♓	7 ♉	7 ♊	0 ♌	24 ♍	0 ♏	17 ♐	19 ♑
17	28 ♏	12 ♑	20 ♑	4 ♓	8 ♈	7 ♊	7 ♋	0 ♍	22 ♎	26 ♏	11 ♑	13 ♒
19	22 ♐	6 ♒	14 ♒	0 ♈	6 ♉	7 ♋	7 ♌	28 ♍	18 ♏	21 ♐	5 ♒	7 ♓
21	15 ♑	1 ♓	9 ♓	28 ♈	5 ♊	6 ♌	7 ♍	25 ♎	13 ♐	15 ♑	29 ♒	1 ♈
23	9 ♒	26 ♓	5 ♈	26 ♉	5 ♋	4 ♍	5 ♎	23 ♏	7 ♑	9 ♒	23 ♓	27 ♈
25	4 ♓	23 ♈	3 ♉	25 ♊	4 ♌	2 ♎	3 ♏	17 ♐	1 ♒	3 ♓	19 ♈	23 ♉
27	29 ♓	20 ♉	0 ♊	24 ♋	2 ♍	27 ♎	27 ♏	11 ♑	25 ♒	28 ♓	16 ♉	23 ♊
29	26 ♈		29 ♊	22 ♌	0 ♎	21 ♏	21 ♐	5 ♒	20 ♓	24 ♈	14 ♊	23 ♋
31	23 ♉		27 ♋		25 ♎		14 ♑	29 ♒		22 ♉		23 ♌

MOON Greenwich Mean Midnight (0 h. 0 m.)   1948-1950

1948	Jan.	Feb.	Mar.	April	May	June	July	Aug.	Sep.	Oct.	Nov.	Dec.
1	7 ♍	29 ♎	20 ♏	6 ♑	8 ♒	22 ♓	24 ♈	12 ♊	3 ♌	12 ♍	5 ♏	11 ♐
3	6 ♎	25 ♏	16 ♐	0 ♒	2 ♓	16 ♈	20 ♉	10 ♋	4 ♍	12 ♎	3 ♐	8 ♑
5	2 ♏	19 ♐	10 ♑	24 ♒	26 ♓	12 ♉	17 ♊	10 ♌	4 ♎	11 ♏	0 ♑	3 ♒
7	28 ♏	13 ♑	4 ♒	18 ♓	21 ♈	9 ♊	16 ♋	10 ♍	3 ♏	9 ♐	26 ♑	28 ♒
9	22 ♐	7 ♒	28 ♒	13 ♈	17 ♉	8 ♋	16 ♌	10 ♎	1 ♐	5 ♑	20 ♒	21 ♓
11	16 ♑	1 ♓	16 ♈	8 ♉	14 ♊	7 ♌	16 ♍	8 ♏	26 ♐	0 ♒	14 ♓	15 ♈
13	10 ♒	25 ♓	16 ♈	4 ♊	12 ♋	6 ♍	14 ♎	4 ♐	21 ♑	24 ♒	7 ♈	10 ♉
15	4 ♓	19 ♈	11 ♉	1 ♋	10 ♌	4 ♎	11 ♏	0 ♑	15 ♒	17 ♓	2 ♉	6 ♊
17	28 ♓	14 ♉	7 ♊	29 ♋	7 ♍	28 ♎	7 ♐	24 ♑	9 ♓	11 ♈	27 ♉	3 ♋
19	22 ♈	11 ♊	5 ♋	28 ♌	7 ♎	28 ♏	2 ♑	18 ♒	2 ♈	6 ♉	24 ♊	1 ♌
21	18 ♉	9 ♋	3 ♌	27 ♍	7 ♎	23 ♐	27 ♑	12 ♓	27 ♈	1 ♊	21 ♋	0 ♍
23	16 ♊	9 ♌	3 ♍	25 ♎	1 ♐	18 ♑	21 ♒	5 ♈	21 ♉	27 ♊	19 ♌	28 ♍
25	15 ♋	9 ♍	2 ♎	23 ♏	27 ♐	12 ♒	15 ♓	29 ♈	24 ♉	17 ♋	16 ♍	26 ♎
27	16 ♌	9 ♎	1 ♏	19 ♐	22 ♑	6 ♓	8 ♈	24 ♉	21 ♊	14 ♌	16 ♎	24 ♏
29	16 ♍		28 ♏	14 ♑	16 ♒	0 ♈	3 ♉	21 ♊	12 ♋	21 ♍	14 ♏	20 ♐
31	15 ♎		24 ♐		10 ♓		28 ♉	19 ♋		21 ♎		16 ♑

1949	Jan.	Feb.	Mar.	April	May	June	July	Aug.	Sep.	Oct.	Nov.	Dec.
1	29 ♑	14 ♓	22 ♓	7 ♉	11 ♊	0 ♌	8 ♍	1 ♏	23 ♐	29 ♑	15 ♓	18 ♈
3	23 ♒	7 ♈	16 ♈	1 ♊	6 ♋	27 ♌	6 ♎	29 ♏	20 ♑	24 ♒	9 ♈	11 ♉
5	17 ♓	1 ♉	10 ♉	26 ♊	25 ♋	4 ♎	26 ♎	26 ♐	15 ♒	18 ♓	3 ♉	8 ♊
7	11 ♈	25 ♉	4 ♊	23 ♋	0 ♍	2 ♐	23 ♐	9 ♑	12 ♈	6 ♉	27 ♉	0 ♋
9	5 ♉	21 ♊	0 ♋	21 ♌	29 ♍	0 ♑	0 ♑	18 ♒	3 ♈	6 ♊	21 ♊	26 ♋
11	0 ♊	19 ♋	27 ♋	20 ♍	29 ♎	21 ♐	27 ♑	13 ♓	27 ♈	29 ♊	16 ♋	22 ♌
13	27 ♊	19 ♌	27 ♍	20 ♎	28 ♏	18 ♑	22 ♒	7 ♈	21 ♉	12 ♋	20 ♌	18 ♍
15	26 ♋	19 ♍	27 ♎	20 ♏	27 ♐	14 ♒	17 ♓	0 ♉	15 ♊	19 ♌	9 ♍	18 ♎
17	25 ♌	19 ♎	26 ♏	19 ♐	24 ♑	9 ♓	10 ♈	24 ♉	11 ♋	19 ♍	8 ♎	16 ♏
19	23 ♎	17 ♏	26 ♐	15 ♑	19 ♒	3 ♈	4 ♉	19 ♊	9 ♌	15 ♎	8 ♏	15 ♐
21	20 ♏	14 ♐	23 ♑	10 ♒	13 ♓	26 ♈	28 ♉	14 ♋	6 ♍	15 ♏	8 ♐	15 ♑
23	17 ♐	10 ♑	19 ♒	4 ♈	6 ♉	20 ♉	24 ♊	11 ♌	4 ♎	15 ♐	4 ♑	12 ♒
25	13 ♑	4 ♒	14 ♓	28 ♈	0 ♊	16 ♊	21 ♋	9 ♍	3 ♏	12 ♑	0 ♒	8 ♓
27	7 ♒	29 ♒	8 ♈	22 ♉	25 ♊	12 ♋	19 ♌	6 ♎	1 ♐	9 ♒	24 ♒	2 ♈
29	7 ♒		1 ♉	16 ♊	20 ♋	10 ♌	18 ♍	3 ♏		9 ♓		26 ♈
31	2 ♓		25 ♈		16 ♋		17 ♎	10 ♐		3 ♈		19 ♉

1950	Jan.	Feb.	Mar.	April	May	June	July	Aug.	Sep.	Oct.	Nov.	Dec.
1	1 ♊	17 ♋	25 ♋	15 ♍	23 ♎	17 ♐	24 ♑	14 ♓	29 ♈	1 ♊	15 ♋	18 ♌
3	26 ♊	15 ♌	23 ♌	15 ♎	23 ♏	16 ♑	22 ♒	9 ♈	23 ♉	25 ♊	10 ♌	14 ♍
5	22 ♋	13 ♍	21 ♍	15 ♏	23 ♐	14 ♒	18 ♓	3 ♉	16 ♊	19 ♋	5 ♍	11 ♎
7	19 ♌	11 ♎	21 ♎	14 ♐	22 ♑	10 ♈	13 ♈	27 ♉	11 ♋	14 ♌	2 ♎	11 ♏
9	17 ♍	10 ♏	20 ♏	12 ♑	19 ♒	5 ♈	7 ♉	21 ♊	6 ♌	11 ♍	2 ♏	11 ♐
11	14 ♎	8 ♐	18 ♐	9 ♒	14 ♓	28 ♈	0 ♊	15 ♋	2 ♍	9 ♎	3 ♏	11 ♑
13	13 ♏	5 ♑	16 ♑	4 ♓	8 ♈	22 ♉	25 ♊	11 ♌	1 ♎	9 ♏	3 ♐	10 ♒
15	11 ♐	2 ♒	12 ♒	29 ♓	1 ♉	16 ♊	16 ♋	8 ♍	29 ♎	9 ♐	3 ♑	8 ♓
17	9 ♑	28 ♒	7 ♓	23 ♈	25 ♉	10 ♋	16 ♌	6 ♎	29 ♏	8 ♑	24 ♒	3 ♈
19	7 ♒	23 ♓	2 ♈	16 ♉	19 ♊	5 ♌	12 ♍	4 ♏	27 ♐	6 ♒	18 ♓	27 ♈
21	3 ♓	18 ♈	26 ♈	10 ♊	13 ♋	1 ♍	9 ♎	2 ♐	24 ♑	2 ♓	12 ♈	21 ♉
23	28 ♓	11 ♉	19 ♉	4 ♋	8 ♌	28 ♍	7 ♏	0 ♑	20 ♒	28 ♓	6 ♉	15 ♊
25	22 ♈	5 ♊	13 ♊	29 ♋	5 ♍	27 ♎	5 ♐	28 ♑	16 ♓	22 ♈	0 ♊	9 ♋
27	15 ♉	29 ♊	8 ♋	25 ♌	2 ♎	25 ♏	4 ♑	26 ♒	11 ♈	15 ♉	24 ♊	3 ♌
29	9 ♊		3 ♌	23 ♍	1 ♏	25 ♐	3 ♒	22 ♓	7 ♉	9 ♊		28 ♌
31	4 ♋		1 ♍		1 ♐		0 ♓	17 ♈		3 ♋		24 ♍

TABLE SIX—*continued*

MOON Greenwich Mean Midnight (o h. o m.) 1951–1953

1951	Jan.	Feb.	Mar.	April	May	June	July	Aug.	Sep.	Oct.	Nov.	Dec.
1	7 ♎	29 ♏	10 ♐	3 ♒	11 ♓	29 ♈	2 ♊	16 ♋	2 ♍	6 ♎	27 ♏	5 ♑
3	5 ♏	28 ♐	9 ♑	1 ♓	7 ♈	23 ♉	26 ♊	10 ♌	27 ♍	3 ♏	26 ♐	5 ♒
5	4 ♐	28 ♑	7 ♒	27 ♓	2 ♉	17 ♊	20 ♋	5 ♍	23 ♎	1 ♐	25 ♑	3 ♓
7	4 ♑	26 ♒	5 ♓	23 ♈	26 ♉	11 ♋	13 ♌	0 ♎	21 ♏	28 ♐	23 ♒	0 ♈
9	4 ♒	24 ♓	1 ♈	18 ♉	20 ♊	4 ♌	8 ♍	26 ♎	19 ♐	28 ♑	20 ♓	26 ♈
11	2 ♓	19 ♈	27 ♈	12 ♊	14 ♋	29 ♌	3 ♎	24 ♏	17 ♑	26 ♒	16 ♈	21 ♉
13	29 ♓	14 ♉	22 ♉	5 ♋	8 ♌	24 ♍	0 ♏	22 ♐	15 ♒	26 ♓	12 ♉	16 ♊
15	24 ♈	8 ♊	16 ♊	29 ♋	2 ♍	20 ♎	28 ♏	22 ♑	15 ♓	20 ♈	7 ♊	10 ♋
17	18 ♉	2 ♋	9 ♋	24 ♌	26 ♍	19 ♏	28 ♐	22 ♒	16 ♈	16 ♉	1 ♋	3 ♌
19	12 ♊	26 ♋	4 ♌	20 ♍	26 ♎	19 ♐	28 ♑	20 ♓	16 ♉	11 ♊	25 ♋	27 ♌
21	5 ♋	21 ♌	29 ♌	18 ♎	26 ♏	20 ♑	28 ♒	17 ♈	8 ♊	5 ♋	19 ♌	21 ♍
23	0 ♌	17 ♍	26 ♍	17 ♏	26 ♐	19 ♒	26 ♓	13 ♉	2 ♋	29 ♋	13 ♍	17 ♎
25	25 ♌	14 ♎	24 ♎	17 ♐	24 ♑	17 ♓	22 ♈	7 ♊	27 ♋	23 ♌	9 ♎	14 ♏
27	21 ♍	12 ♏	22 ♏	16 ♑	21 ♒	13 ♈	17 ♉	1 ♋	21 ♌	18 ♍	6 ♏	13 ♐
29	17 ♎		21 ♐	14 ♒	21 ♓	8 ♉	11 ♊	25 ♋	10 ♍	14 ♎	5 ♐	13 ♑
31	15 ♏		20 ♑		16 ♈		5 ♋	19 ♌		12 ♏		14 ♒

1952	Jan.	Feb.	Mar.	April	May	June	July	Aug.	Sep.	Oct.	Nov.	Dec.
1	29 ♒	19 ♈	10 ♉	26 ♊	28 ♋	11 ♍	14 ♎	3 ♐	24 ♑	3 ♓	26 ♈	2 ♊
3	27 ♓	15 ♉	6 ♊	20 ♋	22 ♌	6 ♎	10 ♏	1 ♑	24 ♒	3 ♈	24 ♉	28 ♊
5	23 ♈	10 ♊	0 ♋	14 ♌	16 ♍	2 ♏	8 ♐	1 ♒	24 ♓	2 ♉	20 ♊	24 ♋
7	18 ♉	4 ♋	24 ♋	8 ♍	11 ♎	29 ♏	7 ♑	1 ♓	23 ♈	29 ♉	15 ♋	17 ♌
9	13 ♊	27 ♋	18 ♌	3 ♎	7 ♏	27 ♐	7 ♒	1 ♈	20 ♉	25 ♊	9 ♌	11 ♍
11	7 ♋	21 ♌	12 ♍	29 ♎	5 ♐	25 ♑	7 ♓	29 ♈	17 ♊	20 ♋	3 ♍	5 ♎
13	0 ♌	15 ♍	7 ♎	26 ♏	4 ♑	25 ♒	6 ♈	25 ♉	11 ♋	13 ♌	27 ♍	0 ♏
15	24 ♌	10 ♎	3 ♏	24 ♐	4 ♒	24 ♓	3 ♉	20 ♊	5 ♌	7 ♍	22 ♎	25 ♏
17	18 ♍	6 ♏	29 ♏	24 ♑	3 ♓	23 ♈	29 ♉	14 ♋	29 ♌	1 ♎	18 ♏	23 ♐
19	13 ♎	2 ♐	27 ♐	24 ♒	1 ♈	19 ♉	23 ♊	8 ♌	23 ♍	26 ♎	15 ♐	22 ♑
21	9 ♏	1 ♑	27 ♑	22 ♓	29 ♈	14 ♊	17 ♋	2 ♍	17 ♎	22 ♏	13 ♑	20 ♒
23	7 ♐	0 ♒	27 ♒	18 ♈	26 ♉	8 ♋	11 ♌	26 ♍	12 ♏	19 ♐	11 ♒	18 ♓
25	6 ♑	0 ♓	26 ♓	13 ♉	22 ♊	2 ♌	5 ♍	21 ♎	9 ♐	16 ♑	9 ♓	15 ♈
27	7 ♒	29 ♓	23 ♈	9 ♊	16 ♋	26 ♌	29 ♍	17 ♏	6 ♑	15 ♒	7 ♈	11 ♉
29	7 ♓	27 ♈	18 ♉	4 ♋	9 ♌	20 ♍	23 ♎	12 ♐	4 ♒	14 ♓	6 ♉	11 ♊
31	5 ♈		14 ♊		0 ♍		19 ♏	10 ♑		12 ♈		7 ♋

1953	Jan.	Feb.	Mar.	April	May	June	July	Aug.	Sep.	Oct.	Nov.	Dec.
1	19 ♋	4 ♌	12 ♍	27 ♎	2 ♐	21 ♑	0 ♓	24 ♈	15 ♊	20 ♋	5 ♍	7 ♎
3	13 ♌	27 ♌	6 ♎	22 ♏	28 ♐	19 ♒	29 ♓	21 ♉	11 ♋	15 ♌	29 ♍	1 ♏
5	7 ♍	21 ♍	0 ♏	18 ♐	25 ♑	18 ♓	27 ♈	18 ♊	6 ♌	9 ♍	23 ♎	26 ♏
7	1 ♎	16 ♎	25 ♏	14 ♑	22 ♒	16 ♈	25 ♉	14 ♋	0 ♍	2 ♎	17 ♏	21 ♐
9	25 ♎	12 ♏	21 ♐	12 ♒	21 ♓	14 ♉	21 ♊	9 ♌	23 ♍	26 ♎	12 ♐	17 ♑
11	20 ♏	9 ♐	18 ♑	11 ♓	20 ♈	12 ♊	17 ♋	3 ♍	17 ♎	20 ♏	7 ♑	15 ♒
13	18 ♐	7 ♑	17 ♒	11 ♈	19 ♉	9 ♋	12 ♌	26 ♍	11 ♏	15 ♐	4 ♒	14 ♓
15	16 ♑	6 ♒	17 ♓	9 ♉	17 ♊	4 ♌	6 ♍	20 ♎	6 ♐	11 ♑	2 ♓	14 ♈
17	16 ♒	6 ♓	18 ♈	6 ♊	13 ♋	28 ♌	0 ♎	14 ♏	1 ♑	9 ♒	1 ♈	13 ♉
19	16 ♓	5 ♈	17 ♉	1 ♋	8 ♌	22 ♍	24 ♎	9 ♐	27 ♑	7 ♓	29 ♈	12 ♊
21	15 ♈	3 ♉	14 ♊	25 ♋	2 ♍	16 ♎	18 ♏	4 ♑	25 ♒	7 ♈	29 ♉	10 ♋
23	12 ♉	0 ♊	10 ♋	20 ♌	26 ♍	10 ♏	14 ♐	1 ♒	24 ♓	6 ♉	27 ♊	6 ♌
25	8 ♊	25 ♊	4 ♌	14 ♍	20 ♎	6 ♐	12 ♑	29 ♒	24 ♈	5 ♊	24 ♋	0 ♍
27	2 ♋	19 ♋	28 ♌	8 ♎	15 ♏	3 ♑	10 ♒	27 ♓	23 ♉	3 ♋	20 ♌	24 ♍
29	28 ♋		21 ♍	6 ♏	11 ♐	1 ♒	10 ♓	27 ♈	23 ♊	29 ♋	14 ♍	18 ♎
31	22 ♌		15 ♎		8 ♑		9 ♈	25 ♉		23 ♌		9 ♏

MOON Greenwich Mean Midnight (0 h. 0 m.)   1954–1956

1954	Jan.	Feb.	Mar.	April	May	June	July	Aug.	Sep.	Oct.	Nov.	Dec.
1	21 ♏	7 ♑	15 ♑	5 ♓	14 ♈	8 ♊	15 ♋	3 ♍	19 ♎	21 ♏	5 ♑	9 ♒
3	17 ♐	5 ♒	13 ♒	6 ♈	14 ♉	4 ♌	12 ♌	28 ♍	12 ♏	14 ♐	0 ♒	5 ♓
5	13 ♑	4 ♓	12 ♓	6 ♉	14 ♊	2 ♍	8 ♍	23 ♎	6 ♐	9 ♑	26 ♒	3 ♈
7	10 ♒	3 ♈	12 ♈	6 ♊	12 ♋	0 ♎	6 ♎	16 ♏	0 ♑	4 ♒	24 ♓	2 ♉
9	8 ♓	2 ♉	12 ♉	4 ♋	9 ♌	24 ♍	24 ♎	10 ♐	26 ♑	1 ♓	23 ♈	2 ♊
11	7 ♈	0 ♊	10 ♊	0 ♌	4 ♍	18 ♎	20 ♏	5 ♑	23 ♒	0 ♈	24 ♉	1 ♋
13	5 ♉	27 ♊	7 ♋	25 ♌	28 ♍	12 ♏	15 ♐	1 ♒	22 ♓	0 ♉	24 ♊	1 ♌
15	3 ♊	23 ♋	3 ♌	19 ♍	22 ♎	6 ♐	10 ♑	29 ♒	21 ♈	0 ♊	23 ♋	28 ♌
17	1 ♋	19 ♌	28 ♌	13 ♎	16 ♏	1 ♑	6 ♒	27 ♓	21 ♉	0 ♋	19 ♌	23 ♍
19	27 ♋	13 ♍	22 ♍	7 ♏	10 ♐	27 ♑	3 ♓	26 ♈	20 ♊	27 ♋	15 ♍	18 ♎
21	23 ♌	7 ♎	16 ♎	1 ♐	4 ♑	20 ♒	29 ♓	25 ♉	17 ♋	23 ♌	9 ♎	11 ♏
23	17 ♍	1 ♏	10 ♏	25 ♐	0 ♒	19 ♓	29 ♈	23 ♊	13 ♌	18 ♍	3 ♏	5 ♐
25	11 ♎	25 ♏	4 ♐	20 ♑	24 ♒	17 ♈	28 ♉	20 ♋	8 ♍	12 ♎	27 ♏	29 ♐
27	5 ♏	19 ♐	28 ♐	16 ♒	24 ♓	17 ♉	26 ♊	16 ♌	3 ♎	6 ♏	20 ♐	24 ♑
29	29 ♏		24 ♑	14 ♓	23 ♈	17 ♊	24 ♋	12 ♍	27 ♎	0 ♐	14 ♑	19 ♒
31	24 ♐		21 ♒		23 ♉		20 ♌	7 ♎		23 ♐		15 ♓

1955	Jan.	Feb.	Mar.	April	May	June	July	Aug.	Sep.	Oct.	Nov.	Dec.
1	29 ♓	22 ♉	3 ♊	25 ♋	2 ♍	19 ♎	22 ♏	6 ♑	22 ♒	27 ♓	18 ♉	26 ♊
3	27 ♈	20 ♊	1 ♋	20 ♌	27 ♍	14 ♏	16 ♐	1 ♒	25 ♓	25 ♈	18 ♊	26 ♋
5	26 ♉	19 ♋	28 ♋	18 ♍	22 ♎	7 ♐	10 ♑	26 ♒	23 ♈	23 ♉	17 ♋	25 ♌
7	24 ♊	17 ♌	25 ♌	13 ♎	16 ♏	1 ♑	4 ♒	22 ♓	22 ♉	22 ♊	15 ♌	22 ♍
9	24 ♋	13 ♍	22 ♍	8 ♏	10 ♐	25 ♑	25 ♓	19 ♈	21 ♊	20 ♋	12 ♍	18 ♎
11	22 ♌	9 ♎	17 ♎	2 ♐	4 ♑	19 ♒	25 ♓	16 ♉	18 ♋	18 ♌	8 ♎	12 ♏
13	19 ♍	3 ♏	11 ♏	26 ♐	29 ♑	15 ♓	22 ♈	15 ♊	13 ♌	15 ♍	3 ♏	6 ♐
15	14 ♎	27 ♏	5 ♐	19 ♑	24 ♒	11 ♈	20 ♉	12 ♋	8 ♍	11 ♎	27 ♏	0 ♑
17	8 ♏	21 ♐	29 ♐	14 ♒	19 ♓	9 ♉	10 ♊	10 ♌	2 ♎	7 ♏	21 ♐	23 ♑
19	1 ♐	16 ♑	23 ♑	10 ♓	17 ♈	8 ♊	10 ♋	7 ♍	28 ♎	1 ♐	15 ♑	17 ♒
21	25 ♐	11 ♒	19 ♒	9 ♈	17 ♉	7 ♋	8 ♌	3 ♎	22 ♏	25 ♐	8 ♒	12 ♓
23	20 ♑	9 ♓	16 ♓	8 ♉	17 ♊	5 ♌	6 ♍	27 ♎	16 ♐	18 ♑	3 ♓	8 ♈
25	16 ♒	6 ♈	15 ♈	8 ♊	17 ♋	2 ♍	2 ♎	21 ♏	10 ♑	12 ♒	29 ♓	5 ♉
27	12 ♓	4 ♉	15 ♉	8 ♋	15 ♌	28 ♍	27 ♎	15 ♐	5 ♒	8 ♓	26 ♈	4 ♊
29	10 ♈		13 ♊	6 ♌	12 ♍	23 ♎	21 ♏	9 ♑	3 ♓	5 ♈	26 ♉	4 ♋
31	8 ♉		12 ♋		7 ♎		24 ♐	9 ♒		3 ♉		5 ♌

1956	Jan.	Feb.	Mar.	April	May	June	July	Aug.	Sep.	Oct.	Nov.	Dec.
1	19 ♌	10 ♎	1 ♍	16 ♐	17 ♑	1 ♓	5 ♈	24 ♉	16 ♋	25 ♌	17 ♎	23 ♏
3	18 ♍	5 ♏	26 ♍	10 ♑	11 ♒	26 ♓	1 ♉	22 ♊	15 ♌	24 ♍	14 ♏	18 ♐
5	14 ♎	0 ♐	20 ♎	3 ♒	6 ♓	1 ♈	29 ♉	21 ♋	15 ♍	22 ♎	10 ♐	13 ♑
7	9 ♏	24 ♐	13 ♏	28 ♒	1 ♈	20 ♉	22 ♊	22 ♌	14 ♎	19 ♏	5 ♑	7 ♒
9	3 ♐	18 ♑	7 ♐	23 ♓	28 ♈	20 ♊	22 ♋	22 ♍	11 ♏	15 ♐	29 ♑	1 ♓
11	27 ♐	11 ♒	2 ♑	20 ♈	26 ♉	20 ♋	20 ♌	16 ♎	7 ♐	9 ♑	23 ♒	25 ♓
13	20 ♑	6 ♓	28 ♑	17 ♉	26 ♊	19 ♌	16 ♍	11 ♏	3 ♑	3 ♒	17 ♓	20 ♈
15	14 ♒	1 ♈	24 ♒	16 ♊	24 ♋	16 ♍	11 ♎	5 ♐	25 ♑	27 ♒	12 ♈	16 ♉
17	9 ♓	27 ♈	21 ♓	14 ♋	23 ♌	13 ♎	5 ♏	28 ♐	19 ♒	21 ♓	8 ♉	14 ♊
19	4 ♈	24 ♉	19 ♈	14 ♌	21 ♍	8 ♏	0 ♐	22 ♑	13 ♓	17 ♈	6 ♊	14 ♋
21	0 ♉	22 ♊	17 ♉	12 ♍	17 ♎	3 ♐	24 ♐	16 ♒	8 ♈	13 ♉	5 ♋	14 ♌
23	28 ♉	21 ♋	15 ♊	9 ♎	13 ♏	27 ♐	18 ♑	11 ♓	4 ♉	11 ♊	5 ♌	13 ♍
25	27 ♊	21 ♌	14 ♋	4 ♏	8 ♐	21 ♑	7 ♒	7 ♈	2 ♊	9 ♋	4 ♍	10 ♎
27	27 ♋	20 ♍	12 ♌	29 ♏	2 ♑	16 ♒	7 ♓	4 ♉	1 ♋	9 ♌	2 ♎	7 ♏
29	27 ♌	17 ♎	9 ♍	24 ♐	26 ♑	10 ♓	3 ♈	3 ♊	1 ♌	7 ♍	27 ♎	2 ♐
31	26 ♍		4 ♎		19 ♒		1 ♉			3 ♎		27 ♐

MOON   Greenwich Mean Midnight (0 h. 0 m.)   1957-1959

1957	Jan.	Feb.	Mar.	April	May	June	July	Aug.	Sep.	Oct.	Nov.	Dec.
1	9 ♑	24 ♒	3 ♓	18 ♈	22 ♉	13 ♋	22 ♌	15 ♎	6 ♐	11 ♑	25 ♒	27 ♓
3	3 ♒	18 ♓	27 ♓	13 ♉	19 ♊	12 ♌	21 ♍	13 ♏	5 ♑	5 ♒	19 ♓	21 ♈
5	27 ♒	12 ♈	21 ♈	9 ♊	17 ♋	10 ♍	19 ♎	9 ♐	26 ♑	29 ♒	13 ♈	16 ♉
7	21 ♓	6 ♉	16 ♉	6 ♋	15 ♌	8 ♎	16 ♏	4 ♑	20 ♒	23 ♓	7 ♉	11 ♊
9	15 ♈	2 ♊	12 ♊	4 ♌	13 ♍	6 ♏	12 ♐	29 ♑	14 ♓	16 ♈	3 ♊	8 ♋
11	11 ♉	0 ♋	9 ♋	3 ♍	12 ♎	3 ♐	8 ♑	23 ♒	8 ♈	11 ♉	29 ♊	6 ♌
13	8 ♊	9 ♋	9 ♌	2 ♎	10 ♏	29 ♐	29 ♑	17 ♓	2 ♉	6 ♊	26 ♋	4 ♍
15	7 ♋	0 ♍	9 ♍	1 ♏	7 ♐	24 ♑	26 ♒	11 ♈	26 ♉	2 ♋	23 ♌	3 ♎
17	7 ♌	1 ♎	9 ♎	29 ♏	3 ♑	18 ♒	20 ♓	5 ♉	22 ♊	29 ♋	22 ♍	1 ♏
19	7 ♍	29 ♎	7 ♏	25 ♐	28 ♑	12 ♓	14 ♈	0 ♊	19 ♋	27 ♌	21 ♎	29 ♏
21	7 ♎	26 ♏	4 ♐	20 ♑	22 ♒	6 ♈	8 ♉	26 ♊	18 ♌	27 ♍	20 ♏	26 ♐
23	4 ♏	21 ♐	0 ♑	14 ♒	16 ♓	0 ♉	4 ♊	25 ♋	18 ♍	27 ♎	17 ♐	22 ♑
25	0 ♐	15 ♑	24 ♑	8 ♓	10 ♈	26 ♉	2 ♋	25 ♌	19 ♎	26 ♏	14 ♑	17 ♒
27	24 ♐	9 ♒	18 ♒	2 ♈	5 ♉	23 ♊	1 ♌	25 ♍	18 ♏	23 ♐	11 ♒	11 ♓
29	18 ♑		11 ♓	27 ♈	1 ♊	22 ♋	1 ♍	25 ♎	15 ♐	19 ♑	3 ♓	5 ♈
31	12 ♒		6 ♈		29 ♊		1 ♎	23 ♏		13 ♒		29 ♈

1958	Jan.	Feb.	Mar.	April	May	June	July	Aug.	Sep.	Oct.	Nov.	Dec.
1	11 ♉	27 ♊	5 ♋	26 ♌	5 ♎	28 ♏	5 ♑	24 ♒	9 ♈	11 ♉	26 ♊	1 ♌
3	6 ♊	25 ♋	3 ♌	26 ♍	5 ♏	27 ♐	2 ♒	18 ♓	2 ♉	5 ♊	21 ♋	27 ♌
5	3 ♋	25 ♌	3 ♍	27 ♎	4 ♐	24 ♑	28 ♒	12 ♈	26 ♉	20 ♊	17 ♌	23 ♍
7	2 ♌	25 ♍	3 ♎	26 ♏	3 ♑	20 ♒	22 ♓	6 ♉	20 ♊	25 ♋	15 ♍	23 ♎
9	1 ♍	22 ♎	3 ♏	24 ♐	29 ♑	14 ♓	16 ♈	0 ♊	16 ♋	22 ♌	14 ♎	22 ♏
11	29 ♍	22 ♏	2 ♐	21 ♑	24 ♒	8 ♈	10 ♉	25 ♊	14 ♌	21 ♍	14 ♏	22 ♐
13	28 ♎	19 ♐	29 ♐	16 ♒	18 ♓	2 ♉	4 ♊	22 ♋	13 ♍	21 ♎	14 ♐	22 ♑
15	25 ♏	14 ♑	24 ♑	10 ♓	12 ♈	26 ♉	0 ♋	20 ♌	13 ♎	21 ♏	13 ♑	18 ♒
17	22 ♐	9 ♒	19 ♒	3 ♈	6 ♉	21 ♊	27 ♋	19 ♍	12 ♏	20 ♐	20 ♒	13 ♓
19	18 ♑	4 ♓	13 ♓	27 ♈	0 ♊	18 ♋	25 ♌	18 ♎	11 ♐	18 ♑	5 ♈	8 ♉
21	13 ♒	28 ♓	6 ♈	21 ♉	25 ♊	15 ♌	23 ♍	17 ♏	8 ♑	14 ♒	29 ♈	1 ♊
23	7 ♓	21 ♈	0 ♉	15 ♊	21 ♋	11 ♍	22 ♎	14 ♐	4 ♒	8 ♓	23 ♈	25 ♊
25	1 ♈	15 ♉	24 ♉	11 ♋	18 ♌	11 ♎	20 ♏	11 ♑	29 ♒	2 ♈	17 ♉	19 ♊
27	25 ♈	9 ♊	18 ♊	8 ♌	16 ♍	9 ♏	18 ♐	7 ♒	23 ♓	26 ♈	11 ♊	15 ♋
29	19 ♉		14 ♋	6 ♍	14 ♎	8 ♐	15 ♑	2 ♓	17 ♈	20 ♉	5 ♋	11 ♌
31	14 ♊		12 ♌		14 ♏		11 ♒	27 ♓		14 ♊		8 ♍

1959	Jan.	Feb.	Mar.	April	May	June	July	Aug.	Sep.	Oct.	Nov.	Dec.
1	21 ♍	14 ♏	25 ♏	17 ♑	24 ♒	10 ♈	12 ♉	26 ♊	12 ♌	17 ♍	9 ♏	17 ♐
3	19 ♎	12 ♐	23 ♐	14 ♒	19 ♓	4 ♉	6 ♊	21 ♋	9 ♍	15 ♎	9 ♐	17 ♑
5	17 ♏	10 ♑	20 ♑	9 ♓	13 ♈	27 ♉	0 ♋	17 ♌	5 ♎	15 ♏	9 ♑	16 ♒
7	16 ♐	8 ♒	17 ♒	4 ♈	7 ♉	21 ♊	25 ♋	13 ♍	5 ♏	14 ♐	7 ♒	13 ♓
9	15 ♑	4 ♓	12 ♓	28 ♈	0 ♊	15 ♋	20 ♌	10 ♎	3 ♐	13 ♑	3 ♓	8 ♈
11	13 ♒	29 ♓	7 ♈	21 ♉	24 ♊	10 ♍	16 ♍	8 ♏	0 ♑	10 ♒	29 ♈	3 ♉
13	9 ♓	23 ♈	1 ♉	15 ♊	18 ♋	6 ♎	13 ♎	7 ♐	0 ♒	6 ♓	23 ♈	26 ♉
15	3 ♈	17 ♉	25 ♉	9 ♋	13 ♌	3 ♏	11 ♏	4 ♑	27 ♒	2 ♈	17 ♉	20 ♊
17	27 ♈	11 ♊	19 ♊	4 ♌	10 ♍	1 ♐	11 ♐	4 ♒	27 ♓	27 ♈	11 ♊	14 ♋
19	21 ♉	5 ♋	13 ♋	1 ♍	8 ♎	1 ♑	10 ♑	27 ♒	21 ♈	21 ♉	5 ♋	8 ♌
21	15 ♊	1 ♌	9 ♌	29 ♍	7 ♏	1 ♒	9 ♒	27 ♓	15 ♉	15 ♊	29 ♋	3 ♍
23	10 ♋	29 ♌	7 ♍	29 ♎	8 ♐	1 ♓	6 ♓	22 ♈	9 ♊	10 ♋	24 ♌	29 ♍
25	7 ♌	26 ♎	6 ♎	29 ♏	8 ♑	28 ♓	2 ♈	17 ♉	10 ♊	8 ♎	19 ♍	26 ♎
27	4 ♍		6 ♏	29 ♐	6 ♒	24 ♈	27 ♈	10 ♊	24 ♋	28 ♍	17 ♎	25 ♏
29	2 ♎		5 ♐	27 ♑	3 ♓	19 ♈	20 ♉	4 ♋	20 ♌	25 ♏	17 ♏	25 ♐
31	0 ♏		4 ♑		28 ♓		14 ♊	29 ♋		24 ♐		26 ♑

MOON   Greenwich Mean Midnight (0 h. 0 m.)   1960-1962

1960	Jan.	Feb.	Mar.	April	May	June	July	Aug.	Sep.	Oct.	Nov.	Dec.
1	10 ♒	0 ♈	20 ♈	5 ♊	7 ♋	22 ♌	25 ♍	15 ♏	8 ♑	17 ♒	8 ♈	14 ♉
3	8 ♓	25 ♈	15 ♉	29 ♊	1 ♌	16 ♍	21 ♎	13 ♐	7 ♒	15 ♓	5 ♉	9 ♊
5	5 ♈	20 ♉	9 ♊	23 ♋	25 ♌	12 ♎	19 ♏	13 ♑	6 ♓	13 ♈	0 ♊	3 ♋
7	29 ♈	13 ♊	3 ♋	17 ♌	21 ♍	11 ♏	19 ♐	13 ♒	4 ♈	9 ♉	25 ♊	27 ♋
9	23 ♉	7 ♋	27 ♋	13 ♍	18 ♎	10 ♐	19 ♑	12 ♓	1 ♉	5 ♊	19 ♋	20 ♌
11	17 ♊	1 ♌	22 ♌	10 ♎	17 ♏	11 ♑	19 ♒	10 ♈	27 ♉	29 ♊	12 ♌	14 ♍
13	11 ♋	27 ♌	18 ♍	8 ♏	17 ♐	11 ♒	18 ♓	6 ♉	21 ♊	23 ♋	6 ♍	9 ♎
15	5 ♌	22 ♍	15 ♎	8 ♐	17 ♑	9 ♓	15 ♈	1 ♊	15 ♋	16 ♌	2 ♎	6 ♏
17	0 ♍	19 ♎	13 ♏	7 ♑	15 ♒	6 ♈	10 ♉	25 ♊	9 ♌	11 ♍	28 ♎	5 ♐
19	26 ♍	16 ♏	11 ♐	5 ♒	13 ♓	1 ♉	4 ♊	18 ♋	3 ♍	7 ♎	27 ♏	5 ♑
21	22 ♎	15 ♐	10 ♑	2 ♓	9 ♈	25 ♉	28 ♊	12 ♌	28 ♍	4 ♏	26 ♐	4 ♒
23	20 ♏	13 ♑	8 ♒	29 ♓	4 ♉	19 ♊	22 ♋	7 ♍	25 ♎	2 ♐	26 ♑	4 ♓
25	19 ♐	12 ♒	6 ♓	24 ♈	28 ♉	13 ♋	16 ♌	2 ♎	20 ♏	29 ♐	24 ♒	2 ♈
27	19 ♑	10 ♓	2 ♈	19 ♉	22 ♊	7 ♌	10 ♍	28 ♎	18 ♐	27 ♑	22 ♓	28 ♈
29	18 ♒	7 ♈	28 ♈	13 ♊	16 ♋	1 ♍	5 ♎	25 ♏	18 ♑	27 ♒	18 ♈	23 ♉
31	16 ♓		23 ♉		10 ♌		1 ♏	23 ♐		25 ♓		18 ♊

1961	Jan.	Feb.	Mar.	April	May	June	July	Aug.	Sep.	Oct.	Nov.	Dec.
1	29 ♊	14 ♌	23 ♌	8 ♎	13 ♏	5 ♑	13 ♒	7 ♈	27 ♉	1 ♋	15 ♌	17 ♍
3	24 ♋	8 ♍	17 ♍	4 ♏	11 ♐	4 ♒	13 ♓	4 ♉	22 ♊	25 ♋	9 ♍	11 ♎
5	17 ♌	2 ♎	12 ♎	1 ♐	9 ♑	2 ♓	12 ♈	0 ♊	17 ♋	19 ♌	3 ♎	6 ♏
7	11 ♍	27 ♎	7 ♏	28 ♐	7 ♒	0 ♈	9 ♉	25 ♊	10 ♌	12 ♍	28 ♎	2 ♐
9	5 ♎	24 ♏	4 ♐	26 ♑	6 ♓	27 ♈	5 ♊	20 ♋	4 ♍	7 ♎	23 ♏	0 ♑
11	1 ♏	22 ♐	2 ♑	25 ♒	4 ♈	24 ♉	28 ♊	13 ♌	28 ♍	1 ♏	20 ♐	28 ♑
13	28 ♏	21 ♑	0 ♒	24 ♓	1 ♉	19 ♊	23 ♋	7 ♍	22 ♎	25 ♏	18 ♑	27 ♒
15	28 ♐	21 ♒	0 ♓	22 ♈	28 ♉	14 ♋	16 ♌	1 ♎	17 ♏	21 ♐	16 ♒	25 ♓
17	28 ♑	21 ♓	29 ♓	19 ♉	23 ♊	8 ♌	10 ♍	25 ♎	13 ♐	18 ♑	14 ♓	23 ♈
19	28 ♒	20 ♈	27 ♈	15 ♊	18 ♋	2 ♍	4 ♎	20 ♏	11 ♑	16 ♒	12 ♈	20 ♉
21	27 ♓	16 ♉	24 ♉	10 ♋	11 ♌	25 ♍	28 ♎	17 ♐	9 ♒	16 ♓	10 ♉	17 ♊
23	25 ♈	11 ♊	20 ♊	4 ♌	5 ♍	20 ♎	23 ♏	16 ♑	9 ♓	17 ♈	8 ♊	12 ♋
25	20 ♉	6 ♋	14 ♋	27 ♌	29 ♍	16 ♏	22 ♐	15 ♒	9 ♈	16 ♉	4 ♋	7 ♌
27	15 ♊	29 ♋	7 ♌	21 ♍	23 ♎	14 ♐	22 ♑	16 ♓	8 ♉	13 ♊	29 ♋	1 ♍
29	9 ♋		1 ♍	17 ♎	22 ♏	14 ♑	22 ♒	15 ♈	5 ♊	9 ♋	23 ♌	24 ♍
31	2 ♌		26 ♍		20 ♐		22 ♓	13 ♉		3 ♌		18 ♎

1962	Jan.	Feb.	Mar.	April	May	June	July	Aug.	Sep.	Oct.	Nov.	Dec.
1	1 ♏	18 ♐	26 ♐	17 ♒	26 ♓	20 ♉	27 ♊	14 ♌	29 ♍	1 ♏	17 ♐	22 ♑
3	26 ♏	16 ♑	24 ♑	17 ♓	26 ♈	18 ♊	23 ♋	8 ♍	22 ♎	25 ♏	12 ♑	19 ♒
5	24 ♐	15 ♒	24 ♒	17 ♈	25 ♉	14 ♋	18 ♌	2 ♎	16 ♏	20 ♐	8 ♒	16 ♓
7	23 ♑	16 ♓	24 ♓	17 ♉	23 ♊	10 ♌	12 ♍	26 ♎	11 ♐	15 ♑	6 ♓	15 ♈
9	22 ♒	15 ♈	24 ♈	15 ♊	19 ♋	4 ♍	6 ♎	20 ♏	6 ♑	12 ♒	5 ♈	14 ♉
11	21 ♓	14 ♉	23 ♉	11 ♋	14 ♌	28 ♍	29 ♎	15 ♐	4 ♒	11 ♓	5 ♉	13 ♊
13	20 ♈	10 ♊	20 ♊	6 ♌	8 ♍	22 ♎	24 ♏	11 ♑	3 ♓	12 ♈	5 ♊	11 ♋
15	17 ♉	6 ♋	15 ♋	0 ♍	1 ♎	16 ♏	18 ♐	10 ♒	3 ♈	12 ♉	4 ♋	8 ♌
17	13 ♊	0 ♌	9 ♌	23 ♍	26 ♎	12 ♐	15 ♑	9 ♓	4 ♉	11 ♊	0 ♌	4 ♍
19	9 ♋	24 ♌	3 ♍	17 ♎	20 ♏	7 ♑	12 ♒	10 ♈	3 ♊	9 ♋	25 ♌	28 ♍
21	3 ♌	18 ♍	26 ♍	12 ♏	16 ♐	5 ♒	11 ♓	9 ♉	0 ♋	4 ♌	19 ♍	21 ♎
23	27 ♌	11 ♎	20 ♎	7 ♐	13 ♑	3 ♓	11 ♈	7 ♊	25 ♋	29 ♌	13 ♎	15 ♏
25	21 ♍	5 ♏	15 ♏	3 ♑	10 ♒	1 ♈	11 ♉	3 ♋	20 ♌	23 ♍	7 ♏	10 ♐
27	14 ♎	0 ♐	10 ♐	29 ♑	8 ♓	1 ♉	10 ♊	28 ♋	14 ♍	16 ♎	1 ♐	5 ♑
29	9 ♏		6 ♑	27 ♒	6 ♈	29 ♉	6 ♋	23 ♌	7 ♎	10 ♏	26 ♐	2 ♒
31	4 ♐		3 ♒		5 ♉		1 ♌	17 ♍		4 ♐		29 ♒

MOON   Greenwich Mean Midnight (0 h. 0 m.)   1963-1965

1963	Jan.	Feb.	Mar.	April	May	June	July	Aug.	Sep.	Oct.	Nov.	Dec.
1	13 ♓	7 ♉	17 ♉	9 ♋	14 ♌	0 ♎	2 ♏	16 ♐	2 ♒	7 ♓	0 ♉	8 ♊
3	11 ♈	5 ♊	15 ♊	5 ♌	9 ♍	24 ♎	26 ♏	11 ♑	29 ♒	6 ♈	0 ♊	8 ♋
5	10 ♉	2 ♋	12 ♋	0 ♍	3 ♎	18 ♏	20 ♐	7 ♒	28 ♓	6 ♉	0 ♋	7 ♌
7	8 ♊	28 ♋	8 ♌	24 ♍	27 ♎	12 ♐	15 ♑	4 ♓	27 ♈	6 ♊	28 ♋	4 ♍
9	6 ♋	24 ♌	3 ♍	18 ♎	21 ♏	6 ♑	11 ♒	2 ♈	26 ♉	5 ♋	25 ♌	29 ♍
11	3 ♌	19 ♍	27 ♍	12 ♏	15 ♐	1 ♒	8 ♓	1 ♉	24 ♊	2 ♌	20 ♍	23 ♎
13	28 ♌	13 ♎	21 ♎	6 ♐	9 ♑	28 ♒	6 ♈	29 ♉	21 ♋	28 ♌	14 ♎	17 ♏
15	23 ♍	7 ♏	15 ♏	0 ♑	4 ♒	25 ♓	4 ♉	27 ♊	18 ♌	23 ♍	8 ♏	10 ♐
17	17 ♎	1 ♐	9 ♐	25 ♑	1 ♓	23 ♈	3 ♊	25 ♋	13 ♍	17 ♎	2 ♐	4 ♑
19	11 ♏	25 ♐	3 ♑	22 ♒	29 ♓	23 ♉	1 ♋	21 ♌	8 ♎	11 ♏	25 ♐	29 ♑
21	5 ♐	21 ♑	29 ♑	20 ♓	29 ♈	22 ♊	29 ♋	17 ♍	2 ♏	5 ♐	19 ♑	24 ♒
23	0 ♑	19 ♒	27 ♒	20 ♈	29 ♉	21 ♋	26 ♌	12 ♎	26 ♏	28 ♐	14 ♒	20 ♓
25	27 ♑	18 ♓	26 ♓	21 ♉	29 ♊	18 ♌	22 ♍	6 ♏	20 ♐	23 ♑	10 ♓	18 ♈
27	25 ♒	18 ♈		20 ♊	27 ♋	14 ♍	16 ♎	0 ♐	15 ♑	18 ♒	8 ♈	16 ♉
29	24 ♓		27 ♉	18 ♋	23 ♌	8 ♎	10 ♏	24 ♐	10 ♒	15 ♓	8 ♉	16 ♊
31	22 ♈		25 ♊		18 ♍		4 ♐	19 ♑		14 ♈		16 ♋

1964	Jan.	Feb.	Mar.	April	May	June	July	Aug.	Sep.	Oct.	Nov.	Dec.
1	1 ♌	19 ♍	10 ♎	25 ♏	27 ♐	12 ♒	16 ♓	7 ♉	0 ♋	9 ♌	0 ♎	5 ♏
3	28 ♌	15 ♎	5 ♏	19 ♐	21 ♑	7 ♓	13 ♈	5 ♊	28 ♋	6 ♍	26 ♎	29 ♏
5	25 ♍	9 ♏	29 ♏	13 ♑	15 ♒	3 ♈	11 ♉	4 ♋	27 ♌	3 ♎	21 ♏	23 ♐
7	19 ♎	3 ♐	23 ♐	7 ♒	11 ♓	2 ♉	10 ♊	4 ♌	25 ♍	0 ♏	15 ♐	17 ♑
9	13 ♏	27 ♐	17 ♑	3 ♓	9 ♈	1 ♊	10 ♋	2 ♍	21 ♎	24 ♏	8 ♑	10 ♒
11	7 ♐	21 ♑	12 ♒	1 ♈	8 ♉	2 ♋	10 ♌	0 ♎	16 ♏	18 ♐	2 ♒	5 ♓
13	1 ♑	17 ♒	8 ♓	0 ♉	8 ♊	1 ♌	8 ♍	26 ♎	11 ♐	12 ♑	26 ♒	0 ♈
15	25 ♑	13 ♓	6 ♈	29 ♉	8 ♋	0 ♍	5 ♎	21 ♏	4 ♑	6 ♒	22 ♓	27 ♈
17	21 ♒	11 ♈	5 ♉	29 ♊	7 ♌	26 ♍	0 ♏	14 ♐	28 ♑	1 ♓	19 ♈	25 ♉
19	17 ♓	9 ♉	4 ♊	0 ♋	4 ♍	21 ♎	24 ♏	8 ♑	23 ♒	27 ♓	17 ♉	26 ♊
21	14 ♈	7 ♊	2 ♋	24 ♋	0 ♎	16 ♏	18 ♐	2 ♒	19 ♓	25 ♈	17 ♊	26 ♋
23	12 ♉	5 ♋	0 ♌	20 ♌	24 ♎	9 ♐	12 ♑	26 ♒	16 ♈	23 ♉	17 ♋	25 ♌
25	11 ♊	3 ♌	27 ♌	15 ♍	19 ♏	3 ♑	6 ♒	23 ♓	14 ♉	23 ♊	16 ♌	23 ♍
27	10 ♋	1 ♍	23 ♍	10 ♏	12 ♐	27 ♑	1 ♓	20 ♈	13 ♊	22 ♋	14 ♍	19 ♎
29	8 ♌	28 ♍	19 ♎	4 ♐	6 ♑	21 ♒	26 ♓	18 ♉	11 ♋	20 ♌	10 ♎	14 ♏
31	6 ♍		13 ♏		0 ♒		23 ♈	16 ♊		17 ♍		8 ♐

1965	Jan.	Feb.	Mar.	April	May	June	July	Aug.	Sep.	Oct.	Nov.	Dec.
1	20 ♐	4 ♒	13 ♒	29 ♓	4 ♉	26 ♊	4 ♌	28 ♍	17 ♏	21 ♐	5 ♒	6 ♓
3	14 ♑	29 ♒	7 ♓	25 ♈	2 ♊	4 ♌	25 ♌	21 ♎	12 ♐	15 ♑	28 ♒	0 ♈
5	7 ♒	23 ♓	3 ♈	23 ♉	1 ♋	2 ♍	21 ♍	7 ♏	7 ♑	9 ♒	23 ♓	26 ♈
7	1 ♓	19 ♈	29 ♈	20 ♊	0 ♌	29 ♍	16 ♎	0 ♐	2 ♒	2 ♓	18 ♈	22 ♉
9	26 ♓	15 ♉	26 ♉	19 ♋	28 ♌	25 ♎	10 ♐	24 ♐	24 ♒	27 ♈	14 ♉	20 ♊
11	22 ♈	13 ♊	24 ♊	17 ♌	25 ♍	19 ♏	4 ♑	18 ♑	18 ♓	22 ♉	12 ♊	20 ♋
13	19 ♉	12 ♋	22 ♋	15 ♍	22 ♎	13 ♐	27 ♑	12 ♒	14 ♈	19 ♊	10 ♋	19 ♌
15	18 ♊	12 ♌	21 ♌	13 ♎	18 ♏	7 ♑	21 ♒	6 ♓	10 ♉	18 ♋	8 ♌	17 ♍
17	19 ♋	12 ♍	20 ♍	9 ♏	13 ♐	1 ♒	16 ♓	2 ♈	9 ♊	17 ♌	7 ♍	15 ♎
19	19 ♌	10 ♎	18 ♎	5 ♐	7 ♑	26 ♒	12 ♈	28 ♈	8 ♋	16 ♍	5 ♎	12 ♏
21	18 ♍	7 ♏	14 ♏	29 ♐	1 ♒	22 ♓	9 ♉	25 ♉	8 ♌	15 ♎	2 ♏	7 ♐
23	15 ♎	2 ♐	9 ♐	23 ♑	25 ♒	19 ♈	8 ♊	24 ♊	7 ♍	13 ♏	28 ♏	2 ♑
25	11 ♏	25 ♐	3 ♑	17 ♒	19 ♓	18 ♉	8 ♋	24 ♋	5 ♎	9 ♐	24 ♐	27 ♑
27	5 ♐	19 ♑	27 ♑	11 ♓	15 ♈	18 ♊	7 ♌	21 ♌	3 ♏	3 ♑	18 ♑	20 ♒
29	29 ♐		21 ♒	7 ♈	12 ♉	18 ♋	6 ♍	17 ♍	28 ♏	28 ♐	12 ♒	14 ♓
31	22 ♑		16 ♓		11 ♊		4 ♏	13 ♎		23 ♑		8 ♈

MOON   1963-1965

MOON   Greenwich Mean Midnight (0 h. 0 m.)   **1966–1968**

1966	Jan.	Feb.	Mar.	April	May	June	July	Aug.	Sep.	Oct.	Nov.	Dec.
1	21 ♈	8 ♊	17 ♊	9 ♌	18 ♍	11 ♍	17 ♎	4 ♒	19 ♓	22 ♈	8 ♊	14 ♋
3	16 ♉	6 ♋	15 ♋	8 ♍	17 ♎	8 ♐	13 ♐	28 ♒	13 ♈	16 ♉	3 ♋	3 ♌
5	14 ♊	6 ♌	14 ♌	8 ♎	16 ♏	4 ♑	8 ♒	22 ♓	7 ♉	11 ♊	0 ♌	9 ♍
7	13 ♋	7 ♍	15 ♍	7 ♏	13 ♐	29 ♑	2 ♓	16 ♈	1 ♊	6 ♋	28 ♌	7 ♎
9	13 ♌	7 ♎	15 ♎	5 ♐	9 ♑	24 ♒	25 ♓	10 ♉	27 ♊	4 ♌	27 ♍	6 ♏
11	13 ♍	5 ♏	14 ♏	1 ♑	4 ♒	17 ♓	19 ♈	5 ♊	25 ♋	3 ♍	26 ♎	4 ♐
13	12 ♎	1 ♐	10 ♐	26 ♑	28 ♒	11 ♈	14 ♉	2 ♋	24 ♌	3 ♎	25 ♏	1 ♑
15	9 ♏	26 ♐	5 ♑	20 ♒	21 ♓	6 ♉	10 ♊	1 ♌	25 ♍	3 ♏	23 ♐	28 ♑
17	4 ♐	20 ♑	29 ♑	13 ♓	16 ♈	2 ♊	8 ♋	1 ♍	25 ♎	2 ♐	20 ♑	23 ♒
19	29 ♐	14 ♒	23 ♒	7 ♈	11 ♉	29 ♊	7 ♌	1 ♎	29 ♏	29 ♐	15 ♒	17 ♓
21	23 ♑	8 ♓	17 ♓	2 ♉	28 ♉	28 ♋	7 ♍	0 ♏	20 ♐	25 ♑	9 ♓	11 ♈
23	17 ♒	2 ♈	11 ♈	28 ♉	27 ♋	27 ♌	6 ♎	28 ♏	16 ♑	19 ♒	3 ♈	4 ♉
25	11 ♓	26 ♈	5 ♉	24 ♊	26 ♋	24 ♍	4 ♏	24 ♐	10 ♒	13 ♓	27 ♈	29 ♉
27	5 ♈	21 ♉	1 ♊	21 ♋	0 ♍	24 ♎	1 ♐	19 ♑	4 ♓	6 ♈	21 ♉	26 ♊
29	29 ♈		27 ♊	19 ♌	29 ♍	21 ♏	27 ♐	13 ♒	28 ♓	0 ♉	17 ♊	23 ♋
31	25 ♉		25 ♋		27 ♎		22 ♑	7 ♓		25 ♉		21 ♌

1967	Jan.	Feb.	Mar.	April	May	June	July	Aug.	Sep.	Oct.	Nov.	Dec.
1	6 ♍	29 ♎	9 ♏	0 ♑	5 ♒	20 ♓	22 ♈	6 ♊	22 ♋	28 ♌	20 ♎	29 ♏
3	4 ♎	27 ♏	7 ♐	26 ♑	0 ♓	14 ♈	16 ♉	1 ♋	20 ♌	21 ♍	21 ♏	29 ♐
5	2 ♏	23 ♐	3 ♑	21 ♒	24 ♓	7 ♉	10 ♊	27 ♋	19 ♍	27 ♎	21 ♐	27 ♑
7	0 ♐	19 ♑	29 ♑	15 ♓	17 ♈	2 ♊	6 ♋	25 ♌	19 ♎	27 ♏	19 ♑	24 ♒
9	27 ♐	14 ♒	23 ♒	8 ♈	11 ♉	27 ♊	2 ♌	24 ♍	18 ♏	26 ♐	15 ♒	19 ♓
11	23 ♑	9 ♓	18 ♓	2 ♉	5 ♊	23 ♋	0 ♍	23 ♎	16 ♐	23 ♑	10 ♓	13 ♈
13	18 ♒	3 ♈	11 ♈	26 ♉	0 ♋	20 ♌	28 ♍	21 ♏	13 ♑	19 ♒	4 ♈	7 ♉
15	13 ♓	26 ♈	5 ♉	20 ♊	26 ♋	17 ♎	26 ♏	19 ♐	9 ♒	13 ♓	28 ♈	0 ♊
17	7 ♈	20 ♉	0 ♊	24 ♋	15 ♌	15 ♏	25 ♐	16 ♑	4 ♓	7 ♈	22 ♉	25 ♊
19	0 ♉	15 ♊	24 ♊	13 ♌	21 ♍	14 ♐	23 ♑	12 ♒	29 ♓	1 ♉	16 ♊	20 ♋
21	24 ♉	11 ♋	20 ♋	11 ♍	20 ♎	13 ♑	20 ♒	8 ♓	22 ♈	25 ♉	10 ♋	16 ♌
23	20 ♊	10 ♌	18 ♌	11 ♎	19 ♏	11 ♒	16 ♓	2 ♈	16 ♉	19 ♊	5 ♌	12 ♍
25	17 ♋	9 ♍	17 ♍	11 ♏	19 ♐	8 ♓	12 ♈	26 ♉	10 ♊	13 ♋	2 ♍	10 ♎
27	16 ♌	10 ♎	11 ♎	11 ♐	17 ♑	4 ♈	6 ♉	20 ♊	4 ♌	9 ♍	0 ♎	8 ♏
29	16 ♍		18 ♏	9 ♑	13 ♒	28 ♈	0 ♊	14 ♋	0 ♍	6 ♎	29 ♎	7 ♐
31	15 ♎		16 ♐		8 ♓		9 ♋	9 ♌		5 ♏		7 ♑

1968	Jan.	Feb.	Mar.	April	May	June	July	Aug.	Sep.	Oct.	Nov.	Dec.
1	21 ♑	10 ♓	0 ♈	15 ♉	17 ♊	3 ♌	8 ♍	29 ♎	22 ♐	1 ♒	21 ♓	25 ♈
3	19 ♒	5 ♈	25 ♈	9 ♊	11 ♋	28 ♌	4 ♎	27 ♏	20 ♑	28 ♒	16 ♈	20 ♉
5	15 ♓	29 ♈	19 ♉	2 ♋	6 ♌	24 ♍	2 ♏	26 ♐	18 ♒	24 ♓	11 ♉	13 ♊
7	9 ♈	23 ♉	12 ♊	27 ♋	2 ♍	22 ♎	1 ♐	25 ♑	15 ♓	20 ♈	5 ♊	7 ♋
9	3 ♉	16 ♊	6 ♋	23 ♌	29 ♍	22 ♏	1 ♑	23 ♒	11 ♈	14 ♉	28 ♊	1 ♌
11	27 ♉	11 ♋	2 ♌	21 ♍	28 ♎	22 ♐	1 ♒	20 ♓	0 ♉	8 ♊	22 ♋	25 ♌
13	21 ♊	7 ♌	29 ♌	20 ♎	29 ♏	22 ♑	29 ♒	16 ♈	0 ♊	2 ♋	16 ♌	21 ♍
15	16 ♋	5 ♍	27 ♍	20 ♏	28 ♐	25 ♒	25 ♓	10 ♉	24 ♊	26 ♋	12 ♍	17 ♎
17	12 ♌	3 ♎	27 ♎	20 ♐	28 ♑	17 ♓	20 ♈	4 ♊	18 ♋	21 ♌	9 ♎	16 ♏
19	9 ♍	1 ♏	26 ♏	16 ♑	25 ♒	12 ♈	14 ♉	28 ♊	13 ♌	17 ♍	8 ♏	17 ♐
21	6 ♎	0 ♐	24 ♐	16 ♒	21 ♓	6 ♉	8 ♊	22 ♋	9 ♍	15 ♎	8 ♐	17 ♑
23	4 ♏	28 ♐	22 ♑	11 ♓	15 ♈	29 ♉	2 ♋	18 ♌	7 ♎	15 ♏	9 ♑	16 ♒
25	3 ♐	25 ♑	14 ♒	6 ♈	9 ♉	26 ♊	26 ♌	14 ♍	6 ♏	15 ♐	8 ♒	14 ♓
27	1 ♑	22 ♒	14 ♓	0 ♉	2 ♊	17 ♋	22 ♍	12 ♎	5 ♐	14 ♑	5 ♓	10 ♈
29	29 ♑	18 ♓	9 ♈	24 ♉	26 ♊	12 ♌	18 ♍	10 ♏	3 ♑	12 ♒	1 ♈	5 ♉
31	27 ♒		3 ♉		20 ♋		15 ♎	8 ♐		8 ♓		28 ♉

MOON   Greenwich Mean Midnight (0 h. 0 m.)   1969–1971

1969	Jan.	Feb.	Mar.	April	May	June	July	Aug.	Sep.	Oct.	Nov.	Dec.
1	10 ♊	25 ♋	3 ♌	19 ♍	24 ♎	17 ♐	26 ♑	18 ♓	7 ♉	10 ♊	24 ♋	26 ♌
3	4 ♋	19 ♌	28 ♌	16 ♎	23 ♏	17 ♑	26 ♒	16 ♈	2 ♊	5 ♋	18 ♌	20 ♍
5	28 ♋	14 ♍	24 ♍	14 ♏	23 ♐	16 ♒	24 ♓	12 ♉	27 ♊	28 ♋	12 ♍	15 ♎
7	22 ♌	10 ♎	20 ♎	13 ♐	22 ♑	14 ♓	20 ♈	6 ♊	20 ♋	22 ♌	8 ♎	12 ♏
9	17 ♍	7 ♏	18 ♏	11 ♑	20 ♒	10 ♈	15 ♉	0 ♋	14 ♌	17 ♍	4 ♏	11 ♐
11	13 ♎	5 ♐	16 ♐	9 ♒	17 ♓	6 ♉	9 ♊	24 ♋	9 ♍	13 ♎	3 ♐	11 ♑
13	11 ♏	4 ♑	16 ♑	7 ♓	13 ♈	0 ♊	3 ♋	18 ♌	4 ♎	7 ♏	2 ♑	11 ♒
15	10 ♐	3 ♒	13 ♒	4 ♈	9 ♉	24 ♊	27 ♋	12 ♍	0 ♏	4 ♐	1 ♒	9 ♓
17	10 ♑	2 ♓	11 ♓	0 ♉	3 ♊	18 ♋	21 ♌	7 ♎	27 ♏	2 ♑	29 ♒	6 ♈
19	10 ♒	0 ♈	8 ♈	25 ♉	27 ♊	12 ♌	15 ♍	3 ♏	25 ♐	0 ♒	26 ♓	3 ♉
21	9 ♓	26 ♈	4 ♉	19 ♊	21 ♋	6 ♍	10 ♎	1 ♐	25 ♑	27 ♒	23 ♈	28 ♉
23	6 ♈	21 ♉	29 ♉	13 ♋	15 ♌	1 ♎	6 ♏	28 ♐	22 ♒	23 ♓	19 ♉	23 ♊
25	1 ♉	15 ♊	23 ♊	7 ♌	9 ♍	27 ♎	4 ♐	28 ♑	21 ♓	19 ♈	14 ♊	17 ♋
27	25 ♉	9 ♋	17 ♋	1 ♍	5 ♎	25 ♏	4 ♑	28 ♒	19 ♈	14 ♉	8 ♋	11 ♌
29	19 ♊		11 ♌	27 ♍	2 ♏	25 ♐	4 ♒	27 ♓	15 ♉	8 ♊	2 ♌	4 ♍
31	13 ♋		6 ♍		2 ♐		4 ♈	24 ♈		2 ♋		28 ♍

1970	Jan.	Feb.	Mar.	April	May	June	July	Aug.	Sep.	Oct.	Nov.	Dec.
1	11 ♎	0 ♐	9 ♐	1 ♒	10 ♓	2 ♉	8 ♊	25 ♋	9 ♍	12 ♎	29 ♏	5 ♑
3	7 ♏	27 ♐	7 ♑	0 ♓	8 ♈	29 ♉	3 ♋	18 ♌	3 ♎	6 ♏	25 ♐	3 ♒
5	4 ♐	27 ♑	6 ♒	29 ♓	6 ♉	25 ♊	28 ♋	12 ♍	27 ♎	2 ♐	22 ♑	1 ♓
7	4 ♑	28 ♒	6 ♓	28 ♈	3 ♊	19 ♋	22 ♌	6 ♎	22 ♏	28 ♐	20 ♒	0 ♈
9	5 ♒	27 ♓	5 ♈	25 ♉	0 ♋	13 ♌	15 ♍	0 ♏	18 ♐	26 ♑	19 ♓	29 ♈
11	5 ♓	26 ♈	4 ♉	21 ♊	23 ♋	7 ♍	9 ♎	26 ♏	16 ♑	24 ♒	18 ♈	27 ♉
13	3 ♈	22 ♉	0 ♊	15 ♋	17 ♌	1 ♎	4 ♏	23 ♐	16 ♒	24 ♓	17 ♉	25 ♊
15	0 ♉	17 ♊	25 ♊	9 ♌	11 ♍	26 ♎	0 ♐	22 ♑	15 ♓	23 ♈	14 ♊	22 ♋
17	25 ♉	11 ♋	19 ♋	3 ♍	5 ♎	22 ♏	29 ♐	22 ♒	14 ♈	21 ♉	10 ♋	18 ♌
19	20 ♊	4 ♌	13 ♌	27 ♍	1 ♏	20 ♐	28 ♑	21 ♓	11 ♉	18 ♊	5 ♌	13 ♍
21	14 ♋	28 ♌	7 ♍	22 ♎	28 ♏	20 ♑	28 ♒	19 ♈	6 ♊	13 ♋	29 ♌	6 ♎
23	8 ♌	22 ♍	1 ♎	19 ♏	26 ♐	19 ♒	28 ♓	15 ♉	1 ♋	7 ♌	22 ♍	0 ♏
25	1 ♍	17 ♎	26 ♎	16 ♐	24 ♑	18 ♓	26 ♈	10 ♊	24 ♋	2 ♍	16 ♎	24 ♏
27	25 ♍	12 ♏	21 ♏	14 ♑	23 ♒	16 ♈	23 ♉	4 ♋	18 ♌	26 ♍	11 ♏	19 ♑
29	20 ♎		19 ♐	14 ♒	21 ♓	13 ♉	18 ♊	27 ♋	12 ♍	21 ♎	8 ♐	14 ♒
31	15 ♏		17 ♑		19 ♈		13 ♋	21 ♌		16 ♏		13 ♒

1971	Jan.	Feb.	Mar.	April	May	June	July	Aug.	Sep.	Oct.	Nov.	Dec.
1	28 ♒	21 ♈	0 ♉	21 ♉	25 ♊	10 ♍	11 ♎	25 ♏	12 ♑	18 ♒	11 ♈	20 ♉
3	26 ♓	18 ♉	28 ♉	17 ♊	20 ♋	3 ♎	5 ♏	21 ♐	10 ♒	18 ♓	11 ♉	19 ♊
5	24 ♈	15 ♊	25 ♊	11 ♋	13 ♌	27 ♎	0 ♐	18 ♑	9 ♓	18 ♈	11 ♊	18 ♋
7	22 ♉	10 ♋	20 ♋	5 ♌	7 ♍	22 ♏	26 ♐	16 ♒	9 ♈	18 ♉	8 ♋	14 ♌
9	18 ♊	5 ♌	14 ♌	28 ♌	1 ♎	17 ♐	23 ♑	16 ♓	9 ♉	17 ♊	6 ♌	8 ♍
11	14 ♋	29 ♌	8 ♍	22 ♍	25 ♎	14 ♑	22 ♒	15 ♈	8 ♊	14 ♋	2 ♌	3 ♎
13	8 ♌	23 ♍	1 ♎	17 ♎	21 ♏	11 ♒	20 ♓	14 ♉	5 ♋	10 ♌	26 ♌	27 ♎
15	2 ♍	16 ♎	25 ♎	11 ♏	18 ♐	9 ♓	20 ♈	11 ♊	0 ♌	4 ♍	20 ♍	21 ♏
17	26 ♍	10 ♏	19 ♏	7 ♐	15 ♑	8 ♈	19 ♉	8 ♋	25 ♌	28 ♍	13 ♎	15 ♐
19	20 ♎	5 ♐	15 ♐	4 ♑	13 ♒	6 ♉	17 ♊	3 ♌	19 ♍	21 ♎	6 ♏	11 ♑
21	14 ♏	2 ♑	11 ♑	2 ♒	11 ♓	4 ♊	14 ♋	28 ♌	12 ♎	15 ♏	1 ♐	7 ♒
23	10 ♐	0 ♒	9 ♒	2 ♓	11 ♈	2 ♋	8 ♌	22 ♍	6 ♏	9 ♐	27 ♑	4 ♓
25	8 ♑	0 ♓	8 ♓	2 ♈	9 ♉	28 ♋	2 ♍	16 ♎	1 ♐	4 ♑	23 ♒	2 ♈
27	7 ♒	0 ♈	8 ♈	1 ♉	6 ♊	23 ♌	25 ♍	9 ♏	25 ♐	0 ♒	21 ♓	0 ♉
29	7 ♓		7 ♉	29 ♉	3 ♋	17 ♍	19 ♎	4 ♐	21 ♑	27 ♒	20 ♈	29 ♉
31	6 ♈		5 ♊		28 ♋		13 ♏	29 ♐		26 ♓		28 ♊

MOON Greenwich Mean Midnight (0 h. 0 m.) 1972-1974

1972	Jan.	Feb.	Mar.	April	May	June	July	Aug.	Sep.	Oct.	Nov.	Dec.
1	12 ♋	0 ♍	20 ♍	5 ♏	8 ♐	24 ♑	29 ♒	21 ♈	15 ♊	23 ♋	12 ♍	16 ♎
3	9 ♌	24 ♍	15 ♎	29 ♏	2 ♑	19 ♒	26 ♓	22 ♉	13 ♋	20 ♌	7 ♎	10 ♏
5	4 ♍	18 ♎	8 ♏	23 ♐	27 ♑	16 ♓	24 ♈	18 ♊	10 ♌	15 ♍	1 ♏	4 ♐
7	29 ♍	12 ♏	2 ♐	17 ♑	22 ♒	14 ♈	23 ♉	16 ♋	6 ♍	10 ♎	25 ♏	27 ♐
9	23 ♎	6 ♐	26 ♐	13 ♒	20 ♓	13 ♉	22 ♊	14 ♌	1 ♎	4 ♏	19 ♐	21 ♑
11	16 ♏	1 ♑	22 ♑	11 ♓	19 ♈	13 ♊	21 ♋	10 ♍	26 ♎	28 ♏	12 ♑	16 ♒
13	11 ♐	27 ♑	19 ♒	11 ♈	20 ♉	13 ♋	19 ♌	5 ♎	20 ♏	22 ♐	7 ♒	12 ♓
15	6 ♑	25 ♒	18 ♓	12 ♉	20 ♊	11 ♌	15 ♍	0 ♏	13 ♐	16 ♑	2 ♓	9 ♈
17	3 ♒	24 ♓	18 ♈	12 ♊	19 ♋	7 ♍	10 ♎	24 ♏	8 ♑	11 ♒	0 ♈	7 ♉
19	0 ♓	23 ♈	18 ♉	10 ♋	16 ♌	2 ♎	4 ♏	18 ♐	3 ♒	7 ♓	29 ♈	7 ♊
21	28 ♓	22 ♉	16 ♊	7 ♌	11 ♍	26 ♎	28 ♏	12 ♑	29 ♒	6 ♈	29 ♉	8 ♋
23	27 ♈	20 ♊	14 ♋	2 ♍	5 ♎	19 ♏	22 ♐	8 ♒	28 ♓	6 ♉	0 ♊	7 ♌
25	25 ♉	17 ♋	10 ♍	26 ♍	29 ♎	13 ♐	17 ♑	5 ♓	27 ♈	6 ♊	29 ♋	4 ♎
27	23 ♊	13 ♌	5 ♏	20 ♎	23 ♏	8 ♑	12 ♒	3 ♈	27 ♉	6 ♋	26 ♌	0 ♏
29	20 ♋	8 ♍	29 ♍	14 ♏	17 ♐	3 ♒	9 ♓	2 ♉	26 ♊	3 ♌	22 ♍	25 ♎
31	17 ♌		23 ♎		11 ♑		7 ♈	1 ♊		0 ♍		19 ♏

1973	Jan.	Feb.	Mar.	April	May	June	July	Aug.	Sep.	Oct.	Nov.	Dec.
1	1 ♐	15 ♑	23 ♑	9 ♓	15 ♈	8 ♊	16 ♋	9 ♍	27 ♎	0 ♐	14 ♑	16 ♒
3	24 ♐	9 ♒	5 ♒	7 ♈	14 ♉	8 ♋	16 ♌	2 ♎	22 ♍	24 ♐	7 ♒	10 ♓
5	18 ♑	5 ♓	14 ♓	5 ♉	14 ♊	7 ♌	14 ♍	6 ♏	16 ♐	18 ♑	2 ♓	6 ♈
7	13 ♒	2 ♈	12 ♈	5 ♊	14 ♋	5 ♍	11 ♎	26 ♏	10 ♑	12 ♒	28 ♓	3 ♉
9	9 ♓	29 ♈	10 ♉	1 ♋	12 ♌	1 ♎	6 ♏	20 ♐	4 ♒	7 ♓	25 ♈	2 ♊
11	5 ♈	28 ♉	9 ♊	1 ♌	9 ♍	26 ♎	0 ♐	14 ♑	29 ♒	3 ♈	24 ♉	1 ♋
13	3 ♉	26 ♊	7 ♋	28 ♌	4 ♎	21 ♏	23 ♐	8 ♒	24 ♓	1 ♉	23 ♊	1 ♌
15	1 ♊	25 ♋	5 ♌	25 ♍	29 ♎	14 ♐	17 ♑	3 ♓	21 ♈	29 ♉	23 ♋	1 ♍
17	1 ♋	23 ♌	2 ♍	20 ♎	24 ♏	8 ♑	11 ♒	28 ♈	19 ♉	28 ♊	21 ♌	28 ♍
19	0 ♌	20 ♍	28 ♍	15 ♏	17 ♐	2 ♒	6 ♓	25 ♉	17 ♊	26 ♋	18 ♍	24 ♎
21	29 ♌	16 ♎	24 ♎	9 ♐	11 ♑	26 ♒	26 ♓	22 ♊	15 ♋	24 ♌	15 ♎	19 ♏
23	26 ♍	11 ♏	19 ♏	5 ♑	5 ♒	21 ♓	21 ♈	20 ♋	14 ♌	21 ♍	10 ♏	13 ♐
25	21 ♎	5 ♐	13 ♐	26 ♑	29 ♒	18 ♈	26 ♉	18 ♌	12 ♍	18 ♎	4 ♐	7 ♑
27	15 ♏	28 ♐	21 ♑	21 ♒	25 ♓	16 ♉	25 ♊	18 ♍	9 ♎	13 ♏	28 ♐	1 ♒
29	9 ♐		0 ♒	17 ♓	23 ♈	16 ♊	25 ♋	17 ♎	5 ♏	8 ♐	22 ♑	24 ♒
31	3 ♑		26 ♒		23 ♉		24 ♌	14 ♎		2 ♐		19 ♓

1974	Jan.	Feb.	Mar.	April	May	June	July	Aug.	Sep.	Oct.	Nov.	Dec.
1	1 ♈	20 ♉	0 ♊	23 ♋	2 ♍	24 ♎	29 ♏	15 ♑	29 ♒	2 ♈	20 ♉	26 ♊
3	27 ♈	18 ♊	28 ♊	22 ♌	0 ♎	20 ♏	24 ♐	8 ♒	23 ♓	28 ♈	17 ♊	25 ♋
5	25 ♉	18 ♋	27 ♋	20 ♍	27 ♎	15 ♐	18 ♑	2 ♓	18 ♈	23 ♉	14 ♋	24 ♌
7	25 ♊	18 ♌	27 ♌	18 ♎	24 ♏	9 ♑	11 ♒	26 ♓	13 ♉	20 ♊	13 ♌	22 ♍
9	25 ♋	16 ♍	26 ♍	15 ♏	19 ♐	3 ♒	5 ♓	21 ♈	10 ♊	18 ♋	11 ♍	20 ♎
11	25 ♌	12 ♎	24 ♎	11 ♐	13 ♑	27 ♒	29 ♓	17 ♉	7 ♋	16 ♌	9 ♎	17 ♏
13	24 ♍	7 ♏	20 ♏	5 ♑	7 ♒	21 ♓	24 ♈	14 ♊	6 ♌	15 ♍	7 ♏	13 ♐
15	21 ♎	2 ♐	15 ♐	29 ♑	0 ♓	16 ♈	21 ♉	12 ♋	6 ♍	14 ♎	4 ♐	8 ♑
17	16 ♏	26 ♐	9 ♑	23 ♒	25 ♓	13 ♉	19 ♊	12 ♌	6 ♎	12 ♏	0 ♑	3 ♒
19	10 ♐	20 ♑	3 ♒	17 ♓	18 ♈	11 ♊	19 ♋	12 ♍	4 ♏	7 ♐	24 ♑	20 ♒
21	4 ♑	14 ♒	27 ♒	13 ♈	18 ♉	10 ♋	19 ♌	12 ♎	1 ♐	4 ♑	18 ♒	20 ♓
23	28 ♑	8 ♓	17 ♓	10 ♉	17 ♊	10 ♌	19 ♍	10 ♏	26 ♐	28 ♑	12 ♈	9 ♉
25	21 ♒	4 ♈	11 ♈	7 ♊	16 ♋	10 ♍	17 ♎	5 ♐	20 ♑	22 ♒	6 ♈	9 ♊
27	16 ♓	4 ♉	14 ♉	6 ♋	15 ♌	7 ♎	14 ♏	0 ♑	14 ♒	16 ♓	2 ♉	6 ♋
29	11 ♈		11 ♊	4 ♌	13 ♍	4 ♏	9 ♐	24 ♑	8 ♓	11 ♈	28 ♉	6 ♌
31	7 ♉		9 ♋		11 ♎		3 ♑	17 ♒		7 ♉		4 ♌

MOON   Greenwich Mean Midnight (0 h. 0 m.)   1975-1976

1975	Jan.	Feb.	Mar.	April	May	June	July	Aug.	Sep.	Oct.	Nov.	Dec.
1	19 ♌	13 ♎	21 ♎	11 ♐	15 ♑	29 ♒	1 ♈	15 ♉	2 ♋	9 ♌	3 ♎	11 ♏
3	18 ♍	10 ♏	19 ♏	7 ♑	9 ♒	23 ♓	25 ♈	17 ♊	1 ♌	9 ♍	2 ♏	10 ♐
5	17 ♎	6 ♐	16 ♐	1 ♒	3 ♓	17 ♈	20 ♉	8 ♋	0 ♍	9 ♎	2 ♐	7 ♑
7	13 ♏	1 ♑	10 ♑	25 ♒	27 ♓	12 ♉	16 ♊	7 ♌	1 ♎	9 ♏	0 ♑	4 ♒
9	9 ♐	25 ♑	4 ♒	19 ♓	21 ♈	8 ♊	14 ♋	7 ♍	1 ♏	8 ♐	26 ♑	29 ♒
11	4 ♑	19 ♒	28 ♒	13 ♈	16 ♉	5 ♋	13 ♌	7 ♎	29 ♏	5 ♑	21 ♒	23 ♓
13	28 ♑	13 ♓	22 ♓	7 ♉	12 ♊	3 ♌	12 ♍	6 ♏	26 ♐	0 ♒	15 ♓	16 ♈
15	22 ♒	7 ♈	16 ♈	3 ♊	9 ♋	2 ♍	11 ♎	3 ♐	21 ♑	24 ♒	8 ♈	10 ♉
17	16 ♓	1 ♉	10 ♉	29 ♊	7 ♌	0 ♎	9 ♏	29 ♐	15 ♒	18 ♓	2 ♉	5 ♊
19	10 ♈	26 ♉	5 ♊	26 ♋	5 ♍	28 ♎	6 ♐	24 ♑	9 ♓	12 ♈	27 ♉	1 ♋
21	4 ♉	22 ♊	2 ♋	24 ♌	4 ♎	26 ♏	2 ♑	18 ♒	3 ♈	6 ♉	22 ♊	28 ♋
23	0 ♊	21 ♋	29 ♋	23 ♍	2 ♏	22 ♐	27 ♑	12 ♓	27 ♈	0 ♊	18 ♋	26 ♌
25	28 ♊	21 ♌	29 ♌	23 ♎	0 ♐	18 ♑	21 ♒	6 ♈	21 ♉	25 ♊	15 ♌	24 ♍
27	27 ♋	21 ♍	29 ♍	22 ♏	27 ♐	13 ♒	15 ♓	0 ♉	15 ♊	21 ♋	13 ♍	23 ♎
29	28 ♌		29 ♎	19 ♐	23 ♑	7 ♓	9 ♈	24 ♉	12 ♋	19 ♌	12 ♎	21 ♏
31	28 ♍		28 ♏		17 ♒		3 ♉	19 ♊		18 ♍		18 ♐

| | | | | | | | | | | 1 Jan. 1976 | | 2 ♑ |

TYPICAL CALCULATIONS

Required the Moon position for midnight (0 h. 0 m.) 6 January 1960.

From 0 h. 0 m. on 5 January to 0 h. 0 m. on 6 January = 24 hours.

This is one half of the period shown in the Table above, which covers the 48 hours from 5 to 7 January.

Therefore, motion from 5 to 7 January = 29° –5° = 24° in 48 hours.

In 24 hours this = 12°. Add this to 5 ♈ and we have 17 ♈.

Required the Moon position for noon (12 h. 0 m.) 6 January 1960.

From 0 h. 0 m. on 5 January to 12 h. 0 m. on 6 January = 36 hours.

Motion being 24° in 48 hours, we need to obtain $\frac{36}{48}$ths of 24°.

$\frac{36}{48} \times 24 = \frac{3}{4} \times 24 = 18°$. Add this to 5 ♈ and we have 23 ♈.

NOTES

NOTES

MERCURY 1900-1905

(To nearest degree at Midnight (o h. o m.) G.M.T.)

1900

- Jan. 1 19♐
- 11 3♑
- 21 18♑
- 31 4♒
- Feb. 10 21♒
- 20 9♓
- Mar. 2 27♓
- 12 8♈
- 16 9♈R
- 22 6♈R
- Apr. 1 29♓R
- 8 27♓D
- 11 27♓
- 21 3♈
- May 1 15♈
- 11 0♉
- 21 19♉
- 31 10♊
- June 10 1♋
- 20 19♋
- 30 3♌
- July 10 12♌
- 19 15♌R
- 20 15♌R
- 30 10♌R
- Aug. 9 4♌R
- 11 4♌D
- 19 7♌
- 29 21♌
- Sep. 8 10♍
- 18 28♍
- 28 15♎
- Oct. 8 1♏
- 18 15♏
- 28 28♏
- Nov. 7 6♐
- 10 6♐R
- 17 2♐R
- 27 21♏R
- 29 20♏D
- Dec. 7 24♐
- 17 6♐
- 27 20♐

1901

- Jan. 1 28♐
- 11 13♑
- 21 0♒
- 31 17♒
- Feb. 10 4♓
- 20 19♓
- 27 22♓R
- Mar. 2 21♓R
- 12 12♓R
- 21 8♓D
- 22 8♓
- Apr. 1 13♓
- 11 24♓
- 21 8♈
- May 1 25♈
- 11 15♉
- 21 7♊
- 31 27♊
- June 10 12♋
- 20 22♋
- 30 26♋
- July 1 26♋R
- 10 23♋R
- 20 17♋R
- 25 16♋D
- 30 18♋
- Aug. 9 28♋
- 19 16♌
- 29 6♍
- Sep. 8 24♍
- 18 11♎
- 28 26♎
- Oct. 8 9♏
- 18 18♏
- 25 20♏R
- 28 20♏R
- Nov. 7 9♏R
- 14 4♏D
- 17 5♏
- 27 16♏
- Dec. 7 0♐
- 17 15♐
- 27 1♑

1902

- Jan. 1 9♑
- 11 25♑
- 21 12♒
- 31 28♒
- Feb. 10 5♓R
- 20 28♓R
- Mar. 2 21♒R
- 4 20♒D
- 12 24♒
- 22 3♓
- Apr. 1 17♓
- 11 3♈
- 21 21♈
- May 1 12♉
- 11 3♊
- 21 20♊
- 31 1♋
- June 10 6♋
- 12 6♋R
- 20 4♋R
- 30 28♊R
- July 6 27♊D
- 10 28♊
- 20 7♋
- 30 22♋
- Aug. 9 13♌
- 19 2♍
- 29 20♍
- Sep. 18 19♎
- 28 0♏
- Oct. 8 4♏R
- 18 27♎R
- 28 19♎R
- 29 19♎D
- Nov. 7 25♎
- 17 11♏
- 27 25♏
- Dec. 7 11♐
- 17 27♐
- 27 12♑

1903

- Jan. 1 21♑
- 11 6♒
- 21 18♒
- 25 19♒R
- 31 16♒R
- 14 4♒D
- 20 5♒
- Mar. 2 13♒
- 12 26♒
- Apr. 1 28♓
- 11 18♈
- 21 9♉
- May 1 27♉
- 11 10♊
- 21 16♊
- 22 16♊R
- 31 14♊R
- June 10 9♊R
- 15 8♊D
- 20 8♊
- 30 15♊
- July 10 29♊
- 20 18♋
- 30 9♌
- Aug. 9 29♌
- 19 15♍
- 29 0♎
- Sep. 8 11♎
- 18 18♎
- 21 18♎R
- 28 15♎R
- Oct. 8 5♎R
- 13 3♎D
- 18 5♎
- 28 18♎
- Nov. 7 5♏
- 17 21♏
- 27 7♐
- Dec. 7 22♐
- 17 8♑
- 27 22♑

1904

- Jan. 1 29♑
- 8 3♒R
- 11 2♒R
- 21 21♑R
- 29 17♑D
- Feb. 10 24♑
- Mar. 1 20♒
- 11 6♒
- 21 24♒
- 31 14♈
- Apr. 10 19♉
- 20 19♉
- 30 26♉
- May 2 26♉R
- 10 24♉R
- 20 19♉R
- 26 17♉D
- 30 18♉
- June 9 24♉
- 19 7♊
- 29 24♊
- July 9 15♋
- 19 6♌
- 29 24♌
- Aug. 8 10♍
- 18 22♍
- 28 0♎
- Sep. 2 1♎R
- 7 0♎R
- 17 22♍R
- 25 17♍D
- 27 17♍
- Oct. 7 27♍
- 17 13♎
- 27 0♏
- Nov. 6 17♏
- 16 2♐
- 26 17♐
- Dec. 6 2♑
- 16 14♑
- 22 17♑R
- 26 16♑R

1905

- Jan. 1 8♑R
- 11 1♑D
- 21 6♑
- 31 17♑
- Feb. 10 1♒
- Mar. 2 4♓
- 22 12♈
- Apr. 1 29♈
- 11 7♉
- 13 7♉R
- 21 5♉R
- May 1 29♈R
- 7 27♈D
- 11 28♈
- 21 4♉
- 31 16♉
- June 10 2♊
- 20 23♊
- 30 14♋
- July 10 4♌
- 20 20♌
- Aug. 9 12♍
- 16 14♍R
- 19 14♍R
- 29 7♍R
- Sep. 8 1♍D
- 18 7♍
- Oct. 8 11♎
- 18 28♎
- 28 14♏
- Nov. 7 29♏
- 17 13♐
- 27 26♐
- Dec. 7 1♑R
- 17 22♐R
- 27 15♐D

R = Retrograde. D = Direct. (See page 20.)

MERCURY   1906-1911

(To nearest degree at Midnight (o h. o m.) G.M.T.)

1906
- Jan. 1 17♐
- 11 28♐
- 21 11♑
- 31 26♑
- Feb. 10 12♒
- 20 0♓
- Mar. 2 19♓
- 12 7♈
- 22 18♈
- 27 19♈R
- Apr. 1 17♈R
- 11 10♈R
- 19 8♈D
- 21 8♈
- May 1 13♈
- 11 24♈
- 21 9♉
- 31 28♉
- Jun. 10 20♊
- 20 11♊
- 30 29♊
- July 10 13♌
- 20 22♌
- 30 26♌R
- Aug. 9 22♌R
- 19 15♌R
- 21 14♌D
- 29 17♌
- Sep. 8 0♍
- 18 19♍
- 28 7♎
- Oct. 8 24♎
- 18 9♏
- 28 24♏
- Nov. 7 6♐
- 17 15♐
- 21 15♐R
- 27 11♐R
- Dec. 7 0♐R
- 10 29♏D
- 17 3♐
- 27 14♐

1907
- Jan. 1 21♐
- 11 6♑
- 21 22♑
- 31 8♒
- Feb. 10 26♒
- 20 14♓
- Mar. 2 28♓
- 9 2♈R
- 12 2♈R
- 22 23♓R
- Apr. 1 18♓D
- 11 23♓
- 21 3♈
- May 1 17♈
- 21 25♉
- 31 16♊
- Jun. 10 6♋
- 20 21♋
- 30 2♌
- July 10 7♌
- 20 5♌R
- Aug. 5 26♋D
- 9 27♋
- 19 8♌
- 29 26♌
- Sep. 8 15♍
- 18 3♎
- 28 19♎
- Oct. 8 4♏
- 18 17♏
- 28 27♏
- Nov. 4 0♐R
- 7 29♏R
- 17 18♏R
- 24 14♏D
- 27 14♏
- Dec. 7 24♏
- 17 8♐
- 27 24♐

1908
- Jan. 1 1♑
- 11 17♑
- 21 4♒
- 31 21♒
- Feb. 10 7♓
- 21 15♓R
- Mar. 11 1♓R
- 14 1♓R
- 21 3♓
- 31 12♓
- Apr. 10 20♓
- 20 12♈
- 30 0♉
- May 10 22♉
- 20 13♊
- 30 1♋
- Jun. 9 12♋
- 19 17♋
- 22 18♋R
- 29 16♋R
- July 9 10♋R
- 16 8♋D
- 19 9♋
- 29 16♋
- Aug. 8 2♌
- 18 22♌
- 28 11♍
- Sep. 7 29♍
- 17 14♎
- 27 28♎
- Oct. 7 14♏
- 17 14♏
- 18 14♏R
- 27 7♏R
- Nov. 6 28♏R
- 7 28♏D
- 16 4♐
- 26 18♐
- Dec. 6 4♐
- 16 19♐
- 26 5♑

1909
- Jan. 1 15♑
- 11 1♒
- 21 17♒
- 31 28♒
- Feb. 3 29♒R
- 10 24♒R
- 20 14♒R
- 24 13♒D
- Mar. 2 15♒
- 12 23♒
- 22 6♓
- Apr. 1 21♓
- 11 9♈
- 21 29♈
- May 1 20♉
- 11 9♊
- 21 22♊
- 31 27♊
- Jun. 3 28♊R
- 10 26♊R
- 20 21♊R
- 27 19♊D
- 30 19♊
- July 10 26♊
- 20 10♋
- 30 0♌
- Aug. 9 21♌
- 19 9♍
- 29 26♍
- Sep. 8 10♎
- 18 21♎
- 28 27♎
- Oct. 8 23♎R
- 18 13♎R
- 22 12♎D
- Nov. 7 15♏
- 17 15♏
- 27 1♐
- Dec. 7 16♐
- 17 2♑
- 27 18♑

1910
- Jan. 1 26♑
- 11 9♒
- 18 12♒R
- 21 11♒R
- 31 0♒R
- Feb. 8 27♑D
- 10 27♑
- 20 4♒
- Mar. 2 16♒
- 12 0♓
- 22 17♓
- Apr. 1 5♈
- 11 26♈
- 21 16♉
- May 1 0♊
- 11 7♊
- 15 8♊R
- 21 6♊R
- 31 1♊R
- Jun. 8 29♉D
- 10 29♉
- 20 5♊
- 30 18♊
- July 10 6♋
- 20 27♋
- 30 17♌
- Aug. 9 5♍
- 19 20♍
- 29 2♎
- Sep. 8 10♎
- 14 11♎R
- 18 10♎R
- 28 1♎R
- Oct. 6 26♍D
- 8 27♍
- 18 8♎
- 28 23♎
- Nov. 7 10♏
- 17 26♏
- 27 12♐
- Dec. 7 27♐
- 17 12♑
- 27 24♑

1911
- Jan. 1 26♑
- 2 26♑R
- 11 18♑R
- 21 10♑R
- 22 10♑D
- Feb. 10 26♑
- 20 10♒
- Mar. 2 25♒
- 12 13♓
- 22 2♈
- Apr. 1 22♈
- 11 9♉
- 21 18♉
- May 1 17♉R
- 11 11♉R
- 19 9♉D
- 21 9♉
- 31 14♉
- Jun. 10 26♉
- 20 12♊
- 30 2♋
- July 10 24♋
- 20 13♌
- 30 29♌
- Aug. 9 12♍
- 19 21♍
- 27 24♍R
- 29 24♍R
- Sep. 8 17♍R
- 18 10♍R
- 19 10♍D
- 28 16♍
- Oct. 8 2♎
- 18 19♎
- 28 6♏
- Nov. 7 22♏
- 17 7♐
- 27 22♐
- Dec. 5 5♑
- 16 10♑R
- 17 10♑R
- 27 1♑R

R = Retrograde.   D = Direct.   (See page 20.)

MERCURY   1912-1917

(To nearest degree at Midnight (o h. o m.) G.M.T.)

1912

- Jan. 1 — 26 ♐ R
- 5 — 24 ♐ D
- 11 — 26 ♐
- 21 — 6 ♑
- 31 — 20 ♑
- Feb. 10 — 4 ♒
- 20 — 21 ♒
- Mar. 1 — 9 ♓
- 11 — 28 ♓
- 21 — 16 ♈
- 31 — 28 ♈
- Apr. 6 — 0 ♉ R
- 10 — 29 ♈ R
- 20 — 22 ♈ R
- 29 — 19 ♈ D
- 30 — 19 ♈
- May 10 — 23 ♈
- 20 — 4 ♉
- 30 — 19 ♉
- Jun. 9 — 8 ♊
- 19 — 29 ♊
- 29 — 21 ♋
- July 9 — 8 ♌
- 19 — 22 ♌
- 29 — 2 ♍
- Aug. 8 — 7 ♍
- 9 — 27 ♍ R
- 18 — 3 ♍ R
- 28 — 25 ♌ R
- Sep. 1 — 24 ♌ D
- 7 — 26 ♌
- 17 — 10 ♍
- 27 — 28 ♍
- Oct. 7 — 15 ♎
- 17 — 2 ♏
- 27 — 17 ♏
- Nov. 6 — 2 ♐
- 16 — 15 ♐
- 26 — 24 ♐
- 29 — 25 ♐ R
- Dec. 6 — 20 ♐ R
- 16 — 9 ♐ R
- 19 — 8 ♐ D
- 26 — 12 ♐

1913

- Jan. 1 — 18 ♐
- 11 — 1 ♑
- 21 — 16 ♑
- 31 — 2 ♒
- Feb. 10 — 18 ♒
- 20 — 7 ♓
- Mar. 2 — 25 ♓
- 12 — 9 ♈
- 19 — 12 ♈ R
- 22 — 11 ♈ R
- Apr. 1 — 4 ♈ R
- 11 — 0 ♈ D
- 21 — 4 ♈
- May 1 — 14 ♈
- 11 — 28 ♈
- 21 — 16 ♉
- 31 — 6 ♊
- Jun. 10 — 28 ♊
- 20 — 17 ♋
- 30 — 2 ♌
- July 10 — 13 ♌
- 20 — 18 ♌
- 22 — 18 ♌ R
- 30 — 15 ♌ R
- Aug. 9 — 8 ♌ R
- 14 — 7 ♌ D
- 19 — 8 ♌
- 29 — 18 ♌
- Sep. 8 — 7 ♍
- 18 — 26 ♍
- 28 — 13 ♎
- Oct. 8 — 29 ♎
- 18 — 14 ♏
- 28 — 27 ♏
- Nov. 7 — 7 ♐
- 13 — 9 ♐ R
- 17 — 7 ♐ R
- 26 — 26 ♏ R
- Dec. 3 — 23 ♏ D
- 7 — 24 ♏
- 17 — 4 ♐
- 27 — 19 ♐

1914

- Jan. 1 — 26 ♐
- 11 — 11 ♑
- 21 — 27 ♑
- 31 — 14 ♒
- Feb. 10 — 2 ♓
- 20 — 18 ♓
- Mar. 1 — 25 ♓ R
- 2 — 25 ♓ R
- 12 — 17 ♓ R
- 22 — 11 ♓ R
- 24 — 11 ♓ D
- Apr. 1 — 14 ♓
- 11 — 23 ♓
- 21 — 6 ♈
- May 1 — 23 ♈
- 11 — 12 ♉
- 21 — 3 ♊
- 31 — 24 ♊
- Jun. 10 — 11 ♋
- 20 — 23 ♋
- 30 — 29 ♋
- July 4 — 29 ♋ R
- 10 — 27 ♋ R
- 20 — 21 ♋ R
- 27 — 19 ♋ D
- 30 — 19 ♋
- Aug. 9 — 22 ♋
- 29 — 3 ♍
- Sep. 8 — 22 ♍
- 18 — 9 ♎
- 28 — 24 ♎
- Oct. 8 — 8 ♏
- 18 — 18 ♏
- 28 — 23 ♏ R
- Nov. 7 — 15 ♏ R
- 7 — 7 ♏ D
- 27 — 14 ♏
- Dec. 7 — 28 ♏
- 17 — 13 ♐
- 27 — 29 ♐

1915

- Jan. 1 — 6 ♑
- 11 — 23 ♑
- 21 — 10 ♒
- 31 — 26 ♒
- Feb. 10 — 7 ♓
- 13 — 8 ♓ R
- 20 — 4 ♓ R
- Mar. 2 — 25 ♒ R
- 6 — 23 ♒ D
- 12 — 25 ♒
- 22 — 3 ♓
- Apr. 1 — 15 ♓
- 11 — 0 ♈
- 21 — 18 ♈
- May 1 — 9 ♉
- 11 — 0 ♊
- 21 — 18 ♊
- 31 — 2 ♋
- Jun. 10 — 9 ♋
- 14 — 9 ♋ R
- 20 — 8 ♋ R
- 30 — 3 ♋ R
- July 8 — 0 ♋ D
- 10 — 0 ♋
- 20 — 6 ♋
- 30 — 20 ♋
- Aug. 9 — 9 ♌
- 19 — 0 ♍
- 29 — 18 ♍
- Sep. 8 — 4 ♎
- 18 — 18 ♎
- 28 — 0 ♏
- Oct. 8 — 7 ♏
- 10 — 7 ♏ R
- 18 — 3 ♏ R
- 28 — 22 ♎ R
- 31 — 21 ♎ D
- Nov. 7 — 25 ♎
- 17 — 8 ♏
- 27 — 23 ♏
- Dec. 7 — 9 ♐
- 17 — 25 ♐
- 27 — 10 ♑

1916

- Jan. 1 — 18 ♑
- 11 — 5 ♒
- 21 — 18 ♒
- 31 — 21 ♒ R
- Feb. 10 — 10 ♒ R
- 18 — 6 ♒ D
- 20 — 7 ♒
- Mar. 1 — 13 ♒
- 11 — 25 ♒
- 21 — 9 ♓
- 31 — 26 ♓
- Apr. 10 — 15 ♈
- 20 — 5 ♉
- 30 — 25 ♉
- May 10 — 10 ♊
- 20 — 18 ♊
- 25 — 19 ♊ R
- 30 — 18 ♊ R
- Jun. 9 — 13 ♊ R
- 18 — 11 ♊ D
- 19 — 11 ♊
- 29 — 15 ♊
- July 9 — 27 ♊
- 19 — 16 ♋
- 29 — 6 ♌
- Aug. 8 — 26 ♌
- 18 — 14 ♍
- 28 — 28 ♍
- Sep. 7 — 11 ♎
- 17 — 19 ♎
- 23 — 21 ♎ R
- 27 — 20 ♎ R
- Oct. 7 — 10 ♎ R
- 14 — 5 ♎ D
- 17 — 6 ♎
- 27 — 17 ♎
- Nov. 6 — 2 ♏
- 16 — 19 ♏
- 26 — 4 ♐
- Dec. 6 — 20 ♐
- 16 — 6 ♑
- 26 — 21 ♑

1917

- Jan. 1 — 29 ♑
- 10 — 6 ♒ R
- 11 — 6 ♒ R
- 31 — 20 ♑ D
- Feb. 10 — 25 ♑
- 20 — 6 ♒
- Mar. 2 — 20 ♒
- 12 — 6 ♓
- 22 — 23 ♓
- Apr. 1 — 13 ♈
- 11 — 3 ♉
- 21 — 20 ♉
- May 1 — 29 ♉
- 6 — 29 ♉ R
- 11 — 28 ♉ R
- 21 — 23 ♉ R
- 30 — 21 ♉ D
- 31 — 21 ♉
- Jun. 10 — 25 ♉
- 20 — 7 ♊
- 30 — 23 ♊
- July 10 — 14 ♋
- 20 — 5 ♌
- 30 — 25 ♌
- Aug. 9 — 9 ♍
- 19 — 22 ♍
- 29 — 1 ♎
- Sep. 6 — 4 ♎ R
- 8 — 4 ♎ R
- 18 — 26 ♍ R
- 28 — 20 ♍ D
- Oct. 8 — 27 ♍
- 18 — 13 ♎
- 28 — 0 ♏
- Nov. 7 — 16 ♏
- 17 — 2 ♐
- 27 — 17 ♐
- Dec. 7 — 2 ♑
- 17 — 15 ♑
- 25 — 20 ♑ R
- 27 — 19 ♑ R

R = Retrograde.   D = Direct.   (See page 20.)

MERCURY 1918-1923

(To nearest degree at Midnight (o h. o m.) G.M.T.)

1918	1919	1920	1921	1922	1923
Jan. 1 15♑R	Jan. 1 18♐	Jan. 1 20♐	Jan. 1 1♑	Jan. 1 12♑	Jan. 1 24♑
11 4♑R	11 27♐	11 4♑	11 17♑	11 29♑	11 8♒
14 3♑D	21 10♑	21 19♑	21 3♒	21 15♒	20 15♒R
21 6♑	31 24♑	31 6♒	31 21♒	31 29♒	31 6♒R
31 16♑	Feb. 10 10♒	Feb. 10 23♒	Feb. 10 7♓	Feb. 5 1♓R	Feb. 10 29♑D
Feb. 10 29♑	20 27♒	Mar. 1 28♓	20 17♓	10 29♒R	20 4♒
20 15♒	Mar. 2 16♓	11 5♈R	22 18♓R	20 19♒R	Mar. 2 15♒
Mar. 2 1♓	12 5♈	21 29♈R	Mar. 2 13♓R	27 16♒D	12 28♒
12 20♓	22 19♈	31 22♈R	12 5♓R	Mar. 2 16♒	22 14♓
22 9♈	29 22♈R	Apr. 3 22♓D	16 3♓D	12 23♒	Apr. 1 2♈
Apr. 1 28♈	Apr. 1 22♈R	10 24♓	22 5♓	Apr. 1 19♓	11 23♈
11 9♉	11 15♈R	20 2♈	Apr. 1 13♓	11 7♈	21 13♉
17 10♉R	21 11♈D	30 15♈	11 26♓	21 22♈	May 1 0Π
21 10♉R	May 1 14♈	May 10 2♉	21 11♈	May 1 17♉	11 9Π
May 1 3♉R	11 23♈	20 21♉	May 1 29♈	11 7Π	18 11ΠR
10 0♉D	21 8♉	30 13Π	11 20♉	21 22Π	21 10ΠR
11 0♉	31 25♉	Jun. 9 4♋	21 12Π	31 29Π	31 6ΠR
21 5♉	Jun. 10 16Π	19 20♋	31 29Π	Jun. 6 1♋R	Jun. 10 2ΠD
31 15♉	20 8♋	29 3♌	Jun. 10 13♋	10 0♋R	20 6Π
Jun. 10 0Π	30 27♋	July 9 9♌	20 20♋	20 25ΠR	30 16Π
20 19Π	July 10 12♌	14 10♌R	25 21♋R	22 22ΠD	July 10 3♋
30 11♋	20 23♌	19 9♌R	30 20♌R	July 10 26Π	20 24♋
July 10 1♌	30 29♌	29 3♌R	July 10 14♌R	20 8♋	30 14♌
20 18♌	Aug. 1 29♌R	Aug. 7 29♋R	19 11♋D	30 28♋	Aug. 9 2♍
30 2♍	9 27♌R	8 29♋D	20 11♋	Aug. 9 18♌	19 18♍
Aug. 9 12♍R	19 19♌R	18 6♌	30 17♋	19 7♍	29 1♎
19 17♍R	25 17♌D	28 23♌	Aug. 9 1♌	29 23♍	Sep. 8 10♎
29 13♍R	29 17♌	Sep. 7 12♍	19 21♌	Sep. 9 9♎	16 14♎R
Sep. 8 4♍R	Sep. 8 28♌	17 1♎	29 11♍	18 20♎	18 14♎R
12 3♍D	18 16♍	27 17♎	Sep. 8 28♍	28 29♎	28 5♎R
18 6♍	28 4♎	Oct. 7 2♏	18 14♎	Oct. 3 0♏R	Oct. 8 29♍D
28 21♍	Oct. 8 22♎	17 16♏	28 28♎	8 29♎R	18 6♎
Oct. 8 8♎	18 7♏	27 27♏	Oct. 8 10♏	18 18♎R	28 21♎
18 26♎	28 22♏	Nov. 6 2♐R	18 16♏	24 15♎D	Nov. 7 8♏
28 12♏	Nov. 7 5♐	16 24♏R	20 16♏R	Nov. 7 27♎	17 24♏
Nov. 7 27♏	17 16♐	26 16♏D	28 12♏R	17 13♏	27 10♐
17 12♐	23 18♐R	Dec. 6 23♏	Nov. 7 1♏R	27 29♏	Dec. 7 25♐
27 25♐	27 17♐R	16 7♐	9 0♏D	Dec. 7 14♐	17 11♑
Dec. 7 3♑	Dec. 7 4♐R	26 22♐	17 5♏	17 0♑	27 24♑
9 4♑R	13 2♐D		27 18♏	27 16♑	
17 28♐R	17 3♐		Dec. 7 3♐		
27 18♐R	27 13♐		17 18♐		
29 18♐D			27 4♑		

R = Retrograde.   D = Direct.   (See page 20.)

MERCURY   1918-1923

MERCURY   1924-1929

(To nearest degree at Midnight (0 h. 0 m.) G.M.T.)

1924	1925	1926	1927	1928	1929
Jan. 1 28♑	Jan. 1 0♑R	Jan. 1 17♐	Jan. 1 24♐	Jan. 1 5♑	Jan. 1 18♑
4 29♑R	7 27♐D	11 0♑	11 9♑	11 21♑	11 4♒
11 25♑R	11 28♐	21 14♑	21 25♑	21 8♒	21 19♒
21 14♑R	21 7♑	31 29♑	31 12♒	31 25♒	29 24♒R
24 13♑D	31 19♑	Feb. 10 16♒	Feb. 10 0♓	Feb. 10 9♓	31 24♒R
31 15♑	Feb. 10 4♒	20 4♓	20 17♓	16 11♓R	Feb. 10 14♒R
Feb. 10 25♑	20 20♒	Mar. 2 22♓	Mar. 2 27♓	20 9♓R	20 9♒D
20 8♒	Mar. 2 8♓	12 9♈	4 27♓R	Mar. 1 29♒R	Mar. 2 14♒
Mar. 1 23♒	12 27♓	22 15♈R	12 24♓R	9 26♒D	12 24♒
11 10♓	22 16♈	Apr. 1 9♈R	22 15♓R	11 26♒	22 9♓
21 29♓	Apr. 1 29♈	11 3♈	27 14♓D	31 14♓	Apr. 1 25♓
31 19♈	8 3♉R	16 3♈D	Apr. 1 15♓	Apr. 10 28♓	11 15♈
Apr. 10 7♉	11 2♉R	21 5♈	11 22♓	20 15♈	21 5♉
20 19♉	21 26♈R	May 1 13♈	21 5♈	30 5♉	May 1 25♉
27 21♉R	May 1 22♈R	11 26♈	May 1 20♈	May 10 27♉	11 11♊
30 21♉R	3 22♈D	21 13♉	11 9♉	20 16♊	21 20♊
May 10 16♉R	11 25♈	31 3♊	21 1♊	Jun. 9 10♋	28 22♊R
20 12♉R	21 4♉	Jun. 10 25♊	31 21♊	17 13♋R	31 22♊R
21 12♉D	31 18♉	20 15♋	Jun. 10 9♋	19 12♋R	Jun. 10 18♊R
30 15♉	Jun. 10 7♊	30 1♌	20 23♋	29 8♋R	20 14♊R
Jun. 9 24♉	20 28♊	July 10 13♌	30 1♌	July 9 3♋R	21 14♊D
19 9♊	30 19♋	20 20♌	July 6 2♌R	11 3♋D	30 17♊
29 29♊	July 10 7♌	25 21♌R	10 2♌R	19 7♋	July 10 27♊
July 9 20♋	20 22♌	30 20♌R	20 26♋R	29 18♋	20 14♋
19 10♌	30 3♍	Aug. 9 12♌R	31 22♋D	Aug. 8 6♌	30 5♌
29 27♌	Aug. 9 9♍	18 10♌D	Aug. 9 26♋	18 27♌	Aug. 9 25♌
Aug. 8 11♍	19 7♍R	19 10♌	19 11♌	28 15♍	19 13♍
18 22♍	29 29♌R	29 17♌	29 0♍	Sep. 7 2♎	29 28♍
28 27♍	Sep. 4 26♌D	Sep. 8 4♍	Sep. 8 19♍	17 17♎	Sep. 8 11♎
29 27♍R	8 27♌	18 23♍	18 7♎	27 29♎	18 20♎
Sep. 7 23♍R	18 9♍	28 11♎	28 22♎	Oct. 7 8♏	26 23♎R
17 14♍R	28 27♍	Oct. 8 27♎	Oct. 8 6♏	13 10♏R	Oct. 8 15♎R
21 13♍D	Oct. 8 15♎	18 12♏	18 19♏	17 8♏R	17 8♎R
27 16♍	18 1♏	28 26♏	28 25♏	27 27♎R	18 8♎D
Oct. 7 0♎	28 17♏	Nov. 7 7♐	Nov. 7 21♏R	Nov. 2 24♎D	Nov. 7 2♏
17 17♎	Nov. 7 2♐	17 11♐R	17 11♏R	6 25♎	17 18♏
27 4♏	17 15♐	27 2♐R	20 10♏D	16 7♏	27 4♐
Nov. 6 20♏	27 25♐	Dec. 5 25♏D	27 14♏	26 21♏	Dec. 7 19♐
16 5♐	Dec. 2 27♐R	7 25♏	Dec. 7 26♏	Dec. 6 7♐	17 5♑
26 20♐	7 25♐R	17 3♐	17 11♐	16 22♐	27 21♑
Dec. 6 4♑	17 13♐R	27 17♐	27 27♐	26 8♑	
16 13♑	22 11♐D				
18 13♑R	27 13♐				
26 7♑R					

R = Retrograde.   D = Direct.   (See page 20.)

MERCURY
1930-1935

(To nearest degree at Midnight (0 h. 0 m.) G.M.T.)

1930

Jan.	1	28♑
	11	8♒
	13	8♒R
	21	2♒R
	31	23♑R
Feb.	3	22♑D
	10	25♑
	20	5♒
Mar.	2	18♒
	12	3♓
	22	21♓
Apr.	1	10♈
	11	1♉
	21	19♉
May	1	0♊
	9	3♊R
	11	2♊R
	21	28♉R
	31	24♉R
Jun.	3	24♉D
	10	26♉
	20	6♊
	30	21♊
July	10	11♋
	20	2♌
	30	21♌
Aug.	9	8♍
	19	22♍
	29	2♎
Sep.	8	7♎
	9	7♎R
	18	2♎R
	28	23♍R
Oct.	1	22♍D
	8	25♍
	18	11♎
	28	28♎
Nov.	7	15♏
	17	29♏
	27	15♐
Dec.	7	0♑
	17	14♑
	27	22♑
	28	22♑R

1931

Jan.	1	21♑R
	11	9♑R
	17	6♑D
	21	7♑
	31	15♑
Feb.	10	28♑
	20	13♒
Mar.	2	29♒
	12	17♓
	22	6♈
Apr.	1	26♈
	11	9♉
	20	13♉R
	21	13♉R
May	1	9♉R
	11	4♉R
	14	4♉D
	31	14♉
Jun.	10	28♉
	20	16♊
	30	7♋
July	10	28♋
	20	16♌
	30	1♍
Aug.	9	13♍
	23	20♍R
	29	18♍R
Sep.	8	9♍R
	15	6♍D
	18	7♍
	28	18♍
Oct.	8	6♎
	18	23♎
	28	10♏
Nov.	7	25♏
	17	10♐
	27	24♐
Dec.	7	5♑
	12	6♑R
	17	6♑R
	27	22♐R

1932

Jan.	1	20♐R
	2	20♐D
	11	26♐
	21	8♑
	31	22♑
Feb.	10	8♒
	20	25♒
Mar.	1	13♓
	11	2♈
	21	18♈
	31	25♈
Apr.	2	25♈R
	10	21♈R
	20	14♈R
	24	14♈D
	30	15♈
May	10	23♈
	20	6♉
	30	22♉
Jun.	9	13♊
	19	4♋
	29	24♋
July	9	10♌
	19	23♌
	29	1♍
Aug.	4	2♍R
	8	1♍R
	18	24♌R
	28	19♌D
Sep.	7	27♌
	17	13♍
	27	2♎
Oct.	7	19♎
	17	5♏
	27	20♏
Nov.	6	4♐
	16	16♐
	25	21♐R
	26	20♐R
Dec.	6	11♐R
	15	4♐D
	16	5♐
	26	12♐

1933

Jan.	1	20♐
	11	4♑
	21	19♑
	31	5♒
Feb.	10	22♒
	20	11♓
Mar.	2	28♓
	12	7♈
	14	7♈R
	22	3♈R
Apr.	1	26♈R
	6	25♈D
	11	26♈
	21	3♈
May	1	15♈
	11	1♉
	21	20♉
	31	12♊
Jun.	10	3♋
	20	20♋
	30	3♌
July	10	12♌
	17	13♌R
	20	13♌R
	30	7♌R
Aug.	9	2♌R
	10	2♌D
	19	7♌
	29	22♌
Sep.	8	11♍
	18	0♎
	28	17♎
Oct.	8	2♏
	18	16♏
	28	28♏
Nov.	7	5♐
	9	5♐R
	17	29♏R
	27	19♏R
	29	19♏D
Dec.	7	24♏
	17	7♐
	27	21♐

1934

Jan.	1	29♐
	11	14♑
	21	1♒
	31	18♒
Feb.	10	6♓
	20	19♓
	26	20♓R
Mar.	2	18♓R
	12	9♓R
	20	6♓D
	22	7♓
Apr.	1	13♓
	11	24♓
	21	9♈
May	1	27♈
	11	17♉
	21	9♊
	31	28♊
Jun.	10	12♋
	20	21♋
	29	24♋R
	30	24♋R
July	10	19♋R
	20	14♋D
	23	14♋D
	30	17♋
Aug.	9	29♋
	19	18♌
	29	8♍
Sep.	8	26♍
	18	12♎
	28	27♎
Oct.	8	9♏
	18	18♏
	24	19♏R
	28	17♏R
Nov.	7	6♏R
	12	3♏D
	17	5♏
	27	16♏
Dec.	7	1♐
	17	17♐
	27	2♑

1935

Jan.	1	10♑
	11	27♑
	21	13♒
	31	28♒
Feb.	9	4♓R
	10	4♓R
	20	25♒R
Mar.	2	19♒R
	3	19♒D
	12	23♒
	22	4♓
Apr.	1	17♓
	11	4♈
	21	23♈
May	1	14♉
	11	4♊
	21	21♊
	31	1♋
Jun.	10	4♋R
	20	0♋R
	30	26♊R
July	4	25♊D
	10	27♊
	20	7♋
	30	24♋
Aug.	9	14♌
	19	4♍
	29	21♍
Sep.	8	7♎
	18	20♎
	28	0♏
Oct.	7	3♏
	8	3♏R
	18	24♏R
	28	17♏D
Nov.	7	26♏
	17	11♏
	27	26♏
Dec.	7	12♐
	17	28♐
	27	14♑

R = Retrograde.   D = Direct.   (See page 20.)

MERCURY

(To nearest degree at Midnight (o h. o m.) G.M.T.)

1936	1937	1938	1939	1940	1941
Jan. 1 22♑	Jan. 1 29♑	Jan. 1 5♑R	Jan. 1 17♐	Jan. 1 22♐	Jan. 1 4♑
11 7♒	7 1♒R	10 29♐D	11 28♐	11 7♑	11 20♑
21 17♒	11 29♑R	11 29♐	21 12♑	21 23♑	21 7♒
24 18♒R	21 18♑R	21 6♑	31 27♑	31 9♒	31 24♒
31 12♒R	27 16♑D	31 18♑	Feb. 10 14♒	Feb. 10 27♒	Feb. 10 9♓
Feb. 10 2♒R	31 17♑	Feb. 10 2♒	Mar. 2 20♓	20 15♓	18 13♓R
13 2♒D	Feb. 10 25♑	20 18♒	12 8♈	Mar. 1 28♓	20 13♓R
20 4♒	20 8♒	Mar. 2 5♓	22 17♈	7 0♈R	Mar. 2 4♓R
Mar. 1 14♒	Mar. 2 23♒	12 24♓	25 18♈R	11 29♓R	12 29♒D
11 27♒	12 9♓	22 14♈	Apr. 1 15♈R	21 20♓R	22 4♓
21 12♓	22 28♓	Apr. 1 29♈	11 7♈R	30 17♓D	Apr. 1 14♓
31 0♈	Apr. 1 18♈	11 6♉	17 6♈D	31 17♓	11 28♓
Apr. 10 19♈	21 20♉	12 6♉R	21 6♈	Apr. 10 23♓	May 1 4♉
20 10♉	May 1 24♉R	21 2♉R	May 1 13♈	20 3♈	11 26♉
30 28♉	11 21♉R	May 1 26♈R	11 25♈	30 18♈	21 16Ⅱ
May 10 10Ⅱ	21 16♉R	6 25♈D	21 11♉	May 10 6♉	Jun. 10 12♋
20 14ⅡR	25 15♉D	11 26♈	31 0Ⅱ	20 27♉	20 16♋R
30 11ⅡR	31 17♉	21 4♉	Jun. 10 21Ⅱ	30 18Ⅱ	30 12♋R
Jun. 9 6ⅡR	Jun. 10 25♉	31 17♉	20 12♋	Jun. 9 7♋	July 10 7♋R
13 6ⅡD	20 9Ⅱ	Jun. 10 4Ⅱ	30 0♌	19 22♋	14 6♋D
19 7Ⅱ	30 28Ⅱ	20 24Ⅱ	July 10 13♌	29 2♌	20 8♋
29 15Ⅱ	July 10 19♋	30 16♋	20 22♌	July 9 5♌R	30 18♋
July 9 0♋	20 10♌	July 10 5♌	28 24♌R	19 1♌R	Aug. 9 5♌
19 20♋	30 27♌	20 21♌	30 24♌R	29 25♋R	19 26♌
29 11♌	Aug. 9 12♍	30 3♍	Aug. 9 18♌R	Aug. 3 25♋D	Sep. 8 2♎
Aug. 8 0♍	19 23♍	Aug. 9 11♍	19 12♌R	8 27♋	18 17♎
18 16♍	29 29♍	15 12♍R	21 12♌D	18 9♌	28 1♏
28 0♎	Sep. 2 0♎R	19 11♍R	29 17♌	28 27♌	Oct. 7 8♏
Sep. 7 11♎	8 27♍R	29 4♍R	Sep. 8 1♍	Sep. 7 17♍	16 12♏R
17 16♎	18 18♍R	Sep. 7 29♌D	18 20♍	17 4♎	17 12♏R
19 16♎R	24 15♍D	8 29♌	28 8♎	27 20♎	27 3♏R
27 12♎R	28 17♍	18 8♍	Oct. 8 25♎	Oct. 7 5♏	Nov. 5 26♎D
Oct. 7 2♎R	Oct. 8 29♍	28 24♍	18 10♏	17 18♏	6 26♎
10 1♎D	18 16♎	Oct. 8 12♎	28 24♏	27 27♏	16 5♏
17 5♎	28 3♏	18 29♎	Nov. 7 7♐	Nov. 2 29♏R	26 19♏
27 19♎	Nov. 7 19♏	28 15♏	17 14♐	6 26♏R	Dec. 6 5♐
Nov. 6 6♏	17 5♐	Nov. 7 0♐	19 14♐R	16 15♏R	16 20♐
16 22♏	27 20♐	17 14♐	27 8♐R	22 12♏D	26 6♑
26 8♐	Dec. 7 4♑	27 26♐	Dec. 7 28♏R	26 14♏	
Dec. 6 23♐	17 14♑	Dec. 5 0♑R	9 28♏D	Dec. 6 25♏	
16 9♑	21 16♑R	7 29♐R	17 3♐	16 9♐	
26 23♑	27 12♑R	17 18♐R	25 15♐	26 25♐	
		25 13♐D			
		27 14♐			

R = Retrograde.   D = Direct.   (See page 20.)

MERCURY   1942-1947

(To nearest degree at Midnight (o h. o m.) G.M.T.)

1942	1943	1944	1945	1946	1947
Jan. 1 16♑	Jan. 1 27♑	Jan. 1 25♑R	Jan. 1 23♐R	Jan. 1 19♐	Jan. 1 27♐
11 2♒	11 9♒	11 15♑R	2 23♐D	11 2♑	11 12♑
21 18♒	16 11♒R	20 9♑D	11 27♐	21 17♑	21 29♑
31 27♒	21 8♒R	21 9♑	21 8♑	31 3♒	31 16♒
Feb. 2 27♒R	31 27♑R	31 15♑	31 22♑	Feb. 10 20♒	Feb. 10 3♓
10 21♒R	Feb. 6 25♑D	Feb. 10 27♑	Feb. 10 7♒	20 8♓	28 23♓R
20 12♒R	10 26♑	20 11♒	20 24♒	Mar. 2 26♓	Mar. 2 23♓R
23 12♒D	20 4♒	Mar. 1 26♒	Mar. 2 12♓	17 10♈R	12 15♓R
Mar. 2 14♒	Mar. 2 16♒	11 14♓	12 1♈	22 8♈R	22 9♓R
12 24♒	12 1♓	21 3♈	22 19♈	Apr. 1 1♈R	23 9♓D
22 7♓	22 18♓	31 23♈	Apr. 1 28♈	9 28♓D	Apr. 1 13♓
Apr. 1 23♓	Apr. 1 7♈	Apr. 10 9♉	4 28♈R	11 28♓	11 23♓
11 11♈	11 28♈	20 16♉	11 25♈R	21 3♈	21 7♈
21 1♉	21 17♉	21 16♉R	21 18♈R	May 1 14♈	May 1 24♈
May 1 22♉	May 1 0♊	30 14♉R	28 17♈D	11 29♈	11 14♉
11 10♊	11 6♊	May 10 8♉R	May 1 17♈	21 17♉	21 5♊
21 21♊	13 6♊R	16 7♉D	11 24♈	31 8♊	31 26♊
31 26♊	21 3♊R	20 7♉	21 6♉	Jun. 10 0♋	Jun. 10 11♋
Jun. 1 26♊R	31 28♉R	30 14♉	31 22♉	20 18♋	20 22♋
10 23♊R	Jun. 5 27♉D	Jun. 9 26♉	Jun. 10 11♊	30 3♌	30 27♋
20 18♊R	10 28♉	19 13♊	20 3♋	July 10 13♌	July 2 27♋R
25 17♊D	20 5♊	July 9 25♋	30 23♋	20 16♌R	10 24♋R
30 18♊	30 19♊	19 14♌	July 10 10♌	30 12♌R	20 18♋R
July 10 26♊	July 10 7♋	29 0♍	20 24♌	Aug. 9 6♌R	26 17♋D
20 12♋	20 29♋	Aug. 8 13♍	30 2♍	13 5♌D	Aug. 9 27♋
30 2♌	30 19♌	18 21♍	Aug. 7 5♍R	19 7♌	19 15♌
Aug. 9 22♌	Aug. 9 6♍	25 22♍R	9 5♍R	29 20♌	29 5♍
19 11♍	19 20♍	28 22♍R	19 29♌R	Sep. 8 8♍	Sep. 8 23♍
29 27♍	29 2♎	Sep. 7 14♍R	29 22♌R	18 27♍	18 10♎
Sep. 8 10♎	Sep. 8 9♎	17 9♍D	31 22♌D	28 14♎	28 25♎
18 21♎	12 9♎R	27 17♍	Sep. 8 27♌	Oct. 8 0♏	Oct. 8 8♏
28 26♎	18 7♎R	Oct. 7 3♎	18 13♍	18 15♏	18 18♏
29 26♎R	28 27♍R	17 21♎	28 1♎	28 27♏	26 21♏R
Oct. 8 21♎R	Oct. 4 25♍D	27 7♏	Oct. 8 18♎	Nov. 7 6♐	28 21♏R
18 11♎R	8 26♍	Nov. 6 23♏	18 5♏	12 7♐R	Nov. 7 11♏R
20 10♎D	18 8♎	16 8♐	28 20♏	17 5♐R	16 6♏D
28 16♎	28 25♎	Dec. 6 5♑	Nov. 7 4♐	27 23♏R	17 6♏
Nov. 7 0♏	Nov. 7 12♏	14 9♑R	17 17♐	Dec. 2 21♏D	27 0♐
17 16♏	17 28♏	16 8♑R	27 23♐	17 5♐	Dec. 7 29♏
27 2♐	27 13♐	26 27♐R	28 23♐R	27 19♐	17 14♐
Dec. 7 18♐	Dec. 7 28♐		Dec. 7 16♐R		27 0♑
17 3♑	17 13♑		17 7♐R		
27 19♑	27 24♑		18 7♐D		
	31 25♑R		27 13♐		

R = Retrograde.   D = Direct.   (See page 20.)

MERCURY   1942-1947

MERCURY 1948–1953

(To nearest degree at Midnight (o h. o m.) G.M.T.)

1948	1949	1950	1951	1952	1953
Jan. 1 8♑ 11 24♑ 21 11♒ 31 27♒ Feb. 10 6♓ 12 6♓R 20 1♓R Mar. 1 22♒R 4 22♒D 11 24♒ 21 3♓ 31 16♓ Apr. 10 2♈ 20 20♈ 30 10♉ May 10 2♊ 20 19♊ 30 1♋ Jun. 9 7♋ 12 7♋R 19 5♋R 29 0♋R July 6 28♊D 9 29♊ 19 6♋ 29 21♋ Aug. 8 11♌ 18 1♍ 28 19♍ Sep. 7 5♎ 17 19♎ 27 0♏ Oct. 7 5♏ 9 5♏R 17 0♏R 27 20♎R 29 20♎D Nov. 6 25♎ 16 9♏ 26 24♏ Dec. 6 10♐ 16 26♐ 26 12♑	Jan. 1 21♑ 11 7♒ 21 19♒ 25 20♒R 31 17♒R Feb. 10 6♒R 15 5♒D Mar. 2 14♒ 12 27♒ 22 12♓ Apr. 1 29♓ 11 18♈ 21 9♉ May 1 28♉ 11 11♊ 21 17♊ 24 17♊R 31 15♊R Jun. 10 10♊R 16 9♊D 20 9♊ 30 16♊ July 10 0♋ 20 19♋ 30 10♌ Aug. 9 29♌ 19 16♍ 29 0♎ Sep. 8 12♎ 18 19♎ 22 19♎R 28 16♎R Oct. 8 6♎R 13 4♎D 18 6♎ 28 19♎ Nov. 7 5♏ 17 21♏ 27 7♐ Dec. 7 23♐ 17 8♑ 27 23♑	Jan. 1 29♑ 9 4♒R 11 4♒R 21 23♑R 30 18♑R 31 18♑D Feb. 10 25♑ 20 6♒ Mar. 2 21♒ 12 7♓ 22 25♓ Apr. 1 15♈ 11 5♉ 21 20♉ May 1 27♉ 4 28♉R 11 25♉R 21 20♉R 28 19♉D 31 19♉ Jun. 10 25♉ 20 7♊ 30 25♊ July 10 16♋ 20 7♌ 30 25♌ Aug. 9 10♍ 19 23♍ 29 1♎ Sep. 4 2♎R 8 2♎R 18 23♍R 27 18♍D 28 18♍ Oct. 8 28♍ 18 14♎ 28 1♏ Nov. 7 17♏ 17 3♐ 27 18♐ Dec. 7 3♑ 17 15♑ 24 18♑R 27 17♑R	Jan. 1 12♑R 11 2♑R 14 2♑D 31 17♑ Feb. 10 0♒ 20 16♒ Mar. 2 3♓ 12 21♓ 22 11♈ Apr. 1 28♈ 11 8♉ 21 7♉R May 1 0♉R 9 28♈D 11 29♈ 21 4♉ 31 15♉ Jun. 10 1♊ 20 21♊ 30 13♋ July 10 3♌ 20 19♌ 30 3♍ Aug. 9 12♍ 18 15♍R 19 15♍R 29 9♍R Sep. 8 2♍R 8 2♍D 18 7♍ 28 22♍ Oct. 8 10♎ 18 27♎ 28 13♏ Nov. 7 28♏ 17 13♐ 27 25♐ Dec. 7 2♑ 8 2♑R 17 25♐R 27 16♐R 28 16♐D	Jan. 1 18♐ 11 27♐ 21 10♑ 31 25♑ Feb. 10 11♒ Mar. 1 17♓ 11 6♈ 21 18♈ 28 20♈R 31 19♈R Apr. 10 12♈R 20 9♈D 30 13♈ May 10 24♈ 20 8♉ 30 27♉ Jun. 9 18♊ 19 9♋ 29 28♋ July 9 12♌ 19 23♌ 29 27♌ Aug. 8 24♌R 18 16♌R 24 15♌D 28 17♌ Sep. 7 29♌ 17 17♍ 27 6♎ Oct. 7 23♎ 17 8♏ 27 23♏ Nov. 6 6♐ 16 15♐ 21 16♐R Dec. 6 2♐R 11 0♐D 16 3♐ 26 14♐	Jan. 1 22♐ 11 7♑ 21 22♑ 31 9♒ Feb. 10 26♒ 20 15♓ Mar. 2 29♓ 9 3♈R 12 2♈R 22 25♓R Apr. 1 20♓D 11 24♓ 21 4♈ May 1 18♈ 11 5♉ 21 25♉ 31 17♊ Jun. 10 7♋ 20 22♋ 30 3♌ July 10 8♌ 12 8♌R 20 6♌R 30 29♋R Aug. 9 28♋D 19 8♌ 29 26♌ Sep. 8 16♍ 18 4♎ 28 20♎ Oct. 8 5♏ 18 18♏ 28 28♏ Nov. 4 1♐R 7 0♐R 17 19♏R 24 15♏D 27 15♏ Dec. 7 25♏ 17 9♐ 27 24♐

R = Retrograde.   D = Direct.   (See page 20.)

MERCURY

1954-1959

(To nearest degree at Midnight (o h. o m.) G.M.T.)

1954	1955	1956	1957	1958	1959
Jan. 1 2♑	Jan. 1 14♑	Jan. 1 25♑	Jan. 1 27♑	Jan. 1 27♐R	Jan. 1 18♐
11 18♑	11 0♒	11 9♒	2 27♑R	6 25♐D	11 0♑
21 5♒	31 28♒	20 13♒R	11 20♑R	11 27♐	21 15♑
31 22♒	Feb. 5 0♓R	21 13♒R	21 11♑R	21 7♑	31 1♒
Feb. 10 8♓	10 26♒R	31 2♒R	23 11♑D	31 20♑	Feb. 10 17♒
20 16♓	20 16♒R	Feb. 10 28♑D	31 16♑	Feb. 10 5♒	20 5♓
21 16♓R	26 14♒D	20 4♒	Feb. 10 27♑	20 21♒	Mar. 2 24♓
Mar. 2 10♓R	Mar. 2 15♒	Mar. 1 15♒	20 10♒	Mar. 2 9♓	21 13♈R
12 2♓R	12 23♒	11 29♒	Mar. 2 26♒	12 29♓	22 13♈R
16 2♓D	Apr. 1 20♓	21 16♓	12 13♓	22 17♈	Apr. 1 6♈R
22 4♓	11 8♈	31 4♈	22 2♈	Apr. 1 29♈	11 1♈R
Apr. 1 13♓	21 28♈	Apr. 10 24♈	Apr. 1 23♈	8 18♈R	13 1♈D
11 26♓	May 1 19♉	20 15♉	11 10♉	11 0♉R	21 4♈
21 12♈	11 8♊	30 0♊	21 19♉	21 23♈R	May 1 13♈
May 1 1♉	21 21♊	May 10 8♊	May 1 18♉R	May 1 20♈D	11 27♈
11 22♉	31 28♊	16 9♊R	11 12♉R	11 24♈	21 14♉
21 13♊	Jun. 5 29♊R	20 8♊R	20 10♉D	21 5♉	31 5♊
31 0♋	10 28♊R	30 3♊R	21 10♉	31 19♉	Jun. 10 27♊
Jun. 10 13♋	20 22♊R	Jun. 8 0♊D	31 15♉	Jun. 10 8♊	20 16♋
20 18♋	29 20♊D	9 0♊	Jun. 10 26♉	20 0♋	30 2♌
24 19♋R	30 20♊	19 5♊	20 12♊	30 21♋	July 10 13♌
30 17♋R	July 10 26♊	29 17♊	30 3♋	July 10 9♌	20 19♌
July 10 11♋R	20 9♋	July 9 4♋	July 10 24♋	20 23♌	24 19♌R
18 9♋D	30 29♋	19 25♋	20 14♌	30 3♍	30 17♌R
20 10♋	Aug. 9 19♌	29 16♌	30 0♍	Aug. 9 8♍	Aug. 9 10♌R
30 17♋	19 8♍	Aug. 8 4♍	Aug. 9 13♍	11 8♍R	17 8♌D
Aug. 9 3♌	29 25♍	18 19♍	19 22♍	19 4♍R	19 8♌
19 23♌	Sep. 8 9♎	28 2♎	28 25♍R	29 26♌R	27 5♍
29 12♍	18 21♎	Sep. 7 10♎	29 25♍R	Sep. 3 25♌D	Sep. 8 19♍
Sep. 8 29♍	28 28♎	15 12♎R	Sep. 8 19♍R	8 27♌	28 12♎
18 15♎	Oct. 3 29♎R	17 12♎R	18 11♍R	18 10♍	Oct. 8 28♎
28 29♎	8 26♎R	27 3♎R	20 11♍D	28 28♍	18 13♏
Oct. 8 9♏	18 15♎R	Oct. 7 27♍D	28 17♍	Oct. 8 16♎	28 26♏
18 15♏	24 13♎D	17 7♎	Oct. 8 3♎	18 3♏	Nov. 7 7♐
19 15♏R	28 15♎	27 23♎	18 20♎	28 18♏	15 10♐R
28 8♏R	Nov. 7 28♎	Nov. 6 9♏	28 7♏	Nov. 7 3♐	17 9♐R
Nov. 7 29♎R	17 14♏	16 25♏	Nov. 7 23♏	17 16♐	27 28♏R
9 29♎D	27 0♐	26 11♐	17 8♐	27 25♐	Dec. 5 24♏D
17 5♏	Dec. 7 15♐	Dec. 6 27♐	27 23♐	Dec. 1 26♐R	7 24♏
27 19♏	17 1♑	16 11♑	Dec. 7 5♑	7 22♐R	17 4♐
Dec. 7 4♐	27 17♑	26 24♑	17 12♑R	17 10♐R	27 18♐
17 20♐			27 2♑R	21 9♐D	
27 6♑				27 13♐	

R = Retrograde.   D = Direct.   (See page 20.)

MERCURY

MERCURY 1960–1965

(To nearest degree at Midnight (o h. o m.) G.M.T.)

1960	1961	1962	1963	1964	1965
Jan. 1 25♐	Jan. 1 7♑	Jan. 1 19♑	Jan. 1 29♑	Jan. 1 18♑R	Jan. 1 19♐
11 10♑	11 24♑	11 5♒	11 7♒	11 6♑R	11 28♐
21 26♑	21 11♒	21 19♒	12 7♒R	16 5♑D	21 10♑
31 13♒	31 27♒	28 23♒R	21 29♑R	21 6♑	31 25♑
Feb. 10 1♓	Feb. 10 8♓	Feb. 10 11♒R	31 21♑R	31 16♑	Feb. 10 11♒
20 18♓	12 9♓R	19 7♒D	Feb. 2 21♑D	Feb. 10 29♑	20 28♒
Mar. 1 26♓	20 5♓R	20 8♒	10 25♑	20 14♒	Mar. 2 16♓
3 26♓R	Mar. 2 26♓R	Mar. 2 14♒	20 5♒	Mar. 1 0♓	12 5♈
11 20♓R	7 24♒D	12 25♒	Mar. 2 19♒	11 18♓	22 20♈
21 13♓R	12 26♒	22 10♓	12 5♓	21 8♈	30 23♈R
25 12♓D	22 3♓	Apr. 1 26♓	22 22♓	31 27♈	Apr. 1 23♈R
31 14♓	Apr. 1 16♓	11 15♈	Apr. 1 12♈	Apr. 10 9♉	11 17♈R
Apr. 10 23♓	11 1♈	21 6♉	11 2♉	18 11♉R	21 12♈R
20 6♈	21 19♈	May 1 26♉	21 19♉	20 11♉R	23 12♈D
30 21♈	May 1 9♉	11 11♊	May 1 29♉	30 5♉R	May 1 15♈
May 10 10♉	11 1♊	21 19♊	11 0♊R	May 10 2♉R	11 24♈
20 2♊	21 19♊	27 20♊R	21 25♉R	11 2♉D	21 8♉
30 23♊	31 3♋	31 20♊R	31 22♉D	20 5♉	31 26♉
Jun. 9 10♋	Jun. 10 10♋	Jun. 10 15♊R	Jun. 10 26♉	30 14♉	Jun. 10 17♊
19 23♋	15 10♋R	20 12♊D	20 6♊	Jun. 9 29♉	20 8♋
29 29♋	20 9♋R	30 16♊	30 22♊	19 18♊	30 27♋
July 4 0♌R	30 4♋R	July 10 28♊	July 10 12♋	29 9♋	July 10 13♌
9 29♋R	July 9 1♋D	20 16♋	20 4♌	July 9 0♌	20 24♌
19 23♋R	10 1♋	30 7♌	30 23♌	19 18♌	30 0♍
29 20♋D	20 7♋	Aug. 9 27♌	Aug. 9 9♍	29 2♍	Aug. 3 0♍
Aug. 8 27♋	30 21♋	19 14♍	19 22♍	Aug. 8 13♍	9 28♌R
18 12♌	Aug. 9 10♌	29 29♍	29 5≏	18 18♍	19 20♌R
28 2♍	19 0♍	Sep. 8 12≏	Sep. 7 5≏R	28 18♍R	26 18♌D
Sep. 7 21♍	29 19♍	18 20≏	18 29♍R	Sep. 7 6♍R	29 18♌
17 8≏	Sep. 8 5≏	25 22≏R	28 21♍D	12 4♍D	Sep. 8 29♌
27 23≏	18 19≏	28 21≏R	Oct. 8 26♍	17 6♍	18 17♍
Oct. 7 7♏	28 0♏	Oct. 8 11≏R	18 12≏	27 20♍	28 5≏
17 18♏	Oct. 8 8♏	17 7≏D	28 29≏	Oct. 7 7≏	Oct. 8 22≏
27 24♏	11 8♏R	18 7≏	Nov. 7 15♏	17 25≏	18 8♏
29 24♏R	18 5♏R	28 17≏	17 1♐	27 11♏	28 23♏
Nov. 6 18♏R	28 24≏R	Nov. 7 3♏	27 16♐	Nov. 6 26♏	Nov. 7 6♐
16 8♏R	Nov. 2 22≏D	17 19♏	Dec. 7 1♑	16 11♐	17 17♐
18 8♏D	7 26≏	27 5♐	17 14♑	26 25♐	24 19♐R
26 14♏	17 8♏	Dec. 7 21♐	27 21♑R	Dec. 6 4♑	27 18♐R
Dec. 6 27♏	27 24♏	17 6♑		10 5♑R	Dec. 7 6♐R
16 13♐	Dec. 7 9♐	27 22♑		16 1♑R	13 3♐D
26 28♐	17 25♐			26 19♐R	17 4♐
31 6♑	27 11♑			30 19♐D	27 14♐

R = Retrograde.   D = Direct. · (See page 20.)

MERCURY   1966–1971
(To nearest degree at Midnight (0 h. 0 m.) G.M.T.)

1966	1967	1968	1969	1970	1971
Jan. 1 20♐	Jan. 1 0♑	Jan. 1 11♑	Jan. 1 25♑	Jan. 1 29♑	Jan. 1 2♑R
11 5♑	11 16♑	11 28♑	11 9♒	5 0♒R	9 28♐D
21 20♑	21 2♒	21 14♒	21 16♒R	11 26♑R	11 28♐
31 6♒	31 19♒	31 29♒	31 7♒R	21 15♑R	21 6♑
Feb. 10 24♒	Feb. 10 7♓	Feb. 8 2♓R	Feb. 10 0♒R	31 16♑	31 19♑
20 12♓	20 18♓	10 1♓R	11 0♒D	Feb. 10 26♑	Feb. 10 3♒
Mar. 2 29♓	Mar. 2 15♓R	20 21♒R	20 5♒	20 9♒	20 19♒
12 6♈R	12 6♓R	29 17♒D	Mar. 2 15♒	Mar. 2 24♒	Mar. 2 7♓
22 0♈R	18 5♓D	Mar. 1 17♒	12 29♒	12 11♓	12 26♓
Apr. 1 23♓R	22 5♓	11 23♒	22 15♒	22 29♓	22 15♈
5 23♓D	Apr. 1 13♓	21 4♓	Apr. 1 3♈	Apr. 1 20♈	Apr. 1 29♈
11 25♓	11 25♓	31 18♓	11 23♈	11 8♉	10 4♉R
21 3♈	21 10♈	Apr. 10 5♈	21 14♉	21 20♉	11 4♉R
May 1 16♈	May 1 28♈	20 24♈	May 1 0♊	May 1 22♉	21 29♈R
11 2♉	11 19♉	30 16♉	11 10♊	2 22♉R	May 1 23♈R
21 22♉	21 10♊	May 10 6♊	19 12♊R	11 17♉R	4 23♈D
31 14♊	31 29♊	20 21♊	21 12♊R	21 13♉R	11 25♈
Jun. 10 4♋	Jun. 10 12♋	30 0♋	31 7♉R	23 13♉D	21 4♉
20 21♋	20 20♋	Jun. 7 2♋R	Jun. 10 3♉R	31 16♉	31 18♉
30 3♌	27 22♋R	9 2♋R	11 3♉D	Jun. 10 25♉	Jun. 10 5♊
July 10 11♌	30 21♋R	19 27♊R	20 7♊	20 10♊	20 26♊
16 11♌R	July 10 16♋R	29 23♊R	30 17♊	30 29♊	30 18♋
20 10♌R	20 12♋R	July 2 23♊D	July 10 3♋	July 10 21♋	July 10 6♌
30 4♌R	21 12♋D	9 26♊	20 24♋	20 11♌	20 22♌
Aug. 9 0♌D	30 17♋	19 8♋	30 15♌	30 28♌	30 3♍
19 7♌	Aug. 9 0♌	29 25♋	Aug. 9 3♍	Aug. 9 12♍	Aug. 9 10♍
29 23♌	19 19♌	Aug. 8 16♌	19 19♍	19 23♍	13 11♍R
Sep. 8 13♍	29 9♍	18 6♍	29 2♎	29 28♍	19 9♍R
18 1♎	Sep. 8 27♍	28 23♍	Sep. 8 12♎	Sep. 2 28♍R	29 1♍R
28 18♎	18 13♎	Sep. 7 8♎	17 15♎R	8 24♍R	Sep. 6 27♌D
Oct. 8 3♏	28 27♎	17 20♎	18 15♎R	18 15♍R	8 28♌
18 17♏	Oct. 8 9♏	27 29♎	28 8♎R	22 14♍D	18 8♍
28 28♏	18 17♏	Oct. 4 1♏R	Oct. 8 0♎D	Oct. 8 0♎	28 26♍
Nov. 3 3♐	22 17♏R	7 0♏R	9 0♎D	18 18♎	Oct. 8 14♎
8 3♐R	28 14♏R	17 21♎R	18 7♎	28 5♏	18 0♏
17 25♏R	Nov. 7 3♏R	25 16♎D	28 22♎	Nov. 7 21♏	28 16♏
27 17♏R	11 1♏D	Nov. 6 26♎	Nov. 7 9♏	17 6♐	Nov. 7 1♐
28 17♏D	17 5♏	16 12♏	17 25♏	27 21♐	17 15♐
Dec. 6 24♏	27 17♏	26 28♏	Dec. 7 26♐	Dec. 7 5♑	27 26♐
17 7♐	Dec. 7 2♐	Dec. 6 13♐	17 11♑	17 14♑R	Dec. 3 28♐R
27 22♐	17 18♐	16 29♐	27 25♑	20 14♑R	7 27♐R
	27 3♑	26 15♑		27 9♑R	17 15♐R
					23 12♐D
					27 13♐

R = Retrograde.   D = Direct.   (See page 20.)

MERCURY

1972–1975

(To nearest degree at Midnight (o h. o m.) G.M.T.)

1972	1973	1974	1975
Jan. 1 17♐ 11 29♐ 27 13♑ 31 28♑ Feb. 10 15♒ 20 3♓ Mar. 1 21♓ 11 8♈ 21 16♈ 22 16♈R 31 11♈R Apr. 10 4♈R 14 4♈D 20 5♈ 30 13♈ May 10 26♈ 20 12♉ 30 2♊ Jun. 9 23♊ 19 14♋ 29 0♌ July 9 13♌ 19 21♌ 25 22♌R 29 22♌R Aug. 8 15♌R 18 10♌D 28 17♌ Sep. 7 3♍ 17 22♍ 27 10♎ Oct. 7 26♎ 17 11♏ 27 25♏ Nov. 6 7♐ 19 12♐R 26 4♐R Dec. 6 26♏D 19 3♐ 26 16♐	Jan. 1 25♐ 11 10♑ 21 26♑ 31 13♒ Feb. 10 0♓ 20 18♓ Mar. 2 28♓ 5 29♓R 12 25♓R 22 16♓R 28 15♓D Apr. 1 16♓ 11 23♓ 21 5♈ May 1 21♈ 11 9♉ 21 1♊ 31 22♊ Jun. 10 10♋ 20 23♋ 30 2♌ July 7 3♌R 10 3♌R 20 28♋R 30 23♋R 31 23♋D Aug. 9 27♋ 19 11♌ 29 1♍ Sep. 8 20♍ 18 7♎ 28 23♎ Oct. 8 7♏ 18 19♏ 28 26♏ 31 27♏R Nov. 7 22♏R 17 11♏R 20 11♏D 27 15♏ Dec. 7 27♏ 17 12♐ 27 27♐	Jan. 1 5♑ 11 21♑ 21 8♒ 31 25♒ Feb. 10 9♓ 16 12♓R 20 10♓R Mar. 2 0♓R 10 27♒D 12 27♒ 22 3♓ Apr. 1 15♓ 11 29♓ 21 16♈ May 1 6♉ 11 27♉ 21 17♊ Jun. 10 11♋ 18 14♋R 20 13♋R 30 9♋R July 10 5♋R 13 4♋D 20 7♋ 30 19♋ Aug. 9 7♌ 19 27♌ 29 16♍ Sep. 8 3♎ 18 17♎ 28 0♏ Oct. 8 9♏ 14 11♏R 18 9♏R 28 29♎R Nov. 4 25♎D 7 26♎ 17 7♏ 27 22♏ Dec. 7 7♐ 17 23♐ 27 9♑	Jan. 1 17♑ 11 3♒ 21 18♒ 31 25♒R Feb. 10 17♒R 20 10♒R 21 10♒D Mar. 2 14♒ 12 25♒ 22 8♓ Apr. 1 24♓ 11 12♈ 21 3♉ May 1 23♉ 11 10♊ 21 21♊ 30 24♊R 31 24♊R Jun. 10 20♊R 20 15♊R 23 15♊D July 10 27♊ 20 13♋ 30 4♌ Aug. 9 24♌ 19 12♍ 29 28♍ Sep. 8 11♎ 18 21♎ 27 24♎R 28 24♎R Oct. 8 17♎R 18 9♎R 19 9♎D 29 17♎ Nov. 7 1♍ 17 17♍ 27 3♐ Dec. 7 19♐ 17 4♑ 27 20♑ 31 26♑

R = Retrograde. D = Direct. (See page 20.)

NOTES

VENUS   (To nearest degree at Midnight (0 h. 0 m.) G.M.T.)   1900–1905

1900	1901	1902	1903	1904	1905
Jan. 1 6♒	Jan. 1 11♐	Jan. 1 23♒	Jan. 1 17♑	Jan. 1 25♏	Jan. 1 22♒
11 19♒	11 23♐	11 0♓	11 0♒	11 7♐	11 4♓
21 1♓	21 6♑	21 3♓	21 12♒	21 19♐	21 15♓
31 13♓	31 18♑	31 3♓R	31 25♒	31 1♑	31 27♓
Feb. 10 26♓	Feb. 10 1♒	Feb. 10 28♒R	Feb. 10 7♓	Feb. 10 13♑	Feb. 10 7♈
20 8♈	20 13♒	20 22♒R	20 19♓	20 25♑	20 17♈
Mar. 2 20♈	Mar. 2 25♒	Mar. 2 18♒R	Mar. 2 2♈	Mar. 1 7♒	Mar. 2 26♈
12 1♉	12 8♓	8 18♒D	12 15♈	11 19♒	12 4♉
22 13♉	22 20♓	12 18♒	22 27♈	21 2♓	22 11♉
Apr. 1 24♉	Apr. 1 3♈	22 21♒	Apr. 1 9♉	31 14♓	Apr. 1 14♉
11 5♊	11 15♈	Apr. 1 27♒	11 21♉	Apr. 10 26♓	7 15♉R
21 16♊	21 28♈	11 5♓	21 3♊	20 8♈	11 14♉R
May 1 26♊	May 1 10♉	21 14♓	May 1 15♊	30 21♈	21 10♉R
11 5♋	11 22♉	May 1 24♓	11 27♊	May 10 3♉	May 1 4♉R
21 13♋	21 5♊	11 4♈	21 8♋	20 15♉	11 29♈R
31 19♋	31 17♊	21 15♈	31 20♋	30 27♉	19 28♈D
Jun. 10 23♋	Jun. 10 29♊	31 26♈	Jun. 10 1♌	Jun. 9 10♊	Jun. 10 6♉
17 24♋R	20 11♋	Jun. 10 7♉	20 12♌	19 22♊	20 14♉
20 24♋R	30 24♋	20 18♉	30 22♌	29 4♋	30 22♉
30 21♋R	July 10 6♌	30 0♊	July 10 2♍	July 9 17♋	July 10 2♊
July 10 15♋R	20 18♌	July 10 11♊	20 11♍	19 29♋	20 12♊
20 8♋R	30 1♍	20 23♊	30 19♍	29 11♌	30 22♊
30 8♋D	Aug. 9 12♍	30 5♋	Aug. 9 26♍	Aug. 8 23♌	Aug. 9 3♋
Aug. 9 9♋	19 25♍	Aug. 9 17♋	28 2♎R	18 6♍	19 14♋
19 14♋	29 7♎	19 29♋	29 2♎R	28 18♍	29 25♋
29 21♋	Sep. 8 19♎	29 11♌	Sep. 8 29♍R	Sep. 7 1♎	Sep. 8 7♌
Sep. 8 29♋	18 1♏	Sep. 8 23♌	18 24♍R	17 13♎	18 19♌
18 9♌	28 13♏	18 6♍	28 18♍R	27 25♎	28 1♍
28 19♌	Oct. 8 24♏	28 18♍	Oct. 8 16♍R	Oct. 7 8♏	Oct. 8 13♍
Oct. 8 29♌	18 6♐	Oct. 8 1♎	18 16♍D	17 20♏	18 25♍
18 10♍	28 18♐	18 13♎	28 22♍	27 2♐	28 8♎
28 22♍	Nov. 7 29♐	28 26♎	Nov. 7 29♍	Nov. 6 14♐	Nov. 7 20♎
Nov. 7 4♎	17 10♑	Nov. 7 8♏	17 7♎	16 27♐	17 3♏
17 16♎	27 21♑	17 21♏	27 17♎	26 9♑	27 15♏
27 28♎	Dec. 7 1♒	27 3♐	Dec. 7 27♎	Dec. 6 21♑	Dec. 7 28♏
Dec. 7 10♏	17 11♒	Dec. 7 16♐	17 8♏	16 3♒	17 10♐
17 22♏	27 20♒	17 28♐	27 19♏	26 15♒	27 23♐
27 5♐		27 11♑			

R = Retrograde.   D = Direct.   (See page 20.)

VENUS (To nearest degree at Midnight (0 h. 0 m.) G.M.T.) 1906-1911

1906	1907	1908	1909	1910	1911
Jan. 1 29♐	Jan. 1 2♐	Jan. 1 6♒	Jan. 1 11♐	Jan. 1 23♒	Jan. 1 18♑
11 12♑	11 7♐	11 18♒	11 24♐	11 28♒	11 1♒
21 24♑	21 15♐	21 1♓	21 6♑	21 1♓	21 13♒
31 7♒	31 24♐	31 13♓	31 19♑	23 1♓R	31 26♒
Feb. 10 19♒	Feb. 10 3♑	Feb. 10 25♓	Feb. 10 1♒	31 29♒R	Feb. 10 8♓
20 2♓	20 14♑	20 7♈	20 14♒	Feb. 10 24♒R	20 21♓
Mar. 2 14♓	Mar. 2 25♑	Mar. 1 19♈	Mar. 2 26♒	20 19♒R	Mar. 2 3♈
12 27♓	12 6♒	11 1♉	12 9♓	Mar. 2 15♒R	12 15♈
22 9♈	22 17♒	21 12♉	22 21♓	5 15♒D	Apr. 1 10♉
Apr. 1 22♈	Apr. 1 29♒	31 24♉	Apr. 1 3♈	12 16♒	11 22♉
11 4♉	11 10♓	Apr. 10 5♊	11 16♈	22 20♒	21 4♊
21 16♉	21 22♓	20 15♊	21 28♈	Apr. 1 27♒	May 1 16♊
May 1 29♉	May 1 4♈	30 25♊	May 1 11♉	21 14♓	11 28♊
11 11♊	11 16♈	May 10 4♋	11 23♉	May 1 24♓	21 9♋
21 23♊	21 28♈	20 11♋	21 5♊	11 4♈	31 20♋
31 5♋	31 10♉	30 17♋	31 17♊	21 15♈	Jun. 10 1♌
Jun. 10 17♋	Jun. 10 22♉	Jun. 9 21♋	Jun. 10 0♋	31 26♈	20 12♌
20 29♋	20 4♊	15 22♋R	20 12♋	Jun. 10 7♉	30 22♌
30 11♌	30 16♊	19 21♋R	30 24♋	20 19♉	July 10 2♍
July 10 23♌	July 10 28♊	29 18♋R	July 10 6♌	30 0♊	20 11♍
20 5♍	20 11♋	July 9 12♋R	20 19♌	July 10 12♊	30 19♍
30 16♍	30 23♋	19 7♋R	30 1♍	20 24♊	Aug. 9 25♍
Aug. 9 28♍	Aug. 9 5♌	28 5♋D	Aug. 9 13♍	30 6♋	19 29♍
19 9♎	19 18♌	29 5♋	19 25♍	Aug. 9 18♋	25 29♍R
29 20♎	29 0♍	Aug. 8 8♋	29 7♎	19 0♌	29 29♍R
Sep. 8 0♏	Sep. 8 12♍	18 13♋	Sep. 8 19♎	29 12♌	Sep. 8 26♍R
18 10♏	18 25♍	28 20♋	18 1♏	Sep. 8 24♌	18 20♍R
28 20♏	28 7♎	Sep. 7 28♋	28 13♏	18 6♍	28 15♍R
Oct. 8 29♏	Oct. 8 20♎	17 8♌	Oct. 8 25♏	28 19♍	Oct. 7 13♍R
18 6♐	18 2♏	27 18♌	18 7♐	Oct. 8 1♎	8 13♍
28 12♐	28 15♏	Oct. 7 29♌	28 18♐	18 14♎	18 16♍
Nov. 7 15♐	Nov. 7 27♏	17 10♍	Nov. 7 29♐	28 26♎	28 21♍
10 15♐R	17 10♐	27 21♍	17 11♑	Nov. 7 9♏	Nov. 7 28♍
17 14♐R	27 22♐	Nov. 6 3♎	27 21♑	17 21♏	17 7♎
27 9♐R	Dec. 7 5♑	16 15♎	Dec. 7 1♒	27 4♐	27 17♎
Dec. 7 3♐R	17 17♑	26 27♎	17 11♒	Dec. 7 17♐	Dec. 7 27♎
17 0♐R	27 29♑	Dec. 6 9♏	27 19♒	17 29♐	17 8♏
21 29♏D		16 22♏		27 12♑	27 20♏
27 0♐		26 4♐			

R = Retrograde.   D = Direct.   (See page 20.)

VENUS (To nearest degree at Midnight (0 h. 0 m.) G.M.T.) 1912–1917

1912

Jan. 1 26♏
11 7♐
21 19♐
31 1♑
Feb. 10 13♑
20 25♑
Mar. 1 8♒
11 20♒
21 2♓
31 15♓
Apr. 10 27♓
20 9♈
30 21♈
May 10 4♉
20 16♉
30 28♉
Jun. 9 10♊
19 23♊
29 5♋
July 9 17♋
19 1♌
29 12♌
Aug. 8 24♌
18 7♍
28 19♍
Sep. 7 1♎
17 14♎
27 26♎
Oct. 7 8♏
17 21♏
27 3♐
Nov. 6 15♐
16 27♐
26 10♑
Dec. 6 22♑
16 4♒
26 16♒

1913

Jan. 1 23♒
11 4♓
21 16♓
31 27♓
Feb. 10 7♈
20 17♈
Mar. 2 26♈
12 4♉
22 10♉
Apr. 1 12♉
4 12♉R
11 11♉R
21 7♉R
May 1 1♉R
11 27♈R
16 26♈D
21 26♈
31 0♉
Jun. 10 6♉
20 13♉
30 22♉
July 10 2♊
20 12♊
30 22♊
Aug. 9 3♋
19 15♋
29 26♋
Sep. 8 8♌
18 20♌
28 2♍
Oct. 8 14♍
18 26♍
28 8♎
Nov. 7 21♎
17 3♏
27 16♏
Dec. 7 28♏
17 11♐
27 23♐

1914

Jan. 1 0♑
11 12♑
21 25♑
31 7♒
Feb. 10 20♒
20 3♓
Mar. 2 15♓
12 27♓
22 10♈
Apr. 1 22♈
11 5♉
21 17♉
May 1 29♉
11 11♊
21 24♊
31 6♋
Jun. 10 18♋
20 0♌
30 12♌
July 10 24♌
20 5♍
30 17♍
Aug. 9 28♍
19 9♎
29 20♎
Sep. 8 1♏
18 11♏
28 20♏
Oct. 8 28♏
18 5♐
28 10♐
Nov. 7 12♐
8 12♐R
17 10♐R
27 5♐R
Dec. 7 0♐R
17 27♏R
18 27♏D
27 28♏

1915

Jan. 1 0♐
11 6♐
21 14♐
31 23♐
Feb. 10 3♑
20 14♑
Mar. 2 25♑
12 6♒
22 18♒
Apr. 1 29♒
11 11♓
21 23♓
May 1 5♈
11 17♈
21 29♈
31 11♉
Jun. 10 23♉
20 5♊
30 17♊
July 10 29♊
20 11♋
30 23♋
Aug. 9 6♌
19 18♌
29 1♍
Sep. 8 13♍
18 25♍
28 8♎
Oct. 8 20♎
18 3♏
28 15♏
Nov. 7 28♏
17 10♐
27 23♐
Dec. 7 5♑
17 18♑
27 0♒

1916

Jan. 1 7♒
11 19♒
21 1♓
31 13♓
Feb. 10 26♓
20 8♈
Mar. 1 20♈
11 1♉
21 13♉
31 24♉
Apr. 10 5♊
20 15♊
30 25♊
May 10 4♋
20 11♋
30 17♋
Jun. 9 20♋
12 20♋R
19 19♋R
29 14♋R
July 9 8♋R
19 4♋R
25 2♋D
29 3♋
Aug. 8 6♋
18 12♋
28 19♋
Sep. 7 28♋
17 8♌
27 18♌
Oct. 7 29♌
17 10♍
27 22♍
Nov. 6 4♎
16 15♎
26 28♎
Dec. 6 10♏
16 22♏
26 5♐

1917

Jan. 1 12♐
11 24♐
21 7♑
31 20♑
Feb. 10 2♒
20 15♒
Mar. 2 27♒
12 9♓
22 22♓
Apr. 1 4♈
11 17♈
21 29♈
May 1 11♉
11 23♉
21 6♊
31 18♊
Jun. 10 0♋
20 13♋
30 25♋
July 10 7♌
20 19♌
30 2♍
Aug. 9 14♍
19 26♍
29 8♎
Sep. 8 20♎
18 2♏
28 14♏
Oct. 8 25♏
18 7♐
28 18♐
Nov. 7 0♑
17 11♑
27 21♑
Dec. 7 1♒
17 11♒
27 18♒

R = Retrograde. D = Direct. (See page 20.)

VENUS

VENUS   (To nearest degree at Midnight (0 h. 0 m.) G.M.T.)   1918–1923

1918	1919	1920	1921	1922	1923
Jan. 1 22♒	Jan. 1 19♑	Jan. 1 26♏	Jan. 1 23♒	Jan. 1 0♑	Jan. 1 29♏
11 27♒	11 1♒	11 8♐	11 5♓	11 13♑	11 6♐
21 28♒R	21 14♒	21 20♐	21 16♓	21 26♑	21 14♐
31 26♒R	31 26♒	31 2♑	31 27♓	31 8♒	31 23♐
Feb. 10 21♒R	Feb. 10 9♓	Feb. 10 14♑	Feb. 10 7♈	Feb. 10 21♒	Feb. 10 4♑
20 15♒R	20 21♓	20 26♑	20 17♈	20 3♓	20 14♑
Mar. 2 13♒R	Mar. 2 4♈	Mar. 1 8♒	Mar. 2 26♈	Mar. 2 16♓	Mar. 2 25♑
3 13♒D	12 16♈	11 21♒	12 3♉	12 28♓	12 7♒
12 14♒	22 28♈	21 3♓	22 8♉	22 11♈	22 18♒
22 19♒	Apr. 1 10♉	31 15♓	Apr. 1 10♉	Apr. 1 23♈	Apr. 1 0♓
Apr. 1 26♒	21 4♊	Apr. 10 27♓	2 10♉R	11 5♉	11 12♓
11 4♓		20 10♈	11 8♉R	21 18♉	21 23♓
21 14♓	May 1 16♊	30 22♈	21 3♉R	May 1 0♊	May 1 5♈
May 1 24♓	11 28♊	May 10 4♉	May 1 27♈R	11 12♊	11 17♈
11 4♈	21 9♋	20 17♉	11 24♈R	21 24♊	21 29♈
21 15♈	31 21♋	30 29♉	14 24♈D	31 6♋	31 11♉
31 26♈	Jun. 10 2♌	Jun. 9 11♊	21 25♈	Jun. 10 18♋	Jun. 10 23♉
Jun. 10 8♉	20 12♌	19 23♊	31 29♈	20 0♌	20 5♊
20 19♉	30 23♌	29 6♋	Jun. 10 5♉	30 12♌	30 18♊
30 1♊	July 10 2♍	July 9 18♋	20 13♉	July 10 24♌	July 10 0♋
July 10 13♊	20 11♍	19 0♌	30 22♉	20 6♍	20 12♋
20 24♊	30 18♍	29 13♌	July 10 2♊	30 17♍	30 25♋
30 6♋	Aug. 9 24♍	Aug. 8 25♌	20 12♊	Aug. 9 28♍	Aug. 9 7♌
Aug. 9 18♋	19 27♍	18 7♍	30 23♊	19 10♎	19 19♌
19 0♌	23 27♍R	28 20♍	Aug. 9 4♋	29 20♎	29 1♍
29 13♌	29 27♍R	Sep. 7 2♎	19 15♋	Sep. 8 1♏	Sep. 8 14♍
Sep. 8 25♌	Sep. 8 22♍R	17 14♎	29 27♋	18 11♏	18 26♍
18 7♍	18 16♍R	27 27♎	Sep. 8 8♌	28 20♏	28 9♎
28 20♍	28 12♍R	Oct. 7 9♏	18 20♌	Oct. 8 28♏	Oct. 8 20♎
Oct. 8 2♎	Oct. 4 11♍D	17 21♏	28 2♍	18 4♐	18 4♏
18 14♎	8 11♍	27 3♐	Oct. 8 14♍	28 9♐	28 16♏
28 27♎	18 14♍	Nov. 6 16♐	18 27♍	Nov. 5 10♐R	Nov. 7 28♏
Nov. 7 10♏	28 20♍	16 28♐	28 9♎	7 10♐R	17 11♐
17 22♏	Nov. 7 28♍	26 10♑	Nov. 7 21♎	17 7♐R	27 23♐
27 5♐	17 7♎	Dec. 6 22♑	17 4♏	27 1♐R	Dec. 7 6♑
Dec. 7 17♐	27 17♎	16 4♒	27 16♏	Dec. 7 26♏R	17 18♑
17 0♑	Dec. 7 28♎	26 16♒	Dec. 7 29♏	16 25♏D	27 1♒
27 12♑	17 9♏		17 12♐	17 25♏	
	27 20♏		27 24♐	27 27♏	

R = Retrograde.   D = Direct.   (See page 20.)

VENUS (To nearest degree at Midnight (o h. o m.) G.M.T.) 1924-1929

1924	1925	1926	1927	1928	1929
Jan. 1 7♒	Jan. 1 13♐	Jan. 1 21♒	Jan. 1 19♑	Jan. 1 26♏	Jan. 1 24♒
11 20♒	11 25♐	11 25♒	11 2♒	11 8♐	11 5♓
21 2♓	21 7♑	18 26♒R	21 14♒	21 20♐	21 16♓
31 14♓	31 20♑	21 26♒R	31 27♒	31 2♑	31 27♓
Feb. 10 26♓	Feb. 10 3♒	31 23♒R	Feb. 10 9♓	Feb. 10 15♑	Feb. 10 8♈
20 8♈	20 15♒	Feb. 10 17♒R	20 22♓	20 27♑	20 17♈
Mar. 1 20♈	Mar. 2 28♒	20 12♒R	Mar. 2 4♈	Mar. 1 9♒	Mar. 2 25♈
11 2♉	12 10♓	28 10♒D	12 17♈	11 21♒	12 2♉
21 13♉	22 23♓	Mar. 2 10♒	22 29♈	21 4♓	22 6♉
31 24♉	Apr. 1 5♈	12 13♒	Apr. 1 11♉	31 16♓	30 8♉R
Apr. 10 5♊	11 17♈	22 18♒	11 23♉	Apr. 10 28♓	Apr. 1 8♉R
20 15♊	21 0♉	Apr. 1 26♒	21 5♊	20 10♈	11 5♉R
30 25♊	May 1 12♉	11 4♓	May 1 17♊	30 23♈	May 1 24♈R
May 10 3♋	11 24♉	21 14♓	11 28♊	May 10 5♉	11 22♈R
20 10♋	21 7♊	May 1 24♓	21 10♋	20 17♉	12 22♈D
30 15♋	31 19♊	11 5♈	31 21♋	30 0♊	21 23♈
Jun. 9 18♋	Jun. 10 1♋	21 16♈	Jun. 10 2♌	Jun. 9 12♊	31 28♈
10 18♋R	20 13♋	31 27♈	20 13♌	19 24♊	Jun. 10 5♉
19 16♋R	30 26♋	Jun. 10 8♉	30 23♌	29 6♋	20 13♉
29 11♋R	July 10 8♌	20 20♉	July 10 2♍	July 9 19♋	30 22♉
July 9 5♋R	20 20♌	30 1♊	20 10♍	19 1♌	July 10 2♊
19 2♋R	30 2♍	July 10 13♊	30 18♍	29 13♌	20 12♊
23 1♋D	Aug. 9 14♍	20 25♊	Aug. 9 22♍	Aug. 8 25♌	30 23♊
29 2♋	19 26♍	30 7♋	20 25♍R	18 8♍	Aug. 9 4♋
Aug. 8 5♋	29 9♎	Aug. 9 19♋	29 24♍R	28 20♍	19 16♋
18 12♋	Sep. 8 20♎	19 1♌	Sep. 8 19♍R	Sep. 7 3♎	29 27♋
28 19♋	18 2♏	29 13♌	18 13♍R	17 15♎	Sep. 8 9♌
Sep. 7 28♋	28 14♏	Sep. 8 25♌	28 9♍R	27 27♎	18 21♌
17 8♌	Oct. 8 25♏	18 8♍	Oct. 2 9♍D	Oct. 7 9♏	28 3♍
27 18♌	18 7♐	28 20♍	8 9♍	17 22♏	Oct. 8 15♍
Oct. 7 29♌	28 18♐	Oct. 8 3♎	18 13♍	27 4♐	18 27♍
17 11♍	Nov. 7 0♑	18 15♎	28 20♍	Nov. 6 16♐	30 10♎
27 22♍	17 11♑	28 28♎	Nov. 7 28♍	16 28♐	Nov. 7 22♎
Nov. 6 4♎	27 21♑	Nov. 7 10♏	17 7♎	26 11♑	17 5♏
16 16♎	Dec. 7 1♒	17 23♏	27 17♎	Dec. 6 23♑	27 17♏
26 28♎	17 10♒	27 5♐	Dec. 7 28♎	16 5♒	Dec. 7 0♐
Dec. 6 10♏	27 18♒	Dec. 7 18♐	17 9♏	26 17♒	17 12♐
16 23♏		17 0♑	27 21♏		27 25♐
26 5♐		27 13♑			

R = Retrograde.   D = Direct.   (See page 20.)

VENUS (To nearest degree at Midnight (o h. o m.) G.M.T.) 1930–1935

1930	1931	1932	1933	1934	1935
Jan. 1 1♑	Jan. 1 28♏	Jan. 1 8♒	Jan. 1 13♐	Jan. 1 20♒	Jan. 1 20♑
11 14♑	11 5♐	11 20♒	11 26♐	11 23♒	11 3♒
				16 24♒R	
21 26♑	21 14♐	21 2♓	21 8♑	21 23♒R	21 15♒
31 9♒	31 23♐	31 15♓	31 21♑	31 19♒R	31 28♒
Feb. 10 21♒	Feb. 10 4♑	Feb. 10 27♓	Feb. 10 3♒	Feb. 10 13♒R	Feb. 10 10♓
20 4♓	20 14♑	20 9♈	20 16♒	20 9♒R	20 23♓
				27 8♒D	
Mar. 2 16♓	Mar. 2 26♑	Mar. 1 21♈	Mar. 2 28♒	Mar. 2 8♒	Mar. 2 5♈
12 29♓	12 7♒	11 2♉	12 11♓	12 12♒	12 17♈
22 11♈	22 19♒	21 14♉	22 23♓	22 18♒	22 29♈
Apr. 1 24♈	Apr. 1 0♓	31 25♉	Apr. 1 6♈	Apr. 1 25♒	Apr. 1 12♉
11 6♉	11 12♓	Apr. 10 5♊	11 18♈	11 4♓	11 24♉
21 18♉	21 24♓	20 15♊	21 0♉	21 14♓	21 6♊
May 1 1♊	May 1 6♈	30 25♊	May 1 13♉	May 1 24♓	May 1 17♊
11 13♊	11 18♈	May 10 3♋	11 25♉	11 5♈	11 29♊
21 25♊	21 0♉	20 10♋	21 7♊	21 16♈	21 10♋
31 7♋	31 12♉	30 14♋	31 20♊	31 27♈	31 22♋
		Jun. 8 15♋R			
Jun. 10 19♋	Jun. 10 24♉	9 15♋R	Jun. 10 2♋	Jun. 10 9♉	Jun. 10 2♌
20 1♌	20 6♊	19 13♋R	20 14♋	20 20♉	20 13♌
30 13♌	30 18♊	29 7♋R	30 26♋	30 2♊	30 23♌
July 10 25♌	July 10 0♋	9 2♋R	July 10 8♌	July 10 14♊	July 10 2♍
20 6♍	20 13♋	19 29♊R	20 21♌	20 26♊	20 10♍
		22 29♊D			
30 18♍	30 25♋	29 0♋	30 3♍	30 7♋	30 17♍
Aug. 9 29♍	Aug. 9 7♌	8 4♋	Aug. 9 15♍	Aug. 9 20♋	Aug. 9 21♍
19 10♎	19 20♌	18 11♋	19 27♍	19 2♌	19 23♍R
29 20♎	29 2♍	28 19♋	29 9♎	29 14♌	29 20♍R
Sep. 8 1♏	Sep. 8 14♍	7 28♋	Sep. 8 21♎	Sep. 8 26♌	Sep. 8 15♍R
18 11♏	18 27♍	17 8♌	18 3♏	18 8♍	18 9♍R
28 19♏	28 9♎	27 19♌	28 15♏	28 21♍	28 7♍R
Oct. 8 27♏	Oct. 8 22♎	7 0♍	Oct. 8 26♏	Oct. 8 3♎	Oct. 8 8♍
18 3♐	18 4♏	17 11♍	18 8♐	18 16♎	18 12♍
28 7♐	28 17♏	27 23♍	28 19♐	28 28♎	28 19♍
Nov. 2 7♐R					
7 7♐R	Nov. 7 29♏	Nov. 6 5♎	Nov. 7 0♑	Nov. 7 11♏	Nov. 7 28♍
17 3♐R	17 12♐	16 17♎	17 11♑	17 23♏	17 7♎
27 27♏R	27 24♐	26 29♎	27 22♑	27 6♐	27 17♎
Dec. 7 23♏R	Dec. 7 7♑	Dec. 6 11♏	Dec. 7 1♒	Dec. 7 19♐	Dec. 7 28♎
13 22♏D					
17 22♏	17 19♑	16 23♏	17 10♒	17 1♑	17 9♏
27 26♏	27 1♒	26 6♐	27 17♒	27 14♑	27 21♏

R = Retrograde.   D = Direct.   (See page 20.)

VENUS (To nearest degree at Midnight (0 h. 0 m.) G.M.T.) 1936–1941

1936	1937	1938	1939	1940	1941
Jan. 1 27♏	Jan. 1 24♒	Jan. 1 2♑	Jan. 1 27♏	Jan. 1 8♒	Jan. 1 14♐
11 9♐	11 6♓	11 14♑	11 5♐	11 21♒	11 26♐
21 21♐	21 17♓	21 27♑	21 14♐	21 3♓	21 9♑
31 3♑	31 27♓	31 9♒	31 23♐	31 15♓	31 21♑
Feb. 10 15♑	Feb. 10 8♈	Feb. 10 22♒	Feb. 10 4♑	Feb. 10 27♓	Feb. 10 4♒
20 27♑	20 17♈	20 5♓	20 15♑	20 9♈	20 16♒
Mar. 1 10♒	Mar. 2 25♈	Mar. 2 17♓	Mar. 2 26♑	Mar. 1 21♈	Mar. 2 29♒
11 22♒	12 1♉	12 0♈	12 7♒	11 3♉	12 11♓
21 4♓	22 5♉	22 12♈	22 19♒	21 14♉	22 24♓
31 16♓	29 6♉ R	Apr. 1 24♈	Apr. 1 1♓	31 25♉	Apr. 1 6♈
Apr. 10 29♓	Apr. 1 5♉ R	11 7♉	11 13♓	Apr. 10 5♊	11 19♈
20 11♈	11 2♉ R	21 19♉	21 24♓	20 15♊	21 1♉
30 23♈	21 26♈ R	May 1 1♊	May 1 6♈	30 24♊	May 1 13♉
May 10 6♉	May 1 21♈ R	11 13♊	11 18♈	May 10 2♋	11 26♉
20 18♉	10 19♈ D	21 26♊	21 0♉	20 9♋	21 8♊
30 0♊	11 20♈	31 8♋	31 13♉	30 13♋	31 20♊
Jun. 9 12♊	21 22♈	Jun. 10 20♋	Jun. 10 25♉	Jun. 6 13♋ R	Jun. 10 2♋
19 25♊	31 27♈	20 2♌	20 7♊	9 13♋ R	20 15♋
29 7♋	Jun. 10 4♉	30 13♌	30 19♊	19 10♋ R	30 27♋
July 9 19♋	20 13♉	July 10 25♌	July 10 1♋	29 4♋ R	July 10 9♌
19 2♌	30 22♉	20 7♍	20 13♋	July 9 29♊ R	20 21♌
29 14♌	July 10 2♊	30 18♍	30 26♋	19 27♊ D	30 3♍
Aug. 8 26♌	20 13♊	Aug. 9 29♍	Aug. 9 8♌	29 29♊	Aug. 9 16♍
18 9♍	30 24♊	19 10♎	19 20♌	Aug. 8 4♋	19 28♍
28 21♍	Aug. 9 5♋	29 21♎	29 3♍	18 11♋	29 10♎
Sep. 7 3♎	19 16♋	Sep. 8 1♏	Sep. 8 15♍	28 19♋	Sep. 8 22♎
17 16♎	29 28♋	18 10♏	18 27♍	Sep. 7 28♋	18 3♏
27 28♎	Sep. 8 9♌	28 19♏	28 10♎	17 8♌	28 15♏
Oct. 7 10♏	18 21♌	Oct. 8 27♏	Oct. 8 22♎	27 19♌	Oct. 8 27♏
17 22♏	28 3♍	18 2♐	18 5♏	Oct. 7 0♍	18 8♐
27 5♐	Oct. 8 16♍	28 5♐	28 17♏	17 12♍	28 20♐
Nov. 6 17♐	18 28♍	31 5♐ R	Nov. 7 0♐	27 23♍	Nov. 7 1♑
16 29♐	Nov. 7 23♎	Nov. 7 4♐ R	17 12♐	Nov. 6 5♎	17 11♑
26 11♑	17 5♏	17 29♏ R	27 25♐	16 17♎	27 22♑
Dec. 6 23♑	27 18♏	27 23♏ R	Dec. 7 7♑	26 29♎	Dec. 7 1♒
16 5♒	Dec. 7 0♐	Dec. 7 20♏ R	17 20♑	Dec. 6 12♏	17 9♒
26 17♒	17 13♐	11 20♏ D	27 2♒	16 24♏	27 16♒
	27 25♐	17 20♏		26 6♐	
		27 24♏			

R = Retrograde.   D = Direct.   (See page 20.)

VENUS (To nearest degree at Midnight (0 h. 0 m.) G.M.T.) 1942-1947

1942	1943	1944	1945	1946	1947
Jan. 1 18♒	Jan. 1 21♑	Jan. 1 27♍	Jan. 1 24♒	Jan. 1 2♑	Jan. 1 27♍
11 21♒	11 3♒	11 9♐	11 6♓	11 15♑	11 4♐
14 21♒R	21 16♒	21 21♐	21 17♓	21 28♑	21 13♐
21 20♒R	31 28♒	31 3♑	31 28♓	31 10♒	31 23♐
31 15♒R	Feb. 10 11♓	Feb. 10 16♑	Feb. 10 8♈	Feb. 10 23♒	Feb. 10 4♑
Feb. 10 9♒R	20 23♓	20 28♑	20 17♈	20 5♓	20 15♑
19 6♒R	Mar. 2 6♈	Mar. 1 10♒	Mar. 2 24♈	Mar. 2 18♓	Mar. 2 26♑
24 6♒D	12 18♈	11 22♒	12 0♉	12 0♈	12 8♒
Mar. 2 6♒	22 0♉	21 5♓	22 3♉	22 13♈	22 20♒
12 10♒	Apr. 1 12♉	31 17♓	26 4♉R	Apr. 1 25♈	Apr. 1 1♓
22 17♒	11 24♉	Apr. 10 29♓	Apr. 1 3♉R	11 7♉	11 13♓
Apr. 1 25♒	21 6♊	20 12♈	11 28♈R	21 20♉	21 25♓
11 4♓	May 1 18♊	30 24♈	21 22♈R	May 1 2♊	May 1 7♈
21 14♓	11 29♊	May 10 6♉	May 1 18♈R	11 14♊	11 19♈
May 1 25♓	21 11♋	20 19♉	7 17♈D	21 26♊	21 1♉
11 5♈	31 22♋	30 1♊	11 18♈	31 8♋	31 13♉
21 16♈	Jun. 10 3♌	Jun. 9 13♊	21 21♈	Jun. 10 20♋	Jun. 10 25♉
31 28♈	20 13♌	19 25♊	31 26♈	20 2♌	20 7♊
Jun. 10 9♉	30 23♌	29 8♋	Jun. 10 4♉	30 14♌	30 20♊
20 21♉	July 10 2♍	July 9 20♋	20 13♉	July 10 26♌	July 10 2♋
30 2♊	20 10♍	19 2♌	30 22♉	20 7♍	20 14♋
July 10 14♊	30 16♍	29 15♌	July 10 2♊	30 18♍	30 26♋
20 26♊	Aug. 9 20♍	Aug. 8 27♌	20 13♊	Aug. 9 0♎	Aug. 9 9♌
30 8♋	16 21♍R	18 9♍	30 24♊	19 10♎	19 21♌
Aug. 9 20♋	19 20♍R	28 22♍	Aug. 9 5♋	29 21♎	29 3♍
19 2♌	29 17♍R	Sep. 7 4♎	19 17♋	Sep. 8 1♏	Sep. 8 16♍
29 15♌	Sep. 8 11♍R	17 16♎	29 28♋	18 10♏	18 28♍
Sep. 8 27♌	18 6♍R	27 28♎	Sep. 8 10♌	28 19♏	28 11♎
18 9♍	28 4♍D	Oct. 7 11♏	18 22♌	Oct. 8 26♏	Oct. 8 23♎
28 22♍	Oct. 8 6♍	17 23♏	28 4♍	18 1♐	18 6♏
Oct. 8 4♎	18 12♍	27 5♐	Oct. 8 16♍	28 3♐	28 18♏
18 17♎	28 19♍	Nov. 6 17♐	18 29♍	29 2♐R	Nov. 7 0♐
28 29♎	Nov. 7 27♍	16 0♑	28 11♎	Nov. 7 1♐R	17 13♐
Nov. 7 12♏	17 7♎	26 12♑	Nov. 7 23♎	17 25♏R	27 25♐
17 24♏	27 18♎	Dec. 6 24♑	17 6♏	27 20♏R	Dec. 7 7♑
27 7♐	Dec. 7 29♎	16 6♒	27 18♏	Dec. 7 17♏R	17 20♑
Dec. 7 19♐	17 10♏	26 18♒	Dec. 7 1♐	9 17♏D	27 3♒
17 2♑	27 22♏		17 14♐	17 19♏	
27 14♑			27 26♐	27 23♏	

R=Retrograde.   D=Direct.   (See page 20.)

VENUS (To nearest degree at Midnight (o h. o m.) G.M.T.) 1948-1953

1948	1949	1950	1951	1952	1953
Jan. 1 9♒	Jan. 1 15♐	Jan. 1 17♒	Jan. 1 21♑	Jan. 1 28♏	Jan. 1 25♒
11 21♒	11 27♐	11 19♒R	11 4♒	11 10♐	11 6♓
21 4♓	21 10♑	21 17♒R	21 16♒	21 22♐	21 17♓
31 16♓	31 22♑	31 11♒R	31 29♒	31 4♑	31 28♓
Feb. 10 28♓	Feb. 10 5♒	Feb. 10 5♒R	Feb. 10 11♓	Feb. 10 16♑	Feb. 10 8♈
20 10♈	20 17♒	22 3♒D	20 24♓	20 29♑	20 16♈
Mar. 1 22♈	Mar. 2 0♓	Mar. 2 5♒	Mar. 2 6♈	Mar. 1 11♒	Mar. 2 24♈
11 3♉	12 12♓	12 9♒	12 19♈	11 23♒	12 29♈
21 14♉	22 24♓	22 16♒	22 1♉	21 5♓	22 1♉
31 25♉	Apr. 1 7♈	Apr. 1 25♒	Apr. 1 13♉	31 18♓	24 1♉R
Apr. 10 6♊	11 19♈	11 4♓	11 25♉	Apr. 10 0♈	Apr. 1 0♉R
20 15♊	21 2♉	21 14♓	21 7♊	20 12♈	11 25♈R
30 24♊	May 1 14♉	May 1 25♓	May 1 0♋	30 25♈	21 19♈R
May 10 2♋	11 26♉	11 6♈	11 11♋	May 10 7♉	May 1 15♈R
20 8♋	21 9♊	21 17♈	31 22♋	20 19♉	5 15♈D
30 11♋	31 21♊	31 28♈	Jun. 10 3♌	30 1♊	11 16♈
Jun. 4 11♋R	Jun. 10 3♋	Jun. 10 10♉	20 13♌	Jun. 9 14♊	21 20♈
9 10♋R	20 15♋	20 21♉	30 23♌	19 26♊	31 26♈
19 6♋R	30 28♋	30 3♊	July 10 2♍	29 8♋	Jun. 10 4♉
29 0♋R	July 10 10♌	July 10 15♊	20 9♍	July 9 21♋	20 13♉
July 9 26♊R	20 22♌	20 27♊	30 15♍	19 3♌	30 22♉
17 25♊D	30 4♍	30 9♋	Aug. 9 18♍	29 15♌	July 10 3♊
19 25♊	Aug. 9 16♍	Aug. 9 21♋	14 18♍R	Aug. 8 28♌	20 13♊
29 28♊	19 28♍	19 3♌	19 18♍R	18 10♍	30 24♊
Aug. 8 3♋	29 10♎	29 15♌	29 14♍R	28 22♍	Aug. 9 6♋
18 10♋	Sep. 8 22♎	Sep. 8 27♌	Sep. 8 8♍R	Sep. 7 5♎	19 17♋
28 19♋	18 4♏	18 10♍	18 3♍R	17 17♎	29 29♋
Sep. 7 28♋	28 16♏	28 22♍	25 2♍D	27 29♎	Sep. 8 11♌
17 9♌	Oct. 8 27♏	Oct. 8 5♎	28 2♍	Oct. 7 11♏	18 23♌
27 19♌	18 9♐	18 17♎	Oct. 8 5♍	17 24♏	28 5♍
Oct. 7 1♍	28 20♐	28 0♏	18 11♍	27 6♐	Oct. 8 17♍
17 12♍	Nov. 7 1♑	Nov. 7 12♏	28 18♍	Nov. 6 18♐	18 29♍
27 24♍	17 11♑	17 25♏	Nov. 7 27♍	16 0♑	28 12♎
Nov. 7 6♎	27 21♑	27 7♐	17 7♎	26 12♑	Nov. 7 24♎
16 18♎	Dec. 7 1♒	Dec. 7 20♐	27 18♎	Dec. 6 24♑	17 7♏
26 0♏	17 9♒	17 3♑	Dec. 7 29♎	16 6♒	27 19♏
Dec. 6 12♏	27 15♒	27 15♑	17 10♏	26 18♒	Dec. 7 2♐
16 25♏			27 22♏		17 14♐
26 7♐					27 27♐

R = Retrograde.   D = Direct.   (See page 20.)

VENUS (To nearest degree at Midnight (0 h. 0 m.) G.M.T.) 1954-1959

1954	1955	1956	1957	1958	1959
Jan. 1 3♑	Jan. 1 26♍	Jan. 1 10♒	Jan. 1 15♐	Jan. 1 15♒	Jan. 1 22♑
11 16♑	11 4♐	11 22♒	11 28♐	9 16♒R	11 5♒
21 28♑	21 13♐	21 4♓	21 10♑	11 16♒R	21 17♒
31 11♒	31 24♐	31 16♓	31 23♑	21 13♒R	31 0♓
Feb. 10 23♒	Feb. 10 4♑	Feb. 10 28♓	Feb. 10 5♒	31 7♒R	Feb. 10 12♓
20 6♓	20 15♑	20 10♈	20 18♒	Feb. 10 2♒R	20 25♓
Mar. 2 18♓	Mar. 2 27♑	Mar. 1 22♈	Mar. 2 0♓	19 1♒D	Mar. 2 7♈
12 1♈	12 8♒	11 4♉	12 13♓	20 1♒	12 19♈
22 13♈	22 20♒	21 15♉	22 25♓	Mar. 2 3♒	22 1♉
Apr. 1 26♈	Apr. 1 2♓	31 26♉	Apr. 1 8♈	12 9♒	Apr. 1 13♉
11 8♉	11 14♓	Apr. 10 6♊	11 20♈	22 16♒	11 25♉
21 20♉	21 26♓	20 15♊	21 2♉	Apr. 1 25♒	21 7♊
May 1 3♊	May 1 8♈	30 24♊	May 1 15♉	11 4♓	May 1 19♊
11 15♊	11 20♈	May 10 1♋	11 27♉	21 14♓	11 0♋
21 27♊	21 2♉	20 7♋	21 9♊	May 1 25♓	21 12♋
31 9♋	31 14♉	30 9♋	31 22♊	11 6♈	31 23♋
Jun. 10 21♋	Jun. 10 26♉	Jun. 1 9♋R	Jun. 10 4♋	21 17♈	Jun. 10 3♌
20 3♌	20 8♊	9 8♋R	20 16♋	31 29♈	20 13♌
30 14♌	30 20♊	19 3♋R	30 28♋	Jun. 10 10♉	30 23♌
July 10 26♌	July 10 2♋	29 27♊R	July 10 10♌	20 22♉	July 10 1♍
20 8♍	20 15♋	July 9 23♊R	20 23♌	30 4♊	20 8♍
30 19♍	30 27♋	14 23♊D	30 5♍	July 10 15♊	30 14♍
Aug. 9 0♎	Aug. 9 9♌	19 23♊	Aug. 9 17♍	20 27♊	Aug. 9 16♍
19 11♎	19 22♌	29 26♊	19 29♍	30 9♋	12 16♍R
29 21♎	29 4♍	Aug. 8 2♋	29 11♎	Aug. 9 21♋	19 15♍R
Sep. 8 1♏	Sep. 8 16♍	18 10♋	Sep. 8 23♎	19 4♌	29 10♍R
18 10♏	18 29♍	28 19♋	18 4♏	29 16♌	Sep. 8 4♍R
28 18♏	28 11♎	Sep. 7 29♋	28 16♏	Sep. 8 28♌	18 0♍
Oct. 8 25♏	Oct. 8 24♎	17 9♌	Oct. 8 28♏	18 11♍	23 0♍D
18 29♏	18 6♏	27 20♌	18 9♐	28 23♍	28 0♍
26 0♐R	28 19♏	Oct. 7 1♍	28 20♐	Oct. 8 5♎	Oct. 8 4♍
28 0♐R	Nov. 7 1♐	17 13♍	Nov. 7 1♑	18 18♎	18 10♍
Nov. 7 27♏R	17 14♐	27 24♍	17 12♑	28 0♏	28 18♍
17 21♏R	27 26♐	Nov. 7 7♎	27 21♑	Nov. 7 13♏	Nov. 7 27♍
Dec. 6 15♏D	Dec. 7 9♑	17 20♎	Dec. 7 0♒	17 26♏	17 7♎
7 15♏	17 21♑	27 2♏	17 8♒	27 8♐	27 18♎
17 17♏	27 3♒	Dec. 6 13♏	27 14♒	Dec. 7 21♐	Dec. 7 29♎
27 22♏		16 25♏		17 3♑	17 11♏
		26 8♐		27 16♑	27 22♏

R=Retrograde. D=Direct. (See page 20.)

VENUS (To nearest degree at Midnight (0 h. 0 m.) G.M.T.) 1960–1965

1960	1961	1962	1963	1964	1965
Jan. 1 28♏	Jan. 1 25♒	Jan. 1 4♑	Jan. 1 25♏	Jan. 1 10♒	Jan. 1 16♐
11 10♐	11 7♓	11 16♑	11 4♐	11 22♒	11 28♐
21 22♐	21 17♓	21 29♑	21 13♐	21 5♓	21 11♑
31 5♑	31 28♓	31 11♒	31 24♐	31 17♓	31 23♑
Feb. 10 17♑	Feb. 10 7♈	Feb. 10 24♒	Feb. 10 5♑	Feb. 10 29♓	Feb. 10 6♒
20 29♑	20 16♈	20 7♓	20 16♑	20 11♈	20 18♒
Mar. 1 11♒	Mar. 2 23♈	Mar. 2 19♓	Mar. 2 27♑	Mar. 1 23♈	Mar. 2 1♓
11 24♒	12 28♈	12 2♈	12 9♒	11 4♉	12 13♓
21 6♓	21 29♈R	22 14♈	22 20♒	21 15♉	22 26♓
31 18♓	22 29♈R	Apr. 1 26♈	Apr. 1 2♓	31 26♉	Apr. 1 8♈
Apr. 10 1♈	Apr. 1 27♈R	11 9♉	11 14♓	Apr. 10 6♊	11 21♈
20 13♈	11 21♈R	21 21♉	21 26♓	20 15♊	21 3♉
30 25♈	21 15♈R	May 1 3♊	May 1 8♈	30 24♊	May 1 15♉
May 10 8♉	May 1 13♈R	11 15♊	11 20♈	May 10 1♋	11 28♉
20 20♉	3 13♈D	21 27♊	21 2♉	20 5♋	21 10♊
30 2♊	11 14♈	31 9♋	31 14♉	30 7♋R	31 22♊
Jun. 9 14♊	21 19♈	Jun. 10 21♋	Jun. 10 27♉	Jun. 9 5♋R	Jun. 10 4♋
19 27♊	31 25♈	20 3♌	20 9♊	19 29♊R	20 17♋
29 9♋	Jun. 10 4♉	30 15♌	30 21♊	29 23♊R	30 29♋
July 9 21♋	20 13♉	July 10 27♌	July 10 3♋	July 9 20♊R	July 10 11♌
19 4♌	30 23♉	20 8♍	20 15♋	12 20♊D	20 23♌
29 16♌	July 10 3♊	30 19♍	30 28♋	19 21♊	30 5♍
Aug. 8 28♌	20 14♊	Aug. 9 0♎	Aug. 9 10♌	29 25♊	Aug. 9 17♍
18 11♍	30 25♊	19 11♎	19 22♌	Aug. 8 2♋	19 29♍
28 23♍	Aug. 9 6♋	29 21♎	29 5♍	18 10♋	Sep. 8 23♎
Sep. 7 5♎	19 18♋	Sep. 8 1♏	Sep. 8 17♍	28 19♋	18 5♏
17 17♎	29 29♋	18 10♏	18 0♎	Sep. 7 29♋	28 17♏
27 0♏	Sep. 8 11♌	28 18♏	28 12♎	17 9♌	Oct. 8 28♏
Oct. 7 12♏	18 23♌	Oct. 8 24♏	Oct. 8 24♎	27 20♌	18 9♐
17 24♏	28 5♍	18 27♏	18 7♏	Oct. 7 1♍	28 20♐
27 6♐	Oct. 8 18♍	24 28♏R	28 19♏	17 13♍	Nov. 7 1♑
Nov. 6 19♐	18 0♎	28 27♏R	Nov. 7 2♐	27 25♍	17 12♑
16 1♑	28 12♎	Nov. 7 23♏R	17 14♐	Nov. 6 7♎	27 21♑
26 13♑	Nov. 7 25♎	17 17♏R	27 27♐	16 19♎	Dec. 7 0♒
Dec. 6 25♑	17 7♏	27 13♏R	Dec. 7 9♑	26 2♏	17 7♒
16 7♒	27 20♏	Dec. 2 12♏D	17 22♑	Dec. 6 14♏	27 12♒
26 18♒	Dec. 7 2♐	7 12♏	27 4♒	16 26♏	
31 24♒	17 15♐	17 16♏		26 8♐	
	27 27♐	27 22♏			

R = Retrograde.   D = Direct.   (See page 20.)

VENUS (To nearest degree at Midnight (0 h. 0 m.) G.M.T.) 1966-1971

1966	1967	1968	1969	1970	1971
Jan. 1 13♒	Jan. 1 23♑	Jan. 1 29♏	Jan. 1 26♒	Jan. 1 4♑	Jan. 1 25♏
6 14♒R	11 5♒	11 11♐	11 7♓	11 17♑	11 4♐
11 13♒R	21 18♒	21 23♐	21 18♓	21 0♒	21 13♐
21 9♒R	31 0♓	31 5♑	31 28♓	31 12♒	31 24♐
31 3♒R	Feb. 10 13♓	Feb. 10 17♑	Feb. 10 7♈	Feb. 10 25♒	Feb. 10 5♑
Feb. 10 29♑R	20 25♓	20 0♒	20 15♈	20 7♓	20 16♑
16 28♑D	Mar. 2 7♈	Mar. 1 12♒	Mar. 2 22♈	Mar. 2 20♓	Mar. 2 28♑
20 29♑	12 20♈	11 24♒	12 26♈	12 2♈	12 9♒
Mar. 2 2♒	22 2♉	21 7♓	19 27♈R	22 15♈	22 21♒
12 8♒	Apr. 1 14♉	31 19♓	22 27♈R	Apr. 1 27♈	Apr. 1 3♓
22 16♒	11 26♉	Apr. 10 1♈	Apr. 1 23♈R	11 9♉	11 15♓
Apr. 1 25♒	21 8♊	20 14♈	11 17♈R	21 22♉	21 27♓
11 4♓	May 1 19♊	30 26♈	21 12♈R	May 1 4♊	May 1 9♈
May 1 25♓	11 1♋	May 10 8♉	30 11♈D	11 16♊	11 21♈
11 6♈	21 12♋	20 21♉	May 1 11♈	21 28♊	21 3♉
21 18♈	31 23♋	30 3♊	11 13♈	31 10♋	31 15♉
31 29♈	Jun. 10 3♌	Jun. 9 15♊	21 18♈	Jun. 10 22♋	Jun. 10 27♉
Jun. 10 11♉	20 13♌	19 27♊	31 25♈	20 4♌	20 9♊
20 22♉	30 23♌	29 10♋	Jun. 10 3♉	30 16♌	30 22♊
30 4♊	July 10 1♍	July 9 22♋	20 13♉	July 10 27♌	July 10 4♋
July 10 16♊	20 8♍	19 4♌	30 23♉	20 9♍	20 16♋
20 28♊	30 12♍	29 17♌	July 10 3♊	30 20♍	30 28♋
30 10♋	Aug. 9 14♍R	Aug. 8 29♌	20 14♊	Aug. 9 1♎	Aug. 9 11♌
Aug. 9 22♋	19 12♍R	18 11♍	30 25♊	19 11♎	19 23♌
19 4♌	Sep. 8 1♍R	28 24♍	Aug. 9 7♋	29 21♎	29 5♍
29 16♌	18 28♌R	Sep. 7 6♎	19 18♋	Sep. 8 1♏	Sep. 8 18♍
Sep. 8 29♌	20 28♌D	17 18♎	29 0♌	18 9♏	18 0♎
18 11♍	30 29♌	27 0♏	Sep. 8 12♌	28 17♏	28 13♎
28 24♍	Oct. 8 3♍	Oct. 7 13♏	18 24♌	Oct. 8 22♏	Oct. 8 25♎
Oct. 8 6♎	18 10♍	17 25♏	28 6♍	18 25♏	18 8♏
18 19♎	28 18♍	27 7♐	Oct. 8 18♍	21 25♏R	28 20♏
28 1♏	Nov. 7 27♍	Nov. 6 19♐	18 1♎	28 24♏R	Nov. 7 2♐
Nov. 7 14♏	17 8♎	16 1♑	28 13♎	Nov. 7 20♏R	17 15♐
17 26♏	27 18♎	26 13♑	Nov. 7 25♎	17 14♏R	27 27♐
27 9♐	Dec. 7 0♏	Dec. 6 25♑	17 8♏	27 10♏R	Dec. 7 10♑
Dec. 7 21♐	17 11♏	16 7♒	27 20♏	Dec. 2 10♏D	17 22♑
17 4♑	27 23♏	26 19♒	Dec. 7 3♐	7 10♏	27 5♒
27 16♑			17 16♐	17 14♏	
			27 28♐	27 21♏	

R = Retrograde.   D = Direct.   (See page 20.)

VENUS (To nearest degree at Midnight (0 h. 0 m.) G.M.T.) 1972-1975

1972		1973		1974		1975	
Jan. 1	11♒	Jan. 1	17♐	Jan. 1	11♒	Jan. 1	23♑
11	23♒	11	29♐	4	11♒R	11	6♒
21	5♓	21	12♑	11	10♒R	21	18♒
31	17♓	31	24♑	21	5♒R	31	1♓
Feb. 10	0♈	Feb. 10	7♒	31	29♑R	Feb. 10	13♓
20	11♈	20	19♒	Feb. 10	26♑R	20	26♓
Mar. 1	23♈	Mar. 2	2♓	14	26♑D	Mar. 2	8♈
11	4♉	12	14♓	20	27♑	12	20♈
21	15♉	22	26♓	Mar. 2	1♒	22	3♉
31	26♉	Apr. 1	9♈	12	7♒	Apr. 1	15♉
Apr. 10	6♊	11	21♈	22	15♒	21	8♊
20	15♊	21	4♉	Apr. 1	25♒	May 1	20♊
30	23♊	May 1	16♉	11	4♓	11	1♋
May 10	0♋	11	28♉	21	15♓	21	12♋
20	4♋	21	11♊	May 1	26♓	31	23♋
27	5♋R	31	23♊	11	7♈	Jun. 10	4♌
30	5♋R	Jun. 10	5♋	21	18♈	20	13♌
Jun. 10	1♋R	20	17♋	31	0♉	30	22♌
20	25♊R	30	0♌	Jun. 10	11♉	July 10	0♍
30	20♊R	July 10	12♌	20	23♉	20	7♍
July 9	18♊R	20	24♌	30	5♊	30	11♍
10	18♊D	30	6♍	July 10	17♊	Aug. 7	12♍R
19	20♊	Aug. 9	18♍	20	29♊	9	12♍R
29	25♊	19	0♎	30	11♋	19	9♍R
Aug. 8	1♋	29	12♎	Aug. 9	23♋	29	3♍R
18	10♋	Sep. 8	24♎	19	5♌	Sep. 8	27♌R
28	19♋	18	5♏	29	17♌	18	25♌D
Sep. 7	29♋	28	17♏	Sep. 8	29♌	28	27♌
17	10♌	Oct. 8	28♏	18	12♍	Oct. 8	2♍
27	21♌	18	10♐	28	24♍	18	9♍
Oct. 7	2♍	28	21♐	Oct. 8	7♎	28	18♍
17	14♍	Nov. 7	1♑	18	19♎	Nov. 7	27♍
27	25♍	17	12♑	28	2♏	27	19♎
Nov. 6	7♎	27	21♑	Nov. 7	14♏	Dec. 7	0♏
16	20♎	Dec. 7	29♑	17	27♏	17	12♏
26	2♏	17	6♒	27	9♐	27	23♏
Dec. 6	14♏	27	10♒	Dec. 7	22♐	31	28♏
16	27♏			17	5♑		
26	9♐			27	17♑		

R=Retrograde.   D=Direct.   (See page 20.)

NOTES

MARS (To nearest degree at Midnight (o h. o m.) G.M.T.) 1900-1905

1900	1901	1902	1903	1904	1905
Jan. 1 14♑	Jan. 1 12♍	Jan. 1 29♑	Jan. 1 5≏	Jan. 1 15≈	Jan. 1 23≏
11 22♑	11 13♍	11 7≈	11 9≏	11 23≈	11 29≏
21 29♑	14 13♍R	21 15≈	21 12≏	21 1♓	21 4♏
31 7≈	21 12♍R	31 23≈	31 14≏	31 9♓	31 8♏
Feb. 10 15≈	31 10♍R	Feb. 10 1♓	Feb. 10 16≏	Feb. 10 17♓	Feb. 10 13♏
20 23≈	Feb. 10 8♍R	20 9♓	19 16≏R	20 24♓	20 16♏
Mar. 2 0♓	20 4♍R	Mar. 2 17♓	20 16≏R	Mar. 1 2♈	Mar. 2 20♏
12 9♓	Mar. 2 0♍R	12 24♓	Mar. 2 15≏R	11 10♈	12 22♏
22 16♓	12 27♌R	22 2♈	12 13≏R	21 17♈	22 24♏
Apr. 1 24♓	22 24♌R	Apr. 1 10♈	22 10≏R	31 25♈	Apr. 1 25♏
11 2♈	Apr. 1 23♌R	11 18♈	Apr. 1 6≏R	Apr. 10 2♉	4 25♏R
21 10♈	5 23♌D	21 25♈	11 3≏R	20 10♉	11 25♏R
May 1 17♈	11 23♌	May 1 3♉	21 0≏R	30 17♉	21 23♏R
11 25♈	21 25♌	11 10♉	May 1 28♍R	May 10 24♉	May 1 20♏R
21 3♉	May 1 27♌	21 17♉	10 27♍D	20 1♊	11 17♏R
31 10♉	11 0♍	31 25♉	11 27♍	30 8♊	21 13♏R
Jun. 10 17♉	21 4♍	Jun. 10 2♊	21 28♍	Jun. 9 15♊	31 10♏R
20 25♉	31 8♍	20 9♊	31 0≏	19 22♊	Jun. 10 9♏R
30 2♊	Jun. 10 12♍	30 16♊	Jun. 10 3≏	29 29♊	18 8♏D
July 10 9♊	20 17♍	July 10 23♊	20 6≏	July 9 6♋	20 8♏
20 16♊	30 22♍	20 0♋	30 10≏	19 12♋	30 9♏
30 23♊	July 10 28♍	30 6♋	July 10 15≏	29 19♋	July 10 12♏
Aug. 9 29♊	20 4≏	Aug. 9 13♋	20 20≏	Aug. 8 25♋	20 15♏
19 6♋	30 9≏	19 19♋	30 26≏	18 2♌	30 19♏
29 12♋	Aug. 9 16≏	29 26♋	Aug. 9 1♏	28 8♌	Aug. 9 23♏
Sep. 8 19♋	19 22≏	Sep. 8 2♌	19 7♏	Sep. 7 15♌	19 28♏
18 25♋	29 28≏	18 8♌	29 14♏	17 21♌	29 4♐
28 1♌	Sep. 8 5♏	28 15♌	Sep. 8 20♏	27 27♌	Sep. 8 10♐
Oct. 8 7♌	18 12♏	Oct. 8 20♌	18 27♏	Oct. 7 3♍	18 16♐
18 12♌	28 18♏	18 27♌	28 4♐	17 9♍	28 23♐
28 17♌	Oct. 8 25♏	28 2♍	Oct. 8 11♐	27 16♍	Oct. 8 0♑
Nov. 7 22♌	18 2♐	Nov. 7 8♍	18 18♐	Nov. 6 22♍	18 7♑
17 27♌	28 10♐	17 13♍	28 26♐	16 28♍	28 14♑
27 2♍	Nov. 7 17♐	27 19♍	Nov. 7 3♑	26 3≏	Nov. 7 22♑
Dec. 7 5♍	17 25♐	Dec. 7 24♍	17 10♑	Dec. 6 9≏	17 29♑
17 8♍	27 2♑	17 29♍	27 18♑	16 15≏	27 6≈
27 11♍	Dec. 7 10♑	27 3≏	Dec. 7 26♑	26 20≏	Dec. 7 14≈
	17 18♑		17 4≈		17 22≈
	27 25♑		27 11≈		27 0♓

R = Retrograde. D = Direct. (See page 20.

MARS (To nearest degree at Midnight (o h. o m.) G.M.T.) 1906-1911

1906	1907	1908	1909	1910	1911
Jan. 1 3♓	Jan. 1 9♏	Jan. 1 23♓	Jan. 1 24♏	Jan. 1 18♈	Jan. 1 8♐
11 11♓	11 15♏	11 0♈	11 0♐	11 23♈	11 15♐
21 19♓	21 21♏	21 7♈	21 7♐	21 29♈	21 22♐
31 26♓	31 27♏	31 14♈	31 14♐	31 5♉	31 29♐
Feb. 10 4♈	Feb. 10 3♐	Feb. 10 21♈	Feb. 10 21♐	Feb. 10 11♉	Feb. 10 7♑
20 11♈	20 8♐	20 28♈	20 27♐	20 16♉	20 14♑
Mar. 2 19♈	Mar. 2 14♐	Mar. 1 5♉	Mar. 2 4♑	Mar. 2 22♉	Mar. 2 21♑
12 26♈	12 19♐	11 12♉	12 11♑	12 29♉	12 29♑
22 3♉	22 25♐	21 18♉	22 17♑	22 5♊	22 6♒
Apr. 1 10♉	Apr. 1 0♑	31 25♉	Apr. 1 24♑	Apr. 1 11♊	Apr. 1 13♒
11 18♉	11 4♑	Apr. 10 2♊	11 1♒	11 17♊	11 21♒
21 25♉	21 9♑	20 9♊	21 7♒	21 23♊	21 28♒
May 1 2♊	May 1 12♑	30 15♊	May 1 14♒	May 1 29♊	May 1 6♓
11 8♊	11 15♑	May 10 22♊	11 20♒	11 6♋	11 13♓
21 15♊	21 17♑	20 28♊	21 27♒	21 12♋	21 21♓
31 22♊	31 19♑	30 5♋	31 3♓	31 18♋	31 28♓
Jun. 10 29♊	Jun. 6 19♑R	Jun. 9 11♋	Jun. 10 9♓	Jun. 10 24♋	Jun. 10 6♈
20 5♋	10 19♑R	19 18♋	20 15♓	20 1♌	20 12♈
30 12♋	20 17♑R	29 24♋	30 20♓	30 7♌	30 19♈
July 10 19♋	30 15♑R	July 9 1♌	July 10 25♓	July 10 13♌	July 10 26♈
20 25♋	July 10 12♑R	19 7♌	20 29♓	20 19♌	20 3♉
30 2♌	20 10♑R	29 13♌	30 3♈	30 26♌	30 9♉
Aug. 9 8♌	30 8♑R	Aug. 8 19♌	Aug. 9 5♈	Aug. 9 2♍	Aug. 9 15♉
19 15♌	Aug. 9 7♑R	18 26♌	19 7♈	19 8♍	19 21♉
29 21♌	10 7♑D	28 2♍	24 7♈R	29 15♍	29 26♉
Sep. 8 27♌	19 8♑	Sep. 7 9♍	29 7♈R	Sep. 8 21♍	Sep. 8 1♊
18 3♍	29 10♑	17 15♍	Sep. 8 5♈R	18 27♍	18 5♊
28 10♍	Sep. 8 13♑	27 22♍	18 3♈R	28 4♎	28 8♊
Oct. 8 16♍	18 17♑	Oct. 7 28♍	28 0♈R	Oct. 7 10♎	Oct. 8 10♊
18 22♍	28 21♑	17 4♎	Oct. 8 27♓R	17 16♎	18 11♊
28 29♍	Oct. 8 27♑	27 11♎	18 26♓R	27 23♎	19 11♊R
Nov. 7 5♎	18 3♒	Nov. 6 17♎	24 25♓D	Nov. 7 0♏	28 10♊R
17 11♎	28 9♒	16 24♎	28 26♓	17 7♏	Nov. 7 8♊R
27 17♎	Nov. 7 15♒	26 0♏	Nov. 7 27♓	27 14♏	17 5♊R
Dec. 7 24♎	17 22♒	Dec. 6 7♏	17 29♓	Dec. 7 21♏	27 1♊R
17 0♏	27 29♒	16 13♏	27 2♈	17 27♏	Dec. 7 28♉R
27 6♏	Dec. 7 5♓	26 20♏	Dec. 7 6♈	27 5♐	17 25♉R
	17 12♓		17 10♈		27 24♉R
	27 19♓		27 15♈		30 24♉D

R = Retrograde.   D = Direct.   (See page 20.)

MARS (To nearest degree at Midnight (0 h. 0 m.) G.M.T.) 1912-1917

1912		1913		1914		1915		1916		1917	
Jan. 1	24♉	Jan. 1	23♐	Jan. 1	17♋R	Jan. 1	7♑	Jan. 1	0♍R	Jan. 1	24♑
11	25♉	11	0♑	11	12♋R	11	15♑	11	29♌R	11	1≈
21	27♉	21	8♑	21	9♋R	21	23♑	21	27♌R	21	9≈
31	0♊	31	15♑	31	7♋R	31	1≈	31	24♌R	31	17≈
Feb. 10	4♊	Feb. 10	23♑	Feb. 10	6♋R	Feb. 10	8≈	Feb. 10	20♌R	Feb. 10	25≈
20	8♊	20	1≈	13	6♋D	20	16≈	20	16♌R	20	3♓
Mar. 1	12♊	Mar. 2	8≈	20	6♋	Mar. 2	24≈	Mar. 1	13♌R	Mar. 2	11♓
11	17♊	12	16≈	Mar. 2	7♋	12	2♓	11	11♌R	12	18♓
21	22♊	22	24≈	12	10♋	22	10♓	21	10♌R	22	26♓
31	27♊	Apr. 1	2♓	22	13♋	Apr. 1	18♓	22	10♌D	Apr. 1	4♈
Apr. 10	2♋	11	9♓	Apr. 1	16♋	21	3♈	31	11♌	11	12♈
20	8♋	21	17♓	11	20♋	21	3♈	Apr. 10	12♌	21	19♈
30	14♋	May 1	25♓	21	25♋	May 1	11♈	20	15♌	May 1	27♈
May 10	19♋	11	2♈	May 1	0♌	11	19♈	30	18♌	11	5♉
20	25♋	21	10♈	11	5♌	21	26♈	May 10	22♌	21	12♉
30	1♌	31	17♈	21	10♌	31	4♉	20	26♌	31	19♉
Jun. 9	7♌	Jun. 10	25♈	31	15♌	Jun. 10	11♉	30	1♍	Jun. 10	27♉
19	13♌	20	2♉	Jun. 10	21♌	20	18♉	Jun. 9	6♍	20	4♊
29	19♌	30	9♉	20	26♌	30	26♉	19	11♍	30	11♊
July 9	25♌	July 10	17♉	30	2♍	July 10	3♊	29	16♍	July 10	18♊
19	1♍	20	24♉	July 10	8♍	20	10♊	July 9	22♍	20	25♊
29	7♍	30	0♊	20	14♍	30	17♊	19	28♍	30	1♋
Aug. 8	14♍	Aug. 9	7♊	30	20♍	Aug. 9	23♊	29	4≏	Aug. 9	8♋
18	20♍	19	13♊	Aug. 9	26♍	19	0♋	Aug. 8	10≏	19	14♋
28	26♍	29	20♊	19	3≏	29	6♋	18	16≏	29	21♋
Sep. 7	3≏	Sep. 8	26♊	29	9≏	Sep. 8	12♋	28	22≏	Sep. 8	27♋
17	9≏	18	1♋	Sep. 8	16≏	18	19♋	Sep. 7	29≏	18	3♌
27	16≏	28	7♋	18	22≏	28	24♋	17	6♏	28	10♌
Oct. 7	23≏	Oct. 8	11♋	Oct. 8	6♏	Oct. 8	0♌	27	12♏	Oct. 8	16♌
17	0♏	18	16♋	18	13♏	18	5♌	Oct. 7	19♏	18	21♌
27	6♏	28	19♋	28	20♏	28	11♌	17	26♏	28	27♌
Nov. 6	13♏	Nov. 7	22♋	Nov. 7	27♏	Nov. 7	15♌	27	4♐	Nov. 7	2♍
16	20♏	17	24♋	17	4♐	17	20♌	Nov. 6	11♐	17	8♍
26	27♏	27	25♋R	27	11♐	27	23♌	16	18♐	27	13♍
Dec. 6	4♐	Dec. 7	24♋R	Dec. 7	19♐	Dec. 7	26♌	26	26♐	Dec. 7	17♍
16	11♐	17	22♋R	17	26♐	17	28♌	Dec. 6	3♑	17	22♍
26	19♐	27	18♋R	27	4♑	27	0♍	16	11♑	27	25♍
								26	19♑		

R = Retrograde.   D = Direct.   (See page 20.)

MARS   (To nearest degree at Midnight (o h. o m.) G.M.T.)   1918-1923

1918		1919		1920		1921		1922		1923	
Jan. 1	27♍	Jan. 1	9♒	Jan. 1	17≏	Jan. 1	27♒	Jan. 1	3♏	Jan. 1	15♓
11	0≏	11	17♒	11	21≏	11	4♓	11	9♏	11	22♓
21	2≏	21	25♒	21	26≏	21	12♓	21	15♏	21	0♈
31	3≏	31	3♓	31	0♏	31	20♓	31	20♏	31	7♈
Feb. 4	3≏R	Feb. 10	11♓	Feb. 10	3♏	Feb. 10	28♓	Feb. 10	26♏	Feb. 10	14♈
10	3≏R	20	19♓	20	6♏	20	5♈	20	1♐	20	21♈
20	1≏R	Mar. 2	26♓	Mar. 1	8♏	Mar. 2	13♈	Mar. 2	6♐	Mar. 2	29♈
Mar. 2	29♍R	12	4♈	11	9♏	12	20♈	12	10♐	12	6♉
12	25♍R	22	12♈	15	9♏ R	22	28♈	22	14♐	22	13♉
22	21♍R	Apr. 1	19♈	21	9♏ R	Apr. 1	5♉	Apr. 1	18♐	Apr. 1	20♉
Apr. 1	18♍R	11	27♈	31	7♏ R	11	12♉	11	21♐	11	26♉
11	15♍R	21	4♉	Apr. 10	5♏ R	21	19♉	21	24♐	21	3♊
21	14♍R	May 1	12♉	20	1♏ R	May 1	26♉	May 1	25♐	May 1	10♊
26	14♍D	11	19♉	30	28≏R	11	3♊	8	25♐ R	11	17♊
May 1	14♍	21	26♉	May 10	24≏R	21	10♊	11	25♐ R	21	24♊
11	15♍	31	3♊	20	22≏R	31	17♊	21	24♐ R	Jun. 10	7♋
21	17♍	Jun. 10	10♊	30	21≏R	Jun. 10	24♊	31	22♐ R	20	13♋
31	20♍	20	17♊	Jun. 1	21≏D	20	1♋	Jun. 10	19♐ R	30	20♋
Jun. 10	24♍	30	24♊	9	22≏	30	7♋	20	16♐ R	July 10	26♋
20	28♍	July 10	1♋	19	23≏	July 10	14♋	30	13♐ R	20	3♌
30	3≏	20	8♋	29	26≏	20	21♋	July 10	11♐ R	30	9♌
July 10	8≏	30	14♋	July 9	29≏	30	27♋	17	11♐ D	Aug. 9	15♌
20	13≏	Aug. 9	21♋	19	3♏	Aug. 9	4♌	20	11♐	19	22♌
30	19≏	19	27♋	29	8♏	19	10♌	30	12♐	29	28♌
Aug. 9	25≏	Sep. 8	10♌	Aug. 8	13♏	29	16♌	Aug. 9	15♐	Sep. 8	4♍
19	1♏	18	16♌	18	19♏	Sep. 8	23♌	19	18♐	18	11♍
29	8♏	28	23♌	28	25♏	18	29♌	29	22♐	28	17♍
Sep. 8	14♏	Oct. 8	29♌	Sep. 7	1♐	28	5♍	Sep. 8	27♐	Oct. 8	23♍
18	21♏	18	5♍	17	8♐	Oct. 8	12♍	18	2♑	18	0≏
28	28♏	28	11♍	27	15♐	18	18♍	28	8♑	28	6≏
Oct. 8	5♐	Nov. 7	17♍	Oct. 7	22♐	28	24♍	Oct. 8	15♑	Nov. 7	13≏
18	12♐	17	22♍	17	29♐	Nov. 7	0≏	18	21♑	17	19≏
28	19♐	27	28♍	27	6♑	17	6≏	28	28♑	27	25≏
Nov. 7	27♐	Dec. 7	4≏	Nov. 6	14♑	27	12≏	Nov. 7	5♒	Dec. 7	2♏
17	5♑	17	9≏	16	21♑	Dec. 7	18≏	17	12♒	17	8♏
27	12♑	27	14≏	26	29♑	17	24≏	27	19♒	27	15♏
Dec. 7	20♑			Dec. 6	7♒	27	0♏	Dec. 7	27♒		
17	27♑			16	14♒			17	4♓		
27	5♒			26	22♒			27	11♓		

R = Retrograde.   D = Direct.   (See page 20.)

MARS   1918-1923

MARS (To nearest degree at Midnight (0 h. 0 m.) G.M.T.) 1924-1929

1924	1925	1926	1927	1928	1929
Jan. 1 18♏	Jan. 1 8♈	Jan. 1 3♐	Jan. 1 8♉	Jan. 1 17♐	Jan. 1 26♊R
11 24♏	11 14♈	11 10♐	11 11♉	11 24♐	11 23♊R
21 0♐	21 20♈	21 17♐	21 15♉	21 1♑	21 21♊R
31 7♐	31 27♈	31 23♐	31 19♉	31 9♑	27 21♊D
Feb. 10 14♐	Feb. 10 3♉	Feb. 10 1♑	Feb. 10 24♉	Feb. 10 16♑	31 21♊
20 20♐	20 9♉	20 8♑	20 29♉	20 24♑	Feb. 10 22♊
Mar. 1 26♐	Mar. 2 16♉	Mar. 2 15♑	Mar. 2 4♊	Mar. 1 1♒	20 24♊
11 3♑	12 22♉	12 22♑	12 10♊	11 9♒	Mar. 2 27♊
21 9♑	22 29♉	22 29♑	22 15♊	21 17♒	12 0♋
31 15♑	Apr. 1 5♊	Apr. 1 6♒	Apr. 1 21♊	31 24♒	22 4♋
Apr. 10 21♑	11 12♊	11 14♒	11 26♊	Apr. 10 2♓	Apr. 1 9♋
20 27♑	21 18♊	21 21♒	21 2♋	20 10♓	11 13♋
30 3♒	May 1 24♊	May 1 28♒	May 1 8♋	30 17♓	21 18♋
May 10 9♒	11 1♋	11 5♓	11 14♋	May 10 25♓	May 1 24♋
20 14♒	21 7♋	21 12♓	21 20♋	20 2♈	11 29♋
30 19♒	31 13♋	31 20♓	31 26♋	30 10♈	21 4♌
Jun. 9 24♒	Jun. 10 20♋	Jun. 10 27♓	Jun. 10 2♌	Jun. 9 17♈	Jun. 10 16♌
19 28♒	20 26♋	20 3♈	20 8♌	19 25♈	20 21♌
29 1♓	30 2♌	30 10♈	30 14♌	29 2♉	30 27♌
July 9 4♓	July 10 9♌	July 10 17♈	July 10 21♌	July 9 9♉	July 10 3♍
19 5♓	20 15♌	20 23♈	20 27♌	19 16♉	20 9♍
24 5♓R	30 21♌	30 29♈	30 3♍	29 23♉	30 16♍
29 5♓R	Aug. 9 28♌	Aug. 9 4♉	Aug. 9 9♍	Aug. 8 29♉	Aug. 9 22♍
Aug. 8 4♓R	19 4♍	19 9♉	19 16♍	18 6♊	19 28♍
18 2♓R	29 10♍	29 13♉	29 22♍	28 12♊	29 4♎
28 29♒R	Sep. 8 17♍	Sep. 8 16♉	Sep. 8 28♍	Sep. 7 17♊	Sep. 8 11♎
Sep. 7 27♒R	18 23♍	18 19♉	18 5♎	17 23♊	18 18♎
17 26♒R	28 29♍	28 19♉	28 11♎	27 27♊	28 24♎
22 25♒D	Oct. 8 6♎	29 19♉R	Oct. 8 18♎	Oct. 7 2♋	Oct. 8 1♏
27 25♒	18 12♎	Oct. 8 19♉R	18 25♎	17 5♋	18 8♏
Oct. 7 27♒	28 19♎	18 17♉R	28 1♏	27 8♋	28 15♏
17 29♒	Nov. 7 26♎	28 14♉R	Nov. 7 8♏	Nov. 6 9♋	Nov. 7 22♏
27 3♓	17 2♏	Nov. 7 10♉R	17 15♏	16 9♋R	17 29♏
Nov. 6 7♓	27 9♏	17 7♉R	27 22♏	26 8♋R	Dec. 7 6♐
16 11♓	Dec. 7 16♏	27 5♉R	Dec. 7 29♏	Dec. 6 5♋R	17 13♐
26 17♓	17 23♏	Dec. 7 5♉D	17 6♐	16 2♋R	27 28♐
Dec. 6 22♓	27 29♏	17 5♉	27 13♐	26 28♊R	
16 28♓		27 7♉			
26 4♈					

R=Retrograde. D=Direct. (See page 20.)

MARS   (To nearest degree at Midnight (o h. o m.) G.M.T.)   1930–1935

1930		1931		1932		1933		1934		1935	
Jan. 1	2♑	Jan. 1	16♌R	Jan. 1	17♑	Jan. 1	18♍	Jan. 1	3♒	Jan. 1	10♎
11	9♑	11	13♌R	11	25♑	11	20♍	11	11♒	11	14♎
21	17♑	21	10♌R	21	2♒	20	20♍	21	19♒	21	18♎
31	25♑	31	6♌R	31	10♒	21	20♍R	31	27♒	31	21♎
Feb. 10	3♒	Feb. 10	2♌R	Feb. 10	18♒	31	20♍R	Feb. 10	5♓	Feb. 10	23♎
20	10♒	20	29♋R	20	26♒	Feb. 10	18♍R	20	12♓	20	24♎
Mar. 2	18♒	Mar. 2	28♋R	Mar. 1	4♓	20	15♍R	Mar. 2	20♓	28	25♎R
12	26♒	9	27♋D	11	12♓	Mar. 2	11♍R	12	28♓	Mar. 2	25♎R
22	4♓	22	28♋	21	20♓	12	7♍R	22	6♈	12	24♎R
Apr. 1	12♓	Apr. 1	0♌	31	27♓	22	4♍R	Apr. 1	14♈	22	21♎R
11	19♓	11	3♌	Apr. 10	5♈	Apr. 1	2♍R	11	21♈	Apr. 1	18♎R
21	27♓	21	7♌	20	13♈	11	1♍R	21	29♈	11	14♎R
May 1	5♈	May 1	11♌	May 10	28♈	13	1♍D	May 1	6♉	21	11♎R
11	13♈	11	15♌	20	6♉	21	1♍	11	14♉	May 1	8♎R
21	20♈	21	20♌	30	13♉	May 1	3♍	21	21♉	11	6♎R
31	28♈	31	24♌	Jun. 9	20♉	11	5♍	31	28♉	18	6♎D
Jun. 10	5♉	Jun. 10	0♍	19	28♉	21	9♍	Jun. 10	5♊	21	6♎
20	12♉	20	5♍	29	5♊	31	12♍	20	12♊	31	7♎
30	20♉	30	11♍	July 9	12♊	Jun. 10	17♍	30	19♊	Jun. 10	9♎
July 10	27♉	July 10	16♍	19	19♊	20	21♍	July 10	26♊	20	12♎
20	4♊	20	22♍	29	25♊	30	26♍	20	3♋	30	16♎
30	11♊	30	28♍	Aug. 8	2♋	July 10	2♎	30	9♋	July 10	20♎
Aug. 9	17♊	Aug. 9	5♎	18	9♋	20	7♎	Aug. 9	16♋	20	25♎
19	24♊	19	11♎	28	15♋	30	13♎	19	23♋	30	0♏
29	0♋	29	17♎	Sep. 7	21♋	Aug. 9	19♎	29	29♋	Aug. 9	6♏
Sep. 8	7♋	Sep. 8	24♎	17	28♋	19	25♎	Sep. 8	5♌	19	12♏
18	12♋	18	0♏	27	4♌	29	2♏	18	12♌	29	18♏
28	18♋	28	7♏	Oct. 7	10♌	Sep. 8	8♏	28	18♌	Sep. 8	24♏
Oct. 8	24♋	Oct. 8	14♏	17	15♌	18	15♏	Oct. 8	24♌	18	1♐
18	29♋	18	21♏	27	21♌	28	22♏	18	0♍	28	8♐
28	3♌	28	28♏	Nov. 6	26♌	Oct. 8	29♏	28	6♍	Oct. 8	15♐
Nov. 7	8♌	Nov. 7	5♐	16	1♍	18	6♐	Nov. 7	12♍	18	22♐
17	11♌	17	13♐	26	6♍	28	13♐	17	17♍	28	29♐
27	14♌	27	20♐	Dec. 6	10♍	Nov. 7	21♐	27	23♍	Nov. 7	7♑
Dec. 7	16♌	Dec. 7	28♐	16	14♍	17	28♐	Dec. 7	28♍	17	14♑
17	17♌	17	5♑	26	17♍	27	6♑	17	3♎	27	22♑
19	17♌R	27	13♑			Dec. 7	14♑	27	7♎	Dec. 7	0♒
27	16♌R					17	21♑			17	8♒
						27	29♑			27	15♒

R = Retrograde.   D = Direct.   (See page 20.)

MARS (To nearest degree at Midnight (o h. o m.) G.M.T.) 1936-1941

1936	1937	1938	1939	1940	1941
Jan. 1 19♒	Jan. 1 27♎	Jan. 1 8♓	Jan. 1 13♏	Jan. 1 28♓	Jan. 1 27♏
11 27♒	11 3♏	11 15♓	11 19♏	11 5♈	11 4♐
21 5♓	21 8♏	21 23♓	21 25♏	21 12♈	21 11♐
31 13♓	31 13♏	31 0♈	31 1♐	31 18♈	31 18♐
Feb. 10 21♓	Feb. 10 18♏	Feb. 10 8♈	Feb. 10 7♐	Feb. 10 25♈	Feb. 10 25♐
20 28♓	20 22♏	20 15♈	20 13♐	20 2♉	20 1♑
Mar. 1 6♈	Mar. 2 26♏	Mar. 2 23♈	Mar. 2 19♐	Mar. 1 9♉	Mar. 2 8♑
11 14♈	12 0♐	12 0♉	12 25♐	11 15♉	12 15♑
21 21♈	22 2♐	22 7♉	22 0♑	21 22♉	22 22♑
31 29♈	Apr. 1 4♐	Apr. 1 14♉	Apr. 1 6♑	31 29♉	Apr. 1 29♑
Apr. 10 6♉	11 5♐	11 21♉	11 11♑	Apr. 10 5♊	11 6♒
20 13♉	15 6♐ R	21 28♉	21 16♑	20 12♊	21 13♒
30 20♉	21 5♐ R	May 1 5♊	May 1 21♑	30 19♊	May 1 20♒
May 10 28♉	May 1 4♐ R	11 12♊	11 25♑	May 10 25♊	11 26♒
20 5♊	11 1♐ R	21 19♊	21 29♑	20 2♋	21 3♓
30 12♊	21 28♏ R	31 25♊	31 2♒	30 8♋	31 10♓
Jun. 9 19♊	31 24♏ R	Jun. 10 2♋	Jun. 10 4♒	Jun. 9 14♋	Jun. 10 16♓
19 25♊	Jun. 10 22♏ R	20 9♋	20 5♒	19 21♋	20 23♓
29 2♋	20 20♏ R	30 15♋	23 5♒ R	29 27♋	30 29♓
July 9 9♋	28 20♏ D	July 10 22♋	30 4♒ R	July 9 4♌	July 10 4♈
19 15♋	30 20♏	20 28♋	July 10 3♒ R	19 10♌	20 10♈
29 22♋	July 10 21♏	30 5♌	20 1♒ R	29 16♌	30 14♈
Aug. 8 28♋	30 26♏	Aug. 9 11♌	30 28♑ R	Aug. 8 23♌	Aug. 9 18♈
18 5♌	Aug. 9 0♐	19 17♌	Aug. 9 25♑ R	18 29♌	19 21♈
28 11♌	19 5♐	29 24♌	19 24♑ R	28 5♍	29 23♈
Sep. 7 18♌	29 10♐	Sep. 8 0♍	24 24♑ D	Sep. 7 12♍	Sep. 7 24♈ R
17 24♌	Sep. 8 16♐	18 6♍	29 24♑	17 18♍	8 24♈ R
27 0♍	18 22♐	28 13♍	Sep. 8 25♑	27 24♍	18 23♈ R
Oct. 7 6♍	28 28♐	Oct. 8 19♍	18 28♑	Oct. 7 1♎	28 21♈ R
17 13♍	Oct. 8 5♑	18 25♍	28 2♒	17 7♎	Oct. 8 18♈ R
27 19♍	18 12♑	28 2♎	Oct. 8 6♒	27 14♎	18 15♈ R
Nov. 6 25♍	28 19♑	Nov. 7 8♎	18 11♒	Nov. 6 20♎	28 12♈ R
16 1♎	Nov. 7 26♑	17 14♎	28 16♒	16 27♎	Nov. 7 11♈ R
26 7♎	17 4♒	27 21♎	Nov. 7 22♒	26 3♏	11 11♈ D
Dec. 6 13♎	27 11♒	Dec. 7 27♎	17 28♒	Dec. 6 10♏	17 11♈
16 18♎	Dec. 7 19♒	17 3♏	27 5♓	16 17♏	27 13♈
26 24♎	17 26♒	27 9♏	Dec. 7 11♓	26 23♏	Dec. 7 15♈
	27 4♓		17 18♓		17 19♈
			27 25♓		27 23♈

R = Retrograde.   D = Direct.   (See page 20.)

MARS   (To nearest degree at Midnight (0 h. 0 m.) G.M.T.)   1942–1947

1942	1943	1944	1945	1946	1947
Jan. 1 25♈	Jan. 1 11♐	Jan. 1 5♊R	Jan. 1 26♐	Jan. 1 28♋R	Jan. 1 11♑
11 0♉	11 19♐	11 5♊D	11 4♑	11 24♋R	11 19♑
21 5♉	21 26♐	21 6♊	21 11♑	21 21♋R	21 27♑
31 10♉	31 3♑	31 7♊	31 19♑	31 17♋R	31 4♒
Feb. 10 15♉	Feb. 10 10♑	Feb. 10 10♊	Feb. 10 27♑	Feb. 10 15♋R	Feb. 10 12♒
20 21♉	20 18♑	20 13♊	20 4♒	20 14♋R	20 20♒
Mar. 2 27♉	Mar. 2 25♑	Mar. 1 17♊	Mar. 2 12♒	22 14♋D	Mar. 2 28♒
12 3♊	12 3♒	11 22♊	12 20♒	Mar. 2 15♋	12 6♓
22 9♊	22 10♒	21 26♊	22 28♒	12 16♋	22 14♓
Apr. 1 15♊	Apr. 1 18♒	31 1♋	Apr. 1 5♓	22 18♋	Apr. 1 21♓
11 21♊	11 25♒	Apr. 10 6♋	11 13♓	Apr. 1 21♋	11 29♓
21 27♊	21 3♓	20 12♋	21 21♓	11 25♋	21 7♈
May 1 3♋	May 1 10♓	30 17♋	May 1 29♓	21 29♋	May 1 15♈
11 9♋	11 18♓	May 10 23♋	11 6♈	May 1 4♌	11 22♈
21 15♋	21 25♓	20 29♋	21 14♈	11 9♌	21 0♉
31 21♋	31 3♈	30 4♌	31 21♈	21 14♌	31 7♉
Jun. 10 27♋	Jun. 10 10♈	Jun. 9 10♌	Jun. 10 29♈	31 19♌	Jun. 10 15♉
20 4♌	20 17♈	19 16♌	20 6♉	Jun. 10 24♌	20 22♉
30 10♌	30 24♈	29 22♌	30 14♉	20 0♍	30 29♉
July 10 16♌	July 10 1♉	July 9 28♌	July 10 21♉	30 6♍	July 10 6♊
20 22♌	20 8♉	19 4♍	20 28♉	July 10 11♍	20 13♊
30 29♌	30 15♉	29 10♍	30 5♊	20 17♍	30 20♊
Aug. 9 5♍	Aug. 9 21♉	Aug. 8 17♍	Aug. 9 11♊	30 23♍	Aug. 9 27♊
19 11♍	19 27♉	18 23♍	19 18♊	Aug. 9 0♎	19 3♋
29 18♍	29 3♊	28 29♍	29 24♊	19 6♎	29 10♋
Sep. 8 24♍	Sep. 8 8♊	Sep. 7 6♎	Sep. 8 0♋	29 12♎	Sep. 8 16♋
18 0♎	18 13♊	17 12♎	18 6♋	Sep. 8 19♎	18 22♋
28 7♎	28 16♊	27 19♎	28 12♋	18 26♎	28 28♋
Oct. 8 13♎	Oct. 8 19♊	Oct. 7 26♎	Oct. 8 16♋	28 2♏	Oct. 8 4♌
18 20♎	18 21♊	17 2♏	18 21♋	Oct. 8 9♏	18 9♌
28 27♎	28 22♊	27 9♏	28 25♋	18 16♏	28 15♌
Nov. 7 3♏	Nov. 7 22♊R	Nov. 6 16♏	Nov. 7 29♋	28 23♏	Nov. 7 20♌
17 10♏	17 19♊R	16 23♏	17 1♌	Nov. 7 0♐	17 24♌
27 17♏	27 16♊R	26 0♐	27 3♌	17 7♐	27 28♌
Dec. 7 24♏	Dec. 7 12♊R	Dec. 6 7♐	Dec. 5 3♌R	27 15♐	Dec. 7 2♍
17 1♐	17 9♊R	16 15♐	7 3♌R	Dec. 7 22♐	17 5♍
27 8♐	27 6♊R	26 22♐	17 2♌R	17 0♑	27 7♍
			27 0♌R	27 7♑	

R = Retrograde.   D = Direct.   (See page 20.)

MARS   (To nearest degree at Midnight (0 h. 0 m.) G.M.T.)   1948-1953

1948	1949	1950	1951	1952	1953
Jan. 1 7♍	Jan. 1 27♑	Jan. 1 2♎	Jan. 1 13♒	Jan. 1 21♎	Jan. 1 1♓
9 8♍R	11 5♒	11 6♎	11 21♒	11 26♎	11 9♓
11 8♍R	21 13♒	21 8♎	21 29♒	21 0♏	21 16♓
21 7♍R	31 21♒	31 10♎	31 7♓	31 5♏	31 24♓
31 4♍R	Feb. 10 29♒	Feb. 10 11♎	Feb. 10 15♓	Feb. 10 9♏	Feb. 10 1♈
Feb. 10 1♍R	20 7♓	13 11♎R	20 22♓	20 12♏	20 9♈
20 27♌R	Mar. 2 14♓	20 11♎R	Mar. 2 0♈	Mar. 1 15♏	Mar. 2 17♈
Mar. 1 23♌R	12 22♓	Mar. 2 9♎R	12 8♈	11 17♏	12 24♈
11 20♌R	22 0♈	12 6♎R	22 15♈	21 18♏	22 1♉
21 19♌R	Apr. 1 8♈	22 3♎R	Apr. 1 23♈	25 18♏R	Apr. 1 9♉
30 18♌D	11 16♈	Apr. 1 29♍R	11 0♉	31 18♏R	11 16♉
31 18♌	21 23♈	11 25♍R	21 8♉	Apr. 10 17♏R	21 23♉
Apr. 10 19♌	May 1 1♉	21 23♍R	May 1 15♉	20 14♏R	May 1 0♊
20 21♌	11 8♉	May 1 22♍R	11 22♉	30 11♏R	11 7♊
30 23♌	21 16♉	5 22♍D	21 0♊	May 10 7♏R	21 14♊
May 10 27♌	31 23♉	11 22♍	31 7♊	20 4♏R	31 20♊
20 0♍	Jun. 10 0♊	21 24♍	Jun. 10 14♊	30 2♏R	Jun. 10 27♊
30 5♍	20 7♊	31 26♍	20 20♊	Jun. 9 1♏R	20 4♋
Jun. 9 9♍	30 14♊	Jun. 10 29♍	30 27♊	11 1♏D	30 11♋
19 15♍	July 10 21♊	20 3♎	July 10 4♋	19 2♏	July 10 17♋
29 20♍	20 28♊	30 8♎	20 11♋	29 3♏	20 24♋
July 9 25♍	30 5♋	July 10 12♎	30 17♋	July 9 6♏	30 0♌
19 1♎	Aug. 9 11♋	20 18♎	Aug. 9 24♋	19 10♏	Aug. 9 7♌
29 7♎	19 18♋	30 23♎	19 0♌	29 14♏	19 13♌
Aug. 8 14♎	29 24♋	Aug. 9 29♎	29 7♌	Aug. 8 19♏	29 19♌
18 19♎	Sep. 8 1♌	19 5♏	Sep. 8 13♌	18 24♏	Sep. 8 26♌
28 26♎	18 7♌	29 11♏	18 19♌	28 0♐	18 2♍
Sep. 7 2♏	28 13♌	Sep. 8 18♏	28 26♌	Sep. 7 6♐	28 8♍
17 9♏	Oct. 8 19♌	18 25♏	Oct. 8 2♍	17 13♐	Oct. 8 15♍
27 16♏	18 25♌	28 2♐	18 8♍	27 19♐	18 21♍
Oct. 7 23♏	28 1♍	Oct. 8 9♐	28 14♍	Oct. 7 26♐	28 27♍
17 0♐	Nov. 7 6♍	18 16♐	Nov. 7 20♍	17 3♑	Nov. 7 3♎
27 7♐	17 12♍	28 23♐	17 26♍	27 11♑	17 10♎
Nov. 6 14♐	27 17♍	Nov. 7 1♑	27 2♎	Nov. 6 18♑	27 16♎
16 22♐	Dec. 7 22♍	17 8♑	Dec. 7 7♎	16 26♑	Dec. 7 22♎
26 29♐	17 26♍	27 16♑	17 13♎	26 3♒	17 28♎
Dec. 6 7♑	27 0♎	Dec. 7 23♑	27 18♎	Dec. 6 11♒	27 4♏
16 15♑		17 1♒		16 19♒	
26 22♑		27 9♒		26 26♒	

R = Retrograde.   D = Direct.   (See page 20.)

MARS (To nearest degree at Midnight (o h. o m.) G.M.T.) 1954-1959

1954	1955	1956	1957	1958	1959
Jan. 1 7♏	Jan. 1 20♓	Jan. 1 21♏	Jan. 1 14♈	Jan. 1 6♐	Jan. 1 17♉
11 13♏	11 27♓	11 28♏	11 19♈	11 13♐	11 19♉
21 19♏	21 4♈	21 5♐	21 25♈	21 20♐	21 22♉
31 24♏	31 11♈	31 11♐	31 1♉	31 27♐	31 26♉
Feb. 10 0♐	Feb. 10 18♈	Feb. 10 18♐	Feb. 10 8♉	Feb. 10 4♑	Feb. 10 0♊
20 6♐	20 25♈	20 24♐	20 14♉	20 12♑	20 4♊
Mar. 2 11♐	Mar. 2 3♉	Mar. 1 1♑	Mar. 2 20♉	Mar. 2 19♑	Mar. 2 9♊
12 16♐	12 9♉	11 7♑	12 26♉	12 26♑	12 14♊
22 21♐	22 16♉	21 14♑	22 3♊	22 3≈	22 19♊
Apr. 1 25♐	Apr. 1 23♉	31 20♑	Apr. 1 9♊	Apr. 1 11≈	Apr. 1 25♊
11 29♐	11 0♊	Apr. 10 27♑	11 15♊	11 18≈	11 ♋
21 3♑	21 7♊	20 3≈	21 21♊	21 26≈	21 6♋
May 1 6♑	May 1 13♊	30 10≈	May 1 28♊	May 1 3♓	May 1 12♋
11 8♑	11 20♊	May 10 16≈	11 4♋	11 10♓	11 18♋
21 8♑	21 27♊	20 22≈	21 10♋	21 18♓	21 23♋
23 9♑R	31 3♋	30 28≈	31 17♋	31 25♓	31 29♋
31 8♑R	Jun. 10 10♋	Jun. 9 3♓	Jun. 10 23♋	Jun. 10 2♈	Jun. 10 5♌
Jun. 10 7♑R	20 16♋	19 8♓	20 29♋	20 9♈	20 11♌
20 4♑R	30 23♋	29 13♓	30 5♌	30 16♈	30 17♌
30 1♑R	July 10 29♋	July 9 17♓	July 10 12♌	July 10 23♈	July 10 24♌
July 10 28♐R	20 6♌	19 20♓	20 18♌	20 29♈	20 0♍
20 26♐R	30 12♌	29 23♓	30 24♌	30 5♉	30 6♍
30 26♐D	Aug. 9 18♌	Aug. 8 24♓	Aug. 9 1♍	Aug. 9 11♉	Aug. 9 12♍
Aug. 9 26♐	19 25♌	11 24♓R	19 7♍	19 17♉	19 19♍
19 28♐	29 1♍	18 23♓R	29 13♍	29 22♉	29 25♍
29 2♑	Sep. 8 7♍	28 22♓R	Sep. 8 20♍	Sep. 8 26♉	Sep. 8 1≏
Sep. 8 6♑	18 14♍	Sep. 7 19♓R	18 26♍	18 29♉	18 8≏
18 10♑	28 20♍	17 17♓R	28 2≏	28 1♊	28 14≏
28 16♑	Oct. 8 27♍	27 14♓R	Oct. 8 9≏	Oct. 8 2♊	Oct. 8 21≏
Oct. 8 22♑	18 3≏	Oct. 7 13♓R	18 16≏	11 3♊R	18 28≏
18 28♑	28 9≏	11 13♓D	28 22≏	18 2♊R	28 4♏
28 4≈	Nov. 7 16≏	17 13♓	Nov. 7 29≏	28 0♊R	Nov. 7 11♏
Nov. 7 11≈	17 22≏	27 15♓	17 5♏	Nov. 7 27♉R	17 18♏
17 18≈	27 29≏	Nov. 6 17♓	27 12♏	17 24♉R	27 25♏
27 25≈	Dec. 7 5♏	16 21♓	Dec. 7 19♏	27 20♉R	Dec. 7 2♐
Dec. 7 2♓	17 12♏	26 25♓	17 26♏	Dec. 7 18♉R	17 9♐
17 9♓	27 18♏	Dec. 6 0♈	27 3♐	17 17♉R	27 17♐
27 16♓		16 5♈		21 17♉D	
		26 10♈		27 17♉	

R = Retrograde.   D = Direct.   (See page 20.)

MARS (To nearest degree at Midnight (0 h. 0 m.) G.M.T.)   1960-1965

1960	1961	1962	1963	1964	1965
Jan. 1 20♐	Jan. 1 8♋R	Jan. 1 5♑	Jan. 1 25♌R	Jan. 1 20♑	Jan. 1 24♍
11 28♐	11 4♋R	11 13♑	11 23♌R	11 28♑	11 26♍
21 5♑	21 2♋R	21 21♑	21 20♌R	21 6♒	21 28♍
31 13♑	31 0♋R	31 28♑	31 17♌R	31 14♒	29 28♍R
Feb. 10 20♑	Feb. 7 0♋D	Feb. 10 6♒	Feb. 10 13♌R	Feb. 10 22♒	31 28♍R
20 28♑	10 0♋	20 14♒	20 9♌R	20 0♓	Feb. 10 27♍R
Mar. 1 5♒	20 1♋	Mar. 2 22♒	Mar. 2 7♌R	Mar. 1 8♓	20 25♍R
11 13♒	Mar. 2 3♋	12 0♓	12 5♌R	11 16♓	Mar. 2 22♍R
21 21♒	12 6♋	22 8♓	17 5♌D	21 23♓	12 18♍R
31 28♒	22 9♋	Apr. 1 15♓	22 6♌	31 1♈	22 14♍R
Apr. 10 6♓	Apr. 1 13♋	11 23♓	Apr. 1 7♌	Apr. 10 9♈	Apr. 1 11♍R
20 14♓	11 18♋	21 1♈	11 9♌	20 17♈	11 9♍R
30 21♓	21 22♋	May 1 9♈	21 12♌	30 24♈	21 9♍D
May 10 29♓	May 1 27♋	11 16♈	May 1 15♌	May 10 2♉	May 1 9♍
20 7♈	11 3♌	21 24♈	11 19♌	20 9♉	11 11♍
30 14♈	21 8♌	31 2♉	21 24♌	30 17♉	21 14♍
Jun. 9 22♈	31 13♌	Jun. 10 9♉	31 28♌	Jun. 9 24♉	31 17♍
19 29♈	Jun. 10 19♌	20 16♉	Jun. 10 3♍	19 1♊	Jun. 10 21♍
29 6♉	20 25♌	30 23♉	20 9♍	29 8♊	20 26♍
July 9 13♉	30 1♍	July 10 1♊	30 14♍	July 9 15♊	30 0≏
19 20♉	July 10 7♍	20 8♊	July 10 20♍	19 22♊	July 10 6≏
29 27♉	20 13♍	30 14♊	20 26♍	29 29♊	20 11≏
Aug. 8 4♊	30 19♍	Aug. 9 21♊	30 2≏	Aug. 8 6♋	30 17≏
18 10♊	Aug. 9 25♍	19 28♊	Aug. 9 8≏	18 12♋	Aug. 9 23≏
28 16♊	19 1≏	29 4♋	19 14≏	28 19♋	19 29≏
Sep. 7 22♊	29 8≏	Sep. 8 10♋	29 21≏	Sep. 7 25♋	29 5♏
17 28♊	Sep. 8 14≏	18 16♋	Sep. 8 27≏	17 1♌	Sep. 8 12♏
27 3♋	18 21≏	28 22♋	18 4♏	27 7♌	18 19♏
Oct. 7 8♋	28 27≏	Oct. 8 28♋	28 11♏	Oct. 7 13♌	28 26♏
17 12♋	Oct. 8 4♏	18 3♌	Oct. 8 17♏	17 19♌	Oct. 8 3♐
27 15♋	18 11♏	28 8♌	18 24♏	27 25♌	18 10♐
Nov. 6 17♋	28 18♏	Nov. 7 13♌	28 2♐	Nov. 6 0♍	28 17♐
16 19♋	Nov. 7 25♏	17 17♌	Nov. 7 9♐	16 5♍	Nov. 7 25♐
21 19♋R	17 2♐	27 20♌	17 16♐	26 10♍	17 2♑
26 18♋R	27 9♐	Dec. 7 23♌	27 24♐	Dec. 6 14♍	27 10♑
Dec. 6 17♋R	Dec. 7 17♐	17 24♌	Dec. 7 1♑	16 18♍	Dec. 7 17♑
16 14♋R	17 24♐	27 25♌R	17 9♑	26 22♍	17 25♑
26 11♋R	27 2♑		27 17♑		27 3♒
31 9♋R					

R = Retrograde.   D = Direct.   (See page 20.)

MARS   (To nearest degree at Midnight (o h. o m.) G.M.T.)   1966–1971

1966	1967	1968	1969	1970	1971
Jan. 1 7≈	Jan. 1 14♎	Jan. 1 23≈	Jan. 1 1♏	Jan. 1 12)(	Jan. 1 16♏
11 15≈	11 19♎	11 1)(	11 7♏	11 20)(	11 22♏
21 23≈	21 23♎	21 9)(	21 12♏	21 27)(	21 29♏
31 1)(	31 26♎	31 17)(	31 18♏	31 5♈	31 5♐
Feb. 10 8)(	Feb. 10 29♎	Feb. 10 25)(	Feb. 10 23♏	Feb. 10 12♈	Feb. 10 11♐
20 16)(	20 2♏	20 2♈	20 28♏	20 19♈	20 17♐
Mar. 2 24)(	Mar. 2 3♏	Mar. 1 10♈	Mar. 2 2♐	Mar. 2 26♈	Mar. 2 24♐
12 2♈	9 3♏ R	11 17♈	12 6♐	12 4♉	12 0♑
22 10♈	12 3♏ R	21 25♈	22 10♐	22 11♉	22 6♑
Apr. 1 17♈	22 2♏ R	31 2♉	Apr. 1 13♐	Apr. 1 18♉	Apr. 1 12♑
11 25♈	Apr. 1 0♏ R	Apr. 10 10♉	11 15♐	11 25♉	11 17♑
21 2♉	11 26♎R	20 17♉	21 17♐	21 2♊	21 23♑
May 1 10♉	21 23♎R	30 24♉	28 17♐ R	May 1 8♊	May 1 29♑
11 17♉	May 1 19♎R	May 10 1♊	May 1 17♐ R	11 15♊	11 4≈
21 24♉	11 17♎R	20 8♊	11 16♐ R	21 22♊	21 8≈
31 1♊	21 15♎R	30 15♊	21 13♐ R	31 28♊	31 13≈
Jun. 10 9♊	27 15♎D	Jun. 9 22♊	31 10♐ R	Jun. 10 5♋	Jun. 10 16≈
20 16♊	31 15♎	19 29♊	Jun. 10 7♐ R	20 12♋	20 19≈
30 22♊	Jun. 10 16♎	29 5♋	20 4♐ R	30 18♋	30 21≈
July 10 29♊	20 19♎	July 9 12♋	30 2♐ R	July 10 25♋	July 10 22≈
20 6♋	30 22♎	19 18♋	July 9 2♐ D	20 1♌	20 22≈R
30 13♋	July 10 26♎	29 25♋	10 2♐	30 8♌	30 20≈R
Aug. 9 19♋	20 0♏	Aug. 8 1♌	20 3♐	Aug. 9 14♌	Aug. 9 17≈R
19 26♋	30 5♏	18 8♌	30 5♐	19 20♌	19 15≈R
29 2♌	Aug. 9 10♏	28 14♌	Aug. 9 8♐	29 27♌	29 13≈R
Sep. 8 9♌	19 16♏	Sep. 7 21♌	19 12♐	Sep. 8 3♍	Sep. 8 12≈R
18 15♌	29 22♏	17 27♌	29 17♐	18 9♍	10 12≈D
28 21♌	Sep. 8 29♏	27 3♍	Sep. 8 22♐	28 16♍	18 12≈
Oct. 8 27♌	18 5♐	Oct. 7 10♍	18 28♐	Oct. 8 22♍	28 14≈
18 3♍	28 12♐	17 16♍	28 4♑	18 28♍	Oct. 8 17≈
28 9♍	Oct. 8 19♐	27 22♍	Oct. 8 11♑	28 5♎	18 21≈
Nov. 7 15♍	18 26♐	Nov. 6 28♍	18 17♑	Nov. 7 11♎	28 25≈
17 21♍	28 4♑	16 4♎	28 24♑	17 17♎	Nov. 7 0)(
27 26♍	Nov. 7 11♑	26 10♎	Nov. 7 2≈	27 24♎	17 6)(
Dec. 7 2♎	17 19♑	Dec. 6 16♎	17 9≈	Dec. 7 0♏	27 12)(
17 7♎	27 26♑	16 22♎	27 16≈	17 7♏	Dec. 7 18)(
27 12♎	Dec. 7 4≈	26 28♎	Dec. 7 24≈	27 13♏	17 24)(
	17 12≈		17 1)(		27 0♈
	27 20≈		27 9)(		

R = Retrograde.   D = Direct.   (See page 20.)

MARS   (To nearest degree at Midnight (0 h. 0 m.) G.M.T.)   1972-1975

1972	1973	1974	1975
Jan. 1 3♈	Jan. 1 1♐	Jan. 1 3♉	Jan. 1 15♐
11 10♈	11 8♐	11 6♉	11 22♐
21 16♈	21 15♐	21 11♉	21 29♐
31 23♈	31 22♐	31 16♉	31 7♑
Feb. 10 0♉	Feb. 10 28♐	Feb. 10 21♉	Feb. 10 14♑
20 6♉	20 5♑	20 26♉	20 22♑
Mar. 1 13♉	Mar. 2 12♑	Mar. 2 1♊	Mar. 2 29♑
11 19♉	12 19♑	12 7♊	12 7♒
21 26♉	22 27♑	22 13♊	22 14♒
31 2♊	Apr. 1 4♒	Apr. 1 19♊	Apr. 1 22♒
Apr. 10 9♊	11 11♒	11 24♊	11 29♒
20 15♊	21 18♒	21 0♋	21 7♓
30 22♊	May 1 25♒	May 1 6♋	May 1 15♓
May 10 28♊	11 2♓	11 12♋	11 22♓
20 5♋	21 9♓	21 18♋	21 0♈
30 11♋	31 16♓	31 24♋	31 7♈
Jun. 9 18♋	Jun. 10 23♓	Jun. 10 1♌	Jun. 10 15♈
19 24♋	20 29♓	20 7♌	20 22♈
29 0♌	30 6♈	30 13♌	30 29♈
July 9 7♌	July 10 12♈	July 10 19♌	July 10 6♉
19 13♌	20 18♈	20 25♌	20 13♉
29 19♌	30 23♈	30 2♍	30 20♉
Aug. 8 26♌	Aug. 9 28♈	Aug. 9 8♍	Aug. 9 26♉
18 2♍	19 3♉	19 14♍	19 3♊
28 8♍	29 6♉	29 20♍	29 8♊
Sep. 7 15♍	Sep. 8 8♉	Sep. 8 27♍	Sep. 8 14♊
17 21♍	18 9♉	18 3♎	18 19♊
27 27♍	20 9♉R	28 10♎	28 23♊
Oct. 7 4♎	28 9♉R	Oct. 8 16♎	Oct. 8 27♊
17 10♎	Oct. 8 7♉R	18 23♎	18 0♋
27 17♎	18 4♉R	28 0♏	28 2♋
Nov. 6 23♎	28 1♉R	Nov. 7 7♏	Nov. 7 3♋R
16 0♏	Nov. 7 28♈R	17 13♏	17 2♋R
26 7♏	17 26♈R	27 20♏	27 0♋R
Dec. 6 13♏	26 25♈D	Dec. 7 27♏	Dec. 7 26♊R
16 20♏	27 25♈	17 4♐	17 22♊R
26 27♏	Dec. 7 26♈	27 11♐	27 19♊R
	17 28♈		31 17♊R
	27 1♉		

R = Retrograde.   D = Direct.   (See page 20.)

NOTES

JUPITER, SATURN, URANUS, and NEPTUNE 1900–1905
(0 h. 0 m., G.M.T.)

	1900 ♃	1900 ♄	1900 ♅	1900 ♆	1901 ♃	1901 ♄	1901 ♅	1901 ♆	1902 ♃	1902 ♄	1902 ♅	1902 ♆
Jan. 1	1♐	28♐	10♐	25♊	26♐	8♑	14♐	27♊	21♑	18♑	18♐	0♋
15	4	29	11	25	29	9	15	27	25	19	19	29♊
29	6	1♑	12	25	2♑	11	16	27	28	21	26	29
Feb. 12	8	2	12	24	5	12	16	27	1♒	23	21	29
26	10	3	12	24	7	14	17	26	4	24	21	29
Mar. 12	10	4	12	24	9	15	17	26	7	25	21	29
26	11	5	12	24	11	16	17	27	10	26	21	29
Apr. 9	11	5	12	25	12	16	17	27	12	27	21	29
23	10	5	12	25	13	16	16	27	14	28	21	29
May 7	8	5	11	25	13	16	16	27	17	28	21	0♋
21	7	4	11	26	12	16	16	28	17	28	20	0
Jun. 4	5	3	10	26	11	15	15	28	17	27	20	1
18	3	2	10	27	10	14	14	29	17	27	19	2
July 2	2	1	9	27	8	13	14	29	16	26	18	2
16	1	0	9	28	6	12	13	0♋	15	25	18	2
30	1	29♐	9	28	5	11	13	0	13	24	18	2
Aug. 13	1	29	8	29	4	11	13	1	11	23	17	3
27	2	28	8	29	3	10	13	1	10	22	17	4
Sep. 10	4	28	9	29	3	10	13	1	8	21	17	4
24	6	29	9	29	4	10	13	1	8	21	18	4
Oct. 8	8	29	10	29	5	10	14	1	7	21	18	4
22	11	0♑	10	29	7	11	14	1	8	22	19	4
Nov. 5	13	2	11	29	10	12	15	1	9	22	19	3
19	16	3	12	29	12	13	16	1	11	23	20	3
Dec. 3	19	4	13	28	15	14	17	1	13	25	21	3
17	23	6	13	28	18	16	18	0	15	26	22	3

	1903 ♃	1903 ♄	1903 ♅	1903 ♆	1904 ♃	1904 ♄	1904 ♅	1904 ♆	1905 ♃	1905 ♄	1905 ♅	1905 ♆
Jan. 1	18♒	28♑	23♐	2♋	18♓	8♒	27♐	4♋	21♈	19♒	1♑	7♋
15	22	29	23	2	20	10	27	4	22	20	2	6
29	25	1♒	24	1	23	11	28	4	23	22	2	6
Feb. 12	28	3	25	1	26	13	29	3	26	23	3	6
26	1♓	4	25	1	29	15	29	3	28	25	4	5
Mar. 12	5	6	25	1	3♈	16	0♑	3	0♉	27	4	5
26	8	7	26	1	6	18	0	3	4	28	4	5
Apr. 9	11	8	26	1	9	19	0	3	7	0♓	4	6
23	14	9	25	1	13	20	0	4	11	1	4	6
May 7	17	9	25	2	16	21	0	4	14	2	4	6
21	19	9	25	2	19	21	29♐	4	17	2	4	6
Jun. 4	21	9	24	3	22	21	29	5	20	3	3	7
18	22	9	24	3	24	21	28	5	24	3	2	7
Jul. 2	23	8	23	4	27	20	27	6	26	3	2	8
16	23	7	22	4	28	19	27	6	29	2	1	8
30	23	6	22	5	0♉	18	26	7	2♊	1	1	9
Aug. 13	22	5	22	5	0	17	26	7	4	0	1	9
27	20	4	22	5	0	16	26	8	5	29♒	0	10
Sep. 10	19	3	22	6	29♈	16	26	8	6	28	0	10
24	17	3	22	6	28	15	26	8	6	27	0	10
Oct. 8	15	3	22	6	27	14	26	8	6	27	1	10
22	14	3	23	6	25	14	27	8	5	26	1	10
Nov. 5	13	3	23	6	23	15	27	8	4	26	2	10
19	14	4	24	6	21	15	28	8	2	27	2	10
Dec. 3	14	5	25	5	20	16	29	7	0	27	3	10
17	16	6	26	5	20	17	0♑	7	28♉	28	4	9

R=Retrograde. D=Direct. (See page 20.)

JUPITER, SATURN, URANUS, and NEPTUNE   1906–1911
(o h. o m., G.M.T.)

	1906 ♃	♄	♅	♆	1907 ♃	♄	♅	♆	1908 ♃	♄	♅	♆
Jan. 1	27♉	29♒	5♑	9♋	5♋	10♓	9♑	11♋	12♌	22♓	13♑	14♋
15	27	1♓	6	9	4	12	10	11	10	23	13	13
29	27	2	6	8	2	13	10	11	9	24	14	13
Feb. 12	27	4	7	8	1	15	11	10	7	26	15	12
26	29	6	8	8	1	16	12	10	5	27	16	12
Mar. 12	0♊	7	8	8	1	18	12	10	4	29	16	12
26	3	9	8	8	2	20	13	10	4	1♈	17	12
Apr. 9	5	10	8	8	4	21	13	10	4	3	17	12
23	8	12	8	8	6	23	13	10	4	4	17	12
May 7	11	13	8	8	8	24	13	10	6	6	17	13
21	14	14	8	9	11	25	12	11	7	7	17	13
Jun. 4	17	15	7	9	13	26	12	11	10	8	16	13
18	21	15	7	10	16	27	11	12	12	9	16	14
Jul. 2	24	15	6	10	20	27	11	12	15	10	15	14
16	27	15	6	11	23	27	10	13	18	10	15	15
30	0♋	14	5	11	26	27	10	13	20	10	14	15
Aug. 13	3	13	5	12	29	26	9	14	24	10	14	16
27	5	12	5	12	2♌	26	9	14	27	9	13	16
Sep. 10	7	11	5	12	5	25	9	14	0♍	8	13	17
24	9	10	5	13	7	24	9	15	3	7	13	17
Oct. 8	10	9	5	13	9	23	9	15	5	6	13	17
22	11	9	5	13	11	22	9	15	8	5	13	17
Nov. 5	11	8	6	13	13	21	10	15	10	4	14	17
19	10	8	6	13	13	21	10	15	12	4	14	17
Dec. 3	9	9	7	12	14	21	11	14	13	3	15	17
17	7	9	8	12	13	21	12	14	14	3	16	16

	1909 ♃	♄	♅	♆	1910 ♃	♄	♅	♆	1911 ♃	♄	♅	♆
Jan. 1	15♍	4♈	17♑	16♋	13♎	17♈	21♑	18♋	10♏	0♉	24♑	20♋
15	14	5	17	15	14	17	21	18	12	0	25	20
29	13	6	18	15	15	18	22	18	13	0	26	20
Feb. 12	12	7	19	15	14	19	23	17	14	1	27	19
26	10	9	20	15	13	20	24	17	15	2	28	19
Mar. 12	8	10	20	14	12	22	24	17	14	4	28	19
26	6	12	21	14	10	24	25	17	14	5	29	19
Apr. 9	5	14	21	15	8	25	25	17	14	7	29	19
23	5	16	21	15	7	27	25	17	11	9	29	19
May 7	5	17	21	15	6	29	25	17	9	11	29	19
21	5	19	21	15	5	0♉	25	17	7	12	29	19
Jun. 4	6	20	20	16	5	2	25	18	6	14	29	20
18	8	21	20	16	5	3	24	18	5	16	29	20
Jul. 2	10	22	19	17	6	5	24	19	5	17	28	21
16	12	23	19	17	7	6	23	19	5	18	28	21
30	15	23	18	18	9	6	23	20	6	19	27	22
Aug. 13	17	23	18	18	11	7	22	20	9	20	26	22
27	20	23	17	19	14	7	22	21	9	20	26	23
Sep. 10	23	22	17	19	17	6	21	21	11	20	26	23
24	26	21	17	19	20	5	21	21	14	20	25	23
Oct. 8	29	20	17	19	23	5	21	21	16	19	25	24
22	2♎	19	17	19	26	3	21	22	19	18	26	24
Nov. 5	5	18	18	19	29	2	22	22	22	17	26	24
19	8	17	18	19	2♏	1	22	22	25	16	26	24
Dec. 3	10	17	19	19	4	0	23	21	28	15	27	23
17	12	16	20	19	7	0	24	21	1♐	14	27	23

R = Retrograde.   D = Direct.   (See page 20.)

JUPITER, SATURN, URANUS, and NEPTUNE 1912-1917
(o h. o m., G.M.T.)

	1912				1913				1914			
	♃	♄	♅	Ψ	♃	♄	♅	Ψ	♃	♄	♅	Ψ
Jan. 1	5♐	13♉	28♑	23♋	0♑	28♉	2♒	25♋	25♑	13♊	6♒	27♋
15	7	13	29	22	3	27	3	25	29	12	7	27
29	10	13	0♒	22	6	27	4	24	2♒	11	8	27
Feb. 12	12	14	1	22	9	27	5	24	5	11	8	26
26	14	15	1	21	11	28	5	24	8	11	9	26
Mar. 12	15	16	2	21	14	29	6	23	11	12	10	26
26	15	18	3	21	15	0♊	7	23	14	13	11	25
Apr. 9	15	19	3	21	17	1	7	23	17	14	11	25
23	15	21	3	21	18	3	7	23	19	15	11	26
May 7	13	23	3	21	18	5	8	24	20	17	12	26
21	12	24	3	22	17	6	8	24	22	19	12	26
Jun. 4	10	26	3	22	16	8	7	24	22	20	11	26
18	8	28	3	22	15	10	7	25	22	22	11	27
Jul. 2	7	29	2	23	13	12	7	25	22	24	11	27
16	6	1♊	2	24	12	13	6	26	21	26	10	28
30	6	2	1	24	10	15	6	26	19	27	10	28
Aug. 13	6	3	1	25	9	16	5	27	17	29	9	29
27	6	4	0	25	8	17	4	27	15	0♋	9	29
Sep. 10	8	4	0	25	8	18	4	28	14	1	8	0♌
24	10	4	0	26	9	18	4	28	13	2	8	0
Oct. 8	12	4	0	26	10	18	4	28	12	2	8	0
22	14	3	0	26	11	18	4	28	13	2	8	0
Nov. 5	17	2	0	26	14	17	4	28	14	2	8	0
19	20	1	0	26	16	16	4	28	15	1	8	0
Dec. 3	23	0	1	26	19	15	5	28	17	0	9	0
17	26	29♉	1	25	22	14	5	28	20	29♊	9	0

	1915				1916				1917			
	♃	♄	♅	Ψ	♃	♄	♅	Ψ	♃	♄	♅	Ψ
Jan. 1	22♒	28♊	10♒	0♌	22♓	13♋	14♒	2♌	26♈	28♋	18♒	4♌
15	25	27	11	29♋	25	12	14	1	27	27	18	4
29	29	26	11	29	27	11	15	1	28	26	19	3
Feb. 12	2♓	26	12	28	0♈	10	16	1	0♉	25	20	3
26	5	25	13	28	3	10	17	0	2	24	21	3
Mar. 12	9	26	14	28	7	10	18	0	5	24	21	2
26	12	26	14	28	10	10	18	0	8	24	22	2
Apr. 9	15	27	15	28	13	10	19	0	11	24	23	2
23	18	28	15	28	17	11	19	0	14	24	23	2
May 7	21	0♋	16	28	20	12	20	0	18	25	24	2
21	23	1	16	28	23	14	20	0	21	26	24	2
Jun. 4	25	3	16	28	26	15	20	1	24	28	24	3
18	27	5	15	29	29	17	19	1	28	29	24	3
Jul. 2	28	6	15	29	1♉	19	19	2	1♊	1♌	23	4
16	28	8	15	0♌	3	21	19	2	3	3	23	4
30	28	10	14	0	4	22	18	3	6	5	22	5
Aug. 13	27	12	13	1	5	24	18	3	8	6	22	5
27	26	13	13	1	5	26	17	4	10	8	21	6
Sep. 10	24	14	12	2	5	27	17	4	11	10	21	6
24	23	15	12	2	4	28	16	4	11	11	20	7
Oct. 8	21	16	12	2	2	0♌	16	5	11	12	20	7
22	20	16	12	3	1	0	16	5	11	13	20	7
Nov. 5	19	16	12	3	29♈	1	16	5	9	14	20	7
19	19	16	12	3	27	1	16	5	8	14	20	7
Dec. 3	19	15	12	2	26	0	16	5	6	14	20	7
17	20	14	13	2	25	29♋	17	4	4	14	21	7

R = Retrograde.   D = Direct.   (See page 20.)

JUPITER, SATURN, URANUS, and NEPTUNE   1918-1923
(o h. o m., G.M.T.)

	1918 ♃	♄	♅	♆	1919 ♃	♄	♅	♆	1920 ♃	♄	♅	♆
Jan. 1	3♊	13♌	21♒	6♌	11♋	28♌	25♒	9♌	17♌	12♍	29♒	11♌
15	2	12	22	6	9	27	26	8	16	11	0♓	11
29	1	11	23	6	7	26	27	8	14	10	0	10
Feb. 12	2	10	24	5	6	25	27	8	12	10	1	10
26	3	9	24	5	6	24	28	7	10	8	2	9
Mar. 12	5	8	25	5	6	23	29	7	9	7	3	9
26	7	8	26	4	7	22	0♓	7	8	6	4	9
Apr. 9	9	8	27	4	8	22	0	7	8	5	4	9
23	12	8	27	4	10	21	1	7	9	5	5	9
May 7	15	8	27	4	12	21	1	7	10	5	5	9
21	18	9	28	5	14	22	2	7	11	5	6	9
Jun. 4	21	10	28	5	17	23	2	7	13	6	6	9
18	24	12	28	5	20	24	2	7	16	6	6	10
Jul. 2	27	13	27	6	23	25	1	8	18	7	5	10
16	1♋	15	27	6	26	27	1	8	21	9	5	11
30	4	16	27	7	29	28	1	9	24	10	5	11
Aug. 13	6	18	26	7	2♌	0♍	0	9	27	12	4	12
27	9	20	25	8	5	2	0	10	0♍	14	4	12
Sep. 10	11	22	25	8	8	4	29♒	10	3	15	3	13
24	13	23	24	9	11	5	29	11	6	17	3	13
Oct. 8	15	25	24	9	13	7	28	11	9	19	2	13
22	16	26	24	9	15	8	28	11	11	20	2	14
Nov. 5	16	27	24	9	17	10	28	12	14	22	2	14
19	15	28	24	9	18	11	28	12	16	23	2	14
Dec. 3	14	28	24	9	18	11	28	11	17	24	2	14
17	13	28	25	9	18	12	28	11	18	25	2	13

	1921 ♃	♄	♅	♆	1922 ♃	♄	♅	♆	1923 ♃	♄	♅	♆
Jan. 1	19♍	25♍	3♓	13♌	17♎	7♎	7♓	15♌	13♏	19♎	10♓	18♌
15	19	25	3	13	18	8	7	15	15	20	11	17
29	18	24	4	12	19	7	8	15	17	20	12	17
Feb. 12	17	23	5	12	19	7	9	14	18	20	12	17
26	15	23	6	12	18	6	9	14	19	19	13	16
Mar. 12	13	21	7	11	17	5	10	14	19	19	14	16
26	11	20	7	11	15	4	11	13	18	18	15	16
Apr. 9	10	19	8	11	13	3	12	13	17	17	16	15
23	9	19	9	11	12	2	12	13	16	16	16	15
May 7	9	18	9	11	10	1	13	13	14	15	17	15
21	9	18	9	11	9	1	13	13	12	14	17	16
Jun. 4	10	18	10	11	9	1	14	14	11	13	17	16
18	12	19	10	12	9	1	14	14	10	13	18	16
Jul. 2	13	19	10	12	10	2	14	14	9	14	18	17
16	16	21	9	13	11	2	13	15	9	14	17	17
30	18	22	9	13	13	3	13	15	10	15	17	17
Aug. 13	21	23	8	14	15	5	12	16	11	16	17	18
27	24	25	8	14	18	6	12	16	13	17	16	19
Sep. 10	27	27	7	15	20	8	11	17	15	19	16	19
24	0♎	28	7	15	23	9	11	17	17	20	15	19
Oct. 8	3	0♎	6	16	26	11	10	18	20	22	14	20
22	6	2	6	16	29	13	10	18	23	24	14	20
Nov. 5	9	3	6	16	2♏	15	10	18	26	25	14	20
19	11	5	6	16	5	16	10	18	29	27	14	20
Dec. 3	14	6	6	16	8	17	10	18	2♐	28	14	20
17	16	7	6	16	11	19	10	18	5	0♏	14	20

R = Retrograde.   D = Direct.   (See page 20.)

JUPITER-NEPTUNE   **1918-1923**

JUPITER, SATURN, URANUS, and NEPTUNE 1924–1929

(0 h. 0 m., G.M.T.)

	1924				1925				1926			
	♃	♄	♅	♆	♃	♄	♅	♆	♃	♄	♅	♆
Jan. 1	8♐	1♏	14♓	20♌	3♑	12♏	18♓	22♌	29♑	23♏	22♓	24♌
15	11	2	15	20	6	13	19	22	2♒	24	22	24
29	14	2	15	19	10	14	19	22	6	25	23	24
Feb. 12	16	2	16	19	12	14	20	21	9	26	24	23
26	18	2	17	19	15	14	21	21	12	26	24	23
Mar. 12	19	2	18	18	18	14	21	20	15	26	25	23
26	20	1	19	18	20	13	22	20	18	26	26	22
Apr. 9	20	0	19	18	21	13	23	20	21	25	27	22
23	19	29♎	20	18	22	12	24	20	23	24	27	22
May 7	18	28	21	18	23	11	24	20	25	23	28	22
21	17	27	21	18	22	10	25	20	26	22	29	22
Jun. 4	15	26	21	18	22	9	25	20	27	21	29	22
18	13	26	21	18	20	8	25	20	27	20	29	23
Jul. 2	12	26	22	19	19	8	25	21	27	20	29	23
16	11	26	21	19	17	8	25	21	26	19	29	23
30	10	26	21	20	15	8	25	22	24	19	29	24
Aug. 13	10	27	21	20	14	8	25	22	23	20	29	24
27	11	28	20	21	13	9	24	23	21	20	28	25
Sep. 10	12	0♏	20	21	13	10	24	23	19	21	28	25
24	13	1	19	22	13	12	23	24	18	22	27	26
Oct. 8	16	3	19	22	14	13	23	24	17	24	27	26
22	18	4	18	22	16	15	22	24	17	25	26	27
Nov. 5	21	6	18	22	18	16	22	25	18	27	26	27
19	24	8	18	23	20	18	22	25	19	28	26	27
Dec. 3	27	9	18	23	23	20	22	25	21	0♐	26	27
17	0♑	11	18	22	25	21	22	25	24	2	26	27

	1927				1928				1929			
	♃	♄	♅	♆	♃	♄	♅	♆	♃	♄	♅	♆
Jan. 1	26♒	3♐	26♓	27♌	27♓	14♐	0♈	29♌	1♉	24♐	4♈	1♍
15	29	5	26	26	29	15	0	29	1	25	4	1
29	3♓	6	27	26	1♈	16	1	28	2	27	4	1
Feb. 12	6	7	27	26	4	17	1	28	4	28	5	0
26	9	7	28	25	7	18	2	28	6	29	6	0
Mar. 12	13	8	29	25	11	19	3	27	9	0♑	6	29♌
26	16	8	0♈	25	14	19	4	27	12	0	7	29
Apr. 9	19	7	1	24	17	19	4	27	15	1	8	29
23	22	7	1	24	21	19	5	26	18	0	9	29
May 7	25	6	2	24	24	18	6	26	22	0	10	29
21	28	5	2	24	27	17	6	26	25	29♐	10	29
Jun. 4	0♈	4	3	24	0♉	16	7	27	28	28	11	29
18	2	3	3	25	3	15	7	27	1♊	27	11	29
Jul. 2	3	2	3	25	5	14	7	27	4	26	11	29
16	3	1	3	25	7	13	7	28	7	25	11	0♍
30	3	1	3	26	9	13	7	28	10	25	11	0
Aug. 13	3	1	3	26	10	13	7	29	12	24	11	1
27	2	1	3	27	10	13	7	29	14	24	11	1
Sep. 10	0	2	2	27	10	13	6	0♍	15	24	10	2
24	28♓	3	1	28	9	14	6	0	16	24	10	2
Oct. 8	26	4	1	28	8	15	5	1	16	25	9	3
22	25	5	0	29	6	16	4	1	16	26	9	3
Nov. 5	24	7	0	29	4	17	4	1	15	27	8	3
19	24	9	0	29	3	19	4	1	13	29	8	4
Dec. 3	24	10	0	29	1	20	4	1	11	0♑	8	4
17	25	12	0	29	1	22	3	1	10	2	7	4

R = Retrograde. D = Direct. See page 20.)

JUPITER, SATURN, URANUS, and NEPTUNE 1930–1935

(0 h. 0 m., G.M.T.)

	1930				1931				1932			
	♃	♄	♅	♆	♃	♄	♅	♆	♃	♄	♅	♆
Jan. 1	8♊	4♑	8♈	3♍	16♋	14♑	11♈	6♍	22♌	24♑	15♌	8♍
15	7	5	8	3	14	15	12	5	21	25	16	8
29	6	7	8	3	13	17	12	5	19	27	16	7
Feb. 12	7	8	9	2	11	19	13	5	17	29	16	7
26	7	10	9	2	11	20	13	4	15	0♒	17	7
Mar. 12	9	11	10	2	10	21	14	4	14	2	18	6
26	11	11	11	1	11	22	15	4	13	3	19	6
Apr. 9	13	12	12	1	12	23	15	3	13	4	19	6
23	16	12	13	1	14	23	16	3	13	4	20	5
May 7	19	12	13	1	16	23	17	3	14	5	21	5
21	22	11	14	1	18	23	18	3	15	5	22	5
Jun. 4	25	10	15	1	21	23	18	3	17	4	22	5
18	28	10	15	1	24	22	19	3	19	4	23	5
Jul. 2	1♋	8	15	1	27	21	19	4	22	3	23	6
16	4	7	15	2	0♌	20	19	4	25	2	23	6
30	7	7	15	2	3	19	19	4	27	1	23	7
Aug. 13	10	6	15	3	6	18	19	5	0♍	0	23	7
27	13	5	15	3	9	17	19	5	3	29♑	23	8
Sep. 10	15	5	14	4	12	17	19	6	6	29	23	8
24	17	5	14	4	15	17	18	6	9	28	22	9
Oct. 8	19	6	13	5	17	17	18	7	12	28	22	9
22	20	7	13	5	19	17	17	7	15	28	21	9
Nov. 5	21	8	12	5	21	18	16	8	17	29	21	10
19	20	9	12	6	22	19	16	8	20	0♒	20	10
Dec. 3	19	10	12	6	23	21	16	8	21	1	20	10
17	18	12	11	6	23	22	15	8	23	2	20	10

	1933				1934				1935			
	♃	♄	♅	♆	♃	♄	♅	♆	♃	♄	♅	♆
Jan. 1	23♍	4♒	19♈	10♍	21♎	14♒	23♈	12♍	17♏	25♒	28♈	15♍
15	23	6	20	10	22	16	24	12	19	26	28	14
29	23	7	20	10	23	18	24	12	21	28	28	14
Feb. 12	21	9	20	9	23	19	24	12	22	0♓	28	14
26	20	11	21	9	23	21	25	11	23	1	29	13
Mar. 12	18	12	22	8	22	23	25	11	23	3	29	13
26	16	13	22	8	20	24	26	10	23	5	0♉	13
Apr. 9	15	15	23	8	18	25	27	10	22	6	1	12
23	14	15	24	8	17	26	28	10	21	7	1	12
May 7	13	16	25	7	15	27	28	10	19	9	2	12
21	13	16	25	7	14	28	29	10	17	9	3	12
Jun. 4	14	16	26	7	13	28	0♈	10	15	10	4	12
18	15	16	27	8	13	28	0	10	14	10	4	12
Jul. 2	17	15	27	8	14	28	1	10	14	10	5	12
16	19	15	27	8	15	27	1	10	13	10	5	13
30	22	14	27	9	17	26	1	11	14	9	5	13
Aug. 13	24	13	27	9	19	25	1	11	15	8	6	13
27	27	12	27	10	21	24	1	12	16	7	5	14
Sep. 10	0♎	11	27	10	24	23	1	12	18	6	5	14
24	3	10	26	11	26	22	1	13	21	5	5	15
Oct. 8	6	10	26	11	29	22	0	13	23	4	4	15
22	9	10	25	12	2♏	22	0	14	26	4	4	16
Nov. 5	12	10	25	12	5	22	29♈	14	29	4	3	16
19	15	11	24	12	8	22	28	14	2♐	4	3	17
Dec. 3	17	12	24	12	11	23	28	15	5	4	2	17
17	19	13	24	12	14	24	28	15	8	5	2	17

R = Retrograde. D = Direct. (See page 20.)